*Phoenix in the Twentieth Century*

# Phoenix

## in the Twentieth Century

### ESSAYS IN COMMUNITY HISTORY

Edited by
G. Wesley Johnson, Jr.

UNIVERSITY OF OKLAHOMA PRESS : NORMAN AND LONDON

*For four who cared:*

John Driggs
K. Trimble
Lorraine Frank
Robert A. Trennert

*And in memoriam:*

Wallace Adams

Library of Congress Cataloging-in-Publication Data

Phoenix in the twentieth century : essays in community history /
   edited by G. Wesley Johnson, Jr. — 1st ed.
     304 p.   22 cm.
   Includes bibliographical references and index.
   ISBN 0-8061-2468-7
   1. Phoenix (Ariz.)—History.   I. Johnson, G. Wesley.
F819.P57P59   1993
979.1'73053—dc20                            92-54156
                                                      CIP

The paper in this book meets the guidelines for permanence and durability of the Committee on Production Guidelines for Book Longevity of the Council on Library Resources, Inc.

1    2    3    4    5    6    7    8    9    10

# Contents

# Illustrations

# Maps

# Editor's Preface

THIS volume seeks to fill a void in the historical literature of the western United States by presenting the past century of Phoenix, Arizona, one of the nation's largest metropolises, privately called by one critic "the most ahistorical community in the United States—only Las Vegas would be a serious rival." At its inauspicious founding in 1870, the small desert hamlet of Phoenix, located on a dry river and far from the impendent railroad, seemed unlikely to grow in one short century to become a haven for more than one-and-a-half-million Americans seeking a new way of life in the Great Southwest.

While Arizona's early history of Indian migrations, Spanish conquest, and frontier expansion has been chronicled and studied in depth by some of the nation's most astute western historians, the history of Arizona's capital city has been neglected. Scholars wanting to preserve the history of the Old West made study of the Arizona territorial period a high priority. A major reason for the neglect of Phoenix was the creation of the state historical society in Tucson in the late 1880s, which resulted in a focus on southern Arizona history. Nevertheless, the earlier citizens of Phoenix are in fact principally to blame for the lack of historical interest in their own community; it was not until the mid-1970s that Phoenicians organized a historical society and museum.

To help Phoenicians understand the community they had inherited, certain city fathers, led by former Mayor John Driggs and the new historical society, joined forces in the late 1970s and 1980s to help sponsor the Phoenix History Project. This was a nonprofit community research endeavor dedicated to finding, analyzing, and preserving sources for local Phoenix history and then publishing the results. Many of the essays in this volume are an outgrowth of that project, which sought to integrate the efforts of trained voluntary community historians with professional historians—faculty and graduate students of several universities.

The goal of the Phoenix History Project was to help prepare a community biography, since the sponsoring bodies of the community wanted to know how Phoenix was founded, why it grew, and who was responsible for its development. Such an assignment for most older communities would have been viewed by consulting historians as old hat. However, the Phoenix project faced a community that was indeed in search of its history, of its very identity. The problem was compounded by the migration to Phoenix during the preceding decade of hundreds of thousands of citizens who had no idea of the background or character of the community which was now their home.

The Phoenix History Project was therefore dedicated to old-fashioned community history: finding the sources, characterizing the leaders, and evaluating the major problems in the growth of the city. Spatial and ecological questions, the intricacies of migration and demographic patterns, and comparison of Phoenix with other southwestern communities, all important areas of study, would be examined in subsequent studies issued by the project. The emphasis of this volume, however, is on local and community histories in the best sense of those categories, as historians have rescued them from well-meaning antiquarians. Today historians of all types, whether demographic, public, social, or interdisciplinary, recognize that a major building block for writing American history is to do (or redo in some cases) the basic history of a community. To that end, these essays should be viewed as an attempt to paint a community portrait of Phoenix, delineating the themes and problems that made it unique as a growing metropolis.

Although this volume closely focuses on Phoenix's problems and issues over time, the overall study may suggest how community history might be done in other cities, especially in the western United States, where documentary materials may be sparse. For example, since few written materials on Phoenix have been collected over the years by local libraries and archives, the Phoenix History Project necessarily launched a major oral-history program to find original materials and testimonies, especially for twentieth-century history. As a solid foundation for the oral histories, a basic chronology of events was compiled by Aimée Lykes, using Phoenix newspapers preserved by Arizona State University and the Arizona State Library.

More than five hundred oral-history interviews with a wide variety of people were conducted with the help of K. Trimble, who served as executive assistant of the project in charge of oral history. The interviewees were drawn from a number of occupations, social groups, religions, neighborhoods, and ethnic groups and thus represented a broad range of personal perspectives. Very often these oral interviews, transcribed and indexed, opened the door to finding privately held manuscript collections, diaries, scrapbooks, letters, account books, and other memorabilia that were later acquired in original or copy form. Many of these sources were used by the writers in this volume.

While the resulting essays attempt to re-create a local history, we also believe they stand as an example of a new historical genre, public history, since the Phoenix History Project was at its outset a commissioned historical assignment. Indeed, as public history has developed during the past decade, community history of this type has become an important part of the professional repertoire of the public historian.[1] Many of the graduate students who worked on the Phoenix project came from the Graduate Program in Public Historical Studies of the University of California, Santa Barbara. They cut their teeth, so to speak, on the problems of how to do sponsored research in the community, and some, such as Karen Smith, later became practicing public historians in Phoenix and elsewhere.

It would be a mistake, on the other hand, to view this volume as simply a piece of applied history. From their work on the Phoenix History Project, several students produced master's theses and doctoral dissertations and completed university internships, suggesting that academic considerations can also be fulfilled in doing public history. Graduate students from Arizona State University, particularly those under the mentorship of Professor Brad Luckingham, joined my students from the University of California to push back the frontiers of knowledge on Phoenix.

We would like to acknowledge the help of the Arizona Humanities Council and its director at that time, Lorraine Frank, which helped sponsor a regional conference in which many of the scholars in this volume first presented their findings. We also acknowledge support from the Research Division, National Endowment for the Humanities, Washington, D.C.

We also need to thank several people and groups who helped make this book possible: first, John Driggs, chair of the advisory committee of the Phoenix History Project, for his unswerving support; K. Trimble, oral-history coordinator for the Phoenix History Project, whose long hours went beyond the call of duty; Lawrence J. Fleming, former chair of the Central Arizona Museum trustees; Sylvia Laughlin, chair of the museum's oral-history committee; and Robert A. Trennert, who served as associate director of the project for two years; second, Lorraine Frank and her staff at the Arizona Humanities Council; third, Emmanuel Chiabi, Barbara Hagen, Marian A. Johnson, all formerly at the University of California, Santa Barbara, and Gerald Bradford, formerly of the Hutchins Center for the Study of Democratic Institutions, at UC–Santa Barbara; fourth, Margaret Finnerty and Aimée Lykes of the Phoenix History Project, who stepped in and lent an important hand during a difficult phase of this project; Cynthia Keetch, Charles Hughes, and Dan Cottam, research assistants; and Marilou Conner, staff assistant, at Brigham Young University. Special thanks also goes to Linda Hunter Adams and staff members at the College of Humanities Publications Center of BYU. Charles Vogel and Larry Schweikart also rendered extra services that should be acknowledged on the editing of this volume.

I want to thank the librarians and archivists in Arizona who have helped: the late Bert Fireman, Susie Sato, Dennis Madden, and Marlene Ware of the Arizona Historical Foundation library; Ed Oeting and Chris Marin of the Arizona Room, Hayden Library, Arizona State University; and Janet Michelieu of the Arizona Historical Society Museum Library, Phoenix. At a personal level, I need to express gratitude and thanks to my family, longtime Phoenicians Zoe and Wesley Johnson, Sr., and Janet and Gary Tipton, whose hospitality literally made it possible for me to visit Phoenix regularly from my university posts in California and Utah. I also owe a great debt of encouragement to my wife, Marian, and Cici, Kye, George, and Ben.

Finally, for allaying our initial fears that "the most ahistorical community" held a dearth of source materials, we are most indebted to the citizens of Phoenix, their clubs, churches, community organizations, families, professional groups, ethnic groups, businesses, and other groups and institutions. Judging from the level of participant cooperation in the Phoenix History Project's oral-history program, we had found a major community that yearned to find out about its past, the sooner the better. To list all the organizations and individuals who provided original materials and testimonies for this volume would indeed fill many pages. Phoenicians from all walks of life willingly discussed findings and ideas with the students and professors; their open-door policy was a manifestation of the genuine courtesy and hospitality of a southwestern city.

Many western cities still await their historian or community biographer. If this volume provides some direction and insight for other community historians, we will be pleased with our labors.

G. Wesley Johnson
Director, Phoenix History Project

*Phoenix in the Twentieth Century*

## CHAPTER ONE

# Introduction

## BY G. WESLEY JOHNSON, JR.

PHOENIX in the Twentieth Century
is a volume about historical change in a western community. The essays
presented here explore five basic themes selected to give insight into how
and why Phoenix made such a rapid rise to regional and national prominence in less than a century. These five themes—the social fabric, the
ethnic mix, economic growth, the importance of water, and community
policy in politics, labor, and transportation—are indicative of both the
unique and normal aspects of urban growth. The essays should be viewed
in the French tradition of scholarship, *contributions à l'histoire*, rather
than complete essays on each subject. We have not contemplated presenting a full range of essays on each topic in this volume; instead we
examine those subjects deemed most important by our colleagues for early
investigation. For example, in part two we present studies on ethnic
groups, essays on Italian Americans and American Indians. The reader
who is interested in groups such as Chinese Americans and the Jewish
community in Phoenix should consult an early publication of the
Phoenix History Project, a special issue of the *Journal of Arizona History*.[1]
Or in the case of politics, a subject covered in part five, the reader is
referred to earlier essays on political figures, such as Dwight B. Heard
and Carl T. Hayden.[2] What we have grouped in this volume are essays
that indicate the nature of the five basic topics selected for analysis.
Let us take a closer look at each of these themes and put them into
a larger context.

Part one examines the social fabric of Phoenix and presents two essays
which discuss the role of elites and the emergence of women in the community. Since Phoenix was a relatively sheltered and isolated community
until the advent of World War II, it is not surprising that its early and
middle-range development were dominated by an elite group of leaders
and several generations of families. Although Phoenix had reached the

100,000 population level by 1950, the eve of the decade of its greatest growth, the city was still in reality a small town dominated by business and professional leaders who had deep roots in the past. By contrast, within ten years this group's hold on Phoenix had weakened, and by 1970 it was apparent that Phoenix was no longer led by one group but by a number of groups and individuals, a pluralistic situation characteristic of many great metropolises.

Putting aside the current legitimate concern in our society for equal opportunity and access for all groups, historically the development of an elite made sense in Phoenix since the community started off with few assets and many liabilities. G. Wesley Johnson's essay on Phoenix elites suggests that but for a strong-willed and ambitious leadership group, Phoenix might today be no more than Florence, Arizona, a quiet country farming town which in the 1870s was a twin to Phoenix. Phoenix had dynamic leaders who transformed their town into a city and then a metropolis, whereas Florence never developed such a leadership cadre. Both towns were in river valleys, both had good agricultural potential, both had similar beginnings, yet one rose to greatness while the other never changed.

The other essay in part one, by Aimée Lykes, treats the emergence of women on the Arizona frontier and the contributions they made to the political and cultural development of the community. Women arrived slowly in Arizona after the Civil War as westward migration increased; not until the 1880s did many women arrive in Phoenix, presumably because the completion of the southern transcontinental railroad through Tucson made travel easier. Once in town, however, women did not tarry in organizing for various causes, as Lykes documents in her essay. The situation for women in Phoenix was not unlike that in other western cities; progress appears to have occurred at the same pace as elsewhere. But one should note that most of these women were married and in many instances their marriage situation served as a foundation for their activities. Not until the decade of World War I was there a growing number of working women in the community, a phenomenon which continued until World War II, when women were recruited for traditionally male jobs in factories, hospitals, and government. Lykes's essay shows that the common image of a male elite running Phoenix must be revised to include the participation of many outstanding women.

Part two features essays on the ethnic community in Phoenix. The first, by Robert Trennert, examines the plight of American Indians, and the second, by Phylis Martinelli, the emergence of Italian Americans. American Indians have been romanticized and vilified but rarely ignored by historians. However, as Trennert suggests, the latter has characterized

Phoenix history because few Indians settled in the growing city. Because the federal government created Indian reservations to the east and south of Phoenix, there was little incentive for Pimas and Papagos to move to the city, especially in view of the fact that the city already segregated Hispanics and blacks geographically. The coming of the federal Indian School to Phoenix in the 1890s eventually facilitated integration, because some graduates married and set up households in the city (although many of these Indians—indeed most students at the school—came from communities other than Phoenix).

Unlike the Indians, Italian Americans had no difficulty integrating into urban society. Martinelli shows how several early Italian families, mostly northern Italians, came to occupy a prominent place in the community as assimilated individuals. However, the identification of a self-aware Italian American community in WASPish Phoenix had to await post–World War II years, when larger numbers moved to the expanding metropolis. Martinelli's essay suggests one of the major findings of the Phoenix History Project: underneath the WASP veneer of pre–World War II Phoenix (before the war triggered an influx of workers, technocrats, minorities, and middle-class winter visitors and retired persons), there were indeed many ethnic groups. Most of these were not visible because there was a lack of what social historians call a critical mass, but they were there, nonetheless, making contributions. Thus current studies looking at German Americans, Polish Americans, Syrian and Lebanese Americans are now in progress.

While African-Americans appeared in small numbers in the community by the 1890s, it was not until the eve of World War I that their number began to increase; this fact motivated bigoted politicians to take a step backward by creating separate grammar and high schools for blacks. In this sense, blacks not only suffered the physical separation meted out to Indians and most Hispanics by being forced to live in certain areas, especially in South Phoenix, they also became the only group to be relegated to separate schools. In such a situation, it is not surprising that the black community did not grow until viable economic opportunities arose after World War II. Phoenix was a backwash in the economic tidal wave that started black migrations to Los Angeles and Oakland from the South. In prewar Phoenix, Hispanics and poor whites dominated the migrant labor market; farmers in the Phoenix area long had used not only Mexican Americans but also Mexican workers legally and illegally brought in from across the border. Phoenix society might rail against so-called wetbacks, but the reality was that local prosperity was intimately tied to the availability of cheap migrant labor working the vast farmlands of the valley. The analysis of ethnic groups as part of the social fabric and economic development of Phoenix needs further study; here we can only suggest some of the problems faced by two minority groups in the emerging metropolis.

Part three presents three essays on economic growth and development in Phoenix. First, Bradford Luckingham's overview of development emphasizes promotion of the community. But for boosterism and an intelligent policy of seeking outside help, Phoenix could have stagnated economically. Luckingham's essay may be read as a complement to Johnson's essay on Phoenix elites. Luckingham shows the way in which an infrastructure of transportation helped develop the agribusiness potential of the Salt River Valley, and within several decades Phoenix put forth a new image as the center of the Valley of the Sun, a romantic name coined by local advertising counselors to lure more winter visitors. While it is true that Tucson also offered similar advantages of mild winter climate and sunny skies, Phoenix did a better job of marketing its assets for winter visitors who wanted to settle or invest in the community's business future. For example, John C. Lincoln, who owned Lincoln Electric of Cleveland, Ohio, became a regular visitor to Phoenix in the 1930s and began to invest in land and resorts; he was the silent partner behind the development of Camelback Inn.

Next, two case studies are presented to document specific aspects of Luckingham's overview. Michael Kotlanger focuses on the decade of the 1920s, when Phoenix developed its high-profile downtown area and finally procured a transcontinental railroad (Southern Pacific). This was a time when wholesalers flocked to Phoenix to serve the needs of other Arizona cities and when Phoenix outgrew Tucson, moving toward replacing El Paso as the dominant city in the Far Southwest.

Larry Schweikart's case study examines the financial sector of Phoenix, beginning with the dynamic intervention of Walter Bimson of Chicago in Phoenix financial affairs during the Great Depression. Bimson, an entrepreneurial banker who arrived on the scene of a discouraged Phoenix, with bravura created a climate of confidence by telling his employees to lend money, not hoard it. Schweikart shows how this stimulus to the economy put Phoenix in a strong position to capitalize on wartime and postwar developments by welding together the strong banking system necessary for the transition from sheltered city to expansive metropolis. It was the vision and aggressiveness of bankers like Bimson and Frank Brophy that distinguished Phoenix from a conservative financial city like Tucson. To be sure, infusion of investment capital had characterized Phoenix since the 1880s, when W. J. Murphy sought investors in Chicago, New York, and Edinburgh for construction of the Arizona Canal, or since 1900, when Dwight B. Heard made possible thousands of valley farmland purchases by securing cheap and plentiful Chicago mortgage money. Schweikart's essay suggests that the importance of local financiers, even late in the city's development, was an important ingredient in providing Phoenix with fundamental economic growth.

Part four explores the importance of water in Phoenix in two essays. For historians of the arid American West, water is a subject stressed often since it spells the difference between arable land or desert. Phoenix is favored to the north and east with a belt of mountains that comprise a major watershed. From the Mogollon Rim and the White Mountains rush streams that feed the Verde and Salt rivers, providing Phoenix with water to make the desert fertile. The ancient Hohokam peoples, who arrived in the Salt River Valley about 300 B.C., were the brilliant engineers of the famous system of canals and ditches the whites inherited when they took possession of the valley in the late 1860s. Pioneers, such as John Y. T. Smith and Jack Swilling, discovered that crops could grow in the Salt River Valley on lands which were abandoned by the Hohokam about A.D. 1400 and which had remained uninhabited thereafter. Swilling and his associates cleaned out the Hohokam canals and grew crops that were sought throughout the territory, setting in motion the migration of farm families to Phoenix and the establishment of a settlement by 1870. But as Earl Zarbin shows in his essay, having a good watershed and a system of canals was not enough: a reservoir for water storage to prevent flooding was the major resource lacking in a water system for twentieth-century needs. The eventual construction of Theodore Roosevelt Dam near Phoenix by 1911 provided a plentiful and predictable water supply for agricultural purposes.

Such was not the case for drinking water. Karen Smith's essay tells how the city of Phoenix sought for decades to obtain enough water for municipal use and how this policy was frequently frustrated. This was before the Central Arizona Project and water from the Colorado River, long a dream to Phoenicians, became a reality by 1985. Since Phoenix for several decades was consistently either the fastest-growing major city in the United States or one of the top three or four, growth became a way of life in Arizona. In fact, the eventual size of Phoenix probably will be determined by the availability of water resources, since there is no shortage of desert land to annex. Pollution, crowding, and a deteriorating quality of life may not be as significant, as Phoenix continues to grow unabated as a favored city for relocation from the East and Midwest. The late futurologist Herman Kahn (relying mainly on computer models) predicted unparalleled growth for Phoenix into the twenty-first century. But the question of water resources remains: will nature limit what humans might aspire to do?

Finally, part five examines three aspects of Phoenix history essential for understanding the rise of the modern metropolis: community policy on politics, labor, and transportation. Michael Konig reminds us that the city election of 1949 had more than passing interest because it was in that year Phoenix reformed its municipal government and sent new industries the message that henceforth Phoenix would be a desirable place to locate. During the 1920s and 1930s, while the commercial life of Phoenix was booming or holding its own, few people were attracted to serve in local government, so it became the preserve of many second-rate business people. City commissioners and mayors changed with great frequency, as did city managers. Phoenix had adopted the city-manager form of government just before World War I in a spurt of enthusiasm for progressive reform, but no professionally trained managers were ever appointed and the position became associated with behind-the-scenes control. Konig shows how this situation had to be changed before Phoenix could grow after the war and how a new group of citizens formed the Charter Government Committee, which took charge and cleaned house. For the next twenty-five years, Charter's candidates and its political committee dominated Phoenix politics, usually for the benefit of the city. But by the 1970s, as Phoenix became a pluralistic metropolis, with many directing elites and with a population that mirrored a complex social and ethnic fabric, critics charged that Charter was unrepresentative, insensitive to minorities, and a tool of the old elite and business interests. Margaret Hance was the last mayor to come from Charter stock, although even she had to run as an independent to survive several terms. Konig tells how the old elite, in one of its clearest manifestations of political influence, won the election of 1949 and in the process (coincidentally) launched the career of Barry Goldwater, who was elected city councilman under Charter.

Margaret Finnerty's essay on labor explains much about postwar expansion and the way organized labor was successfully eliminated from the local power structure. Unions were never strong before World War II because Phoenix had no industries and hence no laboring class. But the golden opportunity for union operatives seemed to occur after 1945 as Phoenix readied for expansion. Finnerty suggests how union growth was frustrated and why Phoenix remained a city under right-to-work laws, with relatively cheap labor and weak unions. Phoenix's labor policy remained in character with other Sunbelt capitals and did not emulate a western city such as San Francisco, which developed strong unions.

In the final essay, transportation historian Kevin McCauley chronicles the attempts by Phoenix officials to develop and implement a reasonable transportation system. McCauley shows that plenty of planning took place and that ideas were discussed and options weighed to give Phoenix an innovative freeway system, but somehow from the 1950s onward, there was only partial implementation of these plans. Limited mileage in freeways, inadequate for the mushrooming metropolis, was built, but the net result of planning and politics was an impasse that lasted until the late 1980s. Whether the ultimate responsibility lay with elected officials, city managers, and staff or with a fickle public that voted both for and against freeways in successive elections is difficult to ascertain.

Since the early seventies, discussed by McCauley, it has become apparent that Phoenix, which boasted of being an All-American City in the 1950s (a national competition it won several times), has begun to lose its sense of progressivism and uniqueness. Was it the demise of the old elite or Charter that meant a strong hand was no longer at the helm, or did it mean that Phoenix, following the path taken by most great cities, had finally reached a stage in its development when the scale of problems became so complex that there were no easy solutions? Older residents interviewed for the Phoenix History Project were nostalgic for the earlier era of boosterism, which gave the impression that Phoenix could solve any problem. Newer residents countered that wishful thinking would not solve such problems as adequate housing for minorities, opportunities for all economic groups in the marketplace, and true representation for all districts in the city (as opposed to Charter, which had candidates elected at large).

The reality of regional leadership and metropolitan stature was difficult for many citizens to comprehend, since it was thrust upon a city which a few decades earlier had been a big, sheltered town where all the leading power brokers in the community could gather around one table in the Luhrs Building at the Arizona Club. By the late 1970s, Phoenix had become a community with intense growing pains, struggling to find a new leadership, a new identity, and a new rationale. One wonders what those irascible pioneers, such as John Y. T. Smith or Jack Swilling, who planted the first crops, would say more than a century later upon seeing a metropolis dedicated to industry and consumerism, with agriculture relegated to a secondary role. Or indeed what the vanished Hohokam Indians would think of our marvelous technological age when in fact much of modern irrigation in Phoenix still depends on canals and ditches they first dug and graded centuries ago.

The century we have explored in these essays was in one sense only the prelude to the birth of a great metropolis; in another sense it was the crucial era in which the very character of a city was molded and the stamp of uniqueness put upon it. Today, sister desert city Tucson to the south would not be mistaken for Phoenix even by the casual observer. The first century did indeed develop a sense of special accomplishment that carried Phoenix and its populace forward into its second century. The task of the historian has been to discover this past and to interpret it for present-day citizens so they might not simply take pride in the collective achievement of transforming desert into metropolis and bonanza, but stand with a touch of humility as problems of the future now come into focus.

The five subject areas of this volume are meant to be soundings into the reality that Phoenix has become. By examining a part of the social fabric, ethnicity, economic growth, water resources, and developments in politics, labor, and transportation, the authors have attempted to describe and analyze how Phoenix, as both community and city, has come this far in almost 120 years. It is hoped that these incursions into social, economic, and political history will raise more questions than they attempt to answer.

The chronology prepared by Aimée Lykes will also help the reader keep in mind how events described in these thematic areas related to the year-by-year development of the city. In the conclusion we will return to an assessment of these themes and examine more closely the issues and problems they suggest.

PART ONE

*The Social Fabric of Phoenix*

## CHAPTER TWO

# Directing Elites:
# Catalysts for Social Change

## BY G. WESLEY JOHNSON, JR.

FIVE years after the end of the American Civil War, the advancing waves of pioneers had reached the desert valleys of central Arizona. In the fall of 1870, federal census takers visited a new village established on the banks of the Salt River, a major tributary to the Gila River. Here they found about 300 new settlers who had excavated some of the old Indian canals and had begun irrigating the harsh desert floor. One of these pioneers was Darrell Duppa, an Englishman of some education, who marveled at the great expanse of canals left behind by the Hohokam, the ancients who had first inhabited this Sonoran Desert valley. Infected by American frontier boosterism, Duppa predicted the settlement would one day become a great city, rising Phoenix-like from the ashes of this old civilization. In fact, the Egyptian bird of mythology caught the fancy of the townsfolk and Phoenix was the name given the new town. It proved to be an apt foretelling of the future because in 120 short years that desert hamlet became the ninth-largest city in the nation (983,403), with a metropolitan area of more than 2 million people (2,069,600—U.S. Census, 1990).

Why did Phoenix attain such spectacular growth? Its beginnings were hardly auspicious. It was founded near an unnavigable desert stream, isolated from the mainline railroads for decades, and situated in the middle of the great Sonoran Desert, which rivaled Death Valley in summer temperatures. Phoenix's future seemed similar to that of hundreds of other frontier towns: marginal at best. In this essay I attempt to answer the question "Why did Phoenix grow?" in human terms by looking at the people who presided over its rise to prominence. I look briefly at economic and political factors, but my focus is on social factors, especially the formation and continuity of directing elites in presiding over the development of Phoenix. In his study of Houston elites, William D. Angel found that "natural conditions did not dictate the future success of cities like Houston. The entrepreneurial behavior of a few prosperous capitalists did."[1] In the case of Phoenix, it was the sustained activity of many boosters, entrepreneurs, and civic leaders over several generations that lifted the desert hamlet from obscurity to become a great regional capital. It is my basic argument that a major factor for rapid social change and development in Phoenix was the activity of these community decision-makers, whom I will refer to as the directing elite. Because Phoenix had a number of handicaps, like Houston, the ascension of Phoenix was closely linked to the quality and ability of its leadership class and its capacity for action over several generations.

## METHODOLOGICAL CONSIDERATIONS

Few American cities offer a more striking example of social change in several generations than Phoenix, where most of the period of intense community development has occurred within the memory of people living today. This is fortunate since the citizens of the new city were far too busy to keep systematic written records on society, politics, and economy. When the Phoenix History Project was planned to collect materials for a history of Phoenix, it was determined that oral history interviews should be given a high priority to make up for the lack of written documentation that characterized Phoenix in the 1980s. Lack of a local historical society until 1973 and no city archive meant that the community's written legacy of its past was sparse or nonexistent.[2] Over a six-year period, the Phoenix History Project planned and conducted more than five hundred oral history interviews with a variety of Phoenicians who were chosen as knowledgeable informants. These interviews, most of which were transcribed, are prime evidence for examining the reasons for the rapid growth of Phoenix and the development of local leadership, since many informants had participated in or had firsthand knowledge of community turning points.

The interviewees represented a wide variety of occupations, social classes, family backgrounds, ethnic groups, religions, geographical locations within the city, and educational backgrounds. A number of them served as members of an informal panel to offer advice on who should be interviewed (if still alive) or be studied (if dead or moved from Phoenix). News media publicity about the project resulted in hundreds of telephone calls and letters from the general public, from which suggestions for more interviews were compiled. In addition, local political, economic, and social leaders were asked for suggestions, and their participation became the equivalent of another panel to advise the project.

Interviewees were asked to comment on the development of community leadership and to identify people who were perceived to be key decision or policy makers; data from the interviews were added to data from the informal panels previously mentioned, and the information was compared with research in so-called local biographical dictionaries and an extensive chronological investigation of Phoenix newspapers (from 1878 to 1980) carried out by Aimée Lykes. On the basis of the synthesis of these data, the names of elite Phoenicians were suggested. This essay focuses on some of the leaders and their actions during several generations. From a methodological perspective, the Phoenix History Project used elements of both the reputational and decisional approaches for analyzing elite behavior and power relationships. Decisions on major questions of public policy were analyzed as a source of determining who participated in decision making and this was contrasted with the members of the community nominated by the panels. The result presented here is a synthesis.[3]

The elites under study were divided into different cohorts—not birth cohorts, but period cohorts; that is, periods during which members demonstrated measurable activity within community affairs. As set forth in the pages that follow, the five cohort groups correspond with the three basic periods of growth and social change in Phoenix. One can argue that these three periods of change derive partly from the activity of the cohorts (in addition to economic and political factors) during that time. In fact, the cohorts' activity during all three periods was a prime causal factor for change. As Glen Elder has observed: "An understanding of change thus entails comparative investigation of the setting, composition, and process of cohort flows and their relation to social institutions."[4] These cohort groups of elites built up Phoenix during three successive stages: first as a town, second as a well-defined city, and third as an expanding metropolis. During the first two stages—Phoenix as town and city—this analysis divides each stage into two sections; hence, there are five period cohorts in the urban biography of Phoenix: the Founding Elite, the Town Elite, the Old City Elite, the New City Elite, and the Metropolitan Elites.[5]

## THE TOWN ELITE, 1870–1910
### The Founding Fathers, 1870–1885

The first period cohort, the Founding Elite, provided an initial burst of leadership in Phoenix. By the late 1860s the Salt River Valley was attracting veterans of the Civil War because of lucrative U.S. Army contracts to provision the needs of Fort McDowell. The army camp, situated on the Verde River north of its confluence with the Salt River, was established to protect new settlers and travelers from Apache Indian attacks. John Y. T. Smith was the first to grow hay for army horses on the banks of the Salt River, but it was Jack Swilling, a Confederate veteran, who sized up the ancient Hohokam Indian canals, abandoned for centuries, and realized they could be used to grow crops on a more systematic basis than the capricious river would allow. He organized the Swilling Ditch Company on the banks of the Salt and attracted mustered-out soldiers from Fort McDowell and miners from nearby Wickenburg, where the Vulture and other mines had peaked. William Hancock, who served at McDowell, decided to stay in the Salt River Valley once he was mustered out; in 1870 he was commissioned by leaders of the emerging settlement to survey a townsite. John Alsap, a medical doctor who farmed and later practiced law in Phoenix, was a guiding force in gaining recognition for the young community, and by fall of 1870 a rudimentary local government had been organized.[6]

Smith, Swilling, Hancock, and Alsap joined Darrell Duppa as five of the major founders who supported the name Phoenix for the new town. Of modest means, all of these men had been attracted to life on the frontier for the "main chance": some for mining, such as Swilling and Duppa, some for farming, such as Smith and Hancock (and later Swilling). And in that quest for the main chance, all shared an optimism that looked well beyond the bleak desert that met their gaze at the outset.

Swilling and Duppa had the broadest vision of the future, yet they were reduced to marginal importance within a few years. Swilling stood accused of robbery and murder, was sent to prison at Yuma, and died shortly afterward; Duppa became a saloonkeeper who dabbled in mining. Smith became a prosperous farmer and major landowner and married Phoenix's first schoolmarm. Hancock and Alsap both practiced law at times and traded in real estate, and in 1881, when the settlement was finally incorporated as a city, Alsap was elected first mayor.

Other settlers of greater means and much energy arrived during the 1870s, but apart from Smith, after the mid-1880s all the founding fathers were either dead or no longer influential in the community. One such early newcomer was Charles Trumbull Hayden, a prosperous Tucson merchant who staked a claim to a strategic valley location and built Hayden's Ferry at a point where the Salt River in flood was easiest to cross. He built a flour mill there, and within a few years the second community in Salt River Valley was born. It was called Tempe, named (again by Duppa) for the valley of the gods in Greek mythology. When R. G. Dun, the forerunner of Dun and Bradstreet, conducted the first survey of economic life in the valley, he found Hayden to be the most credit-worthy merchant in Phoenix or Tempe. Others, such as the Goldwater family, were still emerging frontier merchants and were not yet impressive to Dun.[7]

The founding fathers of the Town Elite can be characterized in the following terms: most were marginal actors, people of insubstantial means who came to the frontier in search of opportunity. Only latecomer Hayden was a man of some affluence and, interestingly, only he achieved lasting influence—through his son, Carl, who later sat in Congress for Arizona for more than five decades. Most were from the Midwest or had Yankee origins, although a few, such as Swilling, were southerners. Although the southerners continued to play an important role in town affairs during the first decades, they never succeeded in making Phoenix, like Tucson, a southern city. Phoenix has borne the stamp of the Midwest from its founding down to modern times.[8]

### The Town Elite Entrepreneurs, 1885–1910

It is rather interesting in examining the later Town Elite, the cohort here called the Entrepreneurs, that patterns of continuity characterizing later growth are found; it was this group of aggressive developers who brought two spur railroads to Phoenix, captured the state capital from Prescott and Tucson, and persuaded the federal government to build Roosevelt Dam to provide crucial water storage for extended irrigation. Whereas some frontier towns were limited by the actions of their founders, who settled down to mediocrity, Phoenix in the 1880s and 1890s was able to attract a remarkable group of actors, both men of means and men of vision. This group inherited a small frontier village, built it into a prosperous town that became Arizona's territorial capital in 1889, and set the stage for overtaking Tucson as the territory's largest city by 1910.[9]

Key members of the new Town Elite Entrepreneurs were men with excellent financial connections, such as Col. William Christy, William J. Murphy, Emil Ganz, and Moses H. Sherman. Christy had served as Iowa state treasurer before coming to Arizona for his health; a man of means, he bought large acreage on Phoenix's west side and experimented with new crops. But Christy's main contribution was in helping to found and direct the Valley Bank, which quickly became the area's leading financial institution. Christy, with excellent connections in the Midwest, brought Phoenix a touch of class.[10]

Also arriving in the early 1880s was William J. Murphy, a railroad contractor who had helped build the Atlantic and Pacific Railroad (later renamed the Santa Fe) through northern Arizona. He took over the herculean task of financing and building the Arizona Canal, the valley's largest irrigation canal, which stretched for more than forty miles. Murphy gained access to huge tracts of land that the Behemoth canal would eventually water; then he helped finance the canal by selling bonds in Chicago, New York, and Great Britain. In the process, Murphy more than anyone publicized to the rest of the country and Europe the mild winter climate, the twelve-month growing season, and other unique attractions of Phoenix. Murphy helped form the Arizona Improvement Company, the largest local corporation dealing in land and water rights, and was allied with Christy as a backer of the Valley Bank.[11]

Emil Ganz, a German immigrant who first tried his fortunes in Georgia, later came to Arizona and quickly achieved prominence with his Bank Exchange Hotel. After Phoenix was incorporated in 1881, it had a succession of weak mayors until 1885, when Ganz was elected. Here was the first cosmopolite, a man with a breadth of experience and vision who put the city on a sound financial basis and inaugurated new services. Ganz later became chief of the rival banking group to Christy; Phoenix benefited from the spirited competition between his Phoenix Bank and the Valley Bank as they vied to finance new commercial and real estate projects.[12]

In real estate, none surpassed the shrewd Yankee Moses Hazeltine Sherman. A classic example of the Horatio Alger myth, Sherman came to Prescott, Arizona, from his native New York State as a penniless schoolteacher. He confidently borrowed heavily and invested in cattle when prices were down and sold at a handsome profit when prices skyrocketed. Sherman moved to Phoenix and invested in land before the land boom of the later 1880s, financed the street-railway system in Phoenix, became a prime participant in the Valley Bank, and by 1890 was the largest taxpayer in Phoenix. Sherman had a flair for organizing syndicates and using other people's money to create his own fortune; this was facilitated by the fact that he had married the daughter of an important Southern Pacific official.[13]

In a seminal essay published in 1957, Robert K. Merton separated and compared two archetypes of influential individuals, namely those whose primary interests were local and those who were more cosmopolitan in outlook.[14] One sees this clearly in examining the Founding Elite, who were locally oriented, and the Entrepreneurs, who had wide-ranging connections: Sherman, who had financial allies in San Francisco and Los Angeles; Christy, who had friends in Iowa and adjacent midwestern states; and Murphy, who had bankers in Chicago and the East. It is this type of activity that distinguishes the two generations who made up the Town Elite and it suggests why Phoenix may have taken off economically rather than its neighbors, such as Wickenburg or Florence, where purely local interests and perspectives dominated and where little growth occurred after the 1880s.

The mild climate as a haven for health seekers was probably the single most important factor in attracting high-quality newcomers with experience and expertise to Phoenix.[15] Consider for example young Dwight B. Heard, heir apparent to the largest hardware company in the nation, who forsook Chicago for Phoenix in the hope of being cured of pulmonary illness. His move was influenced by another Chicagoan, John C. Adams, a former attorney for Marshall Field, who had recently moved to Phoenix—also for family health reasons—and had founded the city's premier hostelry, the Adams Hotel. Moreover, both Adams and Heard were influenced by the presence of winter visitor Whitelaw Reid, publisher of the most important newspaper in the nation, the *New York Tribune*. After his unsuccessful bid for the vice-presidency (on the ticket with Benjamin Harrison) in the 1892 election, Reid traveled to regain his health and spent two winters in Phoenix. He boasted to his eastern friends of the pure air, mild winter climate, and abundant sunshine. The image of Phoenix as a hospitable place for winter visitors was enhanced, and soon W. J. Murphy and his son Ralph founded Ingleside Inn, the first resort hotel in Phoenix. There was a snowball effect. Heard wrote to his family in Chicago, justifying his decision to stay on the frontier because people of the quality of Whitelaw Reid recognized the uniqueness and desirability of Phoenix and were investing in it. Heard then emulated Murphy and Sherman by persuading midwestern and New England visitors to invest in Phoenix land; but because his connections were more extensive than Murphy's or Sherman's, he became an even bigger economic success and had more influence on civic affairs.[16]

Other recruits to the entrepreneurial generation of the Town Elite were Jewish merchants, such as the Goldwater and Goldberg families, who each founded leading mercantile houses that survived through the 1980s (Goldwater's and Hanny's). George Luhrs, a German immigrant, built the Luhrs Hotel, and his sons later built a real estate dynasty in Phoenix (Luhrs Building, Luhrs Tower). John C. Adams, mentioned earlier, was soon elected mayor and became Republican party chief for many years.

Still another cosmopolitan example was political entrepreneur Benjamin A. Fowler, who moved to Phoenix just before 1900. Soon after his arrival he led the fight to have a storage dam built on the Salt River so that the capricious water flow could be controlled for irrigation. A major water storage dam had been discussed since the 1880s. Private dams were financed and partly built, but the projects failed in the 1890s, and by 1900 talk centered on persuading the federal government to help. But how could a town of five thousand people in Arizona Territory (statehood was not attained until 1912) persuade Washington, which had not yet financed reclamation projects, to pick Phoenix as its first major venture?[17]

Fowler was a major reason. He had connections in the East, and he used his lobbying influence in Washington to persuade Department of the Interior engineers to pick Phoenix for a massive demonstration project of what could be accomplished in the arid lands of the West. To be sure, other members of the elite, such as Dwight Heard, who was a personal friend and political confidant of President Theodore Roosevelt, helped out. After Roosevelt signed the Reclamation Act of 1902, development of the Salt River was announced as the first major national endeavor. In one bold stroke, Fowler and other elite members had harnessed the financial power and technical know-how of the federal government to do a job where private enterprise had failed. When the dam was formally dedicated (by former President Theodore Roosevelt) in 1911, a new era of agricultural abundance opened for Phoenix and the adjacent Salt River towns of Mesa, Tempe, and Glendale.[18]

Two other major accomplishments of the Town Elite's later cohort were obtaining spur lines to Phoenix from the Southern Pacific to the south and the Santa Fe to the north by 1887 and 1895, respectively. This meant that the agricultural produce of the valley, then still its main economic resource, could now be sent to California and eastern markets. At the same time, as their town grew and its economic potential soared, the Town Elite literally absconded with the state capital. Phoenix community leaders reasoned that if their town were going to have any pretensions for greatness, it must become the territorial capital. In 1889 they induced the legislature, sitting in Prescott, then the capital (it had also been in Tucson for a time), to remove to Phoenix by parlor car, via California, with all expenses paid. Phoenix delegates mustered votes and the victory was celebrated all the way to Phoenix. In one fell swoop, Phoenix entrepreneurs put the ornament in the crown they planned for their city, which was centrally located in a huge agricultural plain. The future of Phoenix seemed certain when Roosevelt Dam was dedicated and regular water assured. In 1912, President Taft signed Arizona into statehood and Phoenix became the state capital. The big desert town had now become a small city.[19]

## THE CITY ELITE, 1910–1960
### The Old City Elite, 1910–1935

Statehood brought a new vista for leading business and civic leaders. For several years until World War I, boosterism flourished and publicity for Phoenix as a garden city and a desert oasis flooded the country. Some members of the Town Elite survived into this period and provided continuing leadership—Heard for example—but Fowler, the prime mover in obtaining the dam, had been succeeded by John Orme as head of the Salt River Valley Water Users Association, which controlled the dam, power, and irrigation districts. Sherman moved to Los Angeles. Others of the elite founding families continued to be active: Lloyd Christy continued for his family, heading the Valley Bank and serving as mayor of Phoenix; Sylvan Ganz followed in his father's footsteps as a leading banker. The Goldwater family produced two sons, Robert and Barry, who became active by the end of this period and who would furnish continuity for this pioneer family for another generation. Ralph Murphy managed Ingleside Inn and other properties of his father, W. J Murphy.[20]

New faces appeared in Phoenix after the dam and statehood. This group is called the Old City Elite. Largely from the Midwest, they sought opportunity in what now appeared to be the largest city in Arizona, for in 1910, Phoenix, at 11,134, was edging up on Tucson at 13,193.[21] George Mickle arrived in the valley soon after statehood, recognized the need for neighborhood markets, and soon founded the largest chain in Arizona, the Pay 'n' Takit markets. In 1927, Mickle sold out to Safeway Stores and plowed his millions into creating Phoenix Title and Trust Company and building a new skyscraper in Phoenix. He changed business interests and became the very model of the successful entrepreneur who made his fortune in Phoenix, unlike Heard who arrived with heavy Chicago backing. Mickle was active until the 1950s.[22]

Another newcomer was Charles A. Stauffer, publisher of the *Arizona Republic* and *Phoenix Gazette*. Stauffer lived in Dwight Heard's shadow for many years as his chief assistant, but when Heard died in 1929, Stauffer took over the *Republic* and merged it with the *Gazette*. Stauffer became Phoenix's first true press lord by the early 1930s. A mild-mannered, sensitive man, he was well liked in the community. He also had a golden touch for investments and learned how to be an anonymous philanthropist from his mentor, Heard. Unlike most members of either the Town or Old City Elite, who had migrated to Phoenix, Stauffer had been reared in the valley. His period of maximum influence was the 1920s and 1930s. Toward the end of the Depression, his brother-in-law, Wesley Knorpp, increasingly ran the newspaper, radio station KTAR, and other enterprises. For an entire generation, Stauffer and his *Republic* editor, J. W. "Uncle Billy" Spear, were the chief opinion molders in the community.[23]

The Town Elite founded and nourished the basic institutions which became so important in helping to define community leadership during this period, but it was the Old City Elite who initiated the service clubs, such as Rotary, Kiwanis, and Lions; the social clubs, such as the Arizona Club, El Zaribah Shrine, and the Phoenix Country Club; and the Phoenix Chamber of Commerce, which grew out of the old board of trade. This group became conscious of having a "correct address," and members sought exclusive neighborhoods like Los Olivos (pioneered by Heard), between Central Avenue and Third Street; Palmcroft, between Seventh and Fifteenth avenues north of McDowell Road; and Country Club Estates, surrounding the clubhouse of the Phoenix Country Club. These prime locations became new seats of power for business, professional, and industrial leaders, with the Country Club area housing affluent winter visitors who now made Phoenix their private residence. The new areas replaced the Bennett and Churchill additions south of McDowell, which had been prime residential locations for the Town Elite.[24]

It is not surprising that during this period an attempt to create a polite society in Phoenix occurred. Since Phoenix had never been a western town with stereotypic frontier manners and mores, there was no uncivilized past to erase or conveniently forget. Since there was little industry in Phoenix, there was no division between blue-collar workers and managerial or bureaucratic workers. Rather, Phoenix was a city dominated by a commercial elite who benefited from the wealth of the farmers who managed the region's agricultural enterprises. (During this period many farmers, laden with profits from cotton, citrus, and melons, moved to the city.) Perceptions of who was to be in polite society centered on the inclusion of a number of families who dated from Town Elite days, a few from the Founding Elite days, and many who were settling in Phoenix. The first edition of the Phoenix Social Register appeared in 1914 and appeared infrequently for the next two decades.[25]

A far more important means of demarcating who was really part of old Phoenix was the construction, shortly after the turn of the century, of Iron Springs, a summer resort in the pine forest near Prescott. Early Phoenix families joined together to organize an exclusive summer vacation retreat for women and children, since most husbands stayed in Phoenix to work during the sweltering summers but took the train to visit on weekends. Acceptance into this self-defining community was far more indicative of a person's status than inclusion in the social register.[26]

The Woman's Club was founded in 1900 and would continue to be a major focal point for feminine activities for the next fifty years. Social life in pre–World War II days was rooted in personal entertainments, informal parties, and several seasonal balls, the most well known of which was St. Luke's Ball, begun in the 1920s and still given today as a benefit for St. Luke's Hospital. Ironically, a woman who remained an outsider at heart was the dominant person in Phoenix social life. This was Maie Bartlett Heard, wife of Dwight, who survived his death in the late 1920s for more than twenty years. Mrs. Heard directed numerous charities, founded the well-known Heard Museum (one of the nation's premiere repositories of American Indian art), privately financed the major community welfare operation (the Social Services Center) before the New Deal, and helped innumerable community service organizations, such as the Boy Scouts. Yet Mrs. Heard never bought a house at Iron Springs, and the guest book at her home, Casa Blanca, kept from about 1902 until her husband's death, reveals precious few Phoenicians who dined at her table; most of her guests were visiting notables. In a sense, she typified a few families who considered themselves above local polite society. In her case, her father was one of Chicago's most respected and influential citizens. Maie Heard took her social status from Chicago, not Phoenix, even though Phoenix was her home for fifty years.[27]

Domination of the chamber of commerce after World War I was in keeping with a Harding-Coolidge era preoccupation with business as gospel; in the Phoenix instance, the 1920s and 1930s became an era of weakness in city government. This was a cruel disappointment to the progressives who had sponsored a new city charter in 1913 and had put Phoenix in the vanguard nationally in moving to a city manager–commission form of government. Unfortunately, no attempt was made to find professional city managers and the position became a part of the Phoenix spoils system. Rarely rising above local squabbles, city politics was dominated by second- and third-echelon community leaders. Petty vice lords arose in the 1930s and 1940s, payoffs were common on municipal contracts, and city life acquired a seamy side. But Phoenix never became a corrupt fiefdom for a city boss or clique; rather, it suffered from neglect of the true community leaders, who were busy in commerce, agriculture, and the professions. In the latter category a host of lawyers and doctors who would become important in local affairs now surfaced; the Old City Elite included such affluent physicians as R. W. Craig, E. Payne Palmer, Sr., and W. J. McLoone and such prominent attorneys as J. L. B. Alexander, Louis Chalmers, Alexis Baker, and Richard Sloan.[28]

A consolidation of power among families also took place: this was the era of most growth for Jewish merchant families like the Goldwaters, Diamonds, and Korricks. The O'Malley family, arriving from St. Louis in the early 1900s, emerged during this time as a major force in lumberyards, building materials, land, and development. The McArthur brothers, Warren and Charles, perhaps best typified the success of family enterprises. Moving from Chicago soon after statehood, they became distributors for Dodge motor cars and by the 1920s had become two of Phoenix's leading entrepreneurs. They conceived of an international resort hotel on the desert in Phoenix—decades ahead of their time—and found backing to build the world-famous Arizona Biltmore, finished in 1929. The McArthurs, with their connections in Chicago, typified the cosmopolitan aspect of the Old City Elite. However, the Depression cut short their plans and the Wrigley family took over the Biltmore. Indeed, the Wrigleys had built the ultimate mansion in Phoenix atop a knoll adjacent to the Biltmore from which they could watch Phoenix at work to the south and the Biltmore crowd at play to the east. (The Wrigleys heralded another group to be considered below, the Expatriate Elites.)[29]

What was the major accomplishment of the Old City Elite? They presided over the transition from town to city by pushing Phoenix into a building boom without precedent in the 1920s. The Phoenix skyline for the next four decades was created as in quick succession the Heard, Luhrs, Security, Luhrs Tower, and Title and Trust buildings were constructed. George Luhrs, second-generation member of the local elite, was put in charge of his family's two major edifices and struggled during the Depression to keep them open. The modernized American skyline of high-rise buildings was this group's main legacy to the city, a reflection of its determination to transform Phoenix from a garden town into a well-defined city with downtown shopping and professional services.[30]

### The New City Elite—1935–1960

Growing out of the Town and Old City Elites, the New City Elite became the group that tightened control of the city by maintaining power at the chamber of commerce and in 1949, by means of charter government reform, taking control of city politics. Little different from the Old City Elite in practice, these people had old names but were a new generation: second-generation O'Malleys, third-generation Goldwaters. This was the group that, after consolidating power, laid plans for postwar expansion of Phoenix and managed to direct and control the city until about 1960, when Phoenix became a metropolitan area far transcending even the most grandiose chamber of commerce projections of 1945.[31]

Another example was Walter Bimson, who personified newer elements in Phoenix. The Colorado native became a talented young executive at Harris Trust in Chicago. Like Heard forty years before him, Bimson, who visited Phoenix on bank investments, saw his future in Arizona and accepted an offer to take over the ailing Valley Bank. Bimson's success in saving the bank provided the foundation for other Phoenix businesses in coping with the Depression and with rebuilding. Bimson founded a banking dynasty and provided cosmopolitan leadership for Phoenicians for three decades. Furthermore, he brought a new level of sophistication and maturity to the city by stressing cultural activities. He assembled his own first-rate art collection, persuaded his bank to invest in art, then became the catalyst for the community to build the Phoenix Art Museum in the 1950s.[32]

In fact, one can argue that, aside from political reform, this elite cohort group's greatest accomplishments were cultural. Dr. Howell Randolph, a physician of taste and sophistication, became the prime mover in creating the Phoenix Symphony Orchestra in the mid-1940s. Pre–World War II Phoenix was a city of limited cultural life, but the postwar surge of population brought with it newcomers who were interested in providing Phoenix with cultural institutions hitherto neglected.[33]

By 1940, as this new group consolidated, other newcomers beyond Bimson appeared. Preeminent among attorneys were Orme Lewis and Frank Snell; within a few years both founded law firms which became the most prestigious firms in town and still bear their names. Snell, especially, emerged during the war as a community power broker when he was able to convince a weak city hall to clamp down on rampant vice conditions, this in part as an inducement to lift restrictions on weekend liberty for thousands of servicemen stationed at nearby Luke and Williams air force bases. After the war Snell joined forces with ally Edward O'Malley on a variety of projects, and a list of his accomplishments in bringing community projects to life (working with Bimson on the art museum and founding the Thunderbird School of Foreign Trade, for example) is long indeed. Snell and O'Malley were successful in helping Phoenix gain control of its second-largest utility, Arizona Public Service, and Snell later served as board chairman. Snell never held public office, preferring to work through a close group of allies to make certain that community affairs went in the "right direction." It was a measure of agreement at the top that no one ever suggested that either Bimson or Snell were city bosses; rather, they personified the aspirations of the directing elite group they led.[34]

The attitude of shared agreement characterized the direction of city life in Phoenix from the beginning; for such a meager population base, perhaps this is not surprising. It proved to be essential as the middle New City Elite period began after World War II. Phoenix had benefited immensely from war industries (for example, Goodyear, AiResearch, and Aluminum Company of America) plus five army air training facilities, a navy depot, and an army training ground. When peace came, the local economy was immediately in trouble because these war industries closed. The business community of Phoenix feared a return to a prewar agricultural economy. Lewis Haas, an experienced executive, was brought in to revivify the chamber of commerce, and under his direction, chamber staff and citizen committees launched an ambitious drive to bring industry back to Phoenix. International events intervened to aid the cause; the Korean War buildup meant that electronics manufacturers, such as Motorola, took a fresh look at Phoenix and constructed plants. By the end of the 1950s, General Electric and Sperry Rand had been lured to the valley, and with them came a host of related smaller manufacturers, jobbers, and suppliers.[35]

Before the economic miracle could succeed, however, it became clear to the directing elite that control of city hall was essential before industry could be persuaded to bank on Phoenix. Although, under Snell's influence, vice had been cleaned up during the war, politics in the immediate postwar period lapsed back into the apathetic situation of the 1930s. In this instance a crusading *Republic* and *Gazette*, now taken over by Hoosier publisher Eugene Pulliam, who had bought out Stauffer and Knorpp, led the way by exposing the unfortunate return of vice, graft, and payoffs at city hall. A citizens committee, appointed by Mayor Ray Busey, who was struggling to reform the system he had inherited, came in with recommendations to revamp the city's charter. The result was that the commission form of government, with each commissioner presiding over certain prerequisites, such as police or streets, was thrown out and a council system with members elected from the city at large was instituted. Moreover, the requirement that the city manager be a legal resident of Phoenix when appointed was abolished, since for years this had precluded the hiring of a professionally trained manager from another city. New elections were called in 1949, and a slate of candidates (henceforth known as the Charter Government Committee ticket) drawn from the New City Elite took over city hall. Nicholas Udall, Mormon lawyer and scion of the well-known Udall family, was elected mayor; Harry Rosenzweig, member of the prominent jewelry family, and others were elected to the council. Rosenzweig made political history by persuading another son of an Old City Elite family to run for council, a man who had made a name for himself as an outstanding photographer and adventurer, organizing boat trips down the Colorado River through Grand Canyon when few mortals attempted such a feat. This newcomer to local politics proved to be so adept and popular that he stayed only one term on the reformed council. In 1952 he audaciously ran against Ernest W. McFarland for Arizona's U.S. Senate seat. McFarland, Harry S Truman's majority leader and mentor of Lyndon B. Johnson, was retired by this brash upstart who had cut his teeth in city politics: Barry Goldwater.[36]

For the next twenty-five years, Phoenix politics was dominated by the Charter Government Committee, which met in secret every two years to handpick a slate of candidates for city office. The committee was dominated by members of the New City Elite, and opponents derided the fact that most of Charter's candidates over the years lived in the more affluent suburbs, belonged to many of the same clubs, and had a WASPish orientation. Charter's managers were not naïve and attempted to provide ethnic and religious representation. Hence at various times Charter handpicked Mexican American, Asian American, and African-American candidates, and regular spots were assigned to Jews, Mormons, and Catholics. One of Charter's wisest decisions was to name Ray Wilson city manager in 1950. Wilson, previously associate manager at Kansas City, Missouri, brought the first hand of professional management to Phoenix and left an indelible mark of expertise that helped transform the city. In a complete turnaround, Phoenix now became a showcase of municipal government. An example of the city's excellence in this regard was the inauguration of a prestigious internship program that ranks today as one of the nation's finest. The reform thereby provided the reputation for honest municipal administration that helped attract the new industry the chamber of commerce was seeking.[37]

Whereas elected city government participants between the wars included relatively few able community leaders, the lists of Charter Government–picked candidates during the 1950s and into the 1970s reads like a who's who of local business and professional leadership. During the 1950s the high point of elite influence was reached because there was still only one major group running Phoenix: Charter. It ran politics and its informal backers, such as Snell, Bimson, O'Malley, and Pulliam (none of whom ever held office), provided the link to the chamber of commerce and Lewis Haas. Politics and economic development worked hand in hand, and when well-known Phoenix broadcaster Jack Williams was elected mayor in the mid-1950s, the news media were recruited as part of the directing group. Williams, whose voice had been known to Phoenicians for twenty years, was an authentic New City Elite member. He had grown up during the Old City Elite period, but he now helped articulate the goals of the newer cohort group. Many Charter members and allies became part of the Goldwater wing of the Republican party, but Williams's successor as mayor after four years, Democrat Sam Mardian, demonstrated that Charter remained essentially bipartisan. Williams went on to become governor of Arizona for several terms—an exception, since most Charter candidates never ran for state office, viewing their turn at city council a civic responsibility.[38]

During the 1950s, Phoenix stayed firmly in the hands of the generation which emerged in the mid- and late-1930s: Bimson; Snell; O'Malley; Orme Lewis; the Rosenzweig brothers, Harry and Newton; and others. They were joined by newcomer publisher Pulliam and chamber of commerce head Haas in the 1940s; indeed, as Phoenix's population quadrupled, other newcomers arrived, but their major influence and activity were deferred to the 1960s and beyond. The 1950s, the decade of Eisenhower normalcy, was also the classical period of one-elite-group rule in Phoenix, with all the economic, political, and media bases covered. It was a time when Frank Snell, as members of the elite had done for several decades, could still sit down for lunch at the Arizona Club with a few friends and develop either public or private policy for Phoenix, as the occasion demanded. It was a time when the directing elite welcomed the onrush of growth in Phoenix, since everyone was becoming affluent; it seemed as if this group had promoted a demographic revolution that would ensure an economic bonanza for the old families.[39]

## THE METROPOLITAN ELITES, 1960–1990

The very success Charter and the chamber of commerce provided proved to be the eventual undoing of the New City Elite. With Phoenix expanding from a population of one hundred thousand in 1950 to more than four times that number in 1960, the unprecedented influx of newcomers meant the ruling elite faced problems of recruitment (who would be allowed to enter their ranks?) and maintenance of power (how to replace aging or dead members). A more serious problem was spatial development because the demographic revolution was spreading Phoenix over hundreds of square miles annexed by the city. The greatest expansion occurred during the regimes of Mayor Jack Williams (late 1950s) and Mayor Sam Mardian (early 1960s). By the late 1960s this Los Angeles–like urban sprawl resulted in the creation of multiple power centers throughout the Salt River Valley.

First, within Phoenix, the midtown area developed when Ralph Burgbacher's new Park Central Mall stimulated decentralization of the downtown nucleus. Soon a host of high-rise buildings mushroomed in the corridor along Central Avenue, housing new corporations, new ventures, and newcomers with different agendas from the old elites. This was particularly true in banking, where old-line institutions like Valley Bank, First National Bank, and Arizona Bank built new headquarters in thirty- and forty-story skyscrapers but placed them downtown, while most of the newer financial entities built in midtown. Walter Bimson of Valley Bank and Sherman Hazeltine of First National Bank committed their institutions to remain in the old town center which had been the home of four generations of elites. With no such nostalgia, the newcomers, the Metropolitan Elites, chose midtown.[40]

Or they preferred other valley locations that proved attractive. Scottsdale, just northeast of Phoenix proper, is an example. Once a tourist mecca with cheap, westernlike store facades, Scottsdale emerged from curiosity status in the 1940s to become a full-fledged modern city by the late 1950s and 1960s. After battling Phoenix and successfully annexing a huge slice of the northeast residential area, Scottsdale increasingly became the home of affluent newcomers; some were retired winter visitors prolonging their stay, and others were ambitious younger professional business people. In fact, Scottsdale became a symbol for an ambitious, often nouveau riche group of people who set up their own standards of exclusivity. Another power center was the Mesa-Tempe complex adjacent to the southeast; these two cities both had more than one hundred thousand residents by 1970 and no longer could be considered mere bedroom communities of Phoenix. Talley Industries located in Mesa and Tempe, home of Arizona State University, so these cities became a center for research and high-tech industries, and together with Chandler farther to the southeast they were the biggest growth area in the valley in the late 1970s and 1980s.[41]

An embryonic power center emerging at the end of this period was Northwest Phoenix–Glendale, an area long dominated by agricultural interests. With completion of the gigantic Metrocenter Mall, the area gained a more specific focus. By the early 1980s, a fourth power center was forming in Phoenix: the Camelback-Biltmore corridor on East Camelback Road, with an axis furnished by Forty-fourth Street (near the resorts that had proliferated after the war and firmly established the desirability of Phoenix climate and lifestyle). Each one of these new centers had its own group of economic and civic leaders. Even such veterans as Frank Snell admitted it was no longer possible to sit down for lunch at the Arizona Club and decide the fortunes of the city. There were now too many clubs, too many players, too many interests.

Phoenix had reached the size and status of a major metropolis by 1980, and this gave rise to what political scientists call pluralistic power centers and pluralistic elites. The decade of the 1960s was the period of transition as the old single-focus elite waned and the multiple new power centers came to the fore. In politics, Charter Government held on but almost lost out under Charter Mayor Milt Graham, whose popularity eventually caused him to abandon Charter and win reelection as an independent. But the die was cast, and after Charter Mayors John Driggs and Tim Barrow had finished their terms, Margaret Hance emerged as an independent by the mid-1970s. An aging Charter Government Committee finally abandoned politics by the end of the decade, and 1980 found Phoenix realigning politically, with ethnic groups and disadvantaged economic groups claiming more representation in the city's councils. The new mayor, Terry Goddard, was the son of a former Arizona governor, but his connections were with the future, not the past.[42]

From an economic perspective, diffused power throughout Phoenix was the order of the day. One exception was the news media, however, which were still firmly in the hands of the old elite (McFarland's and Chauncey's television stations, Pulliam's newspapers). But even the media changed when Chauncey sold out and McFarland and Pulliam died. While one could find examples of younger generations of older elites active in Phoenix (Richard Snell of Ramada Inn, Gary Driggs of Western Savings, and Ed Korrick on the city council), the most obvious fact about Phoenix was that its directing elites had become metropolitan and dispersed.

Another way of looking at leadership in contemporary Phoenix is demonstrated by the five hundred interviews completed for the Phoenix History Project; a broad pattern of influentials has been suggested. This can be seen in a breakdown of the Metropolitan Elites category:

1. *The Technicians.* These are the highly trained bureaucrats who run city hall and its services, who work in the multiple layers of staff and bureaucracy which characterize an expanded state government. These are also the high tech engineers of Motorola, General Electric, Sperry, Honeywell, and McDonnell-Douglas.

2. *The Managers.* With the rise of big industrial corporations in Phoenix, dozens of top executives have invaded the valley. Some, such as the head of Greyhound, who preferred Phoenix to Chicago, have moved the entire corporation to the valley. Phelps-Dodge, the Arizona copper giant, moved its headquarters to Phoenix.

3. *The New Entrepreneurs.* These are the David Murdocks and Karl Ellers, who built syndicates, conglomerates, and skyscrapers. One of them, William Schulz, who became the apartment king of Phoenix, dared to challenge Barry Goldwater for the Senate in 1980—and almost won.

4. *The Cultural Brokers.* Postwar Phoenix needed cultural institutions, and although old elite member Walter Bimson helped move the city in new cultural directions, it was members of the new Metropolitan Elites, such as newcomer Lewis Ruskin and his interest in the Phoenix Symphony, who put a stamp of quality and cosmopolitanism on Phoenix's new cultural institutions. This also includes the Phoenix Zoo, which the Maytag family of Iowa helped found.

5. *The Intellectuals.* Singularly absent from Phoenix life until the 1960s, this group has grown parallel with Arizona State University (more than fifty thousand students by 1990), which has become one of the largest urban centers of research and higher learning in the country. Retirement and attractive climate also have drawn writers, artists, and other professionals to Phoenix.

One can question whether these approximate interest groups belong within a larger elite structure, and it is possible that the notion of multiple power centers and pluralist elites may be tempered by interest groups and coalitions. Groups increasingly interested in gaining access to power include ethnic minorities, retired people, and the economically disadvantaged. All are important factions now willing to take action and seek political remedies for perceived inequities.

Yet another group has made an impact on Phoenix, the so-called Expatriate Elites. Since the beginning of the twentieth century, Phoenix has attracted winter visitors, including men of national influence, such as publisher Whitelaw Reid in the 1890s and Henry Luce of Time, Inc., in the 1950s. Others, such as the Wrigleys, McCormicks, and Lincolns, have been a special force in the community, endowing institutions and making major investments. The fact that both Harris Trust and Northern Trust of Chicago, two of Illinois's largest banks, recently opened branch offices in Scottsdale suggests the scale and importance of expatriate activity in Phoenix.[43]

These preliminary impressions of the new Metropolitan Elites suggest the fluidity of the 1990s situation in Phoenix. It is a period of transition and realignment in all spheres. In a city which has been characterized by rapid social change, the pace of change has accelerated even more since 1960. Frank Snell said he thought Phoenix had always been relatively open for newcomers and that those who aspired to participate in the direction of the community could be accommodated. The bulk of research supports this view—that is, provided you were not a member of a minority or ethnic group.

Phoenix had few original-entry ethnic enclaves; almost all ethnic groups (save some Mexican Americans) had lived elsewhere before migrating to Phoenix; they were what is often called redirects. Thus it was possible for some Italian American and Jewish American families (such as the Donofrios and Goldbergs) to penetrate the ranks of the Old City Elite in the early 1900s. Save for the early country clubs, Phoenician society rarely displayed much anti-Semitism. But access to power for Mexican Americans and blacks had to wait until the 1950s and 1960s, when representatives were admitted to city hall on Charter tickets. By standards of the 1990s, appointing these leaders was probably tokenism, but at the time, Phoenix was proud to admit such ethnic minorities to the levers of power. Only American Indians have been totally excluded from beginning to present, and they are a special case, since most local Indians were excluded from public schools or failed to take advantage (if indeed they could) of the federal Indian school at Phoenix, which trained generations of Indian leaders for such nations as the Navajo, far removed from Phoenix. Local Indians, such as the Maricopas, Papagos, and Pimas, have been less successful in putting enough young people into the education system to bring forth a new generation of aspirants to leadership until the present; perhaps their day at city hall will come.[44]

The data do not allow further speculation on the crucial theoretical question of circulation of elites, but it seems apparent that the post-1960 period will be viewed by future historians as the time when the old elite structure crumbled, when great population increases resulted in new power centers and pluralist elites as well as dramatic spatial expansion, and when minority and other ethnic and special-interest groups became part of the metropolitan structure. No longer does one group direct the political and economic affairs of Phoenix.

Though they have not created a modern Utopia, as some Phoenix boosters have proclaimed, the several generations of successive directing elites have exercised a dominant influence on the development of one of the nation's largest (ninth in 1990), fastest growing, and most cosmopolitan cities. Will this growth continue, as city fathers and most of the Metropolitan Elites wish, or will the momentum of Phoenix slow down for the balance of the twentieth century to assimilate its hundreds of thousands of newcomers? The period 1990 to 2000 may prove to be still another turning point for the community as the city strives to consolidate and create a new formula for leadership.

One other major factor affecting the post-1960 period in Phoenix is the fact that local influentials have lost control, not only because of the demographic explosion that changed the face of Phoenix, but also because Phoenix has become a part of the national Sunbelt phenomenon. Growth of federal government programs has meant that even city hall, originally and ironically the very bastion of Goldwaterism, has become dependent upon Washington for many programs and services. New factories and new service industries, such as American Express, that have located in Phoenix are national in scope and have had few (if any) local ties. By the late 1980s, Phoenix had entered a real estate and financial slump which took a terrible toll on locally owned financial insitutions: Western Savings of the Driggses, MeraBank of the Rices, and Southwest Savings were bought up by Bank of America. The Goldwater department store, which had been sold earlier, now became part of a Southern California chain, Robinson's. The proudest name in local commerce was gone; indeed, the independence of practically every locally owned business had vanished. Only Bimson's Valley Bank and a handful of other firms remained. As we go to press, sale of the venerable Valley Bank to Banc One of Columbus, Ohio, has been anounced. Phoenix had become a metropolis and a national institution, since, as one wit observed, "every winter that plunges below normal temperatures brings ten thousand new recruits to Phoenix." Even the venerable Frank Snell, who helped orchestrate the postwar growth, later admitted that he never imagined Phoenix would become so large.[45]

The larger significance of this study may lie in the fact that as a frontier community Phoenix was able to control its own fortunes until quite late, when other, older cities had succumbed to economic, political, and social forces of a national character. We have seen how during the formative years the quality of leaders attracted made it possible for Phoenix to surpass other frontier communities, to become the state capital, and to obtain federal backing for building a storage dam. Later, other dynamic civic leaders helped garner air force, navy, and army facilities for Phoenix during World War II; and even later, this group of elites, now several generations in time depth, convinced the entire nation of Phoenix's virtues. The result was spectacularly successful. The rich agricultural base was built upon by light manufacturing and service industries and buttressed by tourism and retirement industries of major proportions. To a casual visitor in the 1990s, it might have appeared that after 120 years of growth it was inevitable that Phoenix should have become one of the nation's Sunbelt capitals. But getting from 1870 to 1990 was made possible largely by the willpower and energy of Phoenix's directing elites, whose plucky leadership dramatically transformed the desert hamlet on the banks of the Salt River.[46]

## CHAPTER THREE

# Phoenix Women
## in the Development of Public Policy:
## Territorial Beginnings

### BY AIMÉE DE POTTER LYKES

IT WOULD seem that even people who look somewhat askance at the women's movement of the 1970s and 1980s must credit it with a positive influence on American historiography. Historians seek the truth, and the recapturing of more of the past as lived by women can do nothing but correct the understandable preoccupation of a largely male profession with the pursuits and achievements of men. Women hold up half the sky, as the Chinese say.

From townsite selection in 1870 to Arizona's emergence as a state in 1912, the women of Phoenix were a microcosmic part of the American nation. Toward the close of the territorial era, the census in Phoenix counted only about 13,000 people. Moreover, the tough Arizona frontier was a masculine environment, partly because it had few women, and those were divided by language, color, and class. In the 1882 county census, the Phoenix population of 2,764 listed only about 180 women over twenty-one with non-Spanish surnames, not a few of them foreign born. While the female population would of course grow with time, the achievers discussed here remained a tiny fraction of the population.[1]

Why is such a small group significant to history? This essay grew out of an investigation of women's groups, a phenomenon of particular interest in the Phoenix territorial era because upper-middle-class women, at least, depended on their groups more than they would in later decades. Most led private, home-centered lives. Only an occasional hotel-keeper, even doctor, challenged the exclusive maleness of business and the professions. Without the ballot, women were also peripheral politically. Most entertainment took place in saloons, gambling dens, and red-light districts that the socially acceptable women left to their "public" sisters.[2] With or without a family, certainly without the enter- tainments of modern media, home could be lonely. Besides church involvement, women who had any leisure turned to other women, not only for companionship, but also for intellectual stimulation and sometimes for a sense of social significance.[3]

Women's peripheral public and political situation caused them to address issues through their organizations; their leaders spoke for the group. Territorial groups tended to be restricted, formally or informally, by sex, so that the pattern of women's influence was perhaps more organizationally definable than it would be in later decades. The two sides of the coin of group involvement, personal self-fulfillment and public service, seem dramatically displayed.

Early Phoenix women's groups had significant, sometimes decisive, influence upon a number of important public issues, among them prohibition, organized charity, the public-library movement, and woman suffrage itself.

## PROHIBITION

It is perhaps difficult in the late twentieth century to imagine temperance as the chief focus of a women's movement that sought to enhance women's power, but the temperance movement generally addressed more issues than liquor traffic alone. This is not to say the Women's Christian Temperance Union (WCTU) was the only important women's group or that women could have succeeded without the indispensable support— and votes—of male allies. But in Phoenix, as elsewhere in nineteenth-century America, it was most often the WCTU that initiated or furthered women's other civic efforts.[4]

On May 1, 1884, at the urging of the wife of Colonel Clendenning of Prescott's Whipple Barracks, a Phoenix branch of the one-year-old territorial WCTU was launched in a flower-bedecked ceremony at the Baptist Church. Dr. Eliza Ingalls, a specialist in women's diseases, was elected president. The WCTU's voice now joined the Good Templars, a national temperance organization open to women, which had been in Phoenix for six years.[5]

Beginning with the crowded second territorial WCTU convention that December at the Methodist Church on Washington Street, Phoenix before 1912 would host at least eleven of twenty-three of these annual territorial conventions, assuring its local chapter a key role. The 1884 meeting resulted in Arizona women's political initiation. Appealing directly to the reformist Thirteenth Assembly in Prescott, the WCTU obtained a law forbidding liquor sales on election days, and the assembly went on to punish election corruption and to ban minors under sixteen from saloons. At the 1887 WCTU convention, again in Phoenix, a legislative committee was established that persuaded the legislature to raise the marital age of consent to sixteen. It also lobbied for the harder-won Sunday closing of businesses, finally achieving this in 1889.[6]

However, the 1890s brought a stiffening on both sides. The 1887 WCTU convention had voted to seek the abolition of gambling, but the Fourteenth Assembly raised the prices for saloon and gambling licenses only slightly in 1889. That year the territorial capital moved to Phoenix, where twenty-two saloons for a population of three thousand hardly provided an ambiance for temperance laws. For its part, as reform-mindedness swept 1890s America, the WCTU replaced its goal of temperance—moderating liquor consumption—with prohibition of the manufacture or sale of liquor. Its 1890 territorial convention in Tucson, with Mrs. R. W. Pearson of Phoenix (wife of the Episcopal chaplain to the assembly) presiding, focused on atrocities by drunken Indians and passed a resolution seeking to ban liquor manufacture and sales in the territory.[7]

In 1893, Louis Hughes of Tucson began a three-year term as Arizona's governor. His wife, Josephine, and her friend Frances Willard, national WCTU president, had founded the territorial WCTU in 1883, and in 1890, Josephine Hughes had followed Mrs. Pearson as the territorial WCTU president. The Hugheses together published the prohibitionist *Tucson Star*. As governor, Louis Hughes advocated temperance and woman suffrage, as did Gov. Nathan O. Murphy, who preceded and followed Hughes. But the decade's assemblies remained unmoved, although both the WCTU and the Templars were mushrooming.[8]

By 1898, Phoenix had perhaps the largest of eight WCTU locals in Arizona, all adjured by the territorial WCTU to meet at least monthly and cooperate with ministers. While the aggressive Methodist church was the bellwether, all major Protestant denominations in the Salt River Valley had at least some WCTU involvement. Public meetings were held in churches throughout the territorial years. The thirteenth territorial convention in Tempe in 1901 initiated a hard-hitting program: each local was (1) to appeal to churchgoers with at least four gospel temperance meetings a year, (2) to emphasize youth work, and (3) to visit county jails, Indian reservations, and schools.[9]

That same year, a local focus was created for all prohibitionists, including the national Prohibition party's Phoenix branch. According to historian James McClintock, it was "largely through the influence of the Mormon Church" that a local-option law was pushed through the legislature requiring county boards of supervisors, upon petition, to hold elections in counties or subdivisions on whether liquor should be sold.[10]

Neither the WCTU nor the Templars campaigned for the first local-option election on June 24, 1902. Certain of victory in the election district north of the Salt River but excluding Phoenix, they were proved correct. Of 370 votes, prohibition received 282. However, the astonished saloonkeepers leaped into action, and in February 1903, Phoenician Louis Melzcer secured a decision from District Judge Kent invalidating the election for irregularities and enjoining the county sheriff to issue Melzcer a saloon license in the dry district.[11]

The previous month at its annual meeting, the Phoenix WCTU had pronounced 1902 a good year. Following the national WCTU pattern, the local WCTU was now reaching out to many Phoenicians: "colored" people, prisoners, women wanting the franchise (headed by Mrs. Mary McCormick, to be one of the incorporators of the Phoenix Woman's Club in 1907), "purity and mothers' meetings" (headed by territorial president Imogene LaChance), the press, miners. There were temperance publications, a medal contest, school savings books, the Loyal Temperance Legion (a youth group instituted in Arizona in 1887 by national organizer M. L. Blair and headed by a woman to be of major significance in the WCTU, Christianna Gilchrist), rescue work (with prostitutes), nonalcoholic medication, antinarcotics, Sunday schools, and "parlor meetings." A few days after the annual meeting, eighty women heard Miss Louise Hollister, national WCTU organizer, at a parlor meeting. By June the new "mothers' meetings," held at the WCTU headquarters at Monroe and Center streets, attracted considerable attention.[12]

The second local-option vote in August 1903 followed the pattern of the first. With little preelection activity, the valley's "prudent farmers [were] . . . convinced that drinking was a vice." The vote, taken in nearly all the inhabited valley but Phoenix, Tempe, and Mesa, again went dry, 315 to 152. A few days later, Scottsdale voted dry, 321 to 153. But the district court again voided the election when the saloonkeepers instituted mandamus proceedings.[13] In April 1905, Mrs. L. M. N. Stevens and Miss Anna Gordon, respectively president and vice-president of the national WCTU, were enthusiastically greeted at local WCTU meetings in Phoenix. Perhaps not coincidentally, a strategy to overwhelm the Phoenix wet vote appeared in the news. But WCTU growth apparently had slowed from a 1904 surge and the two-thirds vote required for county-wide prohibition seemed unattainable.[14]

Onto this lackluster scene came W. W. Stevens, New Mexico superintendent of the Anti-Saloon League, by now the nation's most aggressive prohibition group. Masculine in leadership, the twelve-year-old Anti-Saloon League controlled votes and could be direct and pragmatic. Focusing more strictly than the WCTU on prohibition, it specialized in local-option elections. However, the new Phoenix league listened when Eugene ("Bucky") O'Neill, leading Democratic legislator and husband of suffragist Pauline ONeill, advised that voters were not yet up to abolishing saloons and suggested the strategy of higher license fees. For the fall of 1906, the Anti-Saloon League decided to influence legislators rather than back candidates.[15]

Within months, city saloon licenses had risen to one thousand dollars a year. Governor Kibbey, a former judge and husband of a leader of the Friday Club and the Woman's Club, became a powerful Anti-Saloon League ally after his appointment in 1905. He successfully advocated 1907 laws barring women from saloons and abolishing gambling—women had helped secure a Phoenix opinion poll for the abolition of gambling.[16]

The saloonkeepers tried for an injunction to bar a third local-option election, this time countywide, for which Dr. H. A. Hughes, former county physician and now president of the Anti-Saloon League, had filed 504 signatures. But the Arizona Supreme Court unanimously supported District Judge Kent in rejecting the argument of W. H. Stillwell, attorney for Phoenix saloonkeeper Joseph Thalheimer, that the local-option law was unconstitutional in giving county supervisors power to declare local-option districts.[17]

Feelings became so intense before the May 2, 1908, election that the Phoenix city election went largely unnoticed. A prohibition meeting at city hall plaza, in Spanish and English, drew more than five hundred people and was followed by another the next night at the Dorris Opera House and a third meeting on May 1, again in the plaza. The *Republican* opened its columns to all, and economic arguments appeared for the first time. Prohibition had powerful opposition. A *Gazette* editorial by the "Antiprohibitionists" argued that ending the liquor trade would deprive Phoenix of $500,000 a year in tourist money, $186,000 in payrolls, and $100,000 in license fees and other payments. For the drys, Mayor Louis Coggins issued a circular, signed as a private citizen, stating that the high prices for saloon licenses had produced enough revenue for the city to buy a municipal waterworks, the income from which would offset the loss of saloon licenses. "We can run the city on water, instead of whisky." The women in the WCTU charged themselves as never before and, urged on by Dr. Hughes, invited all Sunday schools, including the colored and Catholic schools, to join their protest (the Catholics and Episcopalians demurred). On election day, decorated wagons plied the streets from early morning, laden with children fluttering banners and yelling WCTU-coached college cheers and temperance songs.[18]

But Phoenix voted wet, swamping the almost solidly dry country districts. Saloon spenders and saloon license fees seem to have been preferable to a waterworks, if not to water. Without the license fees, the wets had argued, the sprinkling of Phoenix's dirt streets would stop and the dusty desert town would become not only figuratively but literally dry. Only the two-thirds requirement saved the saloons, however: prohibition received 53 percent of the countywide vote.[19]

The prohibitionists, disenchanted with the 1901 local-option law, with an all-out effort secured a new majority-rule law in March 1909.

However, the wets extracted from the legislature a plan to segregate the votes of incorporated cities. Dr. Hughes had become territorial president of the Anti-Saloon League, which, like the WCTU, was pledged to participate in all local-option elections.[20]

Meantime, the Anti-Saloon League had attacked the saloons with a domino strategy. The WCTU worked closely with the league and gave moral support as it induced the county to close saloons near the Phoenix red light district in November 1907. In May 1909 the city council passed an ordinance dramatically restricting saloons, although it was quickly invalidated. By September 1910, fourteen more of Phoenix's 1906 count of thirty-two saloons had gone, unable to pay for their thousand-dollar licenses. The Anti-Saloon League's lawyer, J. H. Langston, unearthed a 1903 law barring saloons within six miles of a work site employing twenty-five or more men (such as the Center Street Bridge or Adams School), but in March 1912, over Governor Hunt's veto, the saloons obtained exemption for incorporated cities.[21]

With the June 20, 1910, act enabling a state constitution, the Anti-Saloon League led the prohibitionists in backing the initiative and referendum. Candidates for the constitutional convention, meeting in Phoenix in October, were judged on this issue rather than on prohibition, a label considered too controversial to pin on them. The WCTU, however, insisted that prohibition be incorporated into the constitution, presenting the convention with a petition signed by thirty-two hundred women. But the Committee on Separate Submissions passed over the petition and voted thirty-three to fifteen against submitting the issue to the voters. The Maricopa delegates on the committee were "playing to the galleries," filled with prohibitionists, when they all voted for submission.[22]

For the April 1911 local-option election (requested by Dr. Hughes with more than seven hundred names), Mayor Lloyd Christy, a prohibition-minded Methodist and vice-president of the Central Bank, joined the crusaders. Southern evangelist Joseph Smally's temperance speeches moved hundreds of both sexes to sign antisaloon sentiments in the now prohibitionist *Gazette*. The WCTU not only concentrated on the rural areas, but on April 2 held an overflow meeting for all women at Central Methodist Church.[23]

But the city's largest paper, the *Republican*, argued that Phoenix was not a prohibition town and that prohibition liquor would be bootlegged, as was liquor for the Indians. On the other hand, the paper insisted, boys under twenty-one could not even buy beer: the law against sales to minors had received support from public sentiment. An advertisement by twenty-seven businesses and four banks protested the "Whiskey Row" portrayed by some papers and speakers as a fiction damaging the city's image. The antiprohibitionist *Arizona Democrat* suggested that the real election issue was personal liberty.[24]

This time prohibition carried every district but Phoenix, including Mesa and Tempe. Of 2,408 votes in the corporate city, 1,045 were dry; 1,363, or 56 percent, wet. Since more than 72 percent of the rest of the county had voted dry, the county as a whole was 56 percent for prohibition. After May 29, there would not be "a single wet spot in the county . . . except the city of Phoenix." Dr. Hughes announced a municipal local-option election for the earliest favorable moment, and at its 1911 Phoenix convention, the territorial WCTU resolved to work for a constitutional amendment and more financial support for local-option elections.[25]

In 1911 the Phoenix WCTU had 150 members, up from 60 in 1910. Its political influence in these years can only be estimated. Nationally, the WCTU "developed most of the methods of legislative pressure later used by the Anti-Saloon League." Drinking was not respectable for women, and women were often seen as the chief crusaders for prohibition. However, ardent and supportive female prohibitionists could only persuade; without woman suffrage every single territorial vote for prohibition had to be male. Historians can only speculate on the importance of such relationships as that of Ella and Benjamin Fowler. As valley reclamation leader, he had been elected to the assembly on the first prohibitionist ticket in 1900; she was a leader of the Phoenix Woman's Club and its president in 1911.[26]

## ORGANIZED CHARITY

The Phoenix WCTU, like the national WCTU, sought a louder voice for women in public policy generally. By statehood it had developed such diverse concerns as woman suffrage, the censorship of plays and movies, the welcoming of health seekers who arrived in the city, the need for a police matron, the city's "immense and unusual crop of weeds," and the working conditions for salesgirls. Like other organizations, it helped sponsor the new territorial fair, urging its members to attend. Christianna Gilchrist, superintendent of the Phoenix WCTU headquarters and reading room and organizer of the WCTU's 1912 territorial convention in Tucson, headed the city's growing charity movement.[27]

Notices such as the one in 1879 advertising a Ladies Aid Society benefit for a widow attested to the private character of early Phoenix charity. In 1886 when influential Republican and city founding father John Y. T. Smith brought the case of an indigent family before the city council, the council decided it lacked authority to help.[28]

On January 23, 1890, the Reverend Pearson of the Episcopal church—his wife then territorial WCTU president—invited all philanthropically minded women in Phoenix to create the Ladies Benevolent Society for "relief of the indigent and ministry to the sick." In December 1891, six society members paid a surprise visit to the county hospital. Filthy beds, some on the veranda or in tents, patients fetching firewood and doing their own laundry, and a lone attendant on duty verified their suspicions. When told their exposé would give Phoenix a bad name, the women retorted that the town should attend to its paupers. By 1895 the Ladies Benevolent Society had appointed an investigative committee from each of Phoenix's four wards and developed a pattern of monthly meetings and occasional fund-raising balls.[29]

In 1898 the Ministerial Union, meeting at the Baptist Church, originated plans for a central charitable society, Associated Charities, to assist the "worthy" poor and check on the "unworthy." The Associated Charities officer corps consisted almost entirely of ministers.[30]

In October 1904, Miss Gilchrist, who had been in charge of the WCTU's Free Reading Room, was appointed to attend to the WCTU's charity cases. The following month she presented a plan for organized charity to the WCTU's regular meeting and was appointed to meet with the Ministerial Union to initiate a cooperative charity plan for churches, lodges, businesses, and other organizations. The WCTU would appoint and supervise a "competent agent" to administer Associated Charities from the WCTU headquarters, and participating groups would pay small monthly subscriptions into a WCTU-administered general fund and would appoint one or more advisers each. City and county authorities also would participate as advisers. The agent was to "confer with the proper consultant" for each case, to give temporary relief, to keep careful records, and to report to the WCTU monthly and to subscribing organizations as they desired. The Associated Charities office operated from the WCTU Free Reading Room at Monroe and Center streets. The board of supervisors, city council, and board of trade endorsed the plan, seeing it as helping to lower taxes levied to care for indigents who were sick.[31]

In its first year of operation, Associated Charities indeed gave 80 percent of its aid to "utter strangers," whose numbers grew with Phoenix's reputation as a health resort. In January 1907, Miss Gilchrist, Associated Charities superintendent for many years, published a letter to New York journalist and reformer Jacob Riis asking what western towns could do about the worsening strain on their resources. From December to April, she wrote, Phoenix's population increased by one-fourth; 90 percent of the newcomers were tuberculars, most of whom depended on finding work. Ranches and mines needed only able-bodied people, and other jobs were soon filled. Hundreds of newcomers were thrown onto charity almost upon arrival. Charity in Phoenix cost more than in the East, too, since it took twenty-five dollars a month to feed and shelter each indigent.

Ten churches, all the secret societies, and several private charities were strained to the utmost.[32]

The following month, a group of organizations met to set up a board of charities similar to those in other cities. Miss Gilchrist reported that January's disbursement had been ten times that of January 1906 (doubtless partly because of the Panic of 1907). The group at the meeting discussed ways of trying to persuade Congress to limit the migration of ill persons who affected "the health of the entire community."[33]

The WCTU had a strong influence on Associated Charities. In October 1907, Miss Gilchrist, much involved with the WCTU since 1900, was elected its territorial vice-president and presided at the 1908 convention at the Methodist Church, where she was elected territorial secretary. Prohibitionist B. A. Fowler, Associated Charities president in 1907, researched Los Angeles charity while he was there for a National Irrigation Congress convention.[34]

Although its board now included members of the local elite, such as banker H. B. Wilkinson, real estate broker Dwight Heard, and merchant Morris Goldwater, the Associated Charities budget was strained. Miss Gilchrist reported to the annual meeting on May 4, 1908, that since September 1, of the $3,064 that had been received all but $8 was spent; $300 was needed to see Associated Charities to July 1, the end of the fiscal year. Presaging many later Phoenix drives, on November 13, Mrs. Fowler and Mrs. Heard arranged for a Los Angeles–inspired "tag day" by heading a committee of twenty-five women who were as representative and nonsectarian as possible.[35]

Cooperative efforts multiplied. In 1909, Associated Charities took over the twenty-bed tubercular ward in the county hospital. In June 1911, it was the only southwestern organization of its kind invited to join the National Association of Charities and Corrections, which was then expanding annual conventions into a year-round structure. In October of that year, Associated Charities opened a day nursery at the corner of Washington and Fifth streets where working mothers could leave their children for $1.25 a week, and in December it joined the day nurseries and other organizations for the Child Conservation Congress at the WCTU building. The following March, it combined with the Phoenix Humane Society and Crittenton Home for a solicitation of merchants in an early version of Phoenix's united drives. In October 1912, Associated Charities joined the Sisters of St. Joseph's Hospital in a training program for which hospital nurses paid daily visits to people unable to afford professional care. This service eventually led to free clinics with volunteer doctors.[36]

By 1912, Associated Charities culminated two years of great achievement, listing as accomplishments the establishment of the county tuberculosis hospital, the opening of the day nursery, and the initiation of the nurses' training class. The proportion of indigents in Phoenix's population had decreased, but the Associated Charities was handling more of the indigent population. Sixty-three percent were tubercular. Miss Gilchrist, noted the *Republican*, "has her hand, eye and heart upon 73 families in the city of Phoenix each of which owes the Charities . . . for its help . . . when . . . most needed."[37]

## PUBLIC LIBRARY MOVEMENT

Temperance led to another public policy when the reading-room movement merged with the public library movement. As the not unfriendly *Phoenix Herald* remarked, a many-volume library could woo young men from unsavory activities. One library was said to be worth twenty temperance societies to the temperance cause.[38]

However, the earliest efforts for a library do not seem to have been temperance inspired. Phoenix women of the 1870s, in the tradition of the nineteenth century's feminine reading public, sought not only companionship but the "refinements of civilization." In 1878 the Maricopa Literary Society opened to both sexes, although the Phoenix Library Association, meeting weekly, apparently was masculine. Within a year the Ladies Literary Society (previously known as the Maricopa Literary Society) rented a store and raised funds to buy books. Seventy couples attended its second masquerade.[39]

The literary society, however, had faded from the news when the Phoenix WCTU, one month after its founding in 1884, announced its own reading room, open to all, at the corner of Center and Monroe. With refreshments, games, and occasional socials, the room's monthly attendance averaged 210 persons. Rental charges and a shortage of women to tend the reading room closed it in 1885, but in March 1888 "the Ladies of Phoenix as a body" united for a "paper carnival," the "crowning event of the season," to benefit the Free Library Association. While the WCTU reproached a reporter for calling it the carnival's sponsor, the WCTU had created the library association. The *Gazette* suggested placing the Phoenix Library Association's little-used library of three hundred books at the WCTU's disposal, and in 1889 this idea gained support when the WCTU rented a room in Patton's Opera House. But as matters went, in February the territorial WCTU convention elected the Episcopal minister's wife, Mrs. R. W. Pearson, president. Her husband had just been elected a director of the Phoenix Library Association, and in December the association's books were moved to the hall of the Ladies' Guild of the new Trinity Episcopal Church. The Phoenix Library Association now admitted both male and female county residents for ten dollars a year and limited membership to a hundred persons.[40]

By November 1892 the WCTU sought to sell a 25-foot frontage on Monroe Street for a larger one 250 feet to the west in order to accommodate a better reading room: "We are incorporated for just one thing—to keep a public library and a reading room." On July 18, 1894, the WCTU bought a lot at the corner of Center Street and Monroe, and by 1899 its Free Reading Room was the chief pride of its twenty organized sections.[41]

These early efforts certainly seem germane to the public-library movement, but today's Phoenix Public Library dates from the one opened by the Friday Club in June 1898. In November 1897, fourteen women, gathered by Mrs. Clinton-Miller for the "study of history," had seized on the idea of a public library. "There are two free reading rooms in the city, but this one . . . is a library: hence it could not be free of charge." Only a nominal charge would be made, however, for use of any of the seven hundred volumes the women had collected. Perhaps in some spirit of competition, the WCTU purchased another two hundred volumes and now announced a free circulating library, as differentiated from a reading room, to open at headquarters, November 15.[42]

Phoenix's city charter did not provide for a city library. In 1899 J. W. Bentham's territorial bill for tax-supported libraries in first-class cities failed. Supporting the bill, the *Republican* observed that Phoenix women had labored more than a year to Phoenix's advantage: would-be immigrants could be discouraged by the absence of a library, considered a necessity by eastern cities.[43]

The little Friday Club soon found its library duties overwhelming, and apparently on their own initiative twenty-five people met at the courthouse on May 25, 1899, and organized the new Phoenix Library Association, which had an annual membership fee of three dollars. With the capitol completed, quarters just vacated by the territorial government were available at city hall; so for the city, acquiring new books was the only cost. The *Republican* observed that Tucson's expenditure of two thousand dollars a year had for years resulted in a library about to bring the Old Pueblo a prominence Phoenix would not have.[44]

The city council willingly accepted the 1,300-volume library, but taxpayers had to vote on its support. On February 15, 1901, however, a new library law introduced by prohibitionist B. A. Fowler permitted the city to levy one-sixth of a mill on every dollar of valuation to maintain a free public library, and on March 28 the Phoenix Library Association turned the library over to the city. Librarian Blanche F. Chapman reported that in the library's twenty-two months of existence there had been 2,200 reader visits to the library, books had been borrowed 4,099 times, and there were 146 library association members. Receipts, including $22 from a ball, totaled $1,118, while expenditures came to $1,045—$350 for the librarian, $65 for the janitor, and $350 for 309 new books.

On April 1, the city council named the library trustees. Mayor Emil Ganz and Councilman Fickas championed Mrs. Frazier and Mrs. James of the library association board, but Councilman McNeil refused to permit each councilman to appoint one trustee, insisting that all vote for all. Five men were thus elected trustees, although onlookers were reported to favor the vigorous efforts of Ganz and Fickas for the women.[45]

But Phoenix women had hardly finished with the library. In December 1900 a group which had been meeting at the home of Mrs. Anna McClatchie organized officially as the Phoenix Woman's Club. This club, along with the Friday Club, would represent Phoenix in the chartering of the Arizona Federation of Women's Clubs on November 19, 1901. Although the Phoenix Woman's Club had only seventeen members by that date, it included such influential women as Ella Fowler and Dorothy (Mrs. James) McClintock—two of its five incorporators in 1907—and Mayor Talbot's wife, Hattie. By February 1902, Mrs. McClintock and Mrs. Fowler had corresponded with Andrew Carnegie about a library. The millionaire philanthropist offered twenty-five thousand dollars to the city for a library building if a suitable site could be found. A "ridiculous circumstance" soon reduced his grant to fifteen thousand dollars: the census of 1900 reported Tucson as the territory's largest city, Phoenix having a population of only 5,500. However, B. A. Fowler, in Washington during January 1904 with Charles D. Walcott (director of the U.S. Geological Survey and secretary of the Carnegie Institute), persuaded Carnegie that Phoenix should receive the full twenty-five thousand dollars.[46]

On February 1, 1904, Ella Fowler (then president of the Arizona Federation of Women's Clubs), Dorothy McClintock, and Hattie Talbot presented Carnegie's offer to the city council and Mayor Talbot. The library site had obvious significance for valley real estate brokers. The city council received petitions respectively favoring the city park in Neahr's Addition and the city plaza, and Dwight B. Heard presented a Woman's Club–backed plan from the real estate board favoring the "Keefer lots." Not until January 1905 did the council choose the park site between Washington and Jefferson streets and Tenth and Twelfth avenues, wiring Carnegie to ask if his offer was still in force. Building supplies and plans gave difficulties; by the time the city opened the library on February 12, 1908, Mrs. N. A. Morford, sometime president of the Friday Club, had devotedly served in the city hall location for several years. The 1908 city budget allotted the library a nickel of the eighty-five-cent tax on each hundred dollars of valuation.[47]

## WOMAN SUFFRAGE

Organized charity and the acquisition of a public library were non-controversial efforts by women's groups. The struggle for suffrage, on the other hand, at first echoed, then became more consuming than the struggle for prohibition.

Some WCTU leaders realized earlier on how basic suffrage was. The "Mother of Arizona," Josephine Hughes said: "Let us secure the vote for women first—then the victory for protection of our homes and for the cause of temperance will follow." Many women agreed with her. "The woman suffrage idea in Arizona rather had its inception in the prohibition movement," Prescott suffragist Frances Willard Munds wrote later.[48]

The temperance movement was not Phoenix women's sole political motivation, however. As early as 1882 the "ladies" had "graced" Phoenix Republican deliberations for some time. As mothers of school-age children and/or property owners, Arizona women in 1883 were granted the right to vote for and serve on school boards. At first they exercised this franchise somewhat arbitrarily in Phoenix—for instance in 1884, but not in 1886. In the city bond election of 1886, however, women participated excitedly, even though they could only hurry back and forth in carriages driving male voters to the polls.[49]

McClintock's claim that an Equal Rights Association was formed in 1887 when the WCTU's legislative committee failed in some of its goals, "with the main idea that only by putting the ballot in the hands of women could the liquor interests be overthrown," has not been substantiated. When the capital moved to Phoenix in 1889, however, Phoenix women, organized or not, quickly filled the galleries at city hall to observe the Territorial Assembly in action. In 1891 they followed keenly a bill to give Arizona women the vote. Although the WCTU and the county Farmers' Alliance argued for the women's vote, it went down to defeat, as did similar bills in 1893, 1895, and 1897. While the pressures on legislators obviously were not publicized, moving the capital to Phoenix had made it easier for Phoenix saloons and related businesses to lobby. Also, some whiskey-loving legislators may simply have feared surrendering their good lives to the WCTU.[50]

The constitutional convention that met in Phoenix in September 1891 had demonstrated that women's suffrage was not at hand. The future president of the territorial WCTU, Mrs. E. D. Garlick, as president of the Phoenix branch of the National American Woman Suffrage Association (NAWSA) and accompanied by Josephine Hughes, territorial WCTU president, and Mrs. Laura Johns, NAWSA leader, made a strong argument for suffrage before a special September 18 convention hearing. The Maricopa County delegate, Phoenix lawyer H. N. Alexander, presented a prosuffrage petition from county residents. M. E. Collins came before the convention to argue that although a woman's place was in the home she should have a part in regulating places frequented by children and, moreover, should have the ballot as a taxpayer.

Col. William Herring, prominent Tucson lawyer who headed the Committee of the Whole, declared vehemently that meetings in Phoenix and elsewhere showed Arizona women wanted suffrage. The convention left women the school franchise and provided that a majority vote at a general election could extend them general suffrage. But the convention voted fifteen to six against a constitutional provision.[51]

In his 1893 address to the legislature, Republican Gov. N. O. Murphy unequivocally urged woman suffrage. The WCTU territorial convention, meeting in Phoenix in May 1894 with the host community heavily represented, passed its first (and lengthy) resolution for suffrage, and Mrs. Hughes resigned from the presidency to fight for the cause. Louis Hughes's efforts for the suffrage and against gambling made no more headway with the Eighteenth Assembly than his efforts for temperance had.[52]

Meanwhile, the National American Woman Suffrage Association, having decided that territorial legislatures could grant suffrage, turned its sights on Utah, Oklahoma, and Arizona. On December 6, 1895, a Phoenix meeting organized an Arizona Suffrage Association, with Laura Johns again representing the national association. Mrs. Hughes was "quite naturally" chosen president.[53]

But the 1897 assembly gave suffrage an "icy reception." Despite an address by Laura Johns, a suffrage bill was postponed indefinitely. Two years later, Carrie Chapman Catt, chair of the NAWSA's organizing committee, and Mary Garrett Hay were sent to the Twentieth Assembly to help what was now the Arizona Equal Suffrage Association. Murphy, again governor, repeated his call for suffrage, but as the two veterans predicted, legislators again gave suffrage a chilly reception. A bill passed the House without dissent, but Mrs. Catt sadly wrote NAWSA that saloonkeepers and gambling and bawdyhouse operators had threatened council members voting for suffrage. "A strong favorable majority" had vanished with "the clinking of glasses that accompanied the . . . sale of . . . votes to the proprietors of the prosperous saloons." The saloons, Catt later pronounced, checkmated Equal Suffrage Association efforts for eleven years.[54]

In February 1900 the Equal Suffrage Club met at the home of Mrs. Mary McCormick, who was later to head the Phoenix WCTU's "franchise department" and help incorporate the Woman's Club. In March 1901 the Arizona Equal Suffrage Association, convening in Phoenix, chose Mrs. Pauline O'Neill, widow of Bucky O'Neill, to succeed Mrs. Hughes. Phoenician Anna McClatchie, president of the Arizona Federation of Woman's Clubs, became treasurer. Of eight association officers, four were from Phoenix. No doubt it was Phoenix women who filled the galleries as suffrage bills came up before the Twenty-first Assembly, belying opponents' claims of little interest. The lower house heard that the council, tired of being a buffer between it and the furious women, planned to pass the 1901 suffrage bill, so it defeated the bill that had been introduced through the efforts of Phoenician Lida (Mrs. H. F.) Robinson, wife of the adjutant general.[55]

Suffragist Munds later wrote, perhaps correctly, that the territorial organization would have died had not Mrs. Robinson, then president to the Phoenix Equal Suffrage Association (and later Friday Club president) called a convention in January 1903. Addressing this, Mayor Talbot conceded that as taxpayers, women should have a voice in disbursing public funds, but he gave only qualified approval to the suffrage association's aims. A six-woman lobbying committee was selected, including Pauline O'Neill and Hattie Talbot, Frances Munds of Prescott, and Dr. Frances Woods of Kansas, hastily secured from the national organization, for support in lobbying for a suffrage law in the next assembly.[56]

Mrs. Woods toured the territory and secured pledges until only a few votes lacked for suffrage in either house. The House of Representatives now voted unexpectedly for suffrage, sixteen to seven (the galleries applauded wildly). For two weeks the council pondered the bill. A new motive for passage was argued by former Judge Joseph Kibbey, councilman from Maricopa County. Although later to be the arch foe of suffrage, Kibbey pointed out to the council that Arizona's voting population would be nearer New Mexico's if women voted. Joint statehood could thus be defeated. The council decided that if suffrage were to be voted down, the House must do it. The *Republican* credited the bill's passage to the five Republicans on the council and predicted the move would improve Arizona's eastern image and promote the statehood cause. But Republican Governor Brodie proceeded with his first veto of any bill, despite—so they claimed—a bargain with the suffragists for support of the eight-hour law he championed and despite telegrams and petitions pouring into his office. The eight-hour law having passed, Brodie pronounced the organic act governing the territory to be the final word on suffrage until a state constitution gave women the vote. While his veto may have been "much to the relief of legislators generally,"—the *Republican*, changing its view, claimed the bill would have led to endless litigation—there was consternation in the galleries, where a hundred suffragists had gathered to enjoy their triumph.[57]

Four of the eight House votes to override Brodie's veto came from the four Maricopa County representatives. In November, Mrs. Robinson presided over a suffrage convention at Tempe Congregational Church, and delegates from every town in the county passed a resolution thanking the faithful four. No Phoenix officers were chosen for the county association, but in December the *Arizona Equal Suffrage Newsletter* appeared, apparently published and distributed throughout Arizona by

Mrs. Robinson herself. This well-edited paper kept suffragists in touch until Mrs. Robinson moved from the territory in 1907, leaving the Arizona Suffrage Association leaderless.[58]

Mrs. Mary Bradford of Denver, sent by NAWSA to work with the assembly of 1905, received almost no support from local women. Writing later, Frances Munds remembered that the suffrage struggle had seemed in vain as long as Kibbey was governor. This did not mean Phoenix women kept silent politically. The new Arizona Federation of Women's Clubs, while taking no stand in 1903 on suffrage, in 1904 backed municipal abolition of gambling, an issue which peaked in Phoenix in 1905. When the Democrats gathered in May, the *Republican* reported that "many more ladies than voters" attended. Taking an antigambling position, the party lost the 1905 single-issue election, but by January 1906 women helped at the Second and Third Ward polls in an opinion referendum—Arizona's first—which voted 642 to 438 to abolish gambling in Phoenix. Both the city council and the Territorial Assembly took the referendum as a guide and the assembly later abolished gambling.[59]

Suffrage itself, however, languished. While later support for it would demonstrate that many Phoenix women wanted the vote, Brodie's pronouncement on suffrage's unconstitutionality for the territory may well have given women pause, especially since statehood was in the offing. In February 1909, when Miss Laura Clay, NAWSA auditor and president of the Equal Rights Association of Kentucky, stopped at the Adams Hotel with Frances Munds, resident women were described as apathetic. Miss Clay waged a "one-woman fight" to organize the territory's women into suffrage clubs. She led the reorganizing of a territorial association with Munds as president and secured the introduction of yet another suffrage bill. This time both she and Pauline O'Neill blamed the railroads and mines, probably fearful of women's reforms, for the defeat of suffrage. A bill to give women the vote in local-option elections also failed.[60]

With the constitutional convention of 1910, the suffrage issue, after six slow years, became more urgent. Laura Clay, acknowledging the need for more male help, had suggested the unions. Laura Gregg, a NAWSA organizer, was principal speaker at a labor conference on the constitution held in Phoenix in July; the conference made a resolution for woman suffrage. Crowds of suffragettes scurried around the city on the constitutional convention's opening day, October 10, proclaiming "equal rights for women," and a strong suffragist lobby remained to badger delegates until the closing. But convention president and later governor George W. P. Hunt apparently feared President Taft's reaction to a constitution with female suffrage, and the convention gave the women short shrift, voting 119 to 30 against even a popular referendum on suffrage, the suffragists having accepted this in lieu of a constitutional provision.[61]

However, with statehood achieved, Governor Hunt, in his message to the legislature on March 18, proposed such a referendum on a constitutional amendment for equal suffrage. During the constitutional convention the suffragists had become convinced they could prevail via the initiative and with the wording they wanted. On June 15, several hundred people met at the city hall plaza for Phoenix's first big suffrage rally to circulate petitions for the amendment. Suffragists concentrated on Maricopa County for the 3,342 signatures needed for the initiative and filed with 700 excess names on July 5, in just over three weeks.[62]

In early September, with their amendment on the ballot, the suffragists opened headquarters in Phoenix. Frances Mund came down from Prescott to direct the campaign. Her Arizona Equal Suffrage Central Committee included Mary McCormick of the WCTU, Pauline O'Neill, and Mrs. Virgil Partch. Eugene V. Debs, Socialist candidate for president, stopped briefly in Phoenix to address a thousand people at the Coliseum Theater and pleaded for suffrage, his only local reference. On September 14 a "vast throng," predominantly male, gathered at the city hall plaza to hear Laura Gregg, now married to Joseph Cannon of the Western Federation of Miners, and Pauline O'Neill, now president of the Suffrage League of Phoenix, better known as the Woman's Civic League. Gone were the days of 1895 when the *Republican* could write: "Less than a dozen Arizona matrons come forward biennially to champion a cause that appears to have no other adherents than themselves." By early October, all five political parties in Arizona, including the Progressives, Socialists, and Prohibitionists, had platforms favoring equal suffrage. Carrie Chapman Catt attributed the major parties' reversals to the national Progressives' inclusion of a suffrage plank in their platform. The pragmatic suffragists moved their headquarters from the Adams Hotel to the state fairgrounds for the week of the fair. Dr. Anna Howard Shaw, president of NAWSA and a captivating speaker, addressed a huge crowd at the Elks Theater in October, with Governor Hunt the only man on stage. Thousands of badges, hatbands, and black and yellow pennants were distributed in Phoenix and throughout Arizona, and thousands of pounds of literature in "suffrage yellow" were handed out.[63]

On November 5, with Phoenix women at every polling place to demonstrate how to mark the ballot for Arizona's first initiative, the men of the new state rewarded two decades of local, territorial, and national effort with suffrage for Arizona women. Despite its potential for prohibition, Phoenix men voted for equal suffrage 438 to 319.[64]

## CONCLUSION

The women of the Women's Christian Temperance Union and the other women's clubs comprised a small segment of Phoenix's female population;

they were white, largely Protestant, and tended to be of the upper middle class, the class with enough leisure time to form clubs. Even so, the move toward prohibition, the development of organized charity, the library, and women's suffrage were not their only achievements during these years. For example, the Woman's Club secured a territorial juvenile court.[65]

Phoenix women's influence on prohibition, charity, the library movement, and suffrage fit into the national scene in two patterns of growth. In the case of the prohibition and suffrage movements, national organizations came, as it were, to fetch Phoenix women, taking the initiative in absorbing them as small parts of national strategies. Although the relationships between local Phoenix unions and associations and the national WCTU and NAWSA varied during the territorial years, it was the national organizations that consistently led—occasionally seemed to prod—Phoenix women in their respective causes. The less controversial beginnings of organized charity and the public library, on the other hand, developed from local needs and reached upward to become part of national movements.

Both growth patterns, however, meant the local women were parts of a national whole, and the contrast between them can be overstated. The problem of alcoholism challenged Phoenix women before the WCTU, Phoenix women were wetting their feet politically before NAWSA, the WCTU and later organizations communicated down to local charity, and the Carnegie grants were there to be tapped.

In meeting their own needs, Phoenix women helped to bring some of what was considered to be American civilization to the frontier. Their efforts can be seen as enduringly significant. While prohibition, later attained nationally, eventually gave way to modern medicine and psychology as a remedy for alcoholism, the temperance movement's unique catalytic role has been demonstrated. Gathering women motivated to public service, the movement helped launch and support the library, charity, and suffrage movements in Phoenix.

Not only did Phoenix women help bring their city some of the more desirable aspects of American society for Phoenix's economic, cultural, political, and social growth; viewed from another aspect, these Phoenix beginnings were also small examples of women's developing roles in library science, social work, and their gradually increasing participation in politics. More professional and political participation for women meant more alternatives for them, a multiplying of opportunities for personal growth and community service.

# PART TWO
## Ethnic Communities

## CHAPTER FOUR

# Phoenix and the Indians: 1867–1930

## BY ROBERT A. TRENNERT

THE 1980 census reveals that Phoenix, Arizona, supports the nation's fourth-largest urban Indian population, and as the city entered the last decade of the twentieth century, it was recognized as a major center of American Indian services and activities. But the city did not always have such a reputation. A survey of its history shows that almost two-thirds of a century passed before there was a substantial basis for a large resident Indian population. During the early years of Phoenix history, the relationship between white citizens and local Indians was marked by an unusual blend of distrust and discrimination combined with occasional admiration and toleration. If ever a city seemed confused about the role that local Indians should play in society, it was Phoenix between 1867 and 1930.[1]

Part of this phenomenon is explained by the fact that Phoenix is the only major city in the Southwest that has no Hispanic or Indian heritage. The town, founded by whites at a much later date than its neighboring communities of Los Angeles, El Paso, Albuquerque, and Tucson, was in an area devoid of an indigenous population. As a result, the early history of Phoenix and the surrounding Salt River Valley is unique. Although Phoenicians demonstrated the same biases and tendency to restrict ethnic minorities to low economic and social levels as did other western city dwellers, only a few natives lived within the community itself. However, a large native population surrounded the city, making it a veritable island of white settlement in an ocean of Indians. As a consequence, white citizens were able to exercise an unusual amount of control over Indian activities within the city and limit native participation in civic life. Thus, while Indian relations in Phoenix exhibited some similarities to that of other urban areas, there were also noticeable differences.[2]

Prehistoric Indians had lived along the banks of the Salt River as late as A.D. 1400, but when John Y. T. Smith and Jack Swilling began the first settlements in the late 1860s, there were no permanent native residents in the area. Yet just thirty miles to the south lay the massive Gila River Reservation, with its five thousand Pima and Maricopa Indian residents. Aside from an occasional Apache or Yavapai who might stray into the valley, it was primarily the Pimas and Maricopas who interacted with Phoenicians.[3]

The arrival of the first white settlers in the Salt River Valley presented a singular opportunity to establish friendly relations. The Pimas produced a surplus of grain, and their animosity toward the Apaches tended to keep hostile raiders away. Moreover, the Pimas were anxious to purchase manufactured goods from white merchants and were known for their friendship with Americans. Unfortunately, it soon became evident that residents of the growing white community preferred not to have Indians in their midst, no matter how friendly. Like most Anglo-Americans of the day, Phoenicians were suspicious of any Indian. As early as 1868, army officers at nearby Camp McDowell reported clashes between settlers and Indians. These early problems appear to be cases of genuine misunderstanding. When the curious Indians visited white farms, they saw such an abundance of corn and melons that they helped themselves. The settlers frowned on such practices and quickly determined to resist future chicanery. Such incidents sowed seeds of distrust.[4]

Distrust intensified significantly during the next two decades. The Pimas, having lived in the region for centuries, felt free to roam anywhere they pleased, whether on or off the reservation. As a consequence, incidents of alleged cattle theft and pilfering continued to occur. Most incidents were trivial, but they added up to increasing hostility. Moreover, the Pimas seemed to be blamed for any depredation, no matter who caused it, a situation that finally led to bloodshed. In early 1872 a Pima farmer, not having enough water to work his reservation land, moved to the Salt River settlements to find a job. He had been there only a few days when he was murdered in cold blood. John H. Stout, the Pima Indian agent, was concerned about the effects of this attack. He believed this was the first time a Pima had been killed by an American and feared the slaying might lead to raids of retaliation which would claim the lives and property of innocent people. Consequently he began advocating the removal of the Pimas and Maricopas to Indian Territory (Oklahoma), where they would suffer less from the pressure of white settlement and find more water for farming. Gen. O. O. Howard, then investigating conditions in Arizona, agreed with this recommendation.[5]

The proposed removal never took place. For a variety of reasons, the government was unable to complete plans to relocate the Pimas and Maricopas. Meanwhile, Indian problems increased with the population of the Salt River settlements. White settlers persisted in claiming the entire valley despite the fact that diminishing water resources on the Gila River reservation continued to drive Indian families north to the Salt River Valley. All that the native immigrants wanted was to farm in peace, but their presence in the vicinity of Phoenix angered most white residents. Not all the settlers opposed the Indians, however. Charles T. Hayden, who operated a flour mill in Tempe, purchased grain from them, and the Mormon settlers in Mesa, who had been excluded from proselytizing on the reservation, encouraged the Pimas to settle near their community. Still, on the whole, Indians were unwelcome in the Phoenix area, a sentiment that was reinforced when any of them attempted to move into town. As Agent Stout noted in 1873, young Indian men occasionally went to town in search of regular employment but were usually forced to "earn a living by begging|[and] pilfering." To resolve such problems, President Rutherford B. Hayes set aside a reservation in 1879 on the Salt River just east of Phoenix for the displaced Pimas. The reservation eventually contained thirty-five thousand acres and its establishment was supposed to end the conflict between whites and Indians.[6]

Thus after 1879, Phoenix was situated adjacent to a small native community on the east and the more sizable reservation to the south. By 1880 the town boasted a population of two thousand residents and had begun to emerge as the commercial center of the region. The increasing tempo of economic activity tended to attract more Indians. Most of them came to town to sell their handicrafts or firewood, to deliver sacks of wheat to millers, and to purchase such necessities as calico and thread. Others apparently slipped into town to purchase alcohol from unscrupulous white dealers. Indian men and women could be found on the streets of Phoenix at almost any time, and their usual lack of clothing and occasional intoxication irritated most Phoenicians.[7]

Public concern finally resulted in a city ordinance, passed in 1881, requiring every Indian visiting town to wear "sufficient clothing to cover the person." In an attempt to prevent them from remaining in town, the ordinance also required that all Indians, unless employed by a white resident, must leave the city at sundown. Violators were subject to a ten-dollar fine and/or five days at hard labor. The ordinance had an immediate effect on native visitors. Newspaper reports indicated that the Indians were staying off the streets out of fear of being arrested, not understanding that they were required to keep away only at night. Actually, the Pimas rapidly adapted to the ordinance and ingeniously got around the clothing restriction by hiding several pairs of overalls in a mesquite thicket. Anyone with business in town simply borrowed the communal trousers and returned them when finished.[8]

During the 1880s the number of Indians coming to Phoenix increased. Except for a short period in 1883 when a smallpox epidemic among the

Pimas caused city authorities to ban visits, Indians were seen regularly on the streets. The completion of the Maricopa and Phoenix Railway in 1887 apparently increased the number of native transients. The railroad line crossed the Gila Reservation, enabling Indians to catch rides to town. By the late 1880s they were a common sight on city streets during daylight hours. Phoenicians seemed to consider them a harmless nuisance. In 1888 the *Phoenix Daily Herald* described a typical street scene:

The Pima and Maricopa Indians that throng our plazas or idle in fantastic groups on the street corners lend a picturesque effect to our city scenery that is not without its value. They are a harmless race, these swarthy sons and daughters of Arizona soil, and they adapt themselves easily to our laws and customs without changing their own. . . . Seated on the ground at some sunny corner, the mothers nurse the sturdy babes, while the young men and women laugh and talk together, rarely noticing the passer by. They are always idle and always happy, with seemingly no more thought for the future than the birds that flit among the cottonwood branches. . . . Some of them bring stone relics and curios which they sell to collectors, others dispose of ollas and pottery of their own handiwork.[9]

Although Phoenicians may have considered the Indians harmless, they insisted that ordinances regulating their behavior be strictly enforced. Drunken Indians seemed to be a persistent problem, and the sheriff was kept busy making arrests. The harsh punishment occasionally meted out amused local residents. When Sheriff Tom Sherman was called out to arrest several Indian women for drinking, he found them unclothed. Not wanting to parade them through the courthouse on the way to the jail, Sherman and two other men bodily threw them over the jailhouse wall. Less humorous was the Indian habit of camping near town canals and using the ditches (when empty) for stables. This was "not the most pleasing prospect for settlers who get water lower down," wrote the paper. Although town wags made light of such situations, the murder of several Pimas made it clear that feelings still ran high.[10]

Troubled relations between Phoenicians and local Indians might have continued indefinitely had it not been for the opening of the Phoenix Indian School. The decision to establish a major Indian educational facility in central Arizona had a significant effect on race relations. By 1890 the government had scrapped all plans to relocate Arizona's Indians. Educating the native population for citizenship now appeared a better method of solving the Indian problem. The new school was supposed to be located at Fort McDowell, but the remote location and dilapidated condition of that post gave Phoenix an opportunity to secure the school. In the autumn of 1890, Col. William Christy and William J. Murphy, two of the town's leading citizens, suggested that the Indian Bureau might prefer to establish its school in Phoenix. The two promoters were interested in much more than Indian education. As partners in the Arizona Improvement Company, they controlled large sections of land and were well aware that a federal school would boost the local economy and encourage real-estate development. Moreover, securing the institution would enhance the community's effort to become the major metropolis in Arizona.[11]

With such factors in mind, town boosters were hosts to Indian Commissioner Thomas J. Morgan when he toured the West in October 1890. A citizens committee composed of acting Gov. Nathan O. Murphy, Colonel Christy, and a half-dozen other leading personalities met with Morgan and persuaded him to locate the school in Phoenix if the city promised to donate the necessary land. Phoenicians were delighted when the agreement was announced. The *Arizona Republican* reported to its readers that as much as fifty thousand dollars annually would be added to the local economy, and students would be available to work in nearby citrus orchards. Indeed, the economic benefits to be reaped from the federal institution seemed substantial. *Phoenix Daily Herald* editor N. A. Morford wrote that "from a pecuniary standpoint [the school] would be worth to this valley what ten Capitals, Universities or Normal Schools would be."[12]

Because it required several months to secure a permanent school site, the Indian Bureau rented the unoccupied two-story West End Hotel near downtown Phoenix. Plans called for renovating the building in time to begin classes in the spring of 1891. Unfortunately, the devastating floods of that year so disrupted connections with outside suppliers that the classrooms could not be readied. Consequently, school superintendent Wellington Rich decided to wait until the fall term. In the meantime, considerable effort went into finding a permanent location. Finally, in April 1891, the 160-acre Frank C. Hatch ranch on Center Street three miles north of town was purchased for nine thousand dollars. Although the school site was not then within the city limits, a proposed streetcar line promised to end isolation quickly.[13]

The Phoenix Indian School opened on September 3, 1891. Forty-one Pima and Maricopa boys, fresh from the reservation, were squeezed into the cramped rooms of the West End Hotel. Phoenix residents seemed pleased with the opening of the school and expected great things. One newspaper reported that the school produced an immediate effect on city streets, claiming that Indian girls who had worn "into town only such clothing as the municipal ordinances absolutely required" suddenly decided to impress the school boys by dressing "after the manner of their white sisters. They have long-sleeved dresses on, shoes and stockings, and chew their indispensable gum." Such changes in native attire, although probably exaggerated by the paper, were what Phoenicians wanted. Meanwhile, work on the permanent campus progressed rapidly, and on May 6, 1892, the students moved into a new classroom and dormitory building that would serve as the heart of the institution for years to come. Designed initially to accommodate 125 pupils, the new facility was soon at work educating native children of both sexes.[14]

During the 1890s the school grew rapidly as more buildings were constructed, appropriations increased, and children from other tribes added. By 1895 the school housed 365 students and at the turn of the century more than seven hundred native children representing better than a dozen tribes were in class. The presence of these children had a significant effect on the economic and social life of Phoenix and served to modify some of the prevalent stereotypes about native peoples.[15]

Undoubtedly the most significant catalyst for change as far as Phoenicians were concerned was the institution's "outing system." This program, which had been used at other schools, sent school children into the community to work as domestic servants and laborers. School officials believed that such direct contact with the white population enabled students to learn English more rapidly, develop the work ethic, and prepare themselves for citizenship. Phoenicians, of course, supported the program primarily because it provided a pool of cheap labor. School superintendent Harwood Hall remarked in 1894 that "the hiring of an Indian youth is not looked upon by the people of this valley from a philanthropic standpoint. It is simply a matter of business." Once the program began, young Indian boys could be found working at various jobs—as common laborers, field hands, construction workers, even hotel bellhops. The use of Indian girls was even more widespread. Because of a severe shortage of domestic servants, almost every prominent valley family took in an outing girl, who lived with the family and performed domestic chores in return for room, board, and a small wage. By the late 1890s nearly two hundred Indian girls were living with Phoenix families.[16]

The social life of Phoenix was also affected by the school's presence. In a community that could boast of few cultural attractions, the free performances given by schoolchildren were valued highly. Residents quickly adopted the school and regularly visited the campus, which, with its green lawns, shade trees, and fountains, seemed like an oasis in the desert. The memorial exercises each spring became a significant community event. These affairs featured musical selections, patriotic skits, orations by the more advanced students, and a general party atmosphere. The school band, organized in 1894, was by all accounts the most popular feature of the school. Young Indian musicians performed at every major civic event and were used by school authorities to remind skeptics that the assimilation program was working. Indian athletics also became popular. By the mid-1890s the school had organized baseball and football clubs which proved to be highly competitive with such local teams as those representing Phoenix High and Tempe Normal.[17]

Government expenditures to support Indian education served to boost the local economy. The school's budget rose steadily and had reached $130,000 by the turn of the century. Most of this money went to pay staff salaries, purchase supplies, and support construction, and most of it wound up in the cash registers of Phoenix merchants. Even the students bolstered the economy. Those who earned wages from miscellaneous school employment or from the outing system purchased personal items from local stores and were encouraged to deposit their earnings in city banks. All of these factors enhanced the institution's reputation amongst the white population of Phoenix.[18]

Although the presence of the school prompted many Phoenicians to express more hope for the Indians' future, they continued to demand that transient natives be kept under control. The reservation residents who came to town still received rough treatment. Local residents regarded them as a nuisance and encouraged them to stay out of town. Municipal ordinances were strictly enforced, despite the fact that there was little crime, and about the most an Indian was charged with involved a stolen bicycle. Most problems involved reservation residents getting drunk, cutting up in town, and staying on the streets a little too long. A typical penalty for such a transgression was described in the following curt newspaper comment: "Joaquin, an Indian, was found in town after sundown last night by Marshall Blankenship. He will serve five days on the chain gang."[19]

What residents were really concerned about was the bad image reservation Indians seemed to be giving the town. The *Daily Herald* summed up popular feelings in 1893 when it remarked that the Pimas were a good people, but "they have a lazy habit of sitting about on the sidewalks and in the store doors." Such scenes were deemed bad for business:

Not long since a visitor to Phoenix was asked when he returned east what sort of town this is. His reply was that it is a very pretty place, where the Indians sit in the middle of the sidewalks and dogs bark at strangers. Remarks like that keep capital out of this town. It is time right now for the Indians to move along.[20]

Despite the fact that Indians were considered an economic liability, there is strong evidence to suggest that commerce with reservation people became increasingly significant during the 1890s. The Pimas sold large quantities of wheat, cattle, and firewood to city businesses. In good years they were also known to bring in large quantities of mesquite beans and fresh fish. In 1895 the Pimas sold a million pounds of spring wheat to flour millers in Phoenix, Tempe, and Tucson. Two years later, residents of the Salt River Reservation were reported coming to market "each with a sack or two of grain, . . . which they disposed of at the highest barter price for red handkerchiefs, G-strings, bright-colored calico and tobacco." When Chief Antonio Azul (son of the noted Pima leader) came to town to arrange a big livestock or grain sale, he was courted like any other visiting businessman.[21]

By the mid-1890s, Phoenicians were beginning to notice another subtle development: eastern visitors arriving in the city were seeking out the picturesque "dusky sons of the desert." The Indians quickly took notice of this fact and were soon producing craft goods that might interest tourists. Some of the more enterprising natives even manufactured "relics," which they sold to unsuspecting visitors as prehistoric artifacts. At the end of the decade, Indians could be found daily on city streets selling bows and arrows, ollas, and decorated baskets. As local residents began to realize the significance of this attraction, their comments took on a different light. Instead of public nuisances, native entrepreneurs were more often described as "uncut gems . . . decked out in all the gorgeous and dazzling glory of flaming-colored calicoes and many-colored blankets, with a corresponding amount of red and blue paint on their otherwise vacant faces."[22]

All this coincided with the first real effort to market Phoenix as a tourist attraction. As city fathers realized that eastern visitors were eager to get a glimpse of the fast-disappearing "Wild West," they began to cater to their interests. The rise of tourism was aided by several factors. The excellent climate of the Valley of the Sun had already received national notice, especially from health seekers, and by the late 1890s transportation facilities improved to the point that Phoenix was easily reached by rail from any point in the country. The Santa Fe Railway, in particular, began to realize that tourism could significantly enhance its profit margin. In cooperation with Fred Harvey, it began promoting the Southwest as a tourist attraction in which the Indian motif was given a significant role. This same phenomenon accounted for the establishment of dude ranches and resort hotels, all of which were duly noted by Phoenix boosters.[23]

Eastern tourists thus began to show up in Phoenix, many of them armed with their Kodaks. Photo buffs wanted to snap pictures of Indians in traditional garb. Since trips to the reservation were arduous and camera fans often met with hostility from natives who did not want their images placed on film, the city began sponsoring parades, fairs, and carnivals that featured a decidedly western flavor. The winter carnival was started in 1896 and soon developed into the city's major tourist event. Its evolution demonstrates the city's increasing attempts to meet visitors' demands. The early carnival parades tended to incorporate Indians only as a means of emphasizing the success of the assimilation program. Groups of reservation Indians were followed immediately by scores of native schoolchildren marching in perfect order, giving the audience the impression that old Indian ways were about gone. Within a few years, however, the ever present Indian School pupils had been pushed into the background as "Wild Indians" became the main attraction.[24]

The 1899 winter carnival demonstrated the changing emphasis. To improve the attractiveness of the fair, it was moved from February to December and renamed the Phoenix Cowboy and Indian Carnival. The celebration became a weeklong event and attracted a crowd estimated to be one-third the size of the white population of Arizona Territory. Indians played a prominent role in the affair. Approximately five hundred reservation people came to town, camping east of Phoenix Park. Besides those who participated in the Wild West events, Navajo weavers, Apache basket makers, and Pima potters were permitted to display their skills in front of the courthouse. The real heart of the carnival, of course, was the exciting attempt to re-create the Old West. At selected times during the week, cowboys chased Indians through city streets with such commotion that "the yells of the participants will freeze the blood of the tenderfoot." Even more spectacular was a mock attack on Sutter's cabin, which involved "the fight between the Indians and Mrs. Sutter, and the scalping of Sutter and burning him at the stake." A variety of athletic contests between the various tribes rounded out the program, although the Pima athletes refused to run a race against their old Apache enemies.[25]

The fair was such a success that city fathers added the cowboy-and-Indian theme as a permanent feature. The railroads also cashed in on the carnival. In 1900 the Santa Fe transported several potters from Laguna Pueblo in New Mexico to Phoenix so they could display their crafts. Not to be outdone, the Southern Pacific sent in a team of photographers with instructions to record the Wild West events for advertising purposes.[26]

The show format soon became standardized. Each year a large group of reservation Indians was invited to attend the fair. They were supplied with food and permitted to camp in vacant fields. By the time the festivities started, there might be a thousand Indians in the encampment, "with the usual proportion of dogs, tin cans, crude cooking utensils, etc." Tourists and citizens were encouraged to visit the camp, talk with the residents, and take pictures. The carnival usually set aside one day for the Indians, and the tourists flocked in. Newspapers encouraged the spectacle. "The feeding of the Indians will alone be worth coming to see," wrote the *Republican* in 1902. "They will slaughter the cattle which will be provided for them by the carnival committee. The scenes which will be witnessed there will be precisely the same as those which are enacted at the Indian encampment." The Wild West shows featured mounted natives attacking stagecoaches, traditional dances, and massive Indian parades. The parades were usually chaotic: "Yesterday forenoon attired in all their fine feathers and mounted on their cayuses they charged madly through the streets to the delight of all and particularly the tourists visiting the city. It was a great day for Kodaks."[27]

In 1905 the carnival gave way to the territorial fair. Valley businessmen and stockmen had long sought to organize a major agricultural and technological exhibit which would serve to illustrate the growth and progress of Arizona. With financial aid from the territorial legislature, the fair became a reality; a fairgrounds site was purchased, and exhibition halls were constructed. The territorial fair was much more dignified than the previous carnivals, although it attempted to preserve some of the old atmosphere. Tourists were encouraged to attend the weeklong event, and a day was set aside for the Indians. Organizers offered free admission for all native peoples on Indian Day, and large crowds attended the various athletic and rodeo events. Although Indian Day attracted many curiosity seekers, it lacked the excitement of the old Wild West shows. Additionally, fewer Indians participated, largely because they were not fed by fair organizers. Despite a certain amount of disappointment, Indian participation in the territorial fair became a tradition that continued for years.[28]

While Phoenicians grew more tolerant of the visiting "wild" Indians, they remained opposed to anything they considered a public nuisance. This attitude was made evident shortly after the turn of the century when some of the more righteous citizens decided to eliminate some of the more obvious vices that flourished on city streets, particularly drinking, gambling, and prostitution. Public awareness of Indian participation in some of the seedier aspects of city life had been growing for years. It was exacerbated by the severe shortage of domestic help. Despite the success of the Indian School's outing program, cheap menial labor was virtually unobtainable in Phoenix by 1902. Under such circumstances, some unscrupulous residents took to hiring reservation children. These youngsters received little or no supervision. And because they were employed by white citizens, the ordinances requiring Indians to stay out of town at night did not apply. As a result, concerned residents began to notice what they considered to be immoral behavior among Indian teenagers who gathered on city streets after work.[29]

Unrestricted, the youngsters gravitated toward the seedier parts of town and became involved with gambling and drinking establishments. As one observer noted, "It is plain to be seen that the young men and women from the Papago, Pima, and Maricopa reservations are not living respectable lives in Phoenix and the neighboring towns, freed as they are from all restraints of parents, agent or superintendent. It seems that they have to leave the reservation to earn a living, but in general no thought is given to their moral welfare by their employers." To some Phoenicians, these Indian children were arrogant, refusing to maintain reasonable hours and restrict their activities when requested to do so. A local clergyman found that the youngsters insisted on doing as they pleased, expressing the attitude that if their employers did not like it, they would find another job. Besides, the minister remarked, "they are becoming untrustworthy by refusing to do what they are told to do and by picking up their belongings and leaving places where they are employed without notice."[30]

When Phoenicians, under the leadership of the Reverend Lapsley A. McAfee of the Presbyterian Church, began an effort to clean up the situation, they found it hard to distinguish the reservation children from those attending the Indian School. Consequently, students in the school's outing program were blamed for some of the alleged immorality in town. After attending a Sunday band concert, one observer wrote the Bureau of Indian Affairs complaining of the behavior of Indian children in the audience. Although school administrators realized such complaints represented cases of mistaken identity, the Indian Bureau was highly sensitive to charges of immoral conduct among its students and promptly suspended the outing program in Phoenix. Although this hasty move removed the Indian School from any association with community social problems, it failed to solve the basic difficulty.[31]

The years between 1905 and 1920 were marked by a number of small but significant events which helped establish a permanent basis for a resident native population in Phoenix. For one thing, Indian families began living in town. Although the number was insignificant in comparison with the total population, a 1910 report showed that ten young married Indians were maintaining households in the city. Typical of their number was William French, who purchased a house at 918 East Jefferson Street and held down a regular job paying fifty-five dollars per month. The presence of these families caused the public schools to open their doors to native students. By 1910, four Indian pupils were enrolled at Phoenix Union High School and four more Indians were in local grammar schools. Phoenicians seemed to harbor little resentment toward these youngsters. "They are now welcomed into these schools in small numbers," noted an observer, "and keep up in their grades and are respected and kindly treated by their white associates." By 1918 the number of Indian families living in Phoenix had risen to twenty-four.[32]

While most citizens were unaware of these unassuming families, they were most cognizant of the increasing use of nonresident native labor. After a few years in abeyance, the Indian School's outing system was reinstated, regularly sending sixty to a hundred young Indian women into the community to work as domestic servants. More important, perhaps, was the growing use of reservation people on major construction projects. Although many of these jobs, such as work on Roosevelt Dam, were outside the city limits, all influenced the booming economy. A characteristic city project that used large amounts of Indian labor was construction of the Center Street Bridge. Primarily backed by Dwight B. Heard, who owned considerable acreage south of the river, the bridge was intended to develop south-side lands. Taking advantage of the large labor pool, Heard negotiated a contract with the Pima and Maricopa Indians to provide the necessary manpower and then made arrangements with the Indian Bureau to feed the workers. When the bridge was completed in March 1911, the bulk of the work had been done by residents of the Gila River Reservation.[33]

Another development that benefited Phoenix economically involved the opening of the Indian sanatorium in 1909. The idea of establishing a tuberculosis sanatorium for Indian children of school age was first suggested by Indian Commissioner Francis Leupp. Committed to eradicating contagious diseases then raging among the Indian population of the United States, Leupp recommended that farmland owned by the Indian School at Sixteenth Street and Indian School Road be developed into an Indian health center. Between 1910 and 1915, a large hospital building, numerous bungalows, an infirmary, and employees' residences were constructed. By the end of World War I, the sanatorium was caring for well over a hundred patients annually and was supported by a full-time staff. Indian children suffering from contagious diseases from all over the country were sent to Phoenix for professional care and to benefit from the dry climate. The sanatorium was administered by the Indian School until 1931, when it became a separate entity. By that time it had a capacity of 130 beds, admitted adults, and provided health care for Indians suffering from a variety of conditions. During the 1930s the sanatorium evolved into the Phoenix Indian Hospital, a facility which is still in operation and has served as a focal point for the city's native population.[34]

Some things never seemed to change, however, and Phoenicians displayed incredible gullibility on occasion. An incident that occurred in 1914 just after the outbreak of World War I illustrates some of the latent fear of Indians that remained in the minds of white citizens. In August of that year, newspaper headlines announced that a group of socialist agitators had enlisted local Indians in a scheme to loot and ravage Phoenix. According to the rather farfetched story, Mexican leftists in Arizona had persuaded the Yaqui Indian community at Guadalupe and about five hundred Pimas from Sacaton to join their revolution. They planned to gather at Tempe, capture a militia arsenal, then descend on Phoenix, looting stores and banks, dynamiting buildings, and killing "all and sundry who came in their way." Although the scare proved to be more imaginary than real and quickly blew over, the story frightened many Phoenicians, provoking doubts that the Indians in their midst could be trusted.[35]

Much of this fear was dispelled during World War I, when local Indians displayed great patriotism and public spirit. Many of the older boys at the Indian School were members of the National Guard and had received extensive military training. When war was declared in 1917, these boys were informed that they need not serve because noncitizens were not subject to the draft. This circumstance failed to deter the patriotic students, and sixty-four enlisted in the army and navy. A large number of boys were assigned to an all-Indian company in the Fortieth Division and saw action in France. Those schoolchildren who did not go into the military were used on the home front. In 1918 the Indian Bureau ordered that any surplus student labor be used in the effort to increase agricultural production. Indian residents of Phoenix also purchased war bonds, helped in Red Cross drives, and in general did more than their share. It was because of such patriotism that Congress finally granted Indians citizenship in 1924.[36]

In spite of support for the American system during World War I, native peoples remained reluctant to move permanently into Phoenix. The 1920 census showed that although the city's population had reached 29,053, only 105 of these residents were Indians. Indeed, only the Japanese had a smaller contingent. During the twenties, however, Phoenix made additional strides toward building an urban Indian population. As had been the case in previous decades, economic factors dictated the actions of city fathers.[37]

By far the most ambitious effort to increase the native population centered on an Indian Bureau plan to "colonize" reservation Indians in Phoenix. This program started in 1922 when the bureau decided to coordinate the native work force in the Salt River Valley by having the Indian School serve as an employment agency. Instructions were issued in June of that year that citizens wishing to hire Indian labor must contact the school to make the necessary arrangements. This procedure increased employment of adult Indians, promised to check exploitation, and provided more supervision of Indian activities.[38]

At the same time, a severe labor shortage developed in central Arizona. The sudden demand for workers was prompted by a cotton boom and the expectation that irrigation water from Roosevelt Dam would promote a rapid growth in the overall economy. Dissatisfied with having to depend on Mexican laborers, local businessmen and civic leaders asked the Indian Bureau for help. Federal and tribal governments, faced with problems of reservation unemployment and overcrowding, willingly agreed to cooperate. In 1923, Special Agent Charles D. Dagenett was dispatched to Phoenix with instructions to organize a program for bringing Indian laborers from all over Arizona to the Phoenix area. Within a few months, Dagenett had a system of transportation set up and in operation. Most of the laborers were agricultural workers who went to the cotton fields, but others were hired to work on local irrigation projects, public roads, railroads, and industrial construction.[39]

The relocation program had several notable features. Although it was intended primarily to meet a specific economic need, federal officials expected many of the Indians to leave their reservation homes and settle in Phoenix. "It requires no special gift of prophecy to see what the next five years are going to do to the Indians of this State," noted a member of the Board of Indian Commissioners. "It is almost certain that considerable numbers of Hopi, Navajo, Apache, and Papago Indians will settle in and around Phoenix, Mesa, Tempe, Chandler, Glendale, and other towns and cities of this irrigated section." Not only were jobs plentiful, but white residents seemed truly anxious to welcome more Indian residents. Indian Commissioner Charles H. Burke reported that "a white welcome" awaited Indian families, partly because they were expected to displace Mexican laborers. Congressman Carl Hayden added his support to the relocation program, proclaiming that "they will be heartily welcomed by our white people, their children be received in our public schools, and our churches will be open to all of them."[40]

To a degree at least, the colonization program worked as expected. Between 1922 and 1925, hundreds of Indian laborers were brought into the Phoenix area. Although most remained only a few months, a few stayed. Moreover, when the colonization scheme was combined with the Indian School's revitalized work program, it made for a substantial increase in the number of resident Indians. The Indian School reported that for the year ending June 30, 1925, there were 243 Indian women employed in the city, earning a total of $26,357 for the year. Added to this were almost an equal number of males, bringing to about 400 the number of Indians working regularly in Phoenix.[41]

A portion of these people were young married couples who established permanent residences in the city. Thirty-two Indian families reportedly maintained homes in Phoenix by 1925. Although this figure seems small, it represented a considerable advance. Three of the families owned their houses and twelve had purchased automobiles. Ross and Anna Shaw, graduates of the Indian School, were members of this group. During the twenties, Ross worked for the Railway Express Company, which employed several Indians. The ambitious young Pima Indian first drove a delivery truck, but he was quickly promoted to clerk and entrusted with the agency's cash receipts. He and his family lived on East Adams Street in a multiracial neighborhood which housed many Mexican Americans as well as Indians and whites of a number of national origins.[42]

The Shaws and other Indian families did not believe there was excessive discrimination in Phoenix. Unlike black families, their children were not forced to attend segregated schools. Additionally, a relatively large number of jobs were available. Not counting schoolgirls who worked as domestic servants and employees of the government school and sanatorium, Indians were working "as painters, printers, harness makers, in the railroad shops, for the express company, as shipping clerks, as chauffeurs, yard men, janitors, etc." The openly blatant discrimination was in local theaters, which separated Indian and black patrons from whites.[43]

During these same years, the city continued to have social problems with transient Indians who congregated in the wrong part of town. A number of young Indian girls worked as prostitutes, causing some difficulty for county officials, who did not know how to handle them. In September 1923 the situation became so bad that the county board of supervisors asked the Indian commissioner for a determination whether such Indians were under federal protection or could be placed in the county detention home. The government quickly responded that once out of school or off the reservation, Indian girls remaining in the city were subject to local laws and could be arrested. Indian vendors who came to town to sell their wares also continued to cause concern. Many of them gathered at the railroad station and attempted to sell trinkets to tourists. While their unkempt appearance sometimes embarrassed city fathers, those Indians who congregated on city streets to drink or smoke marijuana gave parts of the business district a reputation it never seemed to lose.[44]

The government's relocation program was almost nonexistent by 1927. Largely because of hard times in the cotton industry, the need for agricultural labor declined significantly. The Indian School attempted to make up for the loss by encouraging more educated young native adults to remain in town. Indeed, it became the policy of school authorities to induce all former students to seek employment in Phoenix rather than return to the reservation. Aiding this effort was the continuing encouragement of city leaders. In 1927 an article in the *Arizona Republican* proclaimed that Indians had become an asset. In language that would have outraged earlier Phoenicians, the paper welcomed new native residents. Noting that about one hundred hardworking families now lived in town, the article concluded that "they are an asset because they are not a public charge, because they are producers, because they pay taxes."[45]

By 1930, then, the situation of the Indians in Phoenix had come a long way. The basis for an urban native population had been established. The census of 1930 estimated that three hundred American Indians called Phoenix their home. Although the figure accounted for less than 1 percent of the population, a certain stability had been attained. The basic institutions necessary to serve urban Indians were present. Jobs were available, as were health facilities in the form of the sanatorium and the school hospital. The Phoenix Indian School had begun to phase out its lower grades and emerge as a high school. In the process, the children of Indian residents were directed into the public schools. Indian community centers, such as an all-Indian church, had also been founded. But more important, perhaps, was the fact that Indians were now a recognized part of city life. They had become an economic and social part of Phoenix. Although some residents continued to complain about transient natives loitering on city streets, on the whole Phoenicians seemed to accept the permanent Indian residents, schoolchildren, and those who came to town to shop or attend fairs and celebrations. In an article published in 1929, Goldie Weisberg described the Indians of Phoenix as being fully assimilated. While she undoubtedly exaggerated conditions, she was on the right track in noting that for all practical purposes Indian residents were much like their fellow citizens. In this sense, attitudes indeed had changed.[46]

Were it not for the Great Depression, the urban Indian population might have grown significantly during the thirties. As it was, not until the wartime years of the forties did large numbers of Indians permanently move to Phoenix. By that time the city was prepared to receive them, largely because of developments in the half-century preceding 1930.[47] It would be incorrect to conclude that white attitudes toward American Indians had completely reversed or that all discrimination had been eliminated. Still, when compared with the reaction that black, Hispanic, and other ethnic groups received during these years, the acceptance of Indians after 1890 was remarkable, standing in contrast to such other southwestern cities as Albuquerque and Los Angeles. It must be kept in mind, however, that this attitude was the result of several specific factors that did not apply to other metropolitan areas. The Indians brought visible economic benefits to the city, were relatively few in number, and never grouped together in a specific neighborhood or ghetto. It is also significant that Indian residents did not engage in political activities or seem to endanger the economic interests of whites. Given these circumstances, it is easy to understand why Anglo Phoenicians felt they could tolerate native residents while simultaneously continuing to mistrust others.

## CHAPTER FIVE

# The Transformation of an Ethnic Community: Phoenix's Italians, 1880 to 1980

## BY PHYLIS CANCILLA MARTINELLI

RESEARCH on America's European ethnic groups generally has focused on major cities in the East (New York or Boston) and the Midwest (Chicago and Detroit). One obvious choice for this focus was the concentration of immigrants in both areas; another was the influential Chicago School's ecological approach, which was predicated on ethnic neighborhood analysis. Yet recent research interests have moved beyond this focus and have begun instead to explore ethnic communities in areas as diverse as Florida and Texas.

This study concerns Italian immigrants in Phoenix, Arizona, an area with an image more traditionally associated with Arizona wranglers, outlaws, and pioneers. However, European immigrants were also a part of the West, even if their presence is not reflected as often in popular imagery. While Italians in western states were fewer in number compared with the heavy concentrations in the East, they often comprised a similar percentage of the generally sparser populations in the West. In 1900, for example, foreign-born Italians in Nevada were 3 percent of the total population, in Arizona 2.9 percent, and in New York 2 percent. Certainly these figures do not mean that Italian American migration history needs to be rewritten; eastern concentrations did form the core of Italian American communities. Rather, the figures suggest the need for further emphasis on regional research. As Lawrence Larsen notes, many western frontier cities had almost as much ethnic and religious diversity as their eastern counterparts.[1]

Phoenix's ethnic community represents an interesting variation on the Italian communities that formed in Arizona. Many of these communities were in mining towns such as Globe, Bisbee, Jerome, Clifton, and Morenci. The local Italian communities were often territorial and could be found in a specific locale. In Globe, for example, Italian immigrants were concentrated on the northwest side of town on a few streets such as

Euclid, Broad, and Hackney. Globe's community had several Italian organizations, stores, and an annual celebration, Columbus Day. In contrast, Phoenix's Italian community was largely invisible to the casual observer. This pattern was typical for European groups in Phoenix, where ethnic neighborhoods were not formed; only Chinese and Mexican neighborhoods were readily apparent. However, geographical concentration is not the only valid criterion for the existence of an ethnic community. Groups that choose to interact with one other because of a common heritage can also be viewed as ethnic communities.[2]

The Phoenix Italian community began forming in the 1870s and grew as more immigrants came to Maricopa County. Between 1882 and 1910, approximately 80 percent of Italian-origin individuals appearing in the Maricopa County voter registers were living in Phoenix. The community established in Phoenix by Italian immigrants contained twenty-five stable families by the early 1900s. An examination of Phoenix city directories reveals that almost twice as many families or individuals from Italy moved through Phoenix during the period; however, they settled elsewhere. Most likely, there were even more Italians in Phoenix, since many immigrants often were not recorded in official sources.[3]

Some of the earliest members of the community moved to Phoenix after exploring for gold in Wickenburg, also in Maricopa County. Several of these men had spent several decades exploring America before finally settling in Phoenix. For example, Francisco Purcella, born in Italy in 1832, was naturalized in New York in 1852 in a period when relatively few Italian immigrants had migrated to America. He appeared in the 1864 territorial census at La Paz, Arizona, where he was listed as a clerk, having been in the territory only one year. In 1865 he was in Hardyville, where he appeared as attorney, in fact, for Carlo Perazzo, another early member of the Phoenix Italian community. By 1870, Purcella was living in Wickenburg, where he became involved in the mining and mercantile business. He arrived in Phoenix from Wickenburg in 1875 and died there in 1882 at age fifty. Along with other early arrivals, such as Carlo Perazzo, Charles Salari, James Righetti, Charles Donofrio, and George Bianchi, Purcella had helped form the nucleus of the Phoenix Italian community.[4]

Despite the lack of a focal geographical area such as a church or neighborhood, the Italians were able to form a viable ethnic group. Practical concerns brought the Italians together as did the need to socialize with people of similar origin. Shared ethnic origins have been recognized as the basis for business ties, and this appears to have been a major network among the Italians. Maricopa County land records show more than two dozen property transactions involving Italians from 1880 to 1900. Apparently, early arrivals bought property from non-Italians. Once this group had established itself, however, new Italian arrivals bought their lands from earlier Italian arrivals. For example, Francis Purcella's land, bought in 1875, was sold to Italian Stephano Danieri in 1882. As the number of Italians grew, so did the network. When Felix Bertino decided to move from Globe to Phoenix in 1902, he looked up an Italian realtor, John Biaggiore, to help him find farmland.[5]

The nucleus of this property network involved sixteen families, who were also involved in other types of commercial transactions. A few of the Italians worked at mining interests in Sonora, Mexico. However, the most common business involvement among Phoenix's Italians centered on saloonkeeping. By the 1890s, almost 40 percent of the Italians in Phoenix were working in this business. They were often proprietors, but they also worked for others as bartenders, porters, musicians, or in other positions.

Phoenix was well endowed with saloons at this time, so Italians obviously were not the only people involved. However, in terms of the general trend of Italian employment in Arizona, saloonkeeping does represent a specialization. As shown in the 1900 special census of occupations, 74 percent of the Italians in Arizona clustered in manufacturing, with most of them working in mining. Only 7 percent of the Italians statewide were saloonkeepers or bartenders, a contrast to the higher percentage in Phoenix.[6]

While German beer or Irish whisky might be more commonly associated with frontier bars than Italian chianti, the Italian saloonkeepers in Phoenix, where there was no mining to absorb immigrant labor, represented an adaptation to an occupation which was suitable for recent immigrants. Edna Bonacich has shown that immigrants tend to go into such easily liquidated businesses as truck farming (specializing in rapid turnover crops) or restaurants, or portable skills like barbering, shoe-making, tailoring. Saloonkeeping fit into this general pattern, for it represented, as did the other businesses Bonacich mentions, a low-capital investment that could be easily liquidated. Immigrants, who often view themselves, at least initially, as sojourners, prefer work which does not tie them too permanently to the new country.[7]

Besides being easily liquidated, saloonkeeping was fairly uncomplicated and allowed a saloon owner to employ ethnic networks to start a business and to hire *paesani*. Most of the saloons run by Italians were near the center of Phoenix and involved almost the identical families involved in the previously mentioned property transactions. The location and owner-ship of saloons kept changing as old partnerships dissolved and new ones formed. In 1892, Alexander Barsanti and Company owned a saloon at Montezuma and Monroe streets, while Charles Salari had a saloon near the train depot. By 1897, Barsanti owned the Union Saloon, Charles Salari had moved his saloon to Five Points, John Biaggiore and

Prosper Bardone ran the Board of Trade Saloon, and the Quadri and Roletto Saloon was opened at 322 South Seventh Street. Oduardo Magnani opened the Columbus Saloon in 1898, while Guerino Bianchi ran a saloon on Second Street (the Union Saloon was transferred to Bartolomeo Poli), and Peter Quadri operated the Depot Saloon. The California Wine House at 132 East Washington typified an immigrant business. It was owned and managed by the Bardones. The bartender was Celestino Ceschetti, the porter Giomito Crotta, and Salvatore Esposito ran the bootblack stand in front. All three employees lived in the rear of the bar.[8]

But in 1906 the Phoenix Anti-Saloon League began to put pressure on the saloons with the passage of antigambling legislation. Italians like Oduardo Magnani and other saloon owners began to face arrest and fines if any gambling took place in their bars. By 1914, all of Maricopa County had become dry as the campaign started in 1906 for prohibition succeeded. Some Italians left the saloon business, and others moved to different areas.[9]

Not all Italians were engaged in the saloon business, but they were still usually found in sojourner types of occupations. The Phoenix city directories list Italians working as barbers, clerks, blacksmiths, and laborers. Some ran grocery stores, confectionery shops, and pool halls. Also listed was a stonecutter, a baker, a painter, and a vocal instructor. A few Italians rented out rooms or ran hotels, and at least one hostelry, the Colombo Hotel, catered to Italian bachelors. Generally, Phoenix's immigrants were similar to other Italians who came to the United States: they had some skills and a desire to work.[10]

Casual socializing among families characterized the other important network, besides business, which linked the Italians. Social networks extended throughout the valley. Phoenix families visited frequently with families in Glendale, Scottsdale, and Tempe. For some, visiting extended as far as Jerome, Flagstaff, Prescott, Superior, and Globe.

Socializing, however, was complicated by the regional diversity of the community. Italy is a nation of distinctive regional dialects; a person from Piedmont might find it hard to understand or speak to someone from Sicily. Several Phoenix families were from the north (Liguria, Piedmont, and the Italian cantons of Switzerland), while some were from the south (Calabria and Sicily). To compensate for the lack of a common dialect, the Italians either spoke "real" Italian or English and primarily reserved their local dialect for speaking to family members.

The large proportion of northern Italians in Phoenix, while not typical of the eastern states, is typical of Italians in the West. During the main period of immigration, from 1880 to 1920, most Italian immigrants on the eastern seaboard were from southern Italy, but western states received larger percentages of northern Italians. For example in 1904, as immigration began to rise, 80 percent of eastern immigrants came from southern Italy while 20 percent came from northern Italy. In the western states for the same year, 76 percent came from the north and 24 percent from the south of Italy. Arizona had 89 percent from the north and 11 percent from the south among its new immigrants.[11]

Some claim that a larger number of northern Italians moved west because "the typical northerner was more literate, more prosperous, and more aggressive . . . than the southerner." However, some western states (Colorado had 55 percent southern Italians in 1904 and Texas had 58 percent) had a larger proportion of southern Italians. One reason for the larger number of northern Italians in the West might be that northern-Italian migration to the United States began by the 1840s, early enough to explore the western states and to begin northern-Italian networks. Certainly more research needs to be done on this dimension of immigration history.[12]

Italians in Phoenix did not come from any single region in Italy, which may be a crucial factor in explaining why Phoenix's Italians did not form a more cohesive unit. In many other American cities a common dialect, chain migration, and kinship ties led to the creation of tightly knit enclaves. Such was the case in Globe, where most Italians came from the same part of Piedmont and organized an integrated community.

Phoenix's Italian community did not, even in its early years, establish any formal organizations. Some Italians joined Anglo-Saxon organizations and several joined Hispanic social organizations, such as the local lodge of Alianza Hispano Americana, the Yucatec Hose Company, and the Phoenix Mexican Athletic Club. In all organizations, the Italians who joined were active members, many even holding office.[13]

There were several reasons why Italians joined Hispanic organizations. Both groups were usually Catholic, so there was a shared religious background. Some Italians had business ties in Mexico, and several had Hispanic wives. Further, the many similarities between the Spanish and Italian languages eased communication. In New Mexico, Italians acted as an intermediate group between the Anglos and the Hispanics and often were trilingual. There is also evidence of trilingual Italians in several Arizona mining towns.[14]

The lack of organizations within the Italian community of Phoenix, combined with its basically scattered nature and the distances involved in socializing, meant that women were the least involved in interacting. Women tended to be more homebound than the men, spending their hours raising their children and tending to domestic chores. They even lacked a meeting place, for while the men could gather at the saloons, there were no grocery stores specializing in Italian staples. Instead, Italian women waited for Louie Rosasco, the grocer from Prescott, to visit. From him they bought their olive oil, tomato sauce, sausage, cheeses, and other items.[15]

If the women generally stayed at home, the men, too, usually kept a low profile in the larger community, a tendency which has left an intriguing historical puzzle of the nature of Phoenix Italians. In an article on school segregation in Arizona, Mary E. Gill and John S. Goff note that a Phoenix lawsuit, Bayless v. Dameron et al., which contended that segregation imposed an unfair burden on the children of Samuel Bayless, was financed by Prosper Bardone (also spelled Bordone, Bardoni, and Bordoni)). Bardone was one of the Italians involved in saloonkeeping, originally working at the Board of Trade Saloon with John Baggiore in 1897. By 1898 he was working at the California Wine House, which advertised a full line of French, German, and Italian imports, a barroom in the back with a good free lunch, and a private dining room for women. Bardone eventually moved up from managing the California Wine House to become secretary-treasurer of the California Wine Company. However, there are no clues as to why he supported integrated education for Phoenix. Perhaps he was influenced by Italians in Louisiana, who were active in the 1890s in opposing antiblack legislation.[16]

One advantage of having such a low profile was that the Italians in Phoenix were not subjected to hysterical nativist claims of Italian criminality found in other American cities with immigrants. Phoenix newspapers generally had little to report about members of the Italian community, but there were enough Italian immigrants in Phoenix for the sheriff's office in 1912 to require an Italian interpreter. Most crimes that involved Italians were minor, and often no individuals were identified. There might only be a laconic comment about minor infractions such as the reporting of a brawl between "an Italian and a Swede named Steve." Possibly one of the "biggest" cases was a 1915 incident during Phoenix's dry days when two Italians who had drifted in from California were caught making wine. The local press delightedly reported the wine to be a "delectable imitation of the wine of La Bella Italia."[17]

If, fortuitously, the Italian community avoided involvement in any scandals, some gained positive recognition in the larger community. For example, Charles Donofrio arrived in 1887 and started selling from a sidewalk stand on Washington Street. Prospering, he brought his brothers Dominic and Salvatore (Sam) from Italy. Their sister Theresa, her husband, Michael Grosso, and the couple's children joined them in 1905. Sam later married into the Perazzos, another early Italian family. Donofrio's confectionery store became a landmark for many Phoenix residents. The Grossos opened an ice cream parlor, although in later years family members branched into a variety of occupations and professions.[18]

James Minotto arrived in Arizona in 1919 and settled in Phoenix in 1924. He became involved in ranching in Yavapai County and the Salt River Valley and served three terms in the Arizona Senate and for several years on the board of governors of the Salt River Valley Water Users Association. In the 1950s he served the United States as deputy chief of the Economic Cooperation Administration. Despite his sophistication, Minotto became a thoroughly western man. He took pride in his roping skills and worked to establish the Phoenix Jaycees Rodeo as a landmark event in the city.[19]

Alessio Carraro established another kind of landmark. He moved to Phoenix from California and in 1928 bought Warner Heights in the 5000 block of East Van Buren. With his son Leo he built a three-story house which dominated the Phoenix skyline and became a local attraction. Plans to develop the 277 acres never materialized and the house was sold to the Tovrea family. Moving to Yarnell, Arizona, Alessio began work on another hill where he cleared, blasted, and shaped the rock into Carraro's Grotto, "a rock wonderland filled with interesting and realistic looking formations." Carraro was just one of a small group of Italian immigrants who, with no formal training, left their mark on the landscape of their new country. Others included Umberto Gabello, who dug an unusual cave house in Colorado; Simon Rodia, whose towers in the Watts section of Los Angeles were declared folk art; and Baldasare Forestieri, who dug a whole complex of grottoes and tunnels in Fresno, California.[20]

Another Phoenix landmark builder, Salvatore Pace Bundanza Cudia, arrived in 1939. He dreamed of creating a local film industry, so he built a studio and movie sets near Fortieth Street and Camelback. Cudia City, as it was called, with its western street sets and restaurant, became a popular dining spot. Cudia filmed the television series "Twenty-Six Men," based on the adventures of the Arizona Rangers, but his plans to rival Hollywood did not materialize. As Phoenix grew to the borders of his studio property, he decided to develop the land commercially.[21]

Other members of the Italian community established more modest monuments over the years. The Mangino family is a typical example. The Manginos moved to Phoenix from New Jersey in 1920. Their service station near the Civic Center was run by brothers Tony, John, and Jim and became a landmark for steady customers for fifty-two years.[22]

As the small Italian community gradually grew, it acquired new members who moved to the area for a variety of reasons, and for a brief time, there were some involuntary Italian residents. During World War II, Arizona became a holding place for prisoners of war. Papago Park in Phoenix (the scene of a major escape attempt by German prisoners) and Florence had the main camps, but there were several smaller camps throughout Arizona.

Most Italian POWs were housed at Florence, but there were Italians at Papago Park, where the National Guard headquarters now stands. The Italians were segregated from the Germans because, in the words of a camp official, "put the Italians and Germans together, the Germans would kill the Italians." The Italian POWs were kept busy cleaning ditches and canals for the Salt River Project. The work battalions were also used at the ordnance shops at the state fairgrounds.[23]

After World War II the Italian community grew, paralleling the growth of the larger community. According to the census, by 1980 the number of Italians had increased to 18,915 single-ancestry Italians and 18,203 people of Italian and other ancestry. Rather than coming directly from Italy, most new migrants were born in the northeastern and north-central states.[24]

As the Italian community in Phoenix grew, it took on new dimensions. It became an Italian American community rather than an Italian immigrant community. The new arrivals brought with them some memories of Italian American traditions and organizations, which they soon started to establish in Phoenix. In essence, then, Phoenix has had two distinguishable Italian groups, although there is some overlap between the two. The early one was formed in the 1880s when immigrants settled in the small town. Relatively static, it grew slowly and was almost invisible in the larger community. The later group, in contrast, has been more visible and has grown much faster.

Although still scattered, the new migrants (most of whom were second- and third-generation Italians) have, in the last three decades, begun to establish a more visible community. In 1960 the community welcomed its own newspaper, *La Tribuna Italiana*. It started as a Columbus Day publication, but its popularity encouraged Del Rogers, the founding editor, to continue. After retiring from the state legislature, Rogers began to publish on a regular basis. Many of the sponsors were Italian businesses. The paper shut down in 1971 because of Rogers's illness, but it had attained a peak circulation of twenty thousand. There have been a few Italian-language radio programs, although none has survived on a permanent basis.

In 1980, Phoenix still did not have an Italian Catholic Church or one with a predominantly Italian congregation. However, St. Joseph's Catholic Church now regularly celebrates the Feast of St. Joseph in March. St. Joseph's Day is celebrated by many Italian groups, but it is often associated with the Sicilians. According to tradition, St. Joseph, considered the family protector, ended a severe famine in Sicily. Now, on his feast day, people devoted to him, or those wishing to give thanks for special prayers that were answered, sponsor a table filled with special foods; friends, family, and people in need are invited to share it. The feast, held at St. Joseph's Church (the first was in 1973), follows many of these traditions, although it is seen as an Italian rather than a Sicilian feast. Several Italian clubs in the Phoenix area also have St. Joseph's tables.[25]

Besides Italian Catholics, there are Italian Protestants, although fewer in number, in the area. In 1947, Louise and Alfred Bonfrisco helped found the Italian Christian Church in Phoenix, which provided services in Italian and English.[26]

The Italian American migration to Phoenix has surfaced in yet another way: through the love of traditional food. A 1978 article noted: "Some Italians must be bankers and doctors, and some must drive trucks or fix refrigerators, but it seems that mostly they feed each other—and the rest of us—in a staggering number of Italian restaurants, delis, and groceries." Most of Phoenix's grocery stores carry a wide range of items for Italian cooking. Once a rarity, there are now numerous Italian eating places. They range from family-operated pizzarias to restaurants that feature gourmet Italian cuisine.[27]

The number of professional people in the community has also increased. The special 1900 census of occupations reveals that there were no Italians in Arizona in professions, and Phoenix city directories list no Italian doctors, dentists, or lawyers until the 1920s. Today there are many professionals of Italian heritage in Phoenix. Some are descendants of the members of the early Italian settlers, while others are new arrivals.[28]

In the past, a person who needed an Italian passport, documents for transacting business in Italy, or a pension from the Italian government had to contact the Italian consulate in Los Angeles. However, in 1957, Phoenix gained its own consulate agent. First filled by Foster Mori, the position went to Anthony Nicoli in 1981; in 1982 it was elevated to vice-consulate status. The duties of the office remain the same, with Joseph Martori next serving as vice-consul.[29]

Another change in the Italian community has been the organizing of several clubs, which have provided focal points for some members of the community. The earliest was established in 1939; it merged in 1952 with another club to become the Arizona American Italian club. A clubhouse was built on North Twelfth Street, and the building still provides a place for members to socialize. The club sponsors numerous social events, encourages an interest in Italian culture, and raises funds for scholarships and charitable services.

The Amico Club, founded in 1952 with thirty-two members (most of them professionals), is basically a service club. The group is involved in fund-raising for a variety of charities, the main source being bingo games at the clubhouse on Indian School Road.

The first lodge of the Sons of Italy, a national organization, was established in Phoenix in 1974; it, too, is social and service oriented. Since its founding, a number of lodges have been established in the valley: Scottsdale, Mesa, Glendale, and Paradise Valley. The organization has expanded throughout the state and has lodges in Tucson and Lake Havasu. In 1977 the grand lodge for Arizona was formed, the first organized since 1953. The lodges keep in touch by meeting regularly throughout the year.

Recently developed areas adjacent to Phoenix also have Italian clubs; for example, Sun City, Sun City West, and Fountain Hills had them by 1983. In 1986, the Center for Italian Culture was organized in Phoenix. It is interested in the Italian language and has held classes throughout the city.

Generally the clubs have conducted their own social and fund-raising events; however, they occasionally cooperate, as when they compete in boccie ball, the Italian version of lawn bowling. Several boccie courts, once unknown in the Phoenix area, have been built by the Italian organizations. In 1978, members of several clubs joined other representatives of the Italian community to sponsor the Phoenix People's Pops Concert. The city recreation department sponsored the event, titled "A Night in Italy," while the ad hoc Italian Cultural Committee sponsored the guest soloist, Enrico Di Giuseppe.

The Phoenix clubs make their presence felt annually at the Hello Phoenix! festival, which is produced by Phoenix Festivals. Hello Phoenix! started in 1978 with representatives from thirty-six cultures and by 1982 had become an ethnic celebration with more than fifty cultures. The Italian organizations participate by selling Italian foods. In 1985, various individuals and Italian American associations helped Lou Brugioni plan Phoenix's first annual Columbus Day parade, which has brought members of the Italian community together on an unprecedented scale.[30]

To view the clubs only in terms of their activities would be to miss an important part of their significance. They have sponsored many activities, but they also have provided events or places for people to gather and become friends. At many meetings there often is a feeling of intimacy and informality. People who have moved to Phoenix, leaving behind family and lifelong friends, often hundreds of miles away, frequently have turned to Italian American clubs to establish new ties. Thus, one unofficial function of ethnic organizations in the Phoenix area is to combat feelings of being alone in a new setting.

In the field of ethnic studies, there has been debate about the continued saliency of ethnic identity for the descendants of European immigrants, sometimes called white ethnics. Phoenix's emerging Italian American community may provide some clues to resolving that debate. The question revolves around whether European ethnics are well on their way toward irreversible assimilation, their distinctiveness dissolving in the melting pot, or whether their ethnic identity remains a part of their basic self, not always apparent but still important.[31]

For many of the Italian Americans moving to the Phoenix area, the most distinctive outward aspects of their ethnic identity, such as speaking Italian, wearing distinctive clothes, or observing folk customs, have faded. Further, many do not fit the physical stereotypes of Italians, that is, having dark hair and eyes and a dark complexion. Thus they could "pass" in the general population. There is not even a Little Italy to remind them of their Italian heritage.

However, instead of ignoring their past heritage, many Italians, at least in Phoenix, are actively seeking contact with others of similar ethnic background. Evidence of this is supported by the growth of clubs. One reason for a lack of interest in dropping an Italian American identification is related to ethnic identification as part of an individual's self-identity. In an area where rapid population growth has led to "anomic rootlessness and alienation," a subjective belief in a shared heritage can be a strong force for developing primary ties. However, it is doubtful that these ties will become the basis for a geographically based Italian community in Phoenix. Ethnic ties can be maintained in residentially dispersed groups, especially since in contemporary society an ethnic identity may not encompass the full range of an individual's social identity but instead, to a certain extent, be situational.[32]

Research on Scottsdale, Arizona, adjacent to Phoenix, reveals patterns that are possibly typical of Italian American migration to the Sunbelt. Evidence indicates a chain migration of families and the establishment of ethnic friendships. Ethnic identity was an important element for these Italian Americans and seemed fairly consistent within the sample despite differences in age, education, and occupation. Italian family attitudes were also important, but ethnic activities were rather less so. The study demonstrates that for this community ethnicity has some salience in the developing Sunbelt environment and demonstrates the need for future comparative research.[33]

Within a century, then, Phoenix's Italian community has been transformed. The early immigrants, who were often sojourners, have been succeeded by numerous second- and third-generation Italian Americans who moved to the Sunbelt as part of the general migration to Arizona. While some Italian Americans left their ethnic identity behind, many have kept it alive. Hence the modern Italian community in Phoenix was infused with new ideas, organizations, businesses, professionals, and festivals. Steady population growth in the Phoenix area will include more Italian Americans, providing the basis for an ethnic community in the years to come.

# PART THREE
*Economic Growth and Development*

## CHAPTER SIX

# The Promotion of Phoenix

## BY BRADFORD LUCKINGHAM

COMPARED to El Paso, Tucson, and Albuquerque, Phoenix was a latecomer to the southwestern urban frontier. In 1867 a few Anglo pioneers from the small mining camp of Wickenburg moved fifty miles southeast into the Salt River Valley in central Arizona, admired the remains of the canal system of the ancient Hohokam Indian civilization, and sensed the agricultural possibilities of the area. Homesteading land near the Salt River, they cleared out old irrigation ditches and constructed new ones, planted crops, and negotiated supply contracts with nearby army posts and mining camps. Those pioneers, soon followed by others, created an economic base from which to grow and develop.

In October 1870 the settlers selected a townsite near the geographical center of the valley. Aware that they were revitalizing the land of an ancient agricultural people, they called it Phoenix after the mythical bird that rose from the ashes; it seemed an appropriate symbol of life rising anew from the remains of the past. The gridiron plan was applied, and the center of the new town was located at the intersection of Washington and Center streets (Central Avenue). Growth was slow but steady, and by 1872 the valley had more than one thousand residents, one-third of whom lived in Phoenix. By then Phoenix was the seat of Maricopa County, and the optimism of the inhabitants was mirrored in the description of Phoenix as a promising town. One booster predicted that "when it has become the capital of the territory, and when the 'iron horse' steams through our country, the Salt River Valley will be the garden of the Pacific Slope, and Phoenix the most important inland town."[1]

Once established, Phoenix had to compete with El Paso, Albuquerque, and Tucson for prominence, and local leaders promoted whatever assets the town possessed. By 1880, Phoenix, with a population of 1,708, was a thriving service hub for an active hinterland that included the Salt River

Valley, the most fertile and productive agricultural area in the territory. Phoenix was incorporated as a city in February 1881, and during the next few years it enhanced its standing as an urban center by securing a railroad and becoming the capital of Arizona Territory. In July 1887, a twenty-six-mile branch line of the transcontinental Southern Pacific Railroad, the Maricopa and Phoenix, was completed north to the town, connecting it with the outside world. In January 1889 the importance of Phoenix was recognized by the legislature when it removed the capital from Prescott to the central Arizona city. The coming of the railroad and the acquisition of the capital, along with agricultural and commercial progress, pleased local promoters and outside investors, and they boosted Phoenix as "the future metropolis of the territory."[2]

By 1890 some observers were calling Phoenix "the Denver of the Southwest," for they believed that "the wonderful growth and progress of the 'Queen City of the Plains' is to be more than duplicated in the garden belt of Arizona." The idea that Phoenix might eventually become another Denver was given credence by Denver investors who injected large sums of capital into the Arizona city and by the Arizona press's frequent use of Denver as a model for Phoenix to emulate. Phoenix leaders had high hopes for their town, but they realized that much effort would have to be expended before it could seriously remind anyone of Denver, a city of 107,000 in 1890. Yet the population of the Colorado center had almost tripled from 36,000 in 1880, and some dreamers in Phoenix envisioned a similar high growth rate for their city.

Actually, growth and development continued to be slow but steady, with the population reaching 3,152 in 1890 and 5,544 in 1900. In February 1895, another branch railroad, the Santa Fe, Prescott and Phoenix, connected with the Santa Fe mainline running across northern Arizona, and the city enjoyed the use of two transcontinental outlets. Promoters celebrated, for the new railroad afforded more access to midwestern and eastern markets and encouraged the movement of more people and capital from those regions into Phoenix and the valley.[3]

Amenities as well as opportunities were present. The climate, for example, was used to promote immigration. Those "chasing the cure" were told that Phoenix was "the healthiest city in the known world," and winter tourists were invited to come and enjoy "Phoenix the favored; Phoenix the balmy; Phoenix the sun-kissed." Critics complained that services needed to be improved considerably before the city could seriously call itself a "health resort," but advertisements and personal statements praising the place had their effect. The result was the arrival of more people, and to meet their needs new facilities appeared; St. Joseph's Hospital, for instance, was founded in 1895, and in 1896 the elegant Hotel Adams opened.

A number of small agricultural centers surrounding Phoenix, including Tempe, Mesa, and Glendale, had emerged by 1900, but they all lagged far behind the capital city in population, and none of them ever threatened its prominence. Phoenix remained the hub of central Arizona life, and the adjacent farm towns looked to it for a wide range of urban goods, services, and amenities.[4]

Along with progress, however, came problems, especially those dealing with water. Late in the 1890s a severe drought hit the valley, forcing thousands of acres out of cultivation, and many farmers and city dwellers, feeling defeated, moved away in search of a new "garden of the Pacific Slope." Those who remained recognized that progress resulting from growth was doomed unless they solved the water problem. After much debate, they decided that a water storage system was the answer. Banding together, residents formed the Salt River Valley Water Users Association, and that organization, taking advantage of the Reclamation Act of 1902, supported the federal government in the construction of nearby Roosevelt Dam, completed in 1911. The building of Roosevelt Dam and its support system brought vital stability to the water supply, allowed irrigation control, and ensured agricultural growth. As the valley prospered, so did Phoenix.

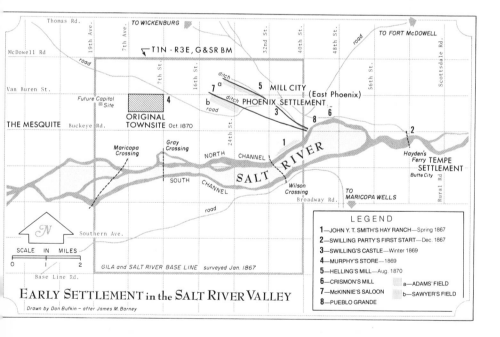

EARLY SETTLEMENT in the SALT RIVER VALLEY

Drawn by Don Bufkin – after James M. Barney

LEGEND

1—JOHN Y. T. SMITH'S HAY RANCH—Spring 1867
2—SWILLING PARTY'S FIRST START—Dec. 1867
3—SWILLING'S CASTLE—Winter 1869
4—MURPHY'S STORE—1869
5—HELLING'S MILL—Aug. 1870
6—CRISMON'S MILL          a—ADAMS' FIELD
7—McKINNIE'S SALOON          b—SAWYER'S FIELD
8—PUEBLO GRANDE

Reproduced from *The Journal of Arizona History*, 18.3 (Autumn, 1977).

With visions of a guaranteed water supply in mind, local boosters and outside investors, including federal-government spokesmen, began to promote the Phoenix area as being more promising than ever. The nation's first reclamation project would bring "water management" to the oasis, and the Phoenix Board of Trade inaugurated a "Tell the World about It" advertising campaign. The Southern Pacific and the Santa Fe railroads published numerous accounts detailing the "marvelous future" awaiting newcomers to the busy city and the rich, irrigated Salt River Valley.[5]

During America's participation in World War I, Phoenix and the valley enjoyed boom times as agricultural activity expanded to new dimensions. At this time long-staple cotton became a vital crop to the war effort. In 1916 cotton production replaced alfalfa growing as the leading industry in the Salt River Valley. Seventy-four hundred acres were planted that year, and by 1920 the crop had increased to 190,000 acres—three-fourths of the irrigated land in the valley. During those years the "cotton craze" pervaded the area, and the enthusiastic "selling of Phoenix" increased.

Unfortunately, the cotton market failed in 1920, causing a short-lived depression, but farmers had learned their lesson. Cotton remained important to the economy, but in the future crop diversification would be encouraged. Moreover, during the boom, the city and the valley had grown rapidly. The 1920 census listed Phoenix's population at 29,053, making it the largest urban center in Arizona and second only to El Paso in the Southwest, a region defined as Arizona, New Mexico, and West Texas.[6]

Despite hard times early in the decade, the 1920s were good to Phoenix and the urban Southwest. As more people and automobiles arrived, the urban area expanded. Amenities and opportunities continued to be promoted. Not only was Phoenix the "commercial and industrial center of Arizona," declared a reporter in December 1928, it was also the city "where winter never comes." The Phoenix-Arizona Club, organized in 1919, spent thousands of dollars each year during the 1920s to advertise "Delightful Phoenix, the Garden Spot of the Southwest." This 550-member booster group promoted Phoenix as a "winter playground" and was instrumental in the growth of tourism and the convention business during the decade. With the arrival of a Southern Pacific mainline in 1926 and the inauguration of scheduled airline service in 1927, investors were encouraged to develop new facilities, and by the end of the decade affluent visitors were flocking to the Westward Ho, the Arizona Biltmore, and other luxury hotels.

By 1930, Phoenix could be called a significant regional urban center. The population rose from 29,053 in 1920 to 48,118 in 1930, and the "metropolis of Arizona" remained the largest city in the region between El Paso and Los Angeles. It was a hive of economic, social, cultural, and governmental activity during the decade. By the end of the 1920s, promoters felt justified in calling Phoenix "truly the capital of Arizona, the hub of new developments, the storehouse and supply house of the state. As Phoenix goes, so goes Arizona."[7]

The Great Depression slowed progress and brought some problems, but public and private investment was evident and the city continued to grow. The population of Phoenix increased 36 percent, from 48,118 in 1930 to 65,414 in 1940, and by that year city boosters felt quite secure about the years to come. As an observer declared in December 1940, "the future of Phoenix is guaranteed as a trade center for a rich agricultural region and a collecting and distributing point for a much greater area." Moreover, he noted, "people of means come here from other parts of the country, just for the delight of living in 'The Valley of the Sun.' "

By this time the Arizona hub claimed to be the "Air Conditioned Capital of the World." As local builder Del Webb asserted in 1940, "air conditioning apparatus has enabled Phoenix to meet and conquer the summer heat, long the bane of southwestern existence." Promoters, who in the past had never mentioned the hot summers in the desert city, now explained that air cooling devices made it no longer necessary for many people to sleep in a yard, on a roof, or on a porch under wet sheets to keep cool during the summer season. Air conditioning increased the livability of residences and other buildings and served to promote and safeguard health. It stimulated business during the summer months and increased the productivity of employees.[8]

Phoenix leaders during the 1930s kept promoting their city as a winter tourist attraction and health mecca, and thousands of people responded. Barry Goldwater and other boosters encouraged this activity as a method of bringing more revenue into Phoenix and the valley. In 1940, Goldwater declared that "the natural thing to which to turn was the capitalization of our climate, our natural beauties, and the romance of our desert." These "natural resources . . . were subjected to a national advertising program," and the "benefits from it can never be fully estimated." According to Goldwater, "the stimulus from the injection of these tourist dollars into the veins of our economic being have been felt by every person doing business in this area. The farmer has sold more produce. The hotels have filled more rooms. The merchants have sold more goods. It is easy to see, therefore, why businessmen are so unanimously enthusiastic about the continuance and enlargement of a proper advertising program."[9]

During the 1930s a Phoenix advertising agency, looking for a more appealing name for the Salt River Valley, came up with "the Valley of the Sun," and its use became popular as the effect of amenities on the economy of Phoenix grew stronger and publicity techniques improved.

During the winter season of 1939–40 it was estimated that thirty-five thousand visitors came to the Phoenix area, and without exception, resort facilities reported gains in the number of guests. For example, the exclusive Camelback Inn, completed in 1936, announced that business in December 1939 represented an increase of 68 percent over December 1938 and a rise of 107 percent over December 1937. The war in Europe encouraged the influx to Phoenix, for tourists, now prohibited from going abroad, often chose to visit Arizona, and those who did so in 1940 spent about thirty million dollars in and around "The City of Palms."[10]

The outbreak of World War II triggered an economic boom and population explosion in Phoenix and the valley. The war years saw the activation of several military installations, including Luke Field west of Phoenix and Williams Field east of Chandler, and in their wake came defense industries, including AiResearch and Goodyear Aircraft. Phoenix organizations, such as the chamber of commerce, worked closely with Arizona's representatives in Washington, especially Sen. Carl T. Hayden, to secure these valuable assets; inducements, including building sites, materialized, and every form of cooperation was extended. As in the past, federal funds and projects stimulated the local economy, and a significant amount of growth and development in Phoenix resulted from both public and private investment.[11]

During the Cold War, military installations such as Luke and Williams Air Force bases continued to serve as part of the national defense effort, and former war plants looked not only to the military but to civilian markets also. A multiplier effect took hold, and as more manufacturers moved to the area, they attracted others. Predominant were light and clean industries, especially electronics firms, and they flourished in the low-humidity climate so necessary to their success. They used little water, yet produced high-value, low-weight products that could easily be shipped anywhere; noting the smallness of the goods, an observer declared that often "a truckload is worth a million dollars." Helpful to these and other concerns was a transportation system that included everything from trucking lines and major highways to transcontinental railroads and international airlines.

Of course, a number of agencies were involved in promoting the Arizona hub. One of the most notable, the Phoenix Chamber of Commerce, advertised the attractions of the area during the postwar years, especially through its monthly publication, *Phoenix Action*. Stressing the opportunities and amenities available in the Valley of the Sun, the chamber sought to make Phoenix "one of most highly publicized cities in America." Citizen organizations, such as the 450-member Phoenix Growth Committee, joined in, especially in support of bond proposals, the effort to make Phoenix a more inviting place in which to live and work.

Maintaining a proper image was important to boosters. For example, it was important to the tourist business in the "clean city" of Phoenix that pollution-free industries settle in the area. Air pollution would hurt tourism, so neat, smokeless plants were encouraged to preserve "the sunshine and pure atmosphere." On the average the sun shone 85 percent of the time and manufacturing concerns appreciated this unusually high norm, for it allowed business schedules to be completed without interruption by adverse weather. Absenteeism was reduced, and outdoor test phases of particular products, such as weapons systems, were rarely disturbed as a result of "nature's battle plan." Executives and workers also appreciated the nearby mountains and man-made lakes and the active but casual year-round lifestyle available in the Valley of the Sun.[12]

The Motorola experience is representative of the sort of success story that would be repeated over and over in Phoenix, and it aptly illustrates the attractions the city held for corporations. Early in 1948 officials of the company, a leading independent concern in the rapidly growing electronics industry, decided to establish in Phoenix a new research and development center devoted exclusively to military electronics. The Cold War and national defense considerations encouraged Motorola to locate in a primary dispersal area in line with the federal government's decentralization program. Phoenix drew attention because of its favorable business climate and its excellent location midway between the national-defense-oriented industrial supply houses of Albuquerque and Southern California. Moreover, nonstop six-hour air service was available between the desert city and Chicago, Motorola's main base, while nearby Arizona State College at Tempe offered the potential for the development of quality engineering programs. The most important factor, however, was the city's "outstanding climate and its nation-wide reputation as a resort and health center." It was felt that the climate and health factors would be a "potent aid in attracting the desired personnel."

The Motorola operation in Phoenix proved to be a success and expansion followed. Only one drawback was noted, and that was "the intense heat of mid-summer." Yet, as Daniel E. Noble, a leading executive, wrote in June 1954, "the agreement is quite general among the Motorola families that they will take the four months of summer weather in preference to the winters in the north and in the east." And "they point out that a hundred-mile drive north from Phoenix will take them into the cool, wooded mountain areas of pine trees and streams. Where, they ask, in the north or in the east, can they drive out of the snow and ice and the cold in a hundred miles? And then there are the coolers." Our "experience with evaporative coolers showed that they worked very well the greater part of the time, but that refrigeration in the laboratories insures perpetually satisfactory working conditions for the staff during the summer months." Many of the "staff members are installing refrigeration units in their homes to provide an equally satisfactory control of temperatures for the family." Noble concluded by stating that "Motorola management feels that refrigeration cooling in the plant and in the home is the complete solution to the Phoenix summer heat problem. Refrigeration cooling has transformed Phoenix into a year-round city of delightful living."[13]

By 1960, Motorola was operating three attractive electronics plants in Phoenix, and the company payroll of five thousand employees was the largest in the city. In 1948, Motorola officials had considered Tucson as a site for their operations, but they chose Phoenix. Unlike Tucson, where considerable opposition from established interests existed, business and civic leaders in the capital openly promoted industrial growth. More than three hundred manufacturing enterprises were established in the Phoenix area between 1948 and 1960, and by 1955 manufacturing had become the city's primary source of income, with farming and tourism placing second and third, respectively. Between 1948 and 1960, manufacturing employment tripled, and the annual income from local concerns rose from less than $5 million in 1940 to more than $435 million in 1963. As a result, urban rivals in the Southwest were left far behind.

In the postwar years, economic diversification was achieved and the new role of Phoenix as a metropolitan center of commerce and industry was assured. The major firms in full operation during the 1950s included AiResearch, General Electric, Goodyear Aircraft, Kaiser Aircraft and Electronics, Motorola, and Sperry Rand, and most of them represented the type of industry promoters wanted to attract. For the most part they were clean and employed thousands of trained workers, many of them engineers, computer experts, electronics technicians, and other highly skilled personnel of white-collar rather than blue-collar nature.

Again it must be emphasized that Phoenix booster organizations worked hard to attract and serve industry. In September 1955, for example, the Municipal Industrial Development Corporation, a group of determined business leaders, played a key role in bringing Sperry Rand to the Valley of the Sun by raising $650,000 in 72 hours. The amount enabled the organization to buy and offer the company a factory site, make improvements to a nearby airport, and arrange other inducements. Influential Phoenicians also helped to secure state tax-law changes that made the business climate of the Phoenix area even more attractive. Most important was the repeal in December 1955 of a state sales tax on manufactured products for sale to the federal government. The day after the tax was repealed, Sperry Rand headquarters in New York announced that it would definitely locate its electronics aviation division plant and research center in Phoenix. The change also encouraged a number of other companies to move and inspired several Phoenix electronics and aerospace firms which did business with the federal government to expand.

Urban leaders in the Southwest wanted their cities to develop economically, but some worked harder than others to realize their goal. Phoenix promoters often led the way, and the recruitment of Sperry Rand served as an example of what could be accomplished. Businessmen elsewhere, urging faster industrial growth in their city, frequently noted the aggressive tactics of ambitious Phoenicians. As one from El Paso declared, in the Arizona capital "industrial scouts are met at the plane, entertained, offered free land, tax deals and an electorate willing to approve millions in business-backed bond issues." By comparison, he lamented, "El Paso does nothing[and] has lost its spot as the number-one city in the Southwest." Moreover, he concluded, "unless we start hustling after new industry, we're going to wind up in serious trouble."[14]

The population of Phoenix increased from 65,414 in 1940 to 439,170 in 1960. Thanks to an aggressive annexation program and immigration, the population increased from 106,818 in 1950 to 439,170 in 1960, a remarkable 311 percent, the highest rate of growth during the decade among the nation's fifty largest cities. By 1960, Phoenix had become the largest city in and the urban capital of the Southwest.[15]

There were problems, of course, but that is another story. The promoters of Phoenix had created an urban center of promise, a major oasis in the rising Sunbelt. Opportunities and amenities seemed to have met in Phoenix, the instant metropolis. As one observer accurately declared in 1960, "the mood is here, the word is out; this is the place. The city is going somewhere, and it is attracting more than an average share of people who want to go somewhere with it."[16]

## CHAPTER SEVEN

# An Overview of Economic Development in Phoenix in the 1920s

## BY MICHAEL KOTLANGER, S.J.

DURING the decade from 1920 to 1930, the economy of Phoenix passed through a cycle of prosperity, depression, recovery, growth, and slippage. The development of agriculture, construction, and transportation illustrates the progress of this economic cycle as well as the growth process of the urban economy.

In 1920, Phoenix was the central city of Arizona and the Southwest. As the state capital, the seat of Maricopa County government, and the home of many regional agencies of the federal government, it was the administrative center; but as the regional wholesale and retail emporium, the service center for many Southwest mining operations, a financial and investment concentration, and the hub of a vast agricultural hinterland in the Salt River Valley, it was also the business core of the region. Economic indicators showed Phoenix to be a prospering city and pointed to the continued growth and progress of the urban center toward metropolitan status during its second fifty years.[1]

Agriculture was the primary economic base for Phoenix and the Salt River Valley. In 1920 valley farmers enjoyed the fourth year of unprecedented earnings for their harvest of long-staple lowland Pima-variety cotton. The regional economy flourished when foreign cotton suppliers were cut off from the American market during the hostilities of World War I. Defense contractors sought new domestic supplies of the long-staple cotton required in the production of tires and airplane fabric. The agricultural lands in the Salt River Valley proved ideal for raising such cotton, and wartime necessity drove the price per pound increasingly higher.

As market prices continued to rise, local growers, speculators, and "cotton plungers" invested in vast acreages of arable land throughout the valley to plant long-staple cotton. The base of the local economy became increasingly unstable as a rapid transition occurred from stability through crop diversity to instability by overdependence on cotton monoculture.

Alfalfa raising, grain farming, cattle ranching, and dairy farming rapidly fell from their positions in the prewar economy as land values rose sharply. Prices ranged from $350 to $600 per acre, and land rental fees for arable acreage rose to a high of $75 per acre. When cotton-market specialists forecast a price of $1.50 per pound ($750 a bale), for the 1920 cotton crop, many growers and investors seriously overextended their financial resources and credit by expanding their acreage in anticipation of quick profits.

In late fall 1920, when more than 180,000 acres (nearly three-fourths of the irrigated land in the valley) was planted in Pima cotton, a market glut occurred. Two international events created it: first, overseas growers dumped nearly a half-million bales of Egyptian long-staple Sakellarides cotton surplus on the American market, and then American defense contractors initiated peacetime production cuts of war matériel. Cotton prices declined, then fell precipitously. Instead of receiving the anticipated price of $1.50 per pound, the few local growers who were able to sell their cotton on a market of limited demand were paid only twenty-eight cents per pound. The regional economy staggered as annual farm income plummeted from a high of nearly $24 million in 1919 to $11.5 million in 1921. A contemporary estimated the financial losses for the 1920 cotton season to equal the entire construction cost of Roosevelt Dam and the valley canal system.

The effects of the cotton market collapse were immediate and widespread. In Phoenix, merchants suffered million-dollar losses when forced to make "charge offs" to keep up with declining sales. In fact, several major department stores—Hanny's, Korrick's, and I. Diamond of Boston—held gigantic merchandise-reduction sales to deplete their inventories.

Numerous cotton workers were stranded in the valley when bankrupted farmers were unable to pay wages. The jobless congregated in Phoenix, hoping to obtain some form of unemployment relief, assistance, or jobs. Several unions and relief organizations attempted to alleviate the suffering and hardship by setting up a soup kitchen at union headquarters near downtown. The press reported incidents of starvation as the depression closed in on Phoenix.

As a result of the cotton market crash, farmers recognized the need to return to the crop diversity that had characterized the regional economy before the craze. The watchword for all concerned was rediversification, which had repercussions in many areas of the urban economy.[2]

In 1921 valley banks, in cooperation with Los Angeles banks, arranged generous low-interest loans for valley farmers who wished to return their acreage to other crops. Farmers replanted nearly fifty thousand acres in alfalfa, while dairymen replaced the thirty thousand dairy cows that had been sold during the cotton boom. The *Arizona Republican* named the dairy cow the "Salvation of the Valley" because of the renaissance of creamery businesses in and around Phoenix. The plentitude of alfalfa as inexpensive forage boosted cattle ranching and livestock feedlot operations into their former positions in the economy.

In spite of the national grain-market depression, many Arizona farmers planted wheat, hegari, barley, sorghum, and corn to meet the supply demands of feedlot operators who "grain finished" their stock before shipping it to local slaughterhouses or West Coast meat packers. Availability of year-round feed supplies led to the construction of the Arizona Packing Company slaughterhouse and stockyards on Tempe Road five miles east of downtown Phoenix. When grain-crop yields increased, farmers marketed them to Phoenix processors. In 1923 the Phoenix Flour Company (Ninth and Van Buren streets) purchased five million pounds of wheat from local farmers for milling purposes. The abundance of grain helped the poultry raising to prosper, and it became such an important export industry that when a national turkey-market glut occurred during the 1924 holiday season, the Phoenix Chamber of Commerce sponsored a successful "Buy A Turkey Day" to get rid of eight thousand surplus birds.

The return to crop diversity illustrated willingness to experiment in all types of agricultural plantings. Citrus groves were redeveloped and expanded to become a major element in the Phoenix economy. North of the city, farmers developed a broad citrus belt that extended from the Arcadia and Ingleside districts westward into the town of Glendale. Citrus exports increased annually during the 1920s to peak in 1930, when 535 carloads of oranges and grapefruit were shipped from Phoenix to markets on the East and West coasts.

Olive and date farming became important agribusiness ventures throughout the valley and helped to advance the processing and canning industry in Phoenix. Arnold's Pickle and Olive Company (Fourteenth and Van Buren streets) specialized as the only packer of green olives in the nation, while Munson's Olive Company (Ninth and Jackson streets) became the major supplier of olives to the East Coast market.

Further crop diversification became possible in middecade when the railroads made available more refrigerated cars to Phoenix shippers, guaranteeing the prompt shipment of such fragile valley-grown produce as melons, cantaloupes, grapes, lettuce, and winter vegetables. Acreages in all these crops increased as Phoenix produce jobbers entered the national market.

Nevertheless, the 1920 cotton crash did not cause the abandonment of cotton as a cash crop; rather, cotton was returned to its proper place in the regional economy. Short-staple upland varieties with higher yields were introduced and became popular as prices in the world market improved. Gradually during the decade, both long- and short-staple cotton planting became popular with valley farmers, with acreage planted in each variety fluctuating annually as farmers and growers responded to market prices.

The recovery of agriculture accompanied the reestablishment or creation of grower, processor, and distributor cooperative associations for each crop group. The associations helped stimulate the growth of another important sector of the Phoenix economy, the construction industry. Each group financed construction of warehouses, packing sheds, canneries, and processing plants throughout the industrial district to handle the produce of their respective memberships.[3]

It should be noted that the essential element for all the agricultural redevelopment and expansion of the 1920s was the construction of Salt River Valley Water Users Association dams along the upper reaches of the Salt River. The series of hydroelectric water storage dams and reservoirs guaranteed adequate year-round water supplies to valley farmers. After middecade the agricultural base of the economy had been nearly fully restored. Figures for farm earnings during 1926 indicated that agriculturalists earned more than $25.5 million for their crops.[4]

While the agricultural sector of the urban economy recovered, construction of commercial, industrial, and residential buildings boomed throughout the city. The sum of this new construction altered the legibility of the cityscape and expanded the already defined patterns of functional zones and neighborhoods. In the central business district, the 1920s marked the beginning of vertical growth, the intensification of land use, and the rapid process of exclusion, segregation, and extension of downtown functions. South of downtown, adjacent to the trunk line and sidings of the railroads, the industrial and warehouse district flourished. This sector continued to grow south and west, with some spillover to the east. High- and middle-income residential neighborhoods continued to be developed outward from the urban core in a northward direction, filling areas previously leapfrogged by builders who had developed subdivisions in the noncontiguous suburbs. The decade-long boom established the construction industry as an important element in the Phoenix economy.[5]

Commercial building construction proceeded at a rapid pace throughout the downtown during 1920. Hotels, churches, retail stores, hospitals, an auditorium, and a theater were constructed that year. Most significantly, the completion of the Heard Building "skyscraper" introduced high-rise development in Phoenix. Vertical growth was rapid during the decade, in which Phoenix acquired a number of the landmark edifices that dominated the skyline for many years.

Following the cotton crash, construction projects slumped and a short-lived but severe depression occurred. One of its victims was the

Phoenix Building and Construction Trades Council, which passed from the scene and was not reorganized until 1930. Construction commenced on only a few buildings during 1921: the Temple Beth Israel–Hebrew Center, the Ellis Building, and the armory. By 1922, however, most contractors had returned to work on projects downtown, and the second phase of the 1920s building boom began. Between 1922 and 1930, such local landmarks as the Newberry Building, the City and County Building, St. Mary's High School, the Korrick's Building, the Phoenix Title and Trust Building, Orpheum Theater, the Professional Building, the Luhrs Building, the San Carlos and Westward Ho hotels, and the expanded Adams Hotel were constructed. Completion of the twelve-story Luhrs Tower in 1930 ended the building boom in downtown Phoenix. As the effects of the Great Depression struck the city, financial resources dried up and many commercial contractors ceased operations.

The warehouse and industrial district was a locus for construction projects throughout the 1920s. The eight miles of railroad-track frontage attracted every conceivable type of industrial and warehouse activity. Between 1919 and 1920, jobbing operations increased 250 percent within the district, and industrial building boomed. Many agricultural processing and jobbing companies enlarged their facilities or built new plants, and new firms were attracted to the district to establish operations. A small manufacturing industry was introduced during the boom years.

Eastward along the railroad tracks, the wholesale produce warehouse district relocated from Jefferson Street and First Avenue to a new concentration area at Twelfth and Madison streets. The Southwestern Packing Company had the only dog-food manufacturing plant in the Trans-Mississippi West. It was forced to double its plant on Madison Street after it introduced its cat chow product to follow its monopoly on dog chow.

Westward along the railroad tracks, various companies built a concentration of refineries and storage tanks and warehouses of nine major petroleum companies from Texas, Oklahoma, and California. The congregation of oil firms between Fifteenth and Nineteenth avenues made Phoenix the petroleum refining and distribution hub of the state.

Many building support manufacturers and suppliers located their firms in the southern section of the district during the 1920s in order to supply contractors' daily construction needs. For example, Phoenix Plaster Company built a one-hundred-thousand-dollar plant at Seventeenth and Jackson streets to supply a hundred tons of plaster a day. Phoenix quickly became the leading producer and distributor of finished steel products in the Southwest when both Western Pipe and Steel Company and Arizona Steel Pipe and Tank Company set up plants and storage yards in the district.

Reproduced from *The Journal of Arizona History*, 18.3 (Autumn, 1977).

A small automobile and automotive-accessory manufacturing industry also emerged to supply the many dealerships along Phoenix's "automobile rows," situated along Central Avenue and on Adams Street, between Fourth Street and Fourth Avenue. The Martin Perry Company of Troy, New York, selected Phoenix, because of its ideal position on the railroads, as the site for its western assembly plant. More than 150 styles of commercial automobile bodies were assembled at the new plant on West Jefferson Street. E. C. Eaton built its carburetor and automotive-parts manufacturing plant adjacent to the Santa Fe tracks west of Phoenix in the Alhambra district. Increasing sales orders caused Phoenix Onyx Company, a processor of Cave Creek onyx, to enlarge its gearshift-ball manufacturing plant in "Acre City" at Twelfth and Harrison streets.

In sum, the building boom of the 1920s extended the industrial and warehouse district of Phoenix and advanced the city as the major distribution hub of Arizona and the Southwest. More important, the growth of a small industrial and manufacturing district and location of the construction support suppliers complemented the already well-established and rapidly expanding agricultural processing, jobbing, and shipping firms in the southern industrial zone. The development of this nascent industrial manufacturing subdistrict introduced another element into the makeup of the urban economy and heralded the future economic development of the city.

Residential housing construction boomed during the 1920s, following a pattern roughly parallel to that of commercial building construction, and marked the beginning of Phoenix's commitment to low-density housing that resulted in the urban sprawl of the 1980s. City officials issued more than 800 residential building permits to contractors in the peak year of the decade, 1920. The cotton crash depressed the housing market and only 343 permits were issued the following year. Permits for new units fell to a low of a 161 in 1922. During the remainder of the decade the number of permits issued annually gradually climbed to more than 500 in 1929.

Initial signs of recovery first appeared in the suburbs beyond the northeast city limits during 1921. Several new estate homes and a club-house were started at the Phoenix Country Club, and new homes were begun in Dwight Heard's high-income Los Olivos suburb. By midsummer, construction had progressed on more than two hundred residences ranging from "modest bungalows to palatial mansions."

The completion of Cave Creek Flood Control Dam in 1923 protected the city west of Central Avenue from the recurrent flooding that had hampered construction of residential neighborhoods. To exemplify the progress of residential construction, the neighborhoods encompassed by the Moreland Corridor freeway-route proposal (of the 1980s) as they developed in the 1920s provide a good illustration. Between Seventeenth and Seventh avenues, the two hundred-acre Story Addition was quickly developed by builders into a popular middle-income housing neighborhood. The adjacent Kenilworth Addition, developed during the 1910s, grew when construction of Kenilworth School in 1920 made the neighborhood between Seventh and Third avenues attractive to prospective home buyers. During the boom, a middle- and high-income residential neighborhood emerged there.

Two additions between Third and Central avenues, Sims and Chelsea, featured high land-value areas of upper-income residential housing that experienced a rapid infilling during the boom. The prime land-value area of Phoenix extended eastward from Central Avenue to Seventh Street. Since 1910, it had become the location of the city's elite upper-income residential housing. During the boom years, Central Place Addition was the site for some development of private housing. Since the late nineteenth century, developers of Brill Addition had promoted it as "being close to the carline," but development slowed in the neighborhood between Seventh and Twelfth streets. After the completion of Deaconess

Hospital (Good Samaritan Hospital) in 1923, a middle-income residential neighborhood was quickly developed throughout the Brill Addition. Extensive development occurred east of the city limits in Grand View Addition, and a low-income, blue-collar residential neighborhood emerged.

North of the Moreland Corridor, the Phoenix Country Club area developed as contractors came in to build the subdivision and the Flower Tract. Despite the boom in residential construction, no single style of indigenous architecture developed in Phoenix; stylistic design in domestic architecture was eclectic. One commentator noted that the city "suffered importations of every type and style of architecture" and that "if popular elsewhere, they became popular here."

The residential building boom firmly established the home-construction industry as an important component of the urban economy. Contractors, skilled craftsmen, and many laborers gained employment from the labor-intensive industry, which poured millions of dollars into the economy. An important building support industry developed as local suppliers provided the needed materials for local contractors. Home building became such a major part of the Phoenix economic scene that when the Great Depression brought the industry to a halt, widespread unemployment and severe economic hardship followed for many Phoenicians.[6]

Civic leaders recognized that the future growth of Phoenix hinged on the development of a system of good roads and the attraction of a main-line railroad through the city. Phoenicians committed themselves to bonded indebtedness to finance the construction, extension, and paving of their street grid and county road system. During 1920, almost every street in the original townsite was paved with expensive bithulithic compound on an asphalt or cement-concrete base. By year's end the city street system had twenty-five miles of pavement. During 1921 the city paved Van Buren Street to the city limits at Sixteenth Street, and the county extended, widened, or paved its roads in the area. The result was a paved highway extending from downtown Phoenix to Mesa. Street paving continued at a rapid pace throughout the decade, and by 1924, Phoenix had risen to eighth place among the first ten U.S. cities of fifty thousand population in the percentage of improved streets.

State highway development in the Phoenix area was predictable when the state opened its central office and main repair yards on a site near the capital complex bounded by Harrison and Jackson streets and Eighteenth and Nineteenth avenues. "Good roads" boosters quickly introduced proposals for the construction of an integrated highway system radiating in all directions from the city.

Los Angeles and Phoenix road boosters cooperated closely from 1922 to 1928 to achieve construction of the Blythe Cutoff Highway. The opening of a five-span bridge over the Colorado River at the Blythe-Ehrenberg crossing shortened the interurban trip by eighty miles and tied the two cities closer together.

In 1925, Van Buren Street and Grand Avenue were put on the official list of federal highways as U.S. 80 and U.S. 89, respectively. The Arizona Highway Commission later designated Van Buren, Washington, and Jefferson streets, Grand Avenue, and a series of interconnecting streets as official state highways. Within the decade, Phoenix became the hub of a system of federal, state, and county highways that strengthened the distribution sector of the city's economy and made Phoenix a major center for the road construction, repair, and maintenance industry.

Railroads fundamentally enhanced Phoenix's urban and economic growth. The 1920s marked a watershed for railroad development because the city acquired a first-class railroad depot, expanded its freight and railroad maintenance facilities, and, most importantly, gained a position on the Southern Pacific mainline.

Phoenicians had labored for many years to acquire a major transcontinental railroad line through their city. From 1913 to 1924, the banner slogan of the *Arizona Gazette* was "Phoenix Must and Will Have a Main-Line Railroad." After encountering continual frustration in their efforts, boosters shifted their emphasis to persuade railroad officials to build a first-class depot. The Arizona Corporation Commission came to the city's assistance by ordering the Southern Pacific and Santa Fe railroads to construct a joint first-class depot. The architectural firm of Lescher and Kibbey planned the $750,000 Spanish-mission-style station. When it opened in 1923, 30,000 people gathered at the Harrison Street site to celebrate the event.

Railroad officials attempted to assuage local disappointment over failure to gain a mainline connection by embarking on an extensive expansion and improvement program for their systems. Santa Fe equipment was upgraded, new heavy "mainline-standard" rails were installed, roadbeds were oiled, and new ballast was added to the tracks. The railroad invested $110,000 in developing additional freight facilities along its tracks in Peoria, Glendale, and Phoenix. Elaborate icing facilities, new switching equipment, and expanded track sidings were added to the Santa Fe railyards. The Southern Pacific countered its rival by carrying out similar improvements.

In 1923, Dr. James Douglas and some financial associates presented plans that would lead directly to the construction of a mainline railroad through Phoenix. They proposed that the Tucson, Phoenix, and Tidewater Railroad connect the Arizona mining belt with the Gulf of California. The proposed first link would connect the Tucson, Phoenix, and Tidewater with the El Paso and Southwestern and the Rock Island System railroads on a direct line through Phoenix. The Phoenix Chamber of Commerce and the Salt River Valley Water Users Association quickly organized and led meetings of the Tidewater Railroad Association to boost the Douglas group's proposal.

The Southern Pacific did not want another competitor in Phoenix and conducted a resistance campaign to thwart the Douglas franchise request. However, as the Douglas proposal gained strength and support, Phelps-Dodge Company, which owned the El Paso and Southwestern line, suddenly moved to purchase the complete holdings of the Tucson, Phoenix, and Tidewater Railroad. Phelps-Dodge then proposed to extend its line into Phoenix. This corporate merger forced the Southern Pacific to move. In June 1924 the Southern Pacific merged operations with the El Paso and Southwestern to establish the Pacific Lines of Southern Pacific. One of the conditions set by the Interstate Commerce Commission for approval of the merger was the construction of a mainline railroad through the Salt River Valley within two years.

A ten-million-dollar mainline project was soon announced. It would include Phoenix on its route and would upgrade and double-track the entire system. Many Phoenicians attended the groundbreaking ceremony at Picacho, but the arrival of the first mainline trains sixteen months later on October 15, 1926, set off a celebration surpassed by none other in the state history. That day, after two special trains arrived carrying delegations from El Paso and Los Angeles, Phoenix staged pageants, band concerts, parades, football contests, and street dances. A "human fly" was hired to scale the Heard Building for the festivities.

Immediate benefits accrued to Phoenix because of the mainline. The Southern Pacific Railroad of Mexico soon built a mainline from Mexico City to the border, then opened the Tepic cutoff. Through this development, Phoenix acquired a direct connection with Mexico's central plateau and thereby extended its market area significantly.

The Santa Fe feared it would lose business to the mainline and began a $350,000 improvement of its Phoenix facilities by constructing a large maintenance yard to tend its rolling stock. The Southern Pacific immediately countered by naming Phoenix divisional headquarters for its new Phoenix Division and moved its regional maintenance facilities from Gila Bend to Phoenix. Within Phoenix, Southern Pacific crews installed bell and light safety crossing signals at all street intersections and company tracks between Seventh Street and Seventh Avenue.

By decade's end, Phoenix was prospering from its mainline position. Local firms had acquired direct rail connections with national and international markets. An important railroad repair industry had taken root in the city, and passenger connections with the nation's major cities nurtured the rapidly growing tourist industry and helped initiate a boom in hotel and resort building. Railroad advertising made Phoenix a focus of national attention and served to attract visitors, winter residents, and permanent residents to the Salt River Valley. The advent of the Great Depression caused a minor setback in railroad development, but by that time Phoenix was well established as an important city in the national railroad system.[7]

Thus in ten years the economy of Phoenix went full cycle from a depression to the Great Depression. During the decade, changes and growth in the agricultural sector returned the city's economy to a firm base. A construction boom introduced an industrial component and caused building support services to locate in Phoenix. The development of transportation through road construction broadened Phoenix's tributary hinterlands and linked the city with the national system of cities. Acquisition of the mainline railroad gave the city links with the national and international markets and nurtured the tourist industry, and rivalry between the Santa Fe and the Southern Pacific fostered the development of a rail maintenance industry. In short, the economy of Phoenix during the 1920s entered a new phase of growth, expansion, and diversification. These are but some of the indicators of urban economic development. They prepared the city to weather the Great Depression, recover, and take off again toward prosperity.[8]

Capt. William A. Hancock, who surveyed the original Phoenix townsite in 1870. He died in 1902.

Charles Pearce (right) and friend, reputedly the first two mail carriers in Phoenix, early 1890s.

Minnie Evans and Helen Guernsey wearing hats fashionable in the mid-1890s.

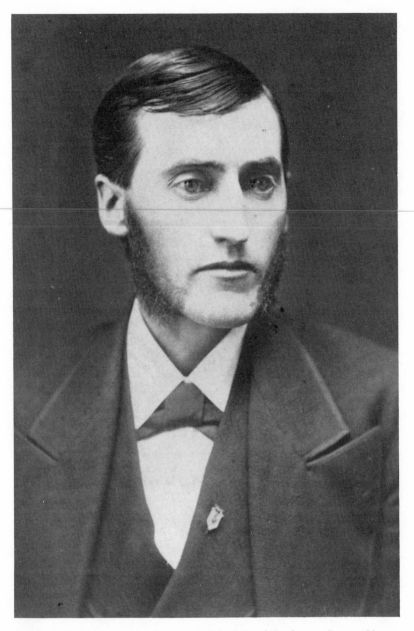

Dr. R. L. Rosson, mayor of Phoenix and builder of the famous Rosson House, now the main architectural attraction in Heritage Square.

Unlike Tombstone, Phoenix could not boast dozens of saloons. Here, however, is one of note: the Old Palace Saloon on Washington Street, about 1905.

A bird's-eye view of Washington Street, the main thoroughfare, about 1906.

Old City Hall, about 1908. When the state government was transferred from Prescott, the building served briefly as the state capitol.

Phoenix Indian School, about 1910. The school's well-known band marched in many parades; each year its football team battled the Phoenix Union High School players.

Theodore Roosevelt Dam was dedicated in 1911 by none other than the former president. Local residents talked for decades about the day Teddy swept into town to dedicate his dam.

The original Salt River Valley Water Users Association building, Van Buren and Second Avenue, about 1914.

An excellent example of decoration in the southwestern style: the residence of Edward and Marie Eisele at 805 North Third Avenue, about 1915.

A. C. Bartlett (extreme left) and his son-in-law, Dwight B. Heard (fourth from left), during a train stop in Nogales. Bartlett was instrumental in securing large amounts of mortgage money in Chicago for Heard's Phoenix firm.

The old Valley Bank branch building, 28 West Adams, about 1915.

Bird's-eye view of Phoenix Union High School, with Camelback Mountain in the background, about 1917. During the first forty years of the twentieth century, this was the main high school.

Looking northward to the Adams Hotel on Central Avenue in the mid-1920s. Note the American Kitchen to the right—known as the best restaurant in Phoenix at the time.

Drivers for Diamond Ice Company helped Phoenicians cool off in the summer by delivering book blocks of ice to family iceboxes, about 1935.

Architecturally one of the most unusual buildings erected in Phoenix in the twentieth century: the Maricopa County Courthouse, with the Phoenix City Hall wing in the rear, about 1935. Note the trademark lampposts.

The famous round table at the Arizona Club in the Luhrs Building. It is said that in the thirties, forties, and fifties, the city's power brokers assembled here to make decisions.

Allesion and Leo Carraro, builders of Tovrea Castle on east Washington Street—a testament to Italian-American craftsmanship.

The Arizona Biltmore in the 1940s. This was the most prestigious resort in Phoenix from the 1920s (when it was built) until the 1970s. Although Frank Lloyd Wright did not design the building, he did serve as consultant. His influence is unmistakable.

# A Record of Revitalization:
# Financial Leadership in Phoenix

## BY LARRY SCHWEIKART

PHOENIX'S rise into the ranks of the major cities in the United States could easily be dated from the depths of the Great Depression. Although few observers would feel comfortable with crediting the 1930s with any benign effects, consider the events that would play a significant part in the revitalization of Phoenix:

1. Walter Reed Bimson took control of Valley Bank in January 1933. His direction and influence rejuvenated it.
2. Frank C. Brophy gained control of the Bank of Douglas (the Arizona Bank) in 1934, ensuring its survival and eventual move to the state capital.
3. First National Bank (now First Interstate Bank) initiated a series of mergers and branch expansions and, under its parent company, Transamerica, brought several powerful banks under its corporate umbrella in 1937.
4. Add to these events the creation of a powerful second tier of banks thirty years later and the financial dominance of the Phoenix metropolitan area was complete.[1]

This essay spans the years 1933 to 1968 because this period, unlike any other in the state's history, witnessed, first, a dynamic reduction in the number of competing banks, combined with the unusual phenomenon of increasing competition, and second, the boom of smaller banks from 1960 to 1968. Moreover, as the number of banks in Arizona diminished and as the major branch-banking establishments competed more heavily, Phoenix took on an increasingly larger role as the state's financial center. This trend is especially evident when one notes that by the end of the thirty-five-year period, few banks had their headquarters in any other city, and by 1970 no major bank had its central office outside Phoenix. (Continental Bank eventually moved to Scottsdale, which is considered part of the Phoenix metropolitan area.) What is intriguing about the trend is that for a variety of reasons new banks again began to spring up in the late 1950s and throughout the 1960s; however, since the hub of financial competition was already set (located in Phoenix), the minor competitors found their fertile fields of business to be in the secondary markets. As a rule, only when these smaller competitors combined did they enter the Phoenix market. There are, of course, exceptions. For example, Guaranty Bank, later United Bank, has competed in Phoenix since the early 1960s, and Continental Bank, later Chase, was a powerful mortgage company before it converted to a bank. Still, no bank today would consider establishing its home office elsewhere in the state.[2]

Here I will detail some of the factors that led to the economic revitalization of Phoenix and then examine some of the consequences of the financial and physical concentration of banking power in the city. Finally, this essay will determine whether the city had a financial policy and, if so, establish its character.

Any discussion of the financial developments of the 1930s in Phoenix must begin with Walter Reed Bimson, who probably had more influence on Arizona banking during the following two decades than any other individual. A blacksmith's son from Berthoud, Colorado, Bimson learned to keep books and was a janitor in the bank his father eventually purchased. At the Harris Trust Company in Chicago he specialized in negotiating farm loans. He was head of the state relief program in Illinois when Valley Bank consulted him about succeeding H. J. McClung (who had resigned) as director and president. Bimson was elected on December 21, 1932, and took over the following New Year's Day. He maintained close contact with Harris Trust; Valley Bank's later ability to continue lending during the Depression suggested to many observers that a Harris pipeline existed.[3]

Even if that were true, Bimson faced, upon arrival at Valley Bank, a less than optimistic situation. Yet he marched in, ordered a 10 percent salary cut, and, as one employee noted, "he made us like it." Bimson immediately allayed most employees' anxieties, however, by assuring them that no more jobs at the bank were endangered. His policy and the bank's policy would be, he told his employees, to make loans. He declared, "I want this period of automatic loan refusal to end and end now!" The Valley Bank was to go into mass production on small loans. Bimson personally set his desk near the entrance of the bank and explained to his loan managers that it was better to make ten loans for $1,500 than one for $15,000. As confidence in the bank's ability to make loans grew, so did deposits, which increased by $200,000 in Bimson's first ten days as president. Thus the entire bank developed a new energy, which, in turn, spread to the community. One example of that energy was the bank's success with new borrowers: less than 1 percent ever defaulted (the number approached 1 percent only in 1942), indicating that Arizona consumers were channeling the money back into the economy.[4] The Valley Bank's flurry of loan activity climaxed in June 1939 when it made installment loans of $68,087 in a single month. Bimson knew that an expanding loan program would return profits to the bank, a point borne out by the $80,000 returned to the bank on its 1 million dollars' worth of installment loans made over a period of several months in the late 1930s. Often overlooked in that period, Walter's brother Carl, in his role as chief promoter and salesman for most of the bank's programs and innovations, constantly drew national attention to the state's geographic advantages and economic opportunities. Carl's influence has been understated far too often.[5]

Of all the banks in Arizona, Valley Bank profited most from the New Deal laws, particularly the National Housing Act of 1934. Carl Bimson was instrumental in getting the law passed and testified before congressional committees. The Federal Housing Administration was empowered to "insure eligible financial institutions against losses upon their loans for the repair, alteration, and improvement of residential properties." The younger Bimson "made a crusade of it, organizing crews to ring doorbells and talk up loans." He realized that the FHA loans under Title I could be applied to appliances, such as ranges and refrigerators, as long as they were considered to be "permanently attached." Carl Bimson's loan officers made more than seven hundred such loans in one week, and more than 600,000 dollar's worth were made in Phoenix in just one year. From 1934 to 1945, Valley Bank made more than 198,000 loans, drawing in people "who had never done business with banks previously." With the home office in Phoenix, Valley gained both profits and power during the Depression, and with it Phoenix gained as well.[6]

With the outbreak of World War II, the state attracted numerous industries that, along with the various government training facilities, caused a growth in local spending by the United States government. As indicated by bank deposits, the effect of this income on the state's economy was substantial. Arizona bank deposits grew by 135 percent more than the national average. From 1939 to 1945, Arizona's deposits increased $271 million, with Valley Bank holding well over half that amount. During the war years, then, the city profited from government investment: directly through the investments themselves and indirectly by assuming the role of Arizona's financial center simply by having major banks that held or controlled government deposits. Valley held 53 percent of the state's total deposits during that period. The convenience of having the government offices in Phoenix further strengthened the city's financial hold on the state's economy.[7]

Another development that contributed to Phoenix's financial revitalization was a tax-law revision pertaining to banks. In 1934, Frank Brophy explained to Lewis Douglas, his close friend, that a coalition of "certain banks, some of the mining companies, and at least one public utility company" had attempted to force "certain Arizona tax officials to desist from practices which result in inequitable and unfair valuation of property that manifestly discriminates against banks and some other corporations." Working through the Maricopa County Taxpayers' League, Brophy succeeded in getting valuations on real property in the county reduced $50 million during a two-year period. Valuations on bank shares and properties of public utilities were not reduced, however, as state officials completely ignored the bankers' protests. As a result, "the burden of taxation was actually being increased on the banks at a time when their actual value was at the lowest point in the history of most of them." Banks took their case to the courts, arguing that taxation had oppressive effects and stymied expansion of bank capitalization. However, under the capitalization method of taxation, a bank could absorb another institution without increasing its own capitalization. Consequently, "the value of the former unit bank just passed out of existence when liquidated." According to state law, the bank was required to sell the acquired real property within five years of purchase. In this way, banks that sold at depressed prices could take advantage of the current tax laws.[8]

Typically, Walter Bimson led the Arizona bankers in presenting their case to the public. As early as 1939 he charged that heavy taxation endangered the entire banking system in Arizona. He maintained that there was "every incentive to pay out too large a proportion of earning in dividends and otherwise to prevent the increase in capital, which affords an increased margin of protection for depositors."[9]

Growing controversy led the Arizona Bankers Association to sponsor a study of taxation problems faced by banks. Using a hypothetical bank with total assets in rough figures of $801,000, deposits of $695,000, other real estate of $9,000, and capital accounts of $104,000, the tax laws of various states were tested. Arizona's tax on this imaginary bank would have been the highest ($5,600) while that of Mississippi and Louisiana ranked second and third ($5,400 and $3,500, respectively).[10]

By 1943 all parties clamored for change. Bankers exerted growing pressure through the Arizona Taxpayers Association. The legislature obliged by passing a new bank-tax law—twice. Both times the governor vetoed it, but the legislature overrode the second veto. According to this law, each bank would pay a tax on its entire net income from all sources, including government or local bonds, at a rate of 5 percent. Additionally, the legislature eliminated the tax on bank shares. Widespread approval greeted the new law, and under it Arizona banks increased their capital substantially.[11]

Another feature of all Arizona banking, but one that benefited Phoenix in particular, was solid advertising. In 1946, Walter Bimson suggested the concept of a publication (*Arizona Progress*) to one of his employees, Herb Leggett, who fleshed out the idea and distributed the resulting pamphlet on a massive scale. The pamphlet depicted all aspects of Arizona's growth, including business, agriculture, and population. Virtually all major banks had a copy, and any person considering a move to Arizona could look at promotional material for the state by picking up a copy of *Arizona Progress* at his or her local bank. Banks in other countries received this publication, and it has probably been the single best piece of promotional material in the state's history, ranking with *Arizona Highways*. Frank Brophy also designed an unorthodox but highly effective advertising campaign for the Bank of Bisbee. The campaign consisted of newspaper advertisements showing pictures of historical subjects but usually presenting a controversial theme. Ironically, it was the advertisement of First National Bank and the Bank of Arizona that prompted Brophy, and possibly Bimson, to advertise.[12]

Armed with new tax laws and bolstered by their five-year opportunity to advertise to a captive audience—the servicemen—bankers took advantage of the postwar period and the increasing population growth of the Southwest. Automobile ownership doubled from 1945 to 1950, contributing, along with an expansion in air travel, to a migration of Americans to warmer climates. Added to this was construction of numerous military installations, training centers, and related industries. Arizona, then, became a haven for scientists and engineers in the defense industry, and they flocked in by the thousands.

This was especially true in the Salt River Valley, where five air-training centers had been established by the government during World War II. Manufacturing followed these installations, and major companies built plants in the valley, such as Garrett Corporation's AiResearch plant, Goodyear Aircraft's plant, and an Allison Steel bridgeworks plant. Even though some of those industries, such as AiResearch, closed at the end of the war, most reopened or were reopened by another company. Motorola, for example, established an electronics plant in Phoenix soon after the war ended. The defense industries drew in even more manufacturing enterprises. Related industries, such as communications, also boomed. In 1951, L. V. Smith of Mountain States Telephone and Telegraph pointed out that his company had spent thirty million dollars since the end of the war. Air-conditioning sales jumped 80 percent from 1940 to 1951, an increase made possible to a great extent by growing home modernization credit. Valley Bank led the entire nation in granting that type of credit.[13]

Along with the contributions of Bimson, Brophy's corporate moves contributed to the revitalization of Phoenix's financial position. With only minority ownership, Brophy eventually gained control of the Bank of Douglas from J. S. ("Rawhide Jimmy") Douglas in 1934 and set up a small branch office in Phoenix in 1945. Brophy lived in the city and realized that it was or would be the financial center of the state. However, it took the death of an important employee to change both the location and corporate direction of the bank.[14]

John B. Crowell, longtime cashier and manager of the Bank of Douglas, was planning to retire, upon the advice of his doctor, after the Phoenix branch opened. He decided to stay on "just one more year" to facilitate development of the new branch, but he died in the spring of 1947. Suddenly burdened with management responsibilities, Brophy decided to make the bank a full-fledged competitor, and in Crowell's absence Brophy moved the home office to Phoenix, where he could manage it himself. He soon acquired an experienced cashier–loan officer named Wesley R. ("Monty") Montgomery from Valley Bank, and Montgomery became executive vice-president in July 1947.[15]

The road to making the Bank of Douglas a major competitor was riddled with organizational, administrative, and economic potholes. When Brophy made the decision to expand in 1946, he told Lewis Douglas the bank's issue of 200,000 dollars' worth of stock would "build up the capital structure in anticipation of future growth." Brophy explained to one New York banker that the bank, as of 1948, was in a "fluid state." To a friend, Brophy wrote in 1949: "[The] general trend of bank deposits for the past year has been downward. . . . After we get our little expansion program set up, then I think we had better settle down and see about making a little more money for the stockholders." By 1950, Brophy reported to Victor H. Rossetti of the Farmers and Merchants Bank in California that he had "completed the financing of the Bank of Douglas and most of the money came from Arizona people."[16]

Although the bank grew as a competitor, some of the money left as quickly as it had arrived. On February 8, 1950, robbers held bank employees of the downtown Phoenix Bank of Douglas at gunpoint as they arrived at work. When the manager appeared, he was forced to open the vault and the employees were herded in. The thieves carried more than $116,000 in a mop bucket to their black Dodge coupe and disappeared. It was the largest bank robbery in Arizona history and was never solved.[17]

A change in the bank's philosophy surfaced despite the robbery and Brophy's original organizational problems. In 1951, Brophy explained to a customer that he had already lent beyond limits set by the board of directors, hardly the act of a conservative banker. The trend was made official by the 1952 annual report:

In the past, the Bank has never solicited accounts, and it is not proposed to change the policy at this time. However, during the coming year, it is anticipated that a new Business Development Department will be set up, and that the various services of the bank will be aggressively presented to business and other potential customers in all areas which we serve.

From that point on, the bank began a vigorous and competitive expansion program. One indication of the new philosophy's success may be found in a memo from Montgomery to Brophy noting that the AiResearch account had a "very handsome balance in it"—more than $300,000.[18]

First National Bank also entered a period of expansion in the late 1930s. Using the merger technique and creating new branch-office facilities, it expanded from three branches in 1939 to forty in 1956. When Transamerica acquired Phoenix National Bank and the Phoenix Savings Bank and Trust Company in 1937, the latter remained a separate entity. However, in 1949 the stockholders supported a full merger of the institutions. First National had continued to expand in the meantime. When the Miners and Merchants Bank branch at Yuma went on the auction block in 1937, First National bought it for $62,500, an acquisition that "proved to be particularly timely in the light of the burgeoning agricultural and military growth which was soon to begin in Yuma." More significantly, a number of former competitors fell under the corporate umbrella of a bank having its home office in Phoenix. Transamerica also acquired Southern Arizona Bank and Trust of Tucson in 1957, but the Tucson bank operated independently of other Transamerica holdings in Arizona until the company divested itself of its Arizona holdings in 1958. The acquisition of these banks by Transamerica marked the beginning of a nationwide expansion program for that company. Transamerica bought banks in six states in addition to the five states in which it already operated banks. Banks affiliated with Transamerica had assets exceeding $3 billion, total deposits of more than $207 billion, and loans of more than $1.4 billion in 1956. Its family of banks had 288 offices and military facilities, and in Southern Arizona Bank and Trust, Transamerica had acquired Arizona's largest state-chartered bank, with assets of $81,645,286.08. In 1958, Transamerica's 329 banking offices in eleven western states fell under the control of newly created Firstamerica Corporation (changed to Western Bancorporation in 1961). As a result of those acquisitions, the second-largest Arizona bank consolidated its power and enhanced the financial strength of Phoenix because of the location of First National Bank's headquarters in the city.[19]

Valley Bank also began a large postwar expansion program by purchasing the First National Bank of Nogales in 1945 and the First National Bank of Winslow the next year. In 1954 a third acquisition, Buckeye

Valley Bank, brought total resources of the three acquired banks to more than thirteen million dollars.[20]

Through the use of a profit-sharing plan, the bank expanded further. Dr. Louis Ricketts had left a sizable block of Valley Bank stock to California Technical Institute; not wanting this stock "hanging over the market," Walter and Carl Bimson negotiated its purchase by paying for it out of the profit-sharing plan. Ultimately, the plan accumulated outstanding shares in three other banks: the Bank of Flagstaff, the First State Bank of Arizona, and the Bank of Douglas.[21]

Brophy had been trying to sell a substantial part of the Bank of Douglas since 1951, and in 1953 he held a meeting with Walter Bimson to encourage Bimson to have Valley Bank buy the stock. Bimson cordially refused. Not only could Valley Bank not afford the stock, but Bimson wanted to preserve competition. "We need more banks in this state, not fewer," he told Brophy. Bimson did agree to help set up a holding company, Arizona Bancorporation, to buy the stock. This company would act as a separate and independent agency "to enable the stockholders of the Valley National Bank to acquire an interest in the Bank of Douglas, the Bank of Flagstaff, and the First State Bank of Arizona and to provide a convenient means of financing the purchase and construction of bank buildings and other bank facilities . . . without using the capital funds of the bank." Valley Bank's profit-sharing fund would act as the vehicle for this purchase.[22]

Valley Bank stockholders received the first two hundred thousand shares of stock issued by the Arizona Bancorporation at an exchange ratio of five Valley Bank shares for one Arizona Bancorporation share. In addition, Arizona Bancorporation obtained holdings in the Professional Building in downtown Phoenix and stock in the Guaranty Life Insurance Company, the Arizona Brewing Company, and the Exchange Finance Corporation with offices in Cottonwood, Sunnyslope, Chandler, and Buckeye. The acquisition of these banks and the related stock exposed Arizona Bancorporation to charges of violating the Bank Holding Act following its passage in 1956. Under that legislation a bank holding company (any company which directly or indirectly owns, controls, or holds with power to vote 25 percent of the voting shares of each of two or more banks) forfeited its control of those companies in which it held 25 percent or more within two years of the law's passage. Further, the comptroller of the currency did not approve the ownership of the Professional Building because the purchase price had been recorded in Valley Bank's books as $1 and the true value of the structure was not disclosed.[23]

In a letter to stockholders, Walter Bimson discussed the possible effects of the Bank Holding Act. He recommended that Arizona Bancorporation sell one hundred shares of voting stock in the Bank of Flagstaff, thereby reducing the total shares to less than 25 percent. Some redefining of Arizona Bancorporation's position had taken place on June 30, 1955, when First State Bank of Arizona merged with the Bank of Douglas. Buckeye Valley Bank and the Bank of Flagstaff had been merged with Valley in 1954. Therefore, Arizona Bancorporation had reduced its holdings to a controlling interest of only the Bank of Douglas—well within the law.[24]

Valley Bank continued its expansion through the creation of branch offices. H. L. ("Doc") Dunham, in a 1959 interview, personally detailed the circumstances surrounding each of the twenty-three branch offices created from December 1939 to December 1956. Those branches gave Valley Bank "the most extensive branch-banking system in the state of Arizona." By the end of the 1950s, it had acquired three more branches, but most offices served Maricopa County.[25]

By 1956, then, two major banks with Phoenix headquarters combined to hold 72 percent of the state's banking assets. But the concentration was even heavier than it appeared. Only eight independent Arizona banks remained, but if one considers Arizona Bancorporation's interest in the Bank of Douglas as a link to Valley Bank and if one realizes that the only non-Phoenix bank of any size, Southern Arizona Bank and Trust, was controlled by Transamerica, the umbrella company of First National Bank, then four banks controlled 93 percent of the state's bank assets, with Phoenix-based banks holding 83 percent.[26]

Disturbed by this concentration, federal examiners instituted an investigation of the Arizona banks in 1956, expressly looking for violations of the Clayton Act. The investigation had been triggered in part by the larger *Board of Governors* v. *Transamerica* case, which received much publicity, but federal examiners kept the investigation quiet throughout the entire fact-finding period. Valley Bank officials knew something was up, of course, when a team of investigators led by Bob Einzig descended on the records department of Valley's main office in Phoenix. Einzig asked for a liaison from Valley Bank, and Carl Bimson, as was frequently the case, drew the tedious and delicate job of baby-sitting a unit of examiners. In turn, Bimson asked Minton Moore, Valley Bank official and researcher, to assist the team.[27]

Previously, as Moore explains, any questionable practices detected by the Board of Governors were handled by a polite message to the bank detailing ways in which the bank could, or should, alter its policy to comply with the law. This was not the case in 1956. No mention of antitrust proceedings was made, and Valley Bank officials were never asked to justify, comment on, or explain data, policies, or procedures.[28]

Like wraiths, the examiners departed as mysteriously as they had come. Their conclusions were compiled into a two-volume report, *Investigation of Banking in Arizona*. Supposedly, the results of the investigation were secret and known only to the Board of Governors of the Federal Reserve Bank of San Francisco. Certainly Arizona banks did not know any of the conclusions.

The report pointed out several areas (a vast majority) in which the banks' actions had not decreased competition: the merger of Holbrook Bank and First National Bank and Transamerica's control of the Bank of Flagstaff and Southern Arizona Bank and Trust. The investigators found acceptable competition in all counties except Pinal and Cochise. Only in those two areas did the investigation reveal a reduction in competition. The report also concluded that a policy of checking with the local bank before making loans in that community "did not forestall competition between the two larger [banking] groups." Having failed to ask for an explanation from bank officials during the investigation, the examiners overlooked obvious, and even blatant, facts which would have altered the conclusions.[29]

For example, Valley Bank was charged with acting to decrease competition in Pinal County. The report showed Valley holding 100 percent of the loans in Pinal County. Minton Moore termed such an accusation ridiculous: Valley Bank was the only bank operating in Pinal County in 1956![30]

The report concluded that Valley Bank and First National were "tending toward monopoly," but no action followed. Not until late 1962 did federal authorities file an antitrust action, and then the only target was Valley Bank and its control of Arizona Bancorporation. In October 1966, Valley relinquished control of Arizona Bancorporation and the case ended with both Valley Bank and The Arizona Bank (as the Bank of Douglas had been renamed) agreeing to refrain from merger activity for a number of years.[31]

As a partial consequence of the antitrust troubles of the major banks, three trends emerged: (1) new banks, such as Guaranty Bank, appeared and took advantage of the merger power denied two of the major banks; (2) many new banks began to compete in secondary markets; and (3) the major banks used branch banking to supplant merger and purchase techniques for expanding.[32]

Meanwhile, right under the nose of Valley, which had pioneered the FHA mortgage lending programs, a powerful new competitor arose— the A. B. Robbs Trust Company, originally an insurance agency. Its founder, A. B. Robbs, Jr., was contacted in 1947 by National Life of Vermont, which arranged to have him originate FHA mortgages in Arizona on behalf of National Life. In essence, Robbs funneled eastern capital into Phoenix and Tucson, with the bulk of the loans going into dwellings in Maricopa County. Robbs Trust Company's growth was phenomenal: in 1953 it had 30 million dollars' worth of mortgages and had long surpassed mighty Valley Bank as the leading mortgage lender in the state. In fact, by 1959, Phoenix ranked eleventh in the nation in home building and Robbs Trust Company led Phoenix financial institutions in lending. Robbs's involvement with eastern investors led him to engage also in extensive Phoenix boosterism, especially promoting the city's residential assets.[33]

After founding two banks—the Bank of Phoenix and Guaranty Bank ("dry runs," Robbs called them)—Robbs pulled a first-of-its-kind conversion, using the mortgage servicing contracts as capital and opening Continental National Bank in 1964. While it was far from being a threat to the Big Three, Robbs still had a lock on the residential mortgage business in Arizona. Given that residential housing grew at continuously strong rates in Phoenix, it was not surprising that Continental yearly stood as one of the top three or four most profitable banks in Arizona. By the 1970s its position as profitability champion was secure, with only one competitor close: Thunderbird Bank in Glendale.[34]

Also established in 1964, Thunderbird found a completely different niche: small business loans. Relying on the Small Business Administration, the management of Thunderbird eschewed general consumer loans to concentrate on the Phoenix business community. Although it remained smaller than Continental, it often ranked equal to or ahead of Continental in profits. Together, Continental and Thunderbird, along with Guaranty (later United Bank), constituted a powerful second tier of specialized banks. When banking was deregulated in the 1980s, it was not surprising that these profitable banks were snatched up by such giants as Chase (Continental), Marshall-Ilsley (Thunderbird), United of Denver (United), and Citicorp (Great Western). It was also predictable that Thunderbird and Continental brought the highest per-share price at the time of sale (roughly 3 and 2.75 times book value, respectively).[35]

Shortly before the Valley Bank lawsuit was settled, another development further underscored Phoenix's dominance in the Arizona financial community. In 1965 the Arizona Bankers Association agreed to set up a permanent office and hire a full-time staff. Before 1965, the association's affairs were rotated annually among the three largest banks in Arizona, namely, Valley, First National, and The Arizona Bank. Association involvement, both legislatively and educationally, became so intense that it was cumbersome, time consuming, and expensive for any one bank to maintain its administration. For some time association officials had been searching for an individual to become the first full-time staff member of the Arizona Bankers Association. Edwin H. Jelliff, formerly with Southern Arizona Bank and Trust Company in Tucson, was selected to fill this position, and on October 29, 1965, he was introduced to delegates attending the association's convention at Del Webb's Townhouse in Phoenix. Soon thereafter the permanent association office was located in the Arizona Title Building in Phoenix. Within ten years the downtown Phoenix skyline was to become enhanced with beautiful new skyscrapers bearing the names of First National Plaza, Valley (Bank) Center, and The Arizona Bank. While he was tempted to move the association offices and take advantage of new, modern, and more convenient quarters available in these buildings, Jelliff declined to do so in order to avoid possible inference of allegiance to any one member bank.[36]

The overall effect of these various actions and consolidations was more significant for Phoenix. By the 1950s the city had become the financial capital of Arizona, with each of the major banks having headquarters in the city. Only Southern Arizona Bank and Trust remained in Tucson, outside the Phoenix circle, and it joined the First Interstate chain in 1974. By the 1970s, even major new banking groups, such as United Bank, Continental Bank, and Great Western Bank, had established their home offices in the Phoenix metropolitan area. Phoenix's financial policy had developed through the individual actions of its bankers. Each bank had independently followed a similar pattern of promoting Arizona and Phoenix, bolstering its position regarding taxation and centralizing its operations in Phoenix. The major banks, through their competition, had fought with the tools available: merger and purchase. Consequently, as the number of banks in Arizona decreased and as the concentration of assets and financial power in Phoenix increased, competition continued at a high level. Thus even when new competition appeared in the 1960s, Phoenix represented the only logical arena for any bank wishing to become a major competitor. No major competition could hope to succeed from a home base in, for example, Yuma.[37]

Most significantly, the banks individually concluded that by promoting Phoenix and Arizona, they were promoting themselves. Ultimately, though, the phenomenon of concentration, combined with competition, growth, and geographical centralization in Phoenix, has enabled the city to become the major financial center of the Southwest between Dallas and Los Angeles. After regional branching started to occur in the 1980s, many large Californian banks, including Bank of America and Security Pacific Bank, started to purchase the relatively smaller Arizona institutions. Eventually, Security Pacific acquired the Arizona Bank and later merged with Bank of America.[38] Even then, they retained the center of their Arizona operations in Phoenix. Perhaps more significant, Valley Bank remained independent until 1992, even after suffering serious real estate–related losses in the early 1980s.[39] Ultimately, interstate banking only reinforced the dominance of the financial institutions head-quartered until the 1990s in Phoenix, while Valley Bank's ability to remain independent underscored the significance of its early decision to develop an extensive branch system based in Phoenix. [As this book goes to press, the sale of Valley Bank to Banc One in Ohio has been announced—Ed.]

PART FOUR

*The Importance of Water*

# CHAPTER NINE

# In Pursuit of a Reservoir

## BY EARL ZARBIN

OF ALL the public-policy issues in the history of Phoenix, none has been—and continues to be—as important as water. The character of the water question, however, has changed from one directed at developing an assured water supply for agriculture to one pointed at satisfying the demands of a still-growing urban industrial center.

To be sure, the responsibility for providing a water supply for farmers never fell upon the city. Rather, the men who served on the city council in the early years knew their interests and those of the city were identical to the interests of those who dug the canals and farmed the land; the income the farmers received for the sale of their wheat and barley was spent primarily in Phoenix. For that reason, while the city at most played a minor role in solving the water question, its storekeepers, lawyers, landowners, civic boosters, and others were deeply involved.

Some of these townspeople were undoubtedly in the crowd that gathered in the Phoenix Plaza for a political rally on Saturday night, October 24, 1884. The last speaker, Lincoln Fowler, a candidate for the territorial assembly, said he would not make a speech because the hour was late. But according to a report of the gathering printed in the *Arizona Gazette*, "in a few minutes' talk he made by far the most practical observations of the evening."[1]

"On the water question," the *Gazette* said, Fowler "took up a proposition new and feasible." He proposed surveys by the federal government of the rivers and streams for the purpose of improving the irrigation of arid western lands and for the construction of reservoirs.[2]

Several days later, the *Phoenix Herald* printed an article signed by Fowler giving a fuller explanation of his proposal. Fowler wrote that "there are many places upon the Salt River, Verde River, Tonto Creek, and

Gila River that could be utilized to store the flood waters of winter for irrigation during the summer months." Fowler had firsthand knowledge about the possibility of building a reservoir on the Salt River. He was among the first white settlers in the Tonto Basin country, which lies about sixty-five miles northeast of Phoenix. The basin is about three thousand feet below the Mogollon Rim, the Mazatzal Mountains, and the Sierra Ancha, and in the late 1880s it was described as being a miniature Salt River Valley with its wealth of cultivated fields, vines, and orchards. The Tonto Basin also was excellent country for grazing cattle and sheep. Tonto Creek flows through the basin from the north, the Salt River from the east. The two water courses come together in the southwestern part of the basin, and a short distance from their confluence the Salt River enters a narrow gorge. It was in this gorge, or box canyon, that Roosevelt Dam was built, with work preliminary to its construction starting in 1903.[3]

The idea for federal assistance in developing the West through the construction of reservoirs dates at least to 1873. In that year, Congress approved a law creating a three-member commission to study ways to improve irrigation in three California valleys. That same year, the governors of nine western states and territories, including Arizona, met in Denver, Colorado, and organized the National Central Committee of Irrigation. The committee, which apparently had no future role in the irrigation movement, submitted a memorial to Congress asking it to aid development of the arid region between the ninety-ninth meridian and the Pacific Ocean. Some of the committee's reasons for federal aid were to be picked up virtually intact in later years by latter-day advocates of a national irrigation program. These included arguments that the needs of the West were "too extensive and costly for either individuals, private corporations, or territorial or state governments" and that the national government had established precedents for providing aid by donating land to various states to aid in canal and railroad construction. The committee's memorial asked Congress to grant the western states one half of all nonmineral arid lands, the sale of which would be used to build canals and reservoirs to reclaim the "arid waste lands." The memorial also asked that the government give the states and territories exclusive control of construction and maintenance of the canals and reservoirs, that the government authorize them to issue bonds to raise funds for construction, and that the laws for settlement of the public domain be made more strict.[4]

In the Salt River Valley, the water question, or problem, was that the Salt River did not supply enough water to irrigate all the land that could be cultivated. The problem did not take long to develop. American settlement of the Salt River Valley began in 1867, and by 1878 the claims to

Salt River water exceeded 6.6 million acre-feet per year, or five-and-a-half times the average yearly normal flow (as measured in later years). Obviously, it would have been impossible for all the claims to water to have been exercised. For the men who dug canals to bring water to the land, farming would have been much easier if the Salt River had provided an even flow the year around, but it did not. The river was erratic, usually reaching its highest level in late fall, winter, and early spring. In that period early farmers cultivated their hay, grain, and vegetables. It also was in that period that the river would flood and wash away the brush and rock dams built by the farmers to divert water into the canals. During the "hot, dry weather of summer, [the river was] sometimes reduced to a mere brook" or the water that remained sank into long, wide stretches of sand, reappearing at a few points where bedrock forced it to the surface. The water problem in this earliest period was not so much a question of supply as an attempt to unite the farmers north of the river so that they would take their water through a single permanent rock heading. A few efforts were made in this direction, but on the whole the farmers would not unite.[5]

In 1878, with the formation of the Grand Canal Company, came a dramatic change. The Grand Canal Company was the first organized specifically to construct a canal and sell water. The canal head was on the north side of the Salt River about one and a half miles northeast of Tempe. Organizers intended the canal to supply water to ten thousand acres of land north of Phoenix and north of the existing Salt River Valley and Maricopa canals. In "the opinion of well informed persons," not much water would remain in the river after the Grand Canal was supplied. Reacting to this threat to the water supply, "a mob tore out the dam of the Grand Canal just after its construction." The dam was rebuilt, and the Grand Canal today is one of two east-west canals still in use north of the Salt River.[6]

Suggestions for remedying the water problem north of the river, in addition to supplying all the canals with water through a single head, included building a concrete dam down to the bedrock to force the water to the surface, growing crops requiring less water, and drilling artesian wells.[7]

On August 30, 1879, stockholders of the Grand Canal Company appointed a committee "to confer with the directors and owners of all the canals in the valley" on the north side about the possibility of consolidating into a single head, but the proposal was met with a lawsuit by the Farmers' Canal Company, Griffin Ditch Company, and Monterey Ditch Company, each of which asserted a priority to the water ahead of the Grand Canal Company and a codefendant, the Mesa Canal Company. While the court agreed with the priority claim, it refused to issue an order stopping the defendants from taking water on grounds that what they took would not make any difference in the amount available to the plaintiffs.[8]

Apparently the first attempt at a legislative solution to the water question came in February 1881 when Assemblyman Peter J. Bolan introduced a bill to establish each canal's priority to water and the amount each could take from the Salt River. While the measure was reported to have support in Phoenix, Tempe Canal water users opposed it and it was overwhelmingly defeated.[9]

Construction of the Arizona Canal starting in 1883 exacerbated the water question. The head was on the north side of the Salt River about a mile below the mouth of the Verde. This put the head above any of the others on both sides of the Salt. The promoters intended to supply water to one hundred thousand acres of land, or twenty thousand acres more than the amount of irrigable land under the existing canals on both sides of the river. Despite reassurances by Arizona Canal representatives that there was enough water for all, the other canal men knew better, and on February 7, 1887, the Arizona Canal Company was sued by the owners of the Salt River Valley, Maricopa, San Francisco, Mesa, Tempe, Utah, and Grand canals. By the time the suit came to trial in March 1890, it had been amended five times and the plaintiffs were Michael Wormser, owner of the San Francisco Canal, and the owners of the Tempe Canal, among them Wormser. Defendants included the Salt River Valley, Maricopa, Grand, Mesa, Utah, Highland, and Arizona canals. The Arizona Canal was then under the control of the Arizona Improvement Company, which also had acquired a majority of the stock in the Salt River Valley, Maricopa, and Grand canal companies in order to remove them as plaintiffs from the suit. The Arizona Improvement Company created the Cross-Cut Canal and Power Company to supply the Salt River Valley, Maricopa, and Grand canals with water from the Arizona Canal, thereby creating a unified north-side system. The Mesa and Utah canal owners withdrew as plaintiffs because they worked out an agreement with the Arizona Improvement Company about how the water of the river should be divided. On July 26, 1890, they signed a contract providing that the Mesa and Utah canals receive one-third of the water and the north-side canals two-thirds after deducting the amounts to which the San Francisco and Tempe canals were entitled.[10]

From time to time in the late 1880s appeared suggestions that reservoirs be built, and in the summer of 1887 reports spread that large syndicates operating on both sides of the Salt River were planning to combine and build large reservoirs on the Salt and Verde rivers. However, nothing materialized, and in September 1888, William A. Hancock, attorney, canal projector, land promoter, and surveyor of the original Phoenix townsite, wrote that the real question confronted by the valley was finding "some means by which money can be secured by the best and most practical means" to build reservoirs. He suggested issuing bonds "secured by a lien upon the property of the county to be benefited by the outlay" and proposed placing the matter in the hands of a board of commissioners appointed for the purpose or giving the authority to the county board of supervisors. Hancock said the time to begin developing water storage was "at once . . . [because] if we delay too long, serious difficulty and possible loss to the farmers and horticultural interests of the valley may be encountered."[11]

Hancock correctly perceived the future, but foresight failed to induce the canal men to stop their squabbling or to induce capitalists to invest money in an enterprise so far away and so uncertain (to them) of success. The reservoir seemed too large a scheme requiring too large an investment. Those who understood the West and the need for irrigation to further its settlement knew that in the absence of private risk taking there was but a single force available to amass the vast sums of money necessary to build reservoirs and irrigation works: government. Thus the majority of farmers, businessmen, and speculators turned to the government to accomplish their purpose. On October 2, 1888, Congress appropriated $100,000 for the United States Geological Survey to survey the arid region of the West to determine to what extent the lands could be reclaimed by irrigation and to select sites for reservoirs for water storage and prevention of floods. All reservoir sites were withdrawn from public settlement.[12]

In February 1889 the U.S. Senate created the Select Committee on Irrigation and Reclamation of Arid lands, and in April the Phoenix Chamber of Commerce invited the committee to visit Phoenix. Sen. William M. Stewart of Nevada, committee chairman, replied that the committee expected to arrive in Arizona in September.[13]

The committee's agreement to visit renewed interest among valley canal men in developing a water storage plan, and it was suggested the county appropriate some money to conduct a survey to locate the best reservoir sites on the Salt and Verde rivers. The board of supervisors appropriated five hundred dollars, and on July 18, a party made up of Maricopa County Surveyor William Breckenridge; John R. Norton, foreman for the Arizona Improvement Company; newspaperman James H. McClintock; and a factotum, L. E. Lamb, departed. They returned August 10 and reported that the most suitable dam site was on the Salt River about four hundred yards below its confluence with Tonto Creek. The river at that point was about two hundred feet wide, and the canyon walls were nearly vertical for about one hundred feet before sloping back about a foot for each foot of rise. The canyon walls were about eight hundred feet high, and a two-hundred-foot-high dam would create a Gothic V-shaped lake, backing water up the Salt River for sixteen miles and up Tonto Creek for ten miles. Said McClintock: "Surely the general government can find at no other place a more eligible site for water storage than this presents."[14]

In 1890, Dexter M. Ferry and C. C. Bowen of D. M. Ferry and Company, a Detroit seed firm, visited the valley at the invitation of Dr. Alexander J. Chandler, the territorial veterinarian. Chandler had done work for the seed company before coming to Arizona in 1887, and he wanted Ferry and Bowen to invest in a scheme for consolidating the canals south of the Salt River and for acquiring land. One of the ideas they considered, and rejected, involved construction of a masonry dam on the Salt River just below its confluence with the Verde northeast of Mesa. However, they began uniting the south-side canals in January 1891 by taking over the management, but not the ownership, of the Mesa Canal, and in March 1892 they incorporated the Consolidated Canal Company.[15]

Controversies over the report of the Senate Select Committee on Irrigation were partly responsible for the calling of the first National Irrigation Congress. It met in Salt Lake City, Utah, September 15–17, 1891, to seek federal help in the construction of irrigation works. The congress adopted a resolution urging the government to cede arid lands to the states and territories so that they could be sold, with the proceeds being used for reclamation projects.[16]

Articles of incorporation for the Rio Verde Canal Company were filed in Phoenix on December 18, 1891. This company filed dam locations on New River and the Verde River, including the Horseshoe site on the Verde. The company bored a 700-foot tunnel through a mountain at the Horseshoe site, sold water rights, and excavated about twenty miles of canals in Paradise Valley, northeast of Phoenix, but it never delivered a drop of water.[17]

In May 1892 the Herald reported that "construction of the dam on the Salt River in the box canyon will probably begin within a year," but the only thing to happen inside that time was the creation of the Hudson Reservoir and Canal Company. Its plans included a 225-foot-high dam in the box canyon on Salt River below Tonto Creek, and the Arizona Republican said:

This is the active beginning of that irrigation scheme which has been the dream of capitalists for years, making a lake of Tonto basin. The profits from its accomplishment have always been apparent, but the stupendous prospective cost until now has stood in the way of the fulfillment of the dream.[18]

Despite the newspaper's hopeful words, "the active beginning" was painfully slow, and in June 1893, shareholders in the Mesa Canal called for a meeting of directors of all canal companies to consider ways to increase the water supply. A number of meetings were held, and again agreement was quickly reached that the only feasible way of boosting the water supply was through construction of a reservoir. The participants could not agree, however, about how to raise funds. In February 1895 the *Herald* said: "It is doubtful whether the old idea of great reservoirs on the rivers will ever materialize."[19]

In 1895, Congress appropriated $3,500 to investigate ways to secure water for the Gila River Indian Reservation, which lies south of the Salt River Valley. As part of the study, hydrographer Arthur Powell Davis of the Geological Survey looked into the possibility of buying water "from companies contemplating storage on Salt River," specifically the Hudson company. Davis examined the Tonto Basin dam site and found it "probable that a safe reservoir could be built capable of impounding an . . . astonishing" eight hundred thousand acre-feet of water. However, he said, the water could not be conveyed by a gravity canal to the eastern end of the reservation, where much of the farming had been done in the past. Although water could be delivered to the central part of the reservation, Davis said, he had been unable to obtain a price for the water from the Hudson company. In any case, he thought it "undesirable to enter into contracts with private companies," a position supported by his supervisor, Frederick H. Newell. In sending Davis's report to the director of the Geological Survey, Newell noted that a number of Salt River water-storage projects had been proposed, but none had been completed "and their achievement depends, to a certain extent, upon the share that the Government may take in the construction" by granting a large body of land. Newell added that Davis had shown

it would be preferable as a business proposition for the Government to do all the work and dispose of the benefitted land, keeping the increased value to repay the cost of the project. The Government, not having exclusive control of the reservoir, would not be sure of the successful completion or of proper maintenance.[20]

In December 1896, Newell attended the fifth National Irrigation Congress, which was held in Phoenix, and there he met attorney George H. Maxwell of California. Newell later said "the campaign for federal reclamation" could be said to date from that congress, for it adopted two resolutions introduced by Maxwell, the first calling for "construction of storage reservoirs by the federal government" and the second all but repudiating the idea of ceding land to the states and territories for that purpose.[21]

Davis revisited Tonto Basin in 1897 and wrote of the site, "It would probably be impossible to find anywhere in the arid region a storage project in which all conditions are as favorable as for this one." The reservoir had enormous capacity, and the "lands to be watered are of remarkable fertility, in a climate which may be classed as almost semi-tropic, and are vastly greater in area than the water can supply." He concluded, "There can be no doubt, . . . that in this reservoir site lies one of the most important possibilities for the future of the agriculture of southern Arizona."[22]

A "lively demand" for water mentioned by Davis became more acute as 1897 passed into 1898 because Arizona and the valley were entering a period of severe drought. In April 1898 a Phoenix piano salesman, Augustus Redewill, said the solution was for Maricopa County to sell two million dollars' worth of bonds and to dam the Salt River.[23]

In the election campaign of 1898, Phoenix merchant Aaron Goldberg promised that if he were elected to the Territorial Council he would call water users and others together to develop a feasible plan to secure water storage. He was elected, and thus began a series of meetings beginning on December 12. During this period Goldberg received a letter from Dwight B. Heard in which Heard outlined the attitude of landowners with early water rights. Heard, who had not arrived in Phoenix until 1895, said owners of ground that was irrigated only when the river flooded "should expect to pay more for storage water than those located under the old canals" because the stored water would give productive value to their land. Similarly, he said, "land under newer canals should bear the principal costs of water storage" since they would "reap the greatest benefit." Heard said the water rights for land under new canals were of indefinite value but "would become decidedly valuable" with water storage. Heard favored construction of the storage works and their operation by the federal government, but he thought it unlikely to happen for many years. The idea that the people should "bond their lands and construct a reservoir themselves would be found impracticable," he said, which meant they must look toward private capital. Goldberg's initiative resulted in the introduction and approval by the legislature of a bill exempting reservoirs and canals constructed for water storage from taxation for a period of fifteen years, but another measure to create an irrigation commission to work on behalf of water storage failed.[24]

The National Irrigation Congress met at Missoula, Montana, September 25–27, 1899, and voted more than ten to one against ceding land to the states and territories for irrigation works. The vote followed a speech opposing cession by former Arizona Gov. Myron H. McCord.[25]

In December 1899, John F. Wilson, Arizona's delegate to Congress, introduced a bill to appropriate $1,040,000 for construction of San Carlos

Dam on the Gila River; construction of the dam was supported by the Geological Survey. Salt River Valley farmers and businessmen adopted a resolution in support of the dam after hearing a speech by Maxwell that the best way to secure reservoirs was to endorse the San Carlos scheme. Maxwell was then chairman of the executive committee of the National Irrigation Association, which had been created the previous September to lobby for federal aid for irrigation throughout the year rather than only at the time of the yearly National Irrigation Congress. The Salt River farmers and ranchers also endorsed resolutions supporting federal construction of water-storage dams and opposing cession.[26]

On the evening of April 17, 1900, the Phoenix and Maricopa County Board of Trade, successor to the Phoenix Chamber of Commerce, appointed a five-member committee on water storage to research the question of selling bonds in the name of the county to build reservoirs. Among the committee members were S. M. McCowan, superintendent of the Phoenix Indian School, and Benjamin A. Fowler, who had spent twenty-seven years in the book publishing business before arriving in the valley in 1899. The committee met with Sims Ely, secretary of the Hudson Reservoir and Canal Company. Ely told the committee it would take at least a year for Congress to approve a bill which would permit the county board of supervisors to call an election asking property owners to approve the sale of bonds. Ely said that if by the end of that time the Hudson company was unable to get financing, the company would find some agreement fair to itself and the people so they could build the reservoir. Meantime, he said, the company was pursuing private investment and construction. Steps in that direction included passage of a law exempting the reservoir from taxation, completion of important engineering work, and the signing of contracts with the canal companies to assure the reservoir company of a profit of three hundred thousand dollars per year.

McCowan reported to the board of trade on May 1, 1900. The committee listed four possible ways to raise money for reservoirs: federal appropriations, federal cession of lands to states and territories, private enterprise, and voting bonds to be sold by Maricopa County. The committee believed that direct government aid was "not worth considering." Similarly, the committee believed that if it waited for government initiative in the ceding of land, "we may, perhaps, in the course of a generation or two, look down from above on the beginning of the undertaking." Committee members pointed out that if the Hudson company built the reservoir, it would be the people, not the canal companies, who paid the $300,000 yearly guarantee made in the contracts between Hudson and the companies. This left the fourth option, bonding the county, which, the committee said, "has many points in its favor over any of the others." Principally, ownership and control of the reservoir would be in the hands of the people. The committee said ownership by the public should include the canal companies, but the lowest estimate of their cost was $4 million. Added to an estimated $2.5 million for building the Tonto Basin dam, the committee doubted that six-and-a-half million dollars' worth of bonds could be sold in a county with an assessed valuation of only $10 million. The committee believed that the Hudson company's reservoir site could be bought and the dam built for between $2 million and $3 million. It recommended preparation of a bill for introduction in Congress and a program "to educate and enlighten the people on the importance, extent and designs of the irrigation movement by the distribution of literature, mass meetings, etc."[27]

In July 1900, editor Charles C. Randolph of the *Arizona Republican* returned to Phoenix from an eastern trip during which he met with some capitalists and talked with them about raising money to build the Tonto dam. Randolph said he was told the drawback to the Hudson company's reservoir was the immense sum of money required, but if the people of Maricopa County showed their faith in the project by issuing five hundred thousand dollars' worth of bonds, that might help raise the funds. On July 19 the *Republican* printed an editorial proposing that the county issue five hundred thousand dollars' worth of bonds contingent upon the Hudson company's raising $2 million to $2.5 million. The newspaper invited comments from its readers.[28]

The *Arizona Gazette* reacted by calling the proposal a plan for grafters to divide half a million dollars, but the *Republican* editorial provoked an outpouring of citizen comments and ideas, leading the *Gazette* to suggest on August 15 that the board of trade call a meeting of citizens to take up the water-storage question. A week later, the board of trade water storage committee and seventy others issued a call for a meeting at 10:00 A.M. August 31 at the Dorris Theater.[29]

The meeting was attended by about six hundred people and led to the creation of the Salt River Valley Water Storage Committee, which was divided into subcommittees to study such matters as importing water from the Colorado River, locating reservoir sites, estimating the quantity of water available for storage, financing, and silting. Benjamin Fowler was elected permanent chairman of the committee, which included representatives from eleven canals, from the cities of Phoenix, Tempe, Mesa and Glendale, and from the board of trade's water storage committee.[30]

In the months that followed, besides presiding over the new committee, Fowler was elected to the Territorial Assembly and represented the committee at the ninth National Irrigation Congress in Chicago. On behalf of the committee, Fowler offered to supply the U.S. Geological Survey with fifteen hundred dollars to aid in the investigation of reservoir sites.[31]

At a meeting on December 11, the Salt River Valley Water Storage Committee outlined a course of action which included drafting a bill for introduction in Congress to allow Maricopa County to sell bonds to build the Tonto Basin dam. Backers planned to send the bill, when completed, to Washington, D.C., where they had sent Fowler to help prepare the way for it.[32]

Davis, meantime, arrived in the valley to study potential reservoir sites on the Verde River. After he informed the water storage committee that his work was limited to the Verde, the committee voted to ask the Geological Survey to extend Davis's work to the Salt River and to raise funds for that purpose.[33]

A two-million-dollar county bonding bill was put in final form January 1, 1901. It included a provision that the U.S. government guarantee the interest on the bonds. Word soon came from Washington that the proposed bill was too complicated, because it would have to be referred to too many departments of government and that in any case it would never be approved with the provision calling for the government guarantee on the bond interest. Arizona's delegate to Congress, Wilson, refused to introduce the bill. He said it should be a simple enabling act. Gov. Nathan O. Murphy seconded Wilson's view and suggested that a pared-down bonding bill be approved by the Territorial Legislature and submitted to Congress for ratification. The water storage committee appointed a committee to draft such legislation.[34]

At Fowler's urging the committee invited Maxwell to Phoenix to advise it while the legislature was in session. The committee also discussed raising fifteen hundred dollars for the Geological Survey. Members thought the county supervisors should contribute the money, but the supervisors insisted they lacked authority to do that. The committee decided to prepare legislation which would permit the use of county money for the Geological Survey's work.[35]

At a meeting February 24, 1901, the water storage committee decided a bill for bonding the county should be drafted for introduction in the legislature. Fowler introduced it on March 11, the same day Maxwell arrived in Phoenix. A few days later, Fowler introduced a substitute for the bonding bill. The substitute provided for the appointment of a five-member board of water storage commissioners by the judge of the U.S. District Court upon the request of the supervisors, who were to seek the creation of the board if petitioned by fifty registered voters. The bill empowered the commissioners to take all steps necessary for construction of reservoirs, including a one-time tax levy of three mills per dollar on all taxable property, which would raise about fifteen thousand dollars.[36]

Maxwell undoubtedly influenced the decision to substitute the commissioners' bill for the bonding bill because he did not believe Congress would pass enabling legislation that would put the burden of taxation for irrigation bonds on the entire county. He told Fowler, legislators, and others at a March 19 meeting that government aid "will come with a rush" as soon as the country's business interests demanded it. Maxwell's plan consisted primarily of getting all businessman in the West to ask their wholesale contacts in the East to write their congressmen in favor of a national irrigation plan. If this were done, Maxwell said, the influence on the congressmen would become irresistible. For the plan to be effective, he said, the movement needed local organizations, and such a group was formed in Phoenix with Fowler selected as one of the men to direct the work.[37]

On March 20 the legislature passed Fowler's bill to create a board of water storage commissioners, amending it to permit the commissioners to levy the property tax for two years instead of one. Murphy signed the bill into law the day it was passed. However, no effort was made to implement it until Davis met with the water storage committee in mid-April and said it would be impossible to do any work at the Tonto Basin unless local funds were contributed. Fowler and others immediately asked the county board of supervisors to ask the U.S. district judge to appoint the commissioners, so on April 18, Judge Webster Street named the five commissioners. One of them was Heard. Immediately after the board organized on April 30, it appropriated five thousand dollars for Davis's work in the Tonto Basin.[38]

Davis submitted a report to the commissioners in July, but for business reasons they refused to disclose his findings. Based on maps prepared by Davis, the commissioners filed an application with the federal land office for a dam site on the Salt River a quarter of a mile downstream from the Hudson Reservoir location. The commissioners attempted to develop with the canal companies a scale of prices for water deliveries, because the old companies objected to paying as much as new companies. In addition, the commissioners worked on a new county bonding bill to be submitted to Congress.[39]

President William McKinley, shot September 6, 1901, in Buffalo, New York, died September 14. His successor, Theodore Roosevelt, delivered his first message to Congress on December 3 and strongly endorsed the national irrigation movement in words that easily could have come from the pen of Maxwell. While the emphasis of Roosevelt's message was on reclamation of arid public lands for settlement, he appeared not to rule out federal aid for lands in private ownership, such as those in the Salt River Valley, by saying that "whatever the nation does for the extension of irrigation should harmonize with, and tend to improve, the condition of those now living on irrigated land."[40]

Phoenix newspapers lauded Roosevelt's words, but they questioned whether a national irrigation program would be of any value to the valley. The *Republican* noted that a bill introduced in the House by Rep. Francis C. Newlands of Nevada would have permitted bringing water to lands already reclaimed, but this provision had been stricken. The newspaper worried that the federal government would confiscate dam sites on the Salt and Verde rivers, construct reservoirs, store all the water the existing ditches could not carry, and then deliver it to new lands. The *Gazette* and the *Phoenix Enterprise* echoed the *Republican*'s concern. The *Republican* continually supported construction of the Tonto Basin reservoir by private capital, but others preferred the issuance of county bonds so the public would own the reservoir.[41]

Fowler left for Washington the morning of January 15, 1902, to represent the board of trade in testifying on behalf of statehood for Arizona and for national irrigation. However, he said that if national irrigation meant opening up thousands of new acres in the Salt River Valley, the county would be better off issuing two million dollars' worth of bonds and building the reservoir itself. Fowler also believed that the Roosevelt administration could be persuaded to abandon an appropriation for the San Carlos reservoir in favor of a dam on the Salt River.[42]

In February the water storage commissioners issued a report on their work. They said that if a dam were built to rise two hundred feet above the riverbed, it would store 981,125 acre-feet of water. The estimated cost of such a dam was $2.5 million, but the cost could be reduced about $700,000 by the manufacture of cement at the site and by the construction of a power plant using falling water to develop electricity. The commissioners said they expected to receive plans, specifications, and estimates in the near future.[43]

They also completed work on a bonding bill, the Maricopa County Enabling Act, and on a second measure prepared by Heard, who, by then, was the National Irrigation Association's representative in Phoenix. The bonding bill, which was sent to attorney John F. Dillon of New York for approval, asked Congress to allow the county to bond itself up to a maximum of $2,250,000 for reservoir work, including "developing and delivering water power." The bill would permit the board of supervisors to appoint a five-member board of water commissioners who would have authority to levy a tax on property within the reservoir district to raise funds to pay principal and interest if revenues from water storage and power works were insufficient. Dillon, according to some, represented "the most eminent authority in the country" on bonding matters, and he was instructed to send the bill to Marcus A. Smith, Arizona's delegate to Congress, once any necessary changes were made. The bill prepared by Heard directed Congress to appropriate $1 million for building the

Salt River dam, provided that the taxpayers of Maricopa County first approved the issuance of bonds.[44]

Fowler wrote from Washington that he expected a reclamation bill to be passed "under the inspiration of the president's powerful personality," and on March 1, 1902, the Senate approved a national irrigation bill introduced by Sen. Henry Hansbrough of North Dakota. The bill was identical to the one introduced in the House by Newlands, which a few days later was reported favorably to the House by a majority of the House Irrigation Committee.[45]

Meantime, the proposed bonding bill came under attack from the water storage committee, which wanted it changed so that the water commissioners would be elected instead of appointed by the board of supervisors and so that the bonds would have to be approved by a two-thirds vote rather than a simple majority of taxpayers. Dillon also proposed some changes, including one to allow 20 percent of the bondholders to begin foreclosure proceedings if interest on the bonds was not paid for six months. This led to such a storm of protest that the water storage commissioners wired Smith in Washington, instructing him not to introduce the enabling act until further notice. After meeting with businessmen and water users from both sides of the river, the commissioners made the default period one year. They also agreed to a two-thirds vote for passage of the bonds, to the election of three commissioners from north of the river and two from south, and to the publication before the bond election of the terms of contracts with at least eight of the twelve canal companies named in the bill. The commissioners sent Heard to Washington to represent them in trying to lobby the measure through Congress.[46]

Davis arrived in Phoenix on April 17, 1902, and reported that a dam built 217 feet above bedrock would cost $1.9 million, and the same day the enabling act was introduced in the House of Representatives. Thereafter, little news arrived about either the Hansbrough-Newlands bill or the enabling act until mid-May. The *Republican* printed a dispatch saying that Roosevelt "was showing lively interest in [the reclamation bill's] status," and the *Prescott Journal-Miner* called attention to a clause in the enabling act that it said threatened the water rights of Verde River farmers in Yavapai County.[47]

At a meeting of businessmen in the Adams Hotel in Phoenix the night of May 27, the group voted to ask the water storage commissioners to amend the enabling act to allow the people to vote on the county's issuing one million dollars' worth of bonds to help a private corporation construct the reservoir should they fail to approve the county's selling two million two hundred fifty thousand dollars' worth of bonds to build it. On May 28 the commissioners agreed to this amendment and two others, the first removing the clause found objectionable by Yavapai County and the second eliminating the requirement that contracts had to be made with at least two-thirds of the canal companies before an election could be held. The commissioners also sent Frank P. Trott to Washington to help lobby the bill.[48]

In Washington, Heard and another south-side water user, Ethelburt W. Wilbur, opposed changing the clause requiring contracts with two-thirds of the canals. Finally, apparently after being pressured by Fowler and Trott, Heard and Wilbur agreed to changing the canal contract clause to six canals, but they would not agree to the other changes recommended in the May 28 resolution of the water storage commissioners. Fowler, Trott, Heard, and Wilbur sent a telegram June 10 saying that nothing but united action could save the enabling act: "We have agreed to change the canal contract clause to six, making no other changes. Let all friends of the valley unite on that basis."[49]

The water storage commissioners met June 12 and wired the four, insisting that the May 28 resolution be followed, but south-side water users expressed opposition to the amendments and support for Heard and Wilbur in objecting to the changes.[50]

The next day, the House passed the Hansbrough-Newlands bill, and on the same day Governor Murphy sent a message saying the enabling act had no chance of passage with or without the amendments. President Roosevelt signed the irrigation law June 17, 1902.[51]

The *Republican* expected Arizona to be the first beneficiary of the national irrigation law because "it is known that the president and the secretary of the interior are very anxious to have the San Carlos reservoir constructed." As to the enabling act, the newspaper said, "if anything has been gained by the agitation which has been going on at Washington, it has been the getting of the bill before the congress and the giving of the people of the valley five months (when Congress would reconvene) in which to get together upon some plan."[52]

But the enabling act was a dead issue because, with Roosevelt's help, Maxwell and Fowler had succeeded in getting into the Hansbrough-Newlands bill a clause which allowed the secretary of the interior to aid lands in private ownership, such as those in the Salt River Valley, with irrigation works. Thus the old arguments, antipathies, and antagonisms among the water users moved into a new arena where, although not all were resolved, most were muted sufficiently to permit formation of the Salt River Valley Water Users Association and construction of Roosevelt Dam by the federal government.

# CHAPTER TEN

# Community Growth and Water Policy

## BY KAREN L. SMITH

EACH day in Phoenix, thousands of residents turn their faucets on, using the 220 million gallons of water the city distributes daily. This in itself seems a remarkable feat for a city born in the middle of an arid region, but because of government reclamation efforts, such as the Salt River Project, or SRP, many Phoenicians take this simple act of turning water on and off for granted; in fact, the average amount of water consumed in Phoenix per capita exceeds the national average.[1]

In the 1970s, Salt River Valley residents worried more about the threat of water in the Salt River blocking transportation routes than the fear of an inadequate water supply stored behind the dams of the SRP. The amount of water available to Phoenicians was not considered a serious problem by city government at the time, despite the desert environment. That has not always been the case.

Between 1940 and 1950, the population of Phoenix (reflecting the activity of war industries in the valley and the return of many servicemen in the postwar period) grew nearly two-thirds, from about 65,000 to nearly 107,000. Water demands brought on by wartime and postwar growth strained the resources of the municipal water system. These demands combined with a serious drought throughout the 1940s caused Phoenix's water supply to be in trouble by 1950.

In contrast to the lack of concern with supply, water quality has always been uppermost in the minds of city policymakers. At one time TCE, DDT, PCBs and other harmful elements in municipal water supplies were a serious health risk; concern for safe drinking water was the primary concern. Town boosters realized as early as the turn of the century that growth would be limited unless Phoenix secured a better-tasting water than the bitter, salt-filled water available from the town's wells. Phoenix water-planning efforts were directed toward finding sources of fresh water to supplement groundwater until World War II, when dynamic growth, drought, and questionable water rights seriously threatened the city's fresh-water supply.

On July 4, 1951, residents of Phoenix awoke to read banner headlines in the *Arizona Republic* declaring a water emergency: the city had only a ten-day supply of fresh water from the Verde River. The crisis of 1951 brought together in a most dramatic way the concerns of adequate water resources and water quality. The crisis also raised, for the first time in Phoenix, the problem of urbanization in an agricultural region. Many Phoenicians wondered how the water crisis had developed, for it seemed that it was an overnight phenomenon. New residents of the city, not knowing of the special reclamation laws governing the SRP, were upset that the city had relatively little control over the valley's water resources. All worried that this might represent the bust to the city's boom cycle. Although the Phoenix press and city government were slow to recognize it, the growing water-resource problems faced by Phoenix had been long in the making.[2]

At the turn of the century, Phoenix had a very meager water system, consisting of little more than a few shallow wells. Some wells furnished a "fairly drinkable water" and others a salt-filled water "hardly fit to use." The remedy at the time consisted of drilling for artesian water, a softer, cooler, and sweeter percolating water. Town leaders were so serious in their belief that artesian wells would provide the answer to the city's water-quality problem that they reminded valley residents of a little publicized law authorizing county boards of supervisors to offer a reward of three thousand dollars for anyone discovering a flowing stream. There were conditions on the reward, of course, but support for finding a pure water supply was clear.[3]

The Reclamation Act of 1902 seemed to solve the valley's agricultural problems because authorization of the SRP ensured a steady supply of developed water for irrigation; farmers at least would no longer be dependent on the capricious nature of the Salt River. While the Reclamation Act did not initially consider the plight of municipalities in the arid region that were dependent upon only a few available water resources for their growing water systems, legislation passed in 1906 provided that government-developed water could be delivered to townsites within the vicinity of irrigation projects. Clarification of this law in 1913 provided that reclamation water could be contracted to city authorities for a municipal water system but not to individuals within the townsite. Municipalities needed to sign a townsite agreement to become eligible; Phoenix signed up about five thousand five hundred acres. This water would be used primarily for public service, such as fighting fires and cleaning streets, not for drinking.[4]

Domestic water was supplied by the privately owned Phoenix Water Company, which held a city franchise. Installation of new water mains underneath Washington Street in 1898 overextended the company's resources, and the city's continued growth to areas outside the city's limits necessitated even more expansion and modernization of facilities. Because Phoenix Water Company was heavily in debt, it appeared that nothing would be done to upgrade the water plant; growth would be stalled, and the city would be the loser unless action was taken. "Once city dwellers had noticed only the presence or absence of a basic service," historian Robert Wiebe wrote of municipal reform at the turn of the century, "they took its existence for granted and scrutinized the details, grumbling over inconveniences and omissions and shoddy work." Municipal ownership provided one answer to the inadequate results of "franchise privileges granted out of a confused need for something at once."[5]

In Phoenix, discussions about building a city-owned water-works surfaced as early as 1903, but the final decision to purchase Phoenix Water Company instead came in 1907. Bonding itself for $300,000, the city paid $150,000 for the waterworks and spent the remaining money on improvements. This proved to be a wise and profitable decision; by 1912 the plant debt had been repaid and more than $135,000 from the earnings of the city-owned service had been channeled back into the facility. Municipal ownership suited the water system because improvements included more than seventy-five miles of pipe and a pump in what is now Verde Park. Phoenix residents were satisfied because, despite the many improvements made to the water system, Phoenix boasted the lowest rate for city water service in Arizona.[6]

While the municipal water system adequately served the city, its water resources consisted almost entirely of pumped water. Even though the city's six to eight wells were said to be capable of supplying a population of fifty thousand, about five times the population of Phoenix in 1912, the problem of salty, bitter-tasting water had yet to be solved. At the same time the city council was deliberating the installation of a municipal water system, it hired Alexander Potter, a New York consulting engineer, to investigate sources of a pure water supply for Phoenix. His final report stated that the Verde River provided the most attractive source and was conveyable to Phoenix by gravity. Not only would the soft water benefit city residents, but Potter insisted that its value would be even higher if Phoenix became a manufacturing center.[7]

The council took no action on Potter's 1906 recommendations, and in 1913 a new city government organized under the commission–city manager system authorized another engineering study. Like Potter, consulting engineers Howard S. Reed, formerly of the U.S. Reclamation Service, and Hiram S. Phillips of Saint Louis condemned the city's groundwater supply as too impure for domestic and manufacturing needs. Both engineers recommended a gravity pipeline which could deliver water under fire or domestic pressure without pumping from the Verde River to the city. V. A. Thompson, superintendent of the city waterworks, asked the city commission for permission to survey a gravity line. The quality of the water was good, the Verde was the only source promising a sufficient supply, and the engineering was simple; Thompson believed the only problem lay in the threat of litigation with the government over water rights.[8]

Despite the Phillips-Reed report and Thompson's strong recommendations, city commissioners delayed action on the Verde project; perhaps the fear of extended litigation dissuaded them. Three years later, however, in 1916, the commission hired another consulting engineer, William L. Church of New York, to investigate further the Verde water source; his findings echoed earlier reports. Rather than assure the commission that it could win any lawsuit, as Thompson had done in 1913, Church recommended that city officials file for additional water rights on the Verde. A notice of appropriation of eleven hundred miner's inches supposedly was made in 1916 with the express provision that the filing was not intended as a waiver of any prior rights the city might have in the river. Although the federal government and the Salt River Valley Water Users Association had claimed all the unappropriated and surplus waters of the Verde River as early as 1906, neither group challenged this appropriation by the city of Phoenix. Perhaps because in that year Roosevelt Dam filled and spilled, water supply seemed more than adequate for everyone in the valley. Still, no reaction from the primary water-resource organization in the valley over their filing must have encouraged the city to pursue its major construction plans for a Verde River water supply.[9]

The number of Phoenicians more than doubled by 1919 (twenty-nine thousand in 1920), and the city's water supply became an acute problem. Earlier estimates of a water supply for fifty thousand had been exaggerated. Thompson, who had been the superintendent of the waterworks and then city manager, directed the waterworks to determine the exact cost for constructing the Verde project, which had been estimated at $1.3 million. Probably because of the immediate need for additional water, the city commission unanimously supported Thompson in his quest to build a twenty-nine-mile-long gravity pipeline from the Verde River to the city's water mains at Twelfth Street and McDowell Road. Voters passed the bond proposal by a wide margin, but because of unsettled national labor conditions throughout this period, local contractors had a difficult time working on the pipeline, so the city finally built most of the project itself under force account. Included within the city's construction plans was a fluctuation reservoir to be built on Thomas Road. The reservoir was not planned for storage but was built to provide sufficient water to cover the city's peak load requirements on the days of heaviest consumption, estimated at five million gallons. The Verde project of the city of Phoenix, completed in 1922, provided fifteen million gallons of pure river water each day to the municipal water system at a cost of $1.5 million.[10]

The Verde project proved less than a panacea for the city's water problems, however, because within the next nine years the pipeline had to be rebuilt to carry thirty million gallons per day. Other piecemeal extensions of the water system throughout the 1920s and early 1930s included ten- and twenty-million-gallon reservoirs, nine new wells sunk along the Verde River, and a new supply line from the well field to the distribution system.[11]

However, instead of long-term water planning, city officials tended to respond to emergency situations. As a result, Phoenix was little prepared for growth, and this became increasingly apparent by 1940. The outbreak of war in Europe encouraged war preparations at home, including the construction of air bases and war factories. Because of its location, Phoenix was selected for two government airfields, and industries like AiResearch and Goodyear Aircraft set up shop in the Salt River Valley. Coupled with these industrial and wartime developments, the city's population expanded from 48,118 in 1930 to more than 100,000 by 1950. This growth, much of it in new areas recently annexed by Phoenix, threw a tremendous load on the somewhat antiquated water supply and distribution system. Since many servicemen were returning to Phoenix after the war to make it their permanent home, population growth would continue unabated. Yet because of the war and a reluctance to plan, city planners considered a large expansion of the water system unnecessary until 1946.

Wartime growth posed several problems for the water system. Phoenicians used one million gallons more of water per day in 1946, during peak consumption periods, than the combined thirty-five-million-gallon capacity of the city's reservoirs. At the same time, water pressure within the city declined rapidly, presenting firefighters, in particular, with serious delays in acquiring water through the hydrant system. New housing for war veterans was suspended in South Phoenix when water for more than twenty families was simply not available from the one well operating in that vicinity. Combined with this deficiency in supply, the salty, bitter-tasting well water had to mix with the city's Verde River supply during the peak summer months. Again the cry of town boosters for fresh water sources to attract new industry could be heard throughout Phoenix. Phoenix needed, city officials thought, an enlarged pipeline from the

Verde to the city, additional reservoirs to maintain pressure and store water for daily needs, an additional grid system of pipe to maintain constant pressure, and a water-treatment plant at the Verde.[12]

Phoenix had to increase its water-supply capacity from thirty million gallons per day to fifty million gallons, and a Kansas City consulting firm of engineers, Burns and McDonnel, presented a program to accomplish this. The firm said Phoenix should develop the Queena Harry well field near the Verde River by drilling eighteen new wells, construct a thirty-million-gallon underground reservoir and pumping station in University Park, and expand the distribution mains. This development project covered four phases, to be carried out over a twenty-year period at an estimated cost of about ten million dollars.[13]

Mayor Ray Busey appointed a citizens committee of five members to examine the water problem and, in effect, evaluate the Burns and McDonnel engineering proposal. The committee, made up of three engineers and two bankers, rejected the consultant's report, chiefly on grounds of expense. Instead of the new well field and a pipeline with a minimum pressure of sixty pounds, the mayor's committee advised the city to build a filtration plant below the proposed site of the McDonnel dam (predicated on construction of the Central Arizona Project) and a parallel water main from Papago Reservoir to the downtown area, increasing the water supply for fire protection and industrial needs there. This scaled-down project would cost the residents of Phoenix about $5.5 million.[14]

The committee thought Phoenix should plan its entire waterworks expansion program with the idea of developing the Verde River as the principal source of supply. Only the Verde, the *Gazette* reported in 1946, had satisfying quality and only the Verde had good water in sufficient quality and sufficient quantity to meet Phoenix's needs. The Verde, in tandem with the Central Arizona Project, would solve the water problem. Phoenix put its largest expansion program ever on a source of supply in which it had limited and questionable rights and on a reclamation project which was not to be approved for more than twenty years. City officials, blind to patterns of growth that were becoming more visible every day, also narrowed their distribution focus to the downtown area. Repeating its previous mistakes of opting for short-term solutions, Phoenix ignored the opportunity to develop a new source of supply in the Queena Harry well field.[15]

Meanwhile, the city water department's ingenuity in meeting the daily demand thrust upon its already strained system was severely tested. In June 1946, Phoenix entered into a six-month contract with Roosevelt Irrigation District to construct a sump at Roosevelt's Twenty-third Avenue and Van Buren Street well. Contingent upon the approval of the Salt

River Valley Water Users Association, which had contracted the well to Roosevelt Irrigation District in the 1920s, the city used the well only when there was an emergency in its water supply. This contract was renegotiated in 1947 for the same purpose. When the association proposed in August 1946 that the city spend eight hundred thousand dollars to build new spillway gates on Horseshoe Dam to impound an additional twenty-five thousand acre-feet of Verde River water for municipal supply, Mayor Busey expressed little interest. He told the association that just because the city was contemplating a new development program did not mean that its consumption of water was going to skyrocket immediately. Consumption did skyrocket, as all indicators had shown it would, and three months later the city of Phoenix and the Salt River Valley Water Users Association signed a contract for construction of the spillway gates.[16]

The dramatic increase in Phoenix water consumption during the 1940s came on the heels of a severe drought that began roughly around 1942. The project's watershed had less than normal rainfall, so that by 1951, with the drought nine years old, water in the storage reservoirs fell to perilously low levels. Throughout the history of Phoenix's water-development programs, the Water Users Association had been more than lenient in allowing the city to divert water from the Verde River. In fact, based on legal filings on the river, the association may have been negligent in allowing the city to proceed as it did. Because the SRP had focused so much on developing its power resources thoroughout the 1920s and on providing storage facilities on the Verde during the 1930s, it had ignored the relatively small amount of water Phoenix diverted. Of some importance, too, was the fact that many of the Water Users Association leaders were also leaders in the informal Phoenix power network. Prolonged drought, the threat in the courts through the *Bristor-Cheatham* case of a change in the use of groundwater, and new management at the SRP suggested that the association might require a different response to the city's illegal diversions.

The city continued to divert more water from the Verde, much more than its entitlement. A 1946 contract with the SRP allowed it about twenty thousand acre-feet in addition to what could be stored behind the Horseshoe spillway gates, but by 1950 some estimates showed the city diverting more than twice that amount. This time the city had taken too much. Bill Pickrell, president of the Water Users Association, told City Manager Ray Wilson that "the existing condition of the Verde River as it pertains to the water supply of the city has become critical." On July 3, 1951, a time of peak water consumption, the SRP told the city it had only a ten-day supply of water in the Verde River.[17]

At the heart of the Phoenix water problem was reclamation law. Much of the land within the city limits held water rights for irrigation purposes, but the organization charged with the responsibility for delivering the water was the Salt River Valley Water Users Association, not the city. As more and more of the valley's farmland was subdivided for residences, fewer and fewer people took their allotted water. But instead of the water reverting to the city system, it went to the farmlands of the SRP.

Although the city, through a vigorous annexation policy, increased in area every year, its water supply from the Verde remained legally fixed. The rapid growth of Phoenix into previously agricultural areas caused problems for the SRP, too. New residents did not understand that land within the boundaries of the project, which included most of the valley, was offered as a lien to the federal government for repayment of the large reclamation debt. Therefore the SRP charged annual assessments to every landowner, whether they held 160 acres or one-fifth of an acre, whether they took irrigation water or not. This posed quite a bookkeeping problem in the days before high-speed computers and data processing. In addition to the paperwork, urbanization resulted in more and more delinquencies in repayment. The SRP faced the impossible task of becoming a collection agency.

Phoenix needed the Verde River to meet its expansion plans, and the SRP was eager to be relieved of the responsibility of collecting delinquent assessments. On July 5, 1951, Pickrell and city engineers indicated that the water crisis might be averted if the city took over delivery of all water to lands within its limits. Chiefly because of editorials in the *Republic*, however, which repeatedly told city residents there was no need for alarm, the true dimensions of the problem remained hidden behind erroneous assurances that the wells would suffice to see the city through the summer without changing water habits drastically. The attitude that Lin Orme, president of the Water Users Association in the 1930s, expressed then, that "it will rain—it always has," seemed to prevail, although city officials asked to meet with SRP officials to work out an agreement. Still, with only five days left before the city's Verde River supply would be depleted, the mayor and city council had yet to institute conservation measures.[18]

Fortunately for Phoenix, Lin Orme was right—it did rain, and it rained long and hard. But the new supply of water did not stop negotiations between the city and the SRP, for this presented a real opportunity to construct a model for the changing uses of agricultural land and water to urban requirements. Early in 1952 the two organizations reached agreement. Included within it were provisions common to a subdivision "master buy": the city would pay the SRP all delinquent assessments on each acre of project land within its limits, which amounted to about two hundred thousand dollars, and would pay the annual assessments and operation and maintenance charges. The SRP would then deliver all the water held for those lands to the city's distribution system for the water department to deliver and manage. Because urban uses require less water than agricultural, the master-buy agreement ensured that Phoenix would have a growing supply of water for years to come.[19]

The 1952 agreement did not, however, provide any additional water for city lands outside the project boundaries, since reclamation law prevented the transporting of project water to nonproject lands. As a result, in 1982 the city faced serious problems because it had annexed large areas to the north and south of the project area; these areas were dependent on the fixed stored-water credits the city had, through its Horseshoe Dam spillway gates, for its fresh water supply. Legal challenges regarding the city's right to divert water from the Verde River and to the master-buy agreement itself may yet appear as the amount of available water pales next to exponential growth in its planned uses. Unlike Tucson, which seems to have managed its much scarcer water supply better, the Phoenix City Council has yet to approve a water conservation policy for the city. As of 1982, Phoenix had a population of one-and-a-half-million people. A city of such numbers cannot long rely on Lin Orme's prophecy that it will always rain when it is needed.

# PART FIVE

*Community Policy on Politics, Labor, and Transportation*

## CHAPTER ELEVEN

# The Election of 1949: Transformation of Municipal Government in Phoenix

## BY MICHAEL F. KONIG

FOR NEARLY two decades after the mayoral and city council elections of November 1949, Phoenix municipal government was dominated by the Charter Government Committee. This committee, composed of prominent civic and business leaders, represented the interests of the larger industries and the more affluent residents of the city. The committee pursued policies to promote sustained metropolitan growth and render Phoenix city government more professional and efficient. In the 1980s, Phoenix citizens argued over the merits of such policies, but during the turbulent municipal election of 1949, candidates endorsed by Charter received overwhelming support from Phoenix voters. This approval demonstrated a pronounced antagonism by most Phoenix residents toward the mismanagement and political maneuvering that had seemed inherent in previous city administrations.

The Charter Government Committee emerged as the result of various reform measures attempted by Phoenix residents after World War II. In an effort to establish an efficient municipal government that could adequately meet the needs of a growing metropolis, voters approved certain city charter amendments in November 1948. These strengthened the power of the city manager in municipal affairs but failed to provide the desired reforms. The office of city manager, regarded as the choicest of political plums, became mired in controversy, and control of the city government remained in the hands of people who opposed progressive change. The candidates and policies endorsed by Charter in the municipal elections of November 1949 gave Phoenix voters an opportunity to end the ceaseless turmoil at city hall and establish a responsible municipal administration that would represent the wishes of the majority of Phoenicians.[1]

From 1914 to 1947, more than twenty individuals held the office of Phoenix city manager. In October 1947, members of the city commission voted William Richards out of office and replaced him with James T. Deppe, the recently resigned secretary of the Citizens Good Government Council. The firing of Richards and the appointment of Deppe caused considerable controversy. City officials raised questions regarding the exact duties of the city manager in municipal affairs. Commission members debated whether the city manager was responsible to the entire commission, to the majority bloc of the commission, or to the mayor alone. At the time of Richards's removal, the majority bloc of the city commission dictated the affairs of the city manager. Minority-bloc members found their influence in the city administration declining and complained that they had not been consulted about the hiring of Deppe.[2]

Deppe served as city manager from October 1947 until January 1950. His comparatively protracted tenure was turbulent, as popular reaction against his actions as city manager translated into support for the candidates and policies of the Charter Government Committee.

Upon taking office, Deppe immediately accused Mayor Ray Busey of causing confusion and discord at city hall because of what Deppe claimed was the vindictiveness and disregard the mayor had for the opinions of the majority-bloc commissioners. In addition to these charges against the mayor, Deppe made several questionable city appointments. He installed a new police chief (Earl O'Clair), a new executive secretary to the city manager, a new street superintendent, and a new city assessor, and he forced out of office several city employees who were working on special projects, such as annexation. Many city officials considered the individuals appointed by Deppe unfit for their new positions. For example, the new assessor, Joe Thurman, had served previously as water superintendent. He had been fired from that position only two months earlier because of a water meter–reading scandal. Thurman had no previous experience in assessing but obviously possessed splendid political recuperative capacities. Such appointments by Deppe contributed to the tension, uncertainty, and inefficiency that grew apace at city hall.[3]

Deppe suffered his first setback when he attempted to fire Eli Wolfson, city sealer of weights and measures, and hire W. O. Kessler. The city commission overruled and sharply rebuked Deppe for attempting this purely political action. The commission also defeated an attempt by Deppe to prohibit the operation of pinball machines in the city bus terminal. Further controversy erupted when Deppe was struck by Police Sgt. John Slaughter during a police department outing at South Mountain Park.[4]

On May 2, 1948, Nicholas Udall took office as mayor. Phoenix citizens hoped his administration would bring peace and efficiency to city government. Expectations for better municipal administration were heightened when the Charter Revision Committee, directed by Charles E. Bernstein, drafted charter amendments that would make the city manager Phoenix's chief administrative officer. Mayor Udall pledged his "highest regard" for the committee's recommendations.[5]

In light of the proposed amendments and because he was dissatisfied with actions of the city manager, Udall sought to remove Deppe from office. Ouster attempts failed during a heated city commission meeting on August 3, 1948. At this meeting Udall accused Deppe of being incompetent, inexperienced, and inefficient, as well as being improperly influenced by Ward H. ("Doc") Scheumack, manager of the Valley Paint and Supply Company and an active participant in behind-the-scenes city politics. The mayor admitted he had taken part in a political switch engineered by Scheumack that had resulted in the appointment of Deppe as city manager. But Udall and Commissioner Charles Walters declared they would not tolerate boss rule of the city by Scheumack. To prove his sincerity, Walters said he and Udall would not enter into a political deal proposed by Commissioner Jack Blaine that would have resulted in the firing of Deppe. According to Udall and Walters, Blaine, who favored firing Deppe, would not vote to do so unless, simultaneously, Aaron Kinney was removed as city clerk and replaced by C. W. Boyer, a former real-estate manager for Blaine. In the deal, Blaine sought to install Boyer as city clerk because in the event of a vacancy on the commission and a deadlock between the remaining four commissioners, the charter authorized the city clerk to break the tie and vote to fill the commission vacancy. Blaine wished to remove Kinney because Kinney would not vote for a new commissioner who favored any faction seeking to gain control of city government. Blaine was one of the first city officials to express dissatisfaction with the city manager and accuse Deppe of riding on the coattails of city boss Scheumack, but he failed to cast the deciding vote that would have removed Deppe from office.[6]

After his defeated attempt to remove the city manager, Udall spoke on two radio stations, KOY and KOOL, both of which gave him broadcast time as a public service. He outlined his reasons for seeking Deppe's ouster and proposed that the strong manager form of government contemplated by the Charter Revision Committee be replaced with a municipal system which would make the mayor administrative head of city government. According to Udall, the mayor would have no vote on the commission but would have veto power. Under this system the mayor would be charged with the operation of the city government and would be empowered to appoint qualified assistants from the civil service to do the work previously done by the city manager.[7]

Deppe vigorously denied the charges of incompetence, inexperience, and inefficiency that were leveled at him. He also maintained that the only boss who provided him with guidance was God and that he always possessed "the most enviable of all titles, the character of an honest man."[8]

Regardless of what claims Deppe made, he kept the municipal political pot boiling by firing Aaron Kinney as city clerk and replacing him with C. W. Boyer. Kinney supported the attempts by Udall and Walters to appoint a successor to Commissioner Roy Stone, who had won the Democratic nomination for one of the two Maricopa County state senate seats and would be forced to resign by January 1, 1949. If Kinney had remained in office after Stone resigned, Udall and Walters would have been in a position to name the new commissioner, thus giving them a majority. But Boyer, who had managed the campaigns of Jack Blaine and William Tate the previous spring, could now be used by Blaine, with the support of Tate, to select the vital fifth commissioner and leave Udall and Walters in the minority and virtually powerless in city affairs.[9]

Against this backdrop of continual political turmoil, Charles E. Bernstein and the Charter Revision Committee labored to secure a special election date on which city voters could decide upon their proposed charter revisions. The committee's task was difficult because of opposition by the majority of the city commissioners and the city manager to the proposed amendments. When the commission demonstrated its reluctance to set the special-election date, Udall and Bernstein threatened to circulate separate initiative petitions to force a special election and place their issues on the ballot. This threat finally motivated the commission to schedule the special election for November 16, 1948. Udall withdrew his strong-mayor proposal because he feared presentation of both plans would result in the defeat of both.[10]

While support for the charter amendments was widespread throughout the city, certain powerful interest groups opposed the measures. The city employees' union, the Central Labor Council of the American Federation of Labor, directed by its executive board member, H. R. Radcliff, saw the strong-manager proposals as a dangerous threat to the civil-service structure of Phoenix. Radcliff said Central Labor Council members objected most particularly to charter amendments that gave the city manager authority to destroy almost any city department. But some city employees who favored the amendments claimed that the union opposition was based on a scheme in which Deppe would seek higher union wages in return for union antagonism toward the strong-manager proposals. Some leaders of the city labor unions preferred the previous form of government because they were able to reach agreements with city officials in behind-the-scenes conferences. With a strong city manager who could not be fired on the political whim of the commission's majority bloc, such agreements would become difficult to reach. According to the *Arizona Republic*, previous city managers had been forced to accept labor agreements they opposed because of commission pressure resulting from union threats of reprisal at the polls.[11]

Despite opposition by the commission majority and Deppe, the charter amendments were approved on November 16, 1948, by a popular vote of 6,595 to 2,949. Support for the amendments by the *Arizona Republic* proved invaluable during the election. An editorial claimed that after passage of the strong-manager proposals, city bosses would be "cut-off from influence with the city purchasing department, the police department, and the city manager himself." The heaviest vote was cast in the comparatively affluent northern section of the city, where the most support for the manager amendments was registered.[12]

The text of the charter amendments included a provision for the removal of the city manager. Five of the seven votes on the expanded city council were required to dismiss the manager without cause. Four votes were required to remove him for incompetence, malfeasance, misfeasance, or neglect of duty.[13]

Deppe's hold on the city manager's office appeared tenuous. Some city officials claimed he had padded the budget by more than eight hundred thousand, but Commissioners Blaine and Stone of the majority bloc rejected offers by Udall and Walters to discuss the names of prospective candidates for the two new council seats created by the charter amendments. The majority bloc ignored the intent of the charter amendments and selected individuals sympathetic to its own desires; Thomas J. Imler, a retired Phoenix businessman, and Wallace W. Caywood, a lunchroom operator, were chosen by the majority bloc to serve on the expanded council. The majority faction voted to retain Deppe as city manager despite the protests of Udall and Walters and the charges of budget padding, so little change occurred in city government despite passage of the charter amendments. Those who controlled city affairs before the special charter election remained in power despite the desires of the Phoenix voting populace. Turmoil and confusion plagued city hall.[14]

The rift between the majority bloc of the city council and the Udall–Walters faction widened when Udall refused to appear on a city-sponsored broadcast on radio station KOY. Udall declared that production of the program had assumed a controversial nature as both factions sought to exploit the broadcast for their own gain. Deppe contributed to the rift when he fired C. W. Boyer as city clerk and John Williams as city auditor. This change occurred as Stone resigned from his position on the council to qualify for the state senate. The ensuing vacancy necessitated the appointment of a new member to the seven-member council. Udall, Walters, and Blaine favored a man named Phoenix Brown, a used-car dealer and president of the Biz-Vets organization. The other three council members, Caywood, Tate, and Imler, with support from Deppe, favored D. S. Horall, a plumbing contractor, or Leo Welnick, a grocer. The council split meant the city clerk would cast the deciding vote in selecting the new council member. Deppe had fired Boyer because of the latter's support for Blaine's choice of city auditor, Phoenix Brown.[15]

The firing of Williams caused heated debates that centered on the Phoenix city budget for 1948–49. Problems with the budget first appeared when municipal revenue fell well below estimates. In addition, the budget was $645,000 higher than anticipated revenues. A $162,000 city-employee wage hike granted the previous year by the former city commission further exacerbated the fiscal situation. An audit of city finances by Max A. Millet, a certified public accountant, revealed that funds and materials had been wasted by city government for a number of years. Udall castigated Deppe for allowing such acute financial problems to develop, and various prominent businessmen balked at a proposal by the city council to levy a 1 percent sales tax.[16]

Public confidence in Deppe eroded further when he fired five high-ranking city officials and reorganized several departments. Among those dismissed were James Girand, popular city water superintendent, and Aaron Kinney, assistant city attorney. Both worked efficiently during their tenure but were fired by Deppe solely because they disagreed with his political views. Kinney questioned the city manager's authority to abolish his civil-service position. Kinney claimed that offices controlled by the civil service were expressly eliminated from the charge of the city manager by the charter amendments. Kinney's arguments were well founded legally and were solidly supported by the *Arizona Republic*. But Kinney received notice he had been relieved of his official duties as both assistant superintendent and legal investigator for the department of the city attorney.[17]

Deppe attracted more criticism when it was discovered he had evaded a law requiring that all purchases by the city be made by advertising for bids. Deppe accomplished this by dividing the orders made by the city into a number of smaller requisitions of less than five hundred dollars.[18]

Incensed by Deppe's actions, Councilman Blaine attempted to have the city manager discharged, describing Deppe's stormy, twenty-month administration as grossly inefficient and berating Deppe for permitting vice and gambling to flourish in Phoenix. Blaine accused Deppe of failing to serve the interests of Phoenix citizens and implied that the city manager, the majority bloc of the city council and Chief of Police Earl O'Clair were controlled by political boss Scheumack. In addition, Blaine charged Deppe and O'Clair with permitting irregularities at the city jail, such as the shaking down of people charged with traffic violations.

Blaine also stated that Deppe and O'Clair received graft from gambling and prostitution establishments and said that the vice squad of the Phoenix Police Department paid nightly visits to a private club where gambling flourished, yet took no action to close the establishment. The councilman further upbraided Phoenix Police Department vice-squad leader Alvin J. Matousek for accepting six hundred dollars' worth of cut glass from various prostitutes in the city. Blaine submitted to the council a resolution calling for Deppe's removal in conformance with procedures outlined in the amended city charter. Udall and Walters voted with Blaine but were defeated by the majority-bloc councilmen: Tate, Imler, Caywood, and C. O. Welnick.[19]

Blaine's charges regarding the proliferation of vice in Phoenix during the Deppe administration were well founded. The city manager continually ignored demands by the mayor to report on the extent of prostitution. Udall even produced a report compiled by Dr. Walter Clarke, clinical professor of public health at Harvard University, who had investigated houses of prostitution in Phoenix. Clarke reported that prostitution was open in the city and that the situation was worse in Phoenix than in other western metropolitan centers. He based his remarks on the findings of surveys of the Phoenix area conducted by the American Social Hygiene Association in June 1949. According to Clarke, officials in Washington, D.C., expressed concern over the vice situation in Phoenix because of the large number of military personnel in the area. He warned of the dangers to public health if the situation were allowed to continue. For a while during World War II, Phoenix was closed to all military personnel because of the vice situation. The association worked closely with the military during the war, watching its reports on venereal disease rates to guide investigations. According to the report by Clarke, open prostitution had been increasing in Phoenix since mid-1947, at which time the city was listed as closed. The survey named eight houses of prostitution and also noted that certain taxicab drivers made contacts for potential customers with prostitutes operating a "good-sized fare's" distance from the downtown area. Clarke also maintained that during the summer and fall of 1949, the vice situation in Phoenix had worsened.[20]

In the face of the charges made by Blaine and the report issued by the American Social Hygiene Association, Deppe, as advised by information provided by O'Clair, reported to the city council that no organized vice existed in the city and that prostitution occurred only as infrequent, isolated instances. According to the city manager, the police department immediately suppressed these isolated occurrences of prostitution.[21]

While the attempt by the minority faction of the city council failed to remove Deppe, the complaints of vice conditions in Phoenix did not go unheard. Secretary of State and Acting Gov. Wesley Bolin ordered an investigation, to be directed by Attorney General Fred O. Wilson, of conditions and possible irregularities in Phoenix municipal government. In particular, the state probe inquired into the death of Henry G. Frederick, a transient, who died of a skull fracture in the city jail after being treated and released from a Phoenix hospital. But at the close of the investigation, the office of the attorney general concluded that there was no need for the state to intervene in city affairs. Some observers maintained that the county attorney's office was the most appropriate agency to conduct such an investigation. Eventually, medical experts determined that Frederick would have died wherever he happened to be and not because of any alleged rough handling he received at the jail.[22]

The Deppe–Scheumack contingent used the findings of the state investigation as a basis from which to strike back at their critics. The city manager triumphantly proclaimed: "I assumed such action on the part of the state officials would be forthcoming after an investigation of the established facts." O'Clair described Blaine's accusations as deliberate and malicious falsehoods and denied that a corrupt political boss controlled his office. The police chief defended himself by calling attention to the fact that he and the South Mountain Police Academy had recently received national recognition in the *Federal Bureau of Investigation Law Enforcement Bulletin* for outstanding strides in modern law enforcement. Yet O'Clair could not deny the existence of baseball betting shops operating openly throughout the city. Deppe attempted to secure a substantial salary increase for himself, and when Blaine objected to this effort, he was referred to as a "contemptible liar" by the city manager. Despite protests by the council's minority faction, Deppe's pay was raised from $8,100 annually to $12,500. Walters described the increase as a "clear and unadulterated raid on the city treasury."[23]

Wearied by the unremitting turmoil at city hall and desirous of executing reforms of the charter amendments, a citizens group of twelve members organized in the summer of 1949. This contingent, thereafter named the Charter Government Committee, formulated plans to run a slate of candidates in the Phoenix municipal elections in November. The committee consisted primarily of representatives from the regular organizations of Phoenix Republicans and Democrats. Essentially a bipartisan organization, it received its strongest support from the upper-income areas of the city.[24]

The Deppe–Scheumack forces immediately attacked the Charter Government Committee. The Reverend Fred A. Barnhill, pastor of First Congregational Church and vice-chairman of the committee, disclosed that he had been telephoned by Scheumack. According to Barnhill, Scheumack said the committee was a mistake and castigated the pastor for participating in such an organization, "which only represented the big corporations" and was antagonistic to the honest administration of City Manager Deppe. Barnhill also claimed that Scheumack accused Alfred Knight, Phoenix philanthropist, patron of the arts and founding member of the committee, of operating a bawdy house.[25]

Udall, who had gained increasing support from the committee as its mayoral candidate, launched a verbal retaliation against the Deppe–Scheumack contingent. These recriminations, regarded by many as the opening guns of the fall election campaign, included the charge that Deppe used time donated to the city by radio station KOY to lay the groundwork for a Deppe–Scheumack ticket which would oppose the Charter candidates in November. Udall called Deppe the administrative boss and Scheumack the political boss and charged they had whipped into line a puppet majority on the city council, which had done their bidding with little protest. The mayor further accused the Deppe–Scheumack faction of imposing censorship on affairs at city hall, extending it even to the minority members of the council. According to Udall, an odd mixture of fear and hate for Deppe existed among department heads, rendering the efficient conduct of city government impossible. Deppe responded to the charges by calling them "insinuations, innuendos, and imagination in place of recorded facts."[26]

As the November elections drew near, the diverse interest groups in the city coalesced into competing political factions. Every member of the council and the city manager played an active role in the campaign. Former mayors and other officials of previous city administrations were also involved. The majority bloc of the council, composed of Caywood, Welnick, Tate, and Imler, formed one ticket. They were joined by Floyd A. Ford, chairman of the civil-service board and former city commissioner. Aligned with Deppe and selecting Imler as its mayoral candidate, the majority bloc ticket, known as the Civic Achievement Group, was supported by Scheumack. Scheumack, who had been active in previous municipal campaigns, served as the principal fund-raiser for the Imler ticket. The Charter Government Committee announced on September 8, 1949, that Udall would head its municipal election ticket. In addition to Udall's candidacy for mayor, the committee endorsed Hohen Foster, Barry M. Goldwater, Margaret B. Kober, Frank G. Murphy, Harry Rosenzweig, and Charles Walter for city council. All of the committee candidates were prominent businessmen and civic leaders. They pledged to install a "trained, experienced, and fully qualified" city manager to administer municipal affairs.[27]

Political lone wolf Blaine lost the backing of his previous supporters, the Biz-Vets, but still sought election as mayor. Realizing that his chances for victory were remote, he stated, "I may not be able to win, but I can keep some of the others [Civic Achievement Group] from winning."

A number of city employees and members of certain labor unions considered sponsoring one or possibly two candidates for the council. In search of backing, Blaine spoke with labor leaders. In radio talks during the campaign, he vowed to reduce taxes, repeal the city sales tax, and reduce bus fares. He also promised to be a crusading mayor who would take strong action against vice.[28]

The Biz-Vets cast about for an individual other than Blaine to head their ticket. They finally offered J. Melvin Goodson, secretary of the state highway commission and unsuccessful gubernatorial aspirant, a campaign fund of $25,000 to enter the race for mayor. Other city officials involved in the campaign as mayoral candidates included former Mayors Ray Busey and J. R. Fleming and former City Manager Roy J. Heyne. Busey was hostile toward Udall's candidacy. W. O. Glick, longtime friend of Busey and former city clerk and magistrate, ran as an independent candidate for the council. John Lane, operator of the P.M. Cocktail Lounge, also entered the race as an independent candidate for mayor but subsequently withdrew because of lack of support.[29]

The city council ordered certain amendments placed on the November 8 election ballot, two of which were controversial. The first proposed to eliminate the inventory tax and limit the city tax on equipment and machinery used exclusively in manufacturing. The second provided for the appointment of a licensed attorney as city magistrate and established a four-year term for that position. While popular with the business interests of the city and supported by all four major candidates, the proposed tax amendment was assailed by Sam S. Levitin, an independent candidate for council. He claimed the amendment would place a disproportionate burden of taxation on homeowners and property-tax payers. He also believed that repeal of the city inventory tax would destroy the workmen's compensation law, cripple school budgets, and reduce old-age pensions. Levitin, whose candidacy was endorsed by an apartment owners' organization called the Home Owners Protective Alliance, observed that a 2 percent state rent tax on business properties had just gone into effect and maintained that if any tax was to be repealed, it ought to be the rent tax, which was eight times as high as the manufacturers' inventory tax.[30]

Despite appeals by Levitin, the More Jobs for More People in Phoenix Committee campaigned for repeal of the inventory tax, citing Tucson's loss of Harland Manufacturing Company as the most compelling reason for Phoenix voters to approve the charter amendment. Marion T. Harland, head of the company, claimed that the move from Tucson to Muscatine, Iowa, was due to the effects of the state inventory tax on his business. Repeal of the Phoenix inventory tax, the committee contended, would remove the inconvenience caused by the tax and make the city more attractive to industry. The committee also claimed that the support it received from all four mayoral candidates dispelled any questions regarding the merits of the proposed amendment.[31]

The opposing political forces assailed each other in earnest as the election drew near. Goldwater branded as false the Civic Achievement Group's claim that it initiated and completed several municipal-improvement projects and rejected the group's assertion that it had participated in various development programs at Sky Harbor Airport. The Phoenix Chamber of Commerce, according to Goldwater, accomplished the development and the entire project was started before Imler or any of his supporters were appointed to the council. Rebutting the claims by the Imler ticket that it had expanded and renovated the city parks and playgrounds, Goldwater asserted that this program was made possible by bonds voted before three of the majority-bloc council members were elected and that Deppe opposed the bond issue. Although the Civic Achievement Group took credit for the slum-clearance project directed by the Phoenix Housing Authority, Goldwater claimed that reputed city boss Scheumack acted openly for his supporters on the council and made every effort to prevent housing authorities from bringing the slum-clearance project before the council for approval of an application for federal funds.[32]

Udall denied that the Civic Achievement Group was responsible, as it claimed, for an annual independent audit of city fiscal affairs. The mayor asserted that the audit was the result of submitting the proposal to Phoenix voters in the municipal elections of 1948 and that not a single member of the Imler group was on the committee then. Deppe, the mayor charged, received bids from a number of accountants for the 1949 city audit but chose to accept one whose daily rate was approximately 50 percent higher than the proposed charges of any other accountant.[33]

Mayoral candidate Busey criticized the Charter Government Committee slogans, saying the election of Udall would end thirty-five years of mal-administration in Phoenix as unwarranted attacks on the "very fine men who, in the past, have served as mayor." Busey maintained that the solution to Phoenix municipal administration problems would be the election of councilmembers by districts. According to Busey, this would ensure that the councilmembers would be responsible to the people of the section of the city they represented. Goldwater disputed the supposed virtues of district election of councilmembers, declaring that Phoenix was a unified metropolitan area with common problems. He also maintained that the task of the city government was to "unify Phoenix, not divide it." Udall also struck at the mayoral candidacy of Busey. He charged that the administration of the former mayor had been marked by emotionalism and inefficiency. Busey, Udall declared, had attempted to abolish the civil-service system and establish a spoils system. The result, according to Udall, was continued agitation and turmoil.[34]

Despite these attacks by Goldwater and Udall, Busey received the endorsement of the Phoenix Central Labor Council, which also supported three members of the Civic Achievement Group ticket, Caywood, Welnick, and Ford, as well as three independents, Ivan V. Larson, E. J. Ranger, and Frank D. Grist. The labor council unanimously opposed the proposed charter amendment removing inventory tax on Phoenix manufacturers.[35]

Other special-interest groups bestowed their support on the various candidates. The Charter slate won endorsement by the Phoenix Ministerial Association because of its promise to hire a "trained and competent" city manager. The *Arizona Republic* and the *Phoenix Gazette* also gave their unequivocal support to the Charter ticket. In an article which appeared on the day before the election, the *Republic* said the Charter ticket was composed of dependable men and women who would give Phoenix the best possible government. According to the paper, if the Charter candidates were not elected, candidates of such high caliber would not enter city politics in the future.[36]

Civic Achievement Group candidate Caywood criticized what he called unfair reporting practices by the *Republic* and the *Gazette*. He claimed that Charter Government Committee candidates benefited unfairly from these practices. In an attempt to prove his argument, Caywood noted that both newspapers announced that Charter mayoral candidate Udall was to speak on the radio on the evening of October 28, 1949. Yet, Caywood said, both newspapers failed to mention that Civic Achievement Group candidate Imler was scheduled to make a radio address later that evening. He further charged that the two newspapers ignored the independent candidates and spied on private political meetings held by the Civic Achievement Group. In a KTAR radio address, Caywood claimed that the newspapers were controlled by professional politicians from outside the state who were reporting half-truths and propaganda in an effort to install their own favorite as city manager. He further stated that these politicians had published stories about a mythical city boss in the two newspapers to serve their own ends.[37]

Scheumack, who had been raising money for the Civic Achievement Group, also criticized the two newspapers, which portrayed him in editorials as the most powerful man in Phoenix city politics. Responding to charges by the newspapers that he controlled the majority bloc on the city council, he said the papers made such accusations to create a smoke screen that would enable the newspapers, which he, too, claimed were controlled from outside the state, to gain control of city hall and name their own manager. The next step, he maintained, was control of the statehouse by the unnamed outside interests. According to Scheumack, the newspapers had deluded some of the outstanding businessmen of the city to seek election.

Deppe also struck at the *Republic* and the *Gazette*, charging that they sought numerous special privileges from city government. His claims carried the inference that because he had denied Phoenix Newspapers Incorporated the use of the entire west side of Second Street between Van Buren and Polk streets for a loading zone, he had been made the object of unfair attacks by the two newspapers.[38]

Charter Government Committee candidates responding to the charges of being manipulated by out-of-state interests declared that five of their members were native Arizonans and the other two were longtime residents of the state. The candidates further pledged that they would represent the interests of all Phoenix citizens because they were too jealous of the city to surrender its control to anyone from outside the state.[39]

S. C. Boyer, the first black candidate for city council in Phoenix history (he ran as an independent), denied that Charter represented the interests of all Phoenix citizens. He castigated both the Charter candidates and the Civic Achievement Group for failing to understand the problems then existing for minorities in the southern sections of the city. Boyer complained that both groups demonstrated little interest in the desire for slum clearance by South Phoenix residents. But at a Lowell School rally for Charter candidates, the principal speaker, Vidal D. Rivera, urged Spanish-speaking citizens to vote for the Charter ticket. He claimed such action would "insure fair treatment for the people of all sections of the city."[40]

Two other important issues surfaced only a few days before the election. The first appeared when Charter council candidate Margaret Kober declared that the city health department was understaffed and had been neglected by previous administrations. The second issue involved a proposal by Busey to consolidate the city bus system with the privately owned and operated Metropolitan Bus Line. Udall, while favoring the proposal, charged that Busey's actions while mayor prevented such a merger and initiated a series of fare increases. The Civic Achievement Group preferred purchase of the private line by the city and reduction of fares, but the four councilmen on the ticket voted to raise bus fares less than five months before the municipal election. Other issues were brought up, but none was so extensively debated as health-department renovation and bus-line consolidation.[41]

Phoenix voters turned out in record numbers on November 8, 1949. Of 41,800 registered voters, 22,353 cast ballots, bringing the entire Charter Government Committee slate into office. Udall lost only four of the fifty-three Phoenix election precincts while receiving almost 10,000 more votes than either Imler or Busey. Goldwater obtained more votes than any municipal candidate, polling 14,498. Rosenzweig was second with 14,387, while Kober, Murphy, Walters, and Foster completed the Charter victory. The Civic Achievement Group ran poorly, winning only one precinct. Support for the Charter ticket, overwhelming in the northern and eastern sections of Phoenix, was also strong in the less-affluent southern precincts. Municipal voters also approved the four proposed charter amendments by considerable majorities.[42]

Within a few days after their victory, the new city councilmembers consulted various city governments and the International Association of City Managers to select a replacement for Deppe. Ray Wilson, former assistant city manager of Kansas City, Missouri, was chosen. But Wilson was unable to assume his role until the new mayor and councilmembers took office.

On January 3, 1950, the new regime took over at a city-hall meeting attended by an overflow crowd of well-wishers. The new city council immediately called for Deppe's resignation as city manager. Deppe, also attending the meeting, refused to resign, claiming that his resignation would merely give substance to what he termed "the illusion of mismanagement, bossism, graft, corruption, inefficiency, and incompetence . . . successfully created by politically ambitious individuals and a ruthless, unprincipled, power-seeking press." Goldwater responded to these charges by stating that Deppe was the only issue in the previous election and declared that because Phoenix voters had so overwhelmingly supported the platform of the Charter Government Committee, the only feasible action for Deppe was to resign. Prolonged applause from the crowd followed this statement by the new councilman, but Deppe still declined to remove himself from office.[43]

In light of this refusal, the council adopted nine resolutions in which it suspended Deppe as city manager. These resolutions, written in accordance with the charter amendments that became law in November 1948, stated that through malfeasance and misfeasance Deppe should be removed from office. The specific charges against Deppe were varied. The first stated that Deppe, despite orders from the council, refused to make deposition of an unfinished airport manager's house at Sky Harbor Airport and convert it into a paying asset for the city. The second declared that Deppe had failed, despite council instructions, to protect property purchased to complete expansion at Sky Harbor. The third maintained that the city manager had failed to exercise the option on the Harry Cordova veterans' emergency housing project with the result that rent on the property doubled.

Resolution 4 charged that through incompetence and lack of fiscal knowledge, Deppe presented the council with a budget for the 1948–49 fiscal year that was out of balance by $645,000 and that because the council followed his recommendations, the city had a $300,000 deficit for the year. The fifth resolution stated that Deppe improperly participated in the campaign by which the council-manager form of government was established and that he acted improperly by publicly ridiculing proponents of the charter amendments. Resolution 6 declared that Deppe improperly conducted himself as city manager by replacing a city clerk in order that he might dictate the selection of a councilman to fill a vacancy. This resolution stated that such an act was outside the city manager's duties and wholly political.

The seventh resolution maintained that Deppe permitted vice conditions to exist in Phoenix during his tenure. Such laxity on the part of the city manager, the resolution said, could be attributed only to his lack of knowledge about the situation or his refusal to enforce city ordinances. Resolution 8 charged that Deppe approved violations of the letter and the spirit of the charter in connection with sales bids on the purchase of property by the city. According to the resolution, these violations made open and competitive bidding impossible. The last of the resolutions claimed that Deppe had not given the necessary administrative assistance to the council to support it as a policy-making body and that he had failed to submit ideas, interpretations, departmental reports, and clear suggestions for sound municipal operations during his administration.[44]

The suspension of Deppe as city manager marked the end of the political importance of the Civic Achievement Group in city affairs. The defeated candidates and major supporters of the Imler ticket faded into obscurity. Deppe, perhaps the central figure in the political turmoil of the preceding months, was shaken by his removal and was in ill health. He committed suicide in a North Hollywood, California, motel a few months after his ouster. His tragic demise forever rendered him an enigma in the history of Phoenix municipal affairs.[45]

Before the municipal elections of November 1949, political turmoil at city hall had retarded demographic and industrial growth in Phoenix. After the election, the Charter Government Committee dominated city elections. Ray Wilson's term as city manager lasted more than eleven years and encompassed one of the most spectacular periods of population growth and increased industrial productivity in the history of the city. Charter consistently secured able candidates for its municipal election slates, and they received overwhelming support from Phoenix voters for the next two decades. As municipal leaders, these individuals brought to Phoenix city government the expertise and efficiency that had made them successful in their own businesses and professions. They transformed Phoenix government into a viable organization which could more adequately meet the needs of a rapidly growing metropolis. Under the watchful eye of the Charter Government Committee, municipal administrators worked closely with business leaders to produce a political and economic climate suited to the growth of technical industry, retail trade, centralized banking institutions, and a burgeoning, comparatively skilled work force. In effect, these individuals linked their own personal success with that of the city. Viewed in this perspective, the municipal elections of 1949 can be seen as a turning point from which Phoenix emerged as the dominant metropolis of the Southwest.[46]

## CHAPTER TWELVE

# The Bug in the Desert: The Labor Movement in Phoenix, 1940–1950

### BY MARGARET FINNERTY

IN 1940, organized labor in Phoenix was, in its own eyes, coming into a wholesome adolescence. As the city's economic base broadened, the population reached sixty thousand and more jobs became available. Organized labor also grew, and orderly, inevitable expansion of unions relative to population growth seemed assured.

Phoenix, a basically midwestern town with strong southern influences, assigned organized labor a negligible role in its power structure. The small but steady stream of health seekers, vacationers, and adventurous entrepreneurs who made up most of the growing population were not interested in promoting organized labor. Unions for the skilled trades were accepted, but labor unions were not encouraged. Where organizing laborers could seriously change economic patterns, for example among agricultural workers, the idea was considered unsound. In general, however, a laissez-faire attitude prevailed; weak unions were an unimportant, only slightly necessary evil.

World War II changed Phoenix. Economically and socially, the change was immediate and drastic. Construction of war plants, airfields, and other military installations drew thousands of workers, many of them union members, to the valley. This influx of union members and the return after the war of many men who had been stationed in Phoenix disrupted the balance.

New businesses joined those attracted by the war effort. Part of the area's appeal was organized labor's limited role in the power structure. Phoenix policymakers, eager to attract companies and to avoid the evils of gangsterism they felt were inevitable with strong unions, were active in introducing union-weakening legislation. Union efforts to help provide jobs for returning veterans proved inadequate; the unemployed often blamed the unions for hoarding available positions.

An emotional battle followed, lasting from 1946 to 1948. Using patriotic themes and working from a strong, traditionally conservative base, those who favored weakened unions operated with an assurance not evident in their impassioned rhetoric. The unions, on the other hand, were plagued with internal disruption and made many blunders. They were forced into a difficult defensive posture. When the excitement subsided, the state did not have a simple statute but a constitutional amendment forbidding closed shops and several other similar practices. Attempts to have the amendment disqualified marked the end of the decade, but even those efforts backfired. The earlier promise of union power implicit in valley growth proved a hollow one for the labor movement.

## BACKGROUND

The dramatic events in Phoenix between 1940 and 1950 had lasting effects on the local labor movement, but the effects had earlier causes. Unions in the city of Phoenix were weak indeed in the town's earliest years, compared to those in the rest of the territory. The miners' unions were the first and strongest; they had bitter struggles for workers' rights and even won representation before statehood. The powerful, feisty miners' unions led a conference of labor organizations held in Phoenix on July 11, 1910. Their purpose was to present the provisions labor wanted in the constitution for the new state. Locals from all over the territory represented carpenters, barbers, pressmen, electrical workers, blacksmiths, plasterers, printers, steam engineers, hod carriers, machinists, and bricklayers. Their shopping list for the constitution included referendum, initiative, and recall provisions; woman suffrage; an anti-injunction law; and the election of United States senators by popular vote. They favored an employer-liability act, abolishment of the fee system in all courts, and the right of the state to seize property of any corporation or person refusing to comply with the law. They wanted the state to defray the costs of the defense as well as the prosecution of criminals; no private police groups were to be allowed to arrest or to give testimony in court. Ironically, they desired that the constitution could be amended by a majority vote of the electors on the initiative of either the legislature or the people.[1]

This same non-Phoenix-based labor organization played a powerful role in the constitutional convention. George W. P. Hunt, a shrewd and portly "friend of labor," steered labor representatives into important committees from his position as president of the convention. The Populist concepts that flavored state constitutions of the era, notably initiative, referendum, and recall, were especially important to both Hunt and the unions. These provisions meant direct legislation, a reaction to existing state constitutions which seemed unresponsive to the will of the people. The recall provision, for example, made judges who called injunctions on strikes answerable to public opinion. These radical ideas caused some concern in conservative circles, both locally and in Washington, D.C.[2]

The liberality of the state's constitution was often honored in the breach. The U.S. Supreme Court extended itself in the cause of protecting business in its labor difficulties. It declared a statute forbidding courts to grant injunctions against picketing (one of labor's favorite themes) unconstitutional. Reflecting the probusiness tenor of the times, Chief Justice Taft explained:

The statute violated due process by protection palpable wrongful injuries to property rights. Moreover, since it singled out certain types of property (that involved in labor disputes) for exposure to wrongful injury, the law violated the equal protection clause of the Fourteenth Amendment.[3]

Despite the power of Arizona miners as a whole, organized labor hardly posed a serious threat to the status quo in Phoenix. A basically agricultural community such as Phoenix, with much southern influence augmented by Old West–style cattle businesses and a new class of commercial entrepreneurs, had no need for unions. Phoenix citizens considered union people outsiders.[4]

Traditionally well-organized groups like the printing trades had unions, even in Phoenix, but there was no such thing as a closed shop, where union membership was necessary to secure employment. Angela Hammer, a pioneer female printer in Arizona, learned typesetting in her teens in Phoenix and wondered at the hostility of union typesetters upset with her working part time. In her autobiography she explains her ignorance of the situation and wishes someone had explained the union position to her. Later, as owner of Messinger Printing, she was remembered favorably by members of the printing unions as a fair and reasonable employer.[5]

## BEFORE WORLD WAR II

The nationwide reaction to union influence after World War I, resulting in yellow-dog contracts and the American plan, found acceptance in conservative Phoenix. A yellow-dog contract forbade union membership to any potential employee. Together with blacklisting, an illegal practice by which employers exchanged names and descriptions of potential troublemakers and agreed not to hire them, these contracts intended to make union membership such a liability that no one would join. The American plan (whose name subtly suggests a bargain: in hotel management, the American plan includes meals, while the European plan does not) promoted an open shop. In a closed or union shop, all employees who were not union members had to join a union within a set time limit. This greatly increased the union's power. An open shop allowed both union and nonunion employees. The presence of nonunion employees reduced the bargaining efficiency of the union members to the advantage of the employers. Yellow-dog contracts eased union members out of the shop and, ideally, out of the bargaining picture. Arguing that each worker should be free to join or not to join a union, anti-union people considered closed shops a limit on the workers' freedom of choice. Union organizers, on the other hand, felt that unorganized workers had no choice but to work under conditions and wages set by the employers, a situation equally in violation of freedom. With superior public-relations sense, the anti-union side grasped the patriotic theme for their own; theirs was the American plan. They fought "against the infiltration of subversive doctrines . . . to combat the dictatorship of individuals and groups."[6]

Attempts to organize by those connected with food production made Phoenix suddenly aware of "subversive doctrines." To counter labor efforts, Associated Farmers of California was created in 1938; its first president was Kemper Marley, at that time a cattleman. The organization's aim, couched in lofty phrases, was to counter any power organized labor might be able to raise.[7]

The rather direct methods used by both Associated Farmers of California and its sister organization in Arizona came under the investigative eye of the U.S. Senate's La Follette Committee in 1940. Early in February of that year the committee subpoenaed records that indicated organizational ties between the two farmer groups despite their denials. Sums of money allegedly donated to wreck unions were disclosed, and Kemper Marley himself was summoned before an inquisitive Senator Thomas.[8] While the *Arizona Labor Journal* pointed out the existence of a "sample copy of an ordinance presented to the city commission of Phoenix like one in Los Angeles," the entire investigation was not considered worthy of coverage by the city's leading paper, the *Arizona Republic*.[9]

Five years earlier, the National Labor Relations Act, also known as the Wagner Act, had given unions a legitimacy they had not possessed before. It extended the protection of government to unions

by encouraging the practice and procedure of collective bargaining and by protecting the exercise by workers of full freedom of association, self-organization, and designation of representatives of their own choosing, for the purpose of negotiating the terms and conditions of their employment or other mutual aid or protection.[10]

Not only did federal legislation aid the cause of organized labor, but even the Supreme Court reversed its usual probusiness stand; on the repressive *Truax* v. *Corrigan* decision of 1921, Alfred H. Kelly and

Winifred A. Harbison observed that "within a generation . . . the Court was to hold that the right to engage in peaceful picketing was guaranteed by the Fourteenth Amendment."[11] The Fourteenth Amendment was the same amendment called up in the original judgment.

Although the full scope of this federal action did not affect Phoenix to the extent that it did the big manufacturing centers of the East, it created a more favorable climate for organized labor. Even more influential was the election of Populist Gov. Sidney Osborn in 1940, a member of one of Phoenix's original families. Like Governor Hunt, Osborn was sympathetic to unions. He was quoted as saying, "When I am in the house of labor, I am in the house of friends."[12] M. A. DeFrance, active in the union movement at that time, remembered Governor Osborn as being helpful to his cause. Said DeFrance: "He did anything that we wanted to ask for, I think, within reason. I don't think . . . we ever asked anything unreasonable . . . that's all we ever asked of any governor, was . . . a fair shake."[13]

The labor movement began to feel its power. According to Max Faulkner, even the smaller organizations could brag that "unions were strong; it [membership] was one-hundred percent before right to work." Even allowing for nostalgia, the might of the movement early in the decade must be admitted.[14] The majority of businessmen were a-union or anti-union in sentiment. Those who viewed the unions as weak were indifferent; those who recognized their potential were opposed to them. "There were unions, oh yes," remembered an early contractor, "but . . . most of the work was open shop; we didn't care whether our men carried a union card or not . . . there was no problem, no labor contracts."[15]

In 1940 and 1941, the *Arizona Labor Journal* could recite a litany of old Phoenix firms that signed contracts, including Valley of the Sun Studio (owned by visionary S. B. B. Cudia), which signed in August 1940, and the Tovrea Meat Packing Company, which signed in December of that year. Bayless Markets offered to lead the crusade for open shops in June of 1940. The Associated Farmers of Arizona backed Bayless up, but its injunction was dissolved a week later. Early the next year, Bayless signed a contract with the union.[16]

## WORLD WAR II: CHANGE AND GROWTH

Pearl Harbor and the resulting war caught Phoenix as unaware as the rest of the nation. Many of its existing industries were converted to war production and new plants also appeared. A parallel activity occurred in the military sphere: Luke Field, named for the Phoenix-born "balloon buster" hero of World War I, soon constituted one of a ring of bases around the city. Construction workers, factory workers, soldiers, and airmen flocked to Phoenix.

Along with the increasing number of jobs brought to Arizona by the war effort, higher wages benefited the state's workers. A War Labor Board ruling placed Arizona in the California Labor Market Area and raised the wages of people working under contract for the government to the California level.[17] Former AFL Secretary-Treasurer Wade Church considered the ruling a major achievement for labor during the war years:

The War Labor Board had broken out "labor market areas," they called it, and it included California and parts of Nevada . . . but Arizona wasn't in it; so I set about, with the help of Dean Sisk (Secretary-Treasurer of the AFL at the time) to have Arizona included in the California Labor Market Area. . . . I went before the war Labor Board and broke it. So the laborers came in and then the painters and the carpenters—finally the whole thing was thrown in, virtually with California.

At the time of the ruling, Church was personnel director for Atkinson-Kier Construction Company, which was heavily involved in government war contracts. He considered his move to the staff of the AFL in February 1943 inevitable because he was quite knowledgeable about the labor movement and its problems. He was interested in public relations and political lobbying—then, as now, primary concerns of the AFL. Individual unions and their locals, by contrast, concentrated on recruiting, collective bargaining, and settling grievances.[18]

Church increasingly saw organized labor's problems as public relations oriented. He admitted that labor presented a "very, very poor image." To remedy the image problem, he became an active member of nearly forty organizations—everything from the Red Cross and United Fund to the Boy Scouts. "I would serve for a while and then I'd get someone else in the labor movement to take over as representing the labor movement." This, he said, "got labor involved with the community in order to build a sound image of contributing and being part of the community."[19]

Elected president of the AFL in March 1943, Church also became editor of the *Arizona Labor Journal*. Among the oldest weeklies in the state, the *Journal* had varied in quality under a succession of editors. Church planned to upgrade the paper and use it as a tool to interest union people in political activity. He hoped to carry some of the more liberal syndicated columns, but he soon learned that the *Arizona Republic* had exclusive rights to them in the Phoenix area. Church asked Wes Knorpp of the *Republic* why the newspaper subscribed to the columns but never printed them. Knorpp responded, "Why do you suppose we have them? So that you can't use them."[20]

The AFL offered support to John Boettiger in 1946 when he attempted to change the *Phoenix Shopping News* from a weekly advertising paper to a daily newspaper in competition with the *Republic*. Boettiger, who tried to buck an established business elite, also was plagued with personal problems and the struggle for survival in a distinctly conservative climate was too much for him. His *Arizona Times* proved to be unsuccessful.[21]

## MINORITY MEMBERSHIP

Among the problems that beset organized labor in the forties was racial prejudice. The social patterns that routinely excluded blacks, Mexicans, and, to a lesser degree, Asians from education, housing, and social activity existed to a certain extent for union members. Barriers to ethnic membership in unions harmed the unions as much as the minorities. Since they were unorganized, minorities existed as an alternative labor pool. Their lower standard of living and willingness to work for lower wages was a rebuke to the goals the labor movement had articulated for all workers.

Yet, as in many other parts of the nation, it was almost impossible for blacks to join trade unions. One of the rules that kept them out stated that a prospective member had to have either three vouchers from union members or have a father in the union. Like a feudal guild, this arrangement kept trades in families and limited the number of new tradesmen, black or white, available. One determined black bricklayer left sunny Phoenix to seek work in snowbound Flagstaff. Of the few bricklayers in the northern town, even fewer were willing to work at jobs during the winter, when a workweek might total three days. Once he had been admitted to the bricklayers' union in Flagstaff, the frozen union member presented his card at the Phoenix local, which had no choice but to admit him.[22]

Union members acknowledged the problem. Said M. A. DeFrance: "We've been as guilty as anyone else of discrimination . . . although we, I think, changed more rapidly than anyone else in recognizing . . . that it was wrong and had to be corrected."[23] Wade Church was in the forefront of this battle. In *Arizona Labor Journal* editorials, he frequently blasted minority prejudice as a danger for the unity of the labor movement as well as being immoral and unpatriotic. Both Church and his successor, Elmer Vickers, were "advocates for that change, early. . . . They spoke for all of labor." Still, unions were slow to respond; it was 1956 before the bricklayers admitted blacks in Phoenix.[24]

## POSTWAR CHALLENGES

The end of World War II brought drastic changes to the Phoenix economy. The end of war-matériel production, the closing of military bases, the return of veterans, and the readjustment of the role of the working woman—all represented problems the city and its population had to face. As early as 1943 the *Arizona Labor Journal* commented editorially that planning should be undertaken to secure postwar prosperity so that Phoenix war plants would continue operation after the conflict had been won. To facilitate this strategy, in January 1946 the Labor Veterans' Job Group was formed. Ross Goodwin, formerly president of the Phoenix Central Labor Council, was appointed president.[25]

Despite heroic efforts on the part of both labor and management, there were simply more workers than jobs. Union members frequently were juggled about to spread what work there was as equally as possible. If unions refused to take on new members when there was not enough work for the existing membership, job seekers became doubly bitter because belonging to a union was essential for many positions.

Many believed the right-to-work movement was born to curb abuses in the labor movement. Others maintained that antilabor forces turned a period of economic instability in a basically conservative area to their political and financial advantage. The right-to-work issue presented the major crisis to organized labor in Phoenix. Until it arose, statutes and judicial decisions, city-state and state-federal power struggles, and disputes

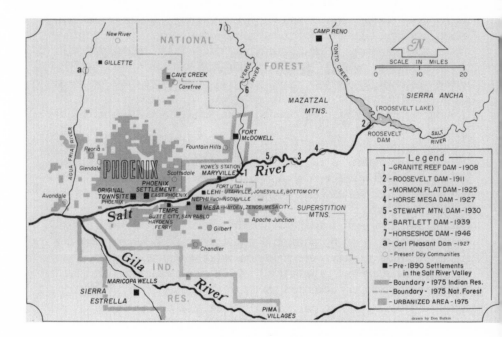

Salt River Valley Irrigation System as of 1975. Reproduced from *The Journal of Arizona History*, 18.3 (Autumn, 1977).

within the unions all followed the seesaw of progressive-conservative growth-recession, mirroring the city's own history.

The Phoenix Chamber of Commerce, since its earliest days as the Phoenix Board of Trade, did yeoman duty as a booster organization for city growth. Its members saw tremendous advantages in attracting eastern money, including federal funds. Roosevelt Dam, one of the earliest federally financed projects of its kind, was strongly endorsed by members of the Phoenix business community. In the early forties, the spiritual descendants of those early entrepreneurs encouraged valuable military installations to settle in the Salt River Valley. They reasoned that the good flying climate and flat land for runways augured well for Phoenix as a home for the young air corps. The ring of air bases and training fields they attracted paid off handsomely for the original effort. Between 1940 and 1950, the population of Phoenix doubled; the population of the valley in general increased even more.[26]

New business came to Phoenix partly as a result of military development. Defense plants found a good supply of skilled workers; many potential employees had come to the area for health reasons, and the start of new factories attracted many more. For these new Phoenicians, housing was constructed, bus lines were routed, and city services were expanded. Even under wartime restrictions Phoenix grew. That growth was, to a large extent, due to the planning of such people as the members of the chamber of commerce.

However, powerful unions to match the dimensions of the new growth did not fit into the chamber's plans. John Mills, of the old and famous Westward Ho Hotel, expressed the view of many businessmen:

We've never been an enthusiastic supporter of the unions as they're being operated. We tried to pay the top wages and treat our employees right, and we didn't think it was necessary for them—for the employees—to pay tribute to the union in order to keep a job, and I was quite active in helping to pass the right-to-work law anywhere where the employer was determined to treat the employees right.[27]

Others echoed these sentiments in rural parts of the state, so the logical way to prevent organized labor from becoming a serious problem was to act at the state level. In 1945, bills introduced in both houses of the legislature guaranteed that a person would not have to join a union in order to hold a job. Norman Fain of Prescott, a rancher, sponsored the Senate bill, urged to do so by I. M. Clausen, a prominent member of the Associated Farmers of Arizona. Fain did not think the bill was controversial and felt it would be passed in a week.[28]

In debate at hearings of the Senate Judiciary Committee, serious divisions of opinion on the matter became evident. Wade Church spoke for labor in opposition to Fain's Senate Bill 61 and pointed out the hardships such legislation would cause for organized labor. He also accused the sponsors of being influenced by a rightist group from Texas called Christian Americans. Church later recalled the battle: "I remember when the people came in from Texas and distributed those right-to-work bills to the legislature." He admitted to the union's plight: "When you say people should have the right to work, it's like coming out for motherhood, or babies, or baths, or something like that . . . you can't argue that everyone doesn't have a right to work, but, you see, they were clever enough to choose that title, so we had a bitter deal."[29]

Fain and Sen. Dan Angius, who sponsored a similar bill, were quick in their denials of outside influence. They were quoted in Michael S. Wade's *The Bitter Issue* as saying: "Despite the Christian American Association's possible attempt, there is no evidence that it was source of, or had any influence whatsoever on, the Right to Work legislation in Arizona."[30]

Considerable organized support was rallied in favor of the bills, but the bills soon encountered political trouble. After much acrimonious debate and parliamentary sidestepping, Fain's bill was killed. Strong labor influence in the Democratic party, under the leadership of Governor Osborn, won the first round of the fight.

In 1946 a new effort was launched by a different group with new tactics. An initiative petition was filed to put a constitutional amendment on the ballot. The amendment was worded in approximately the same way as Senator Fain's doomed bill. The group behind the petition drive consisted of a former serviceman and five of his employees. Herbert M. Williams had lost a bid in a construction job because his men could not get into unions; they could not be hired without union cards. The organization they formed was called the Veterans' Right to Work Committee and it became a very powerful and successful political organization.[31]

Armed with its inspiring name and an exciting cause, the committee attracted politically astute men who would become important forces in Arizona's government. John Rhodes moved from membership in the committee to membership in the U.S. House of Representatives. Guy Stillman worked on the committee and later became Democratic national committeeman for Arizona. Barry Goldwater combined his right-to-work experience with his prominent family name and rose to the U.S. Senate.[32]

While these three leaders were indeed veterans of World War II, the committee was by no means limited to former servicemen. The committee's name was, however, often linked with the proposed amendment. Many union members who had also served in the war resented the monopoly on military experience the opposition claimed. This was only one of several defensive stands the union took.

As the pro and anti forces battled over right to work in Arizona, organized labor nationwide suffered a great deal of bad publicity. There were several strikes in 1946. The image of John L. Lewis defying President Harry S Truman and threatening to cripple the nation by closing down the coal mines drove many uncommitted Americans away from labor's banner. Each alleged abuse in organized labor was pointed out by a press largely controlled by business interests. While no union leaders in Phoenix accepted the standards set by eastern racketeers, the Veterans' Right to Work Committee was quick to point out that they might, given the chance. In reality the union movement in Phoenix was more fragmented than monolithic. Nowhere was this more obvious than in the case of the Culinary Workers Union, which rebelled against the measured low-profile strategy favored by the majority of the unionists.

D. A. Baldwin, head of the Culinary Workers Union, was a controversial figure. "He was a power," recalls Wade Church. "He was a wild one." Because he was an aggressive organizer, Baldwin's enthusiasm was perhaps excessive for a conservative southwestern town like Phoenix. He was "strike happy."

In the middle of the most heated labor controversy of the decade, Baldwin called a strike at the Westward Ho Hotel, a bastion of conservatism in Phoenix at the time. This was a tactical error, according to DeFrance: "He struck some of the largest hotels and resort places, where the patrons . . . care no more about a picket line out in front . . . than the man in the moon . . . they weren't our kind of people. Instead of getting agreements with restaurants who . . . had a lot of union people patronizing them, he struck these big ones first. Well, it went down the drain, that's all." DeFrance even blamed Baldwin for passage of the right-to-work law in Arizona: "Before it was all over, there was hardly anything left. Many people blamed Don Baldwin for the enactment of the right to work law . . . he rubbed people the wrong way so much."[34] The strike was unsuccessful, and it caused hard feelings in and out of the unions.

Meanwhile, the Veterans' Right-to-Work Committee forged ahead, with willing workers pouring time, talent, and money into a media program that presented them as moderates—not in favor of prohibiting unions, but, rather, in favor of curbing excess. The union stand, as a result, took a defensive tone. Feeling cornered, the unions overreacted. While the opposition attempted to sound rational, labor's stand approached paranoia: an editorial in the *Arizona Labor Journal* spoke of "the right to starve."[35]

In March 1946, the state AFL called a special convention of members to rally forces for the battle. In addition to continuing efforts to find jobs for returning veterans and to unite politically, convention delegates proposed to abolish the state sales tax by an initiative. Ray Busey, later Phoenix mayor and a frequent defender of the union position, called the sales tax initiative labor's answer to right to work.[36]

Far more memorable than these positive steps were the heavy-handed messages on the radio, in the press, and in pamphlets. The war of words raged hotter and hotter as election day approached. Both sides tried to sway voters with entreaties to the flag, democracy, the American way, and survival itself. When the smoke cleared, organized labor found itself thoroughly defeated. The *Arizona Labor Journal* handled the defeat in its usual understated way: "Big Employers Succeed in First Attempt To Starve the Workers of Arizona."[37]

It was intended at first that the new right-to-work amendment should stand alone; court injunctions could be used to enforce it. It soon became clear, however, that organized labor and its friends hardly considered the war over. Enabling legislation would be necessary if the amendment were to be effective. In February 1947, Sen. Dan Angius (still antilabor) introduced Senate Bill 65, which not only put teeth into the amendment but contained an emergency clause. Ordinary bills became effective ninety days after receiving the governor's signature. The emergency clause would have made the bill effective immediately after it left the governor's desk. Although the emergency clause was dropped, the bill and its twin in the House, unlike Fain's earlier bill in a much different Senate, sailed through triumphantly and was reluctantly signed by Governor Osborn.

In an effort to regain the initiative, unions circulated petitions to have the bill placed on the November ballot for a vote by the citizenry at large. This gave them one more chance. At the very least, it delayed the law's implementation until after the election.[38]

With substantial money and effort put forth on both sides, another media battle was launched. Once again labor found itself on the defensive. Union people united in their conviction that the Phoenix press was hostile:

They always called us 'labor goons' and 'Gum bosses.' . . . we're not the bosses, they're the bosses . . . that's the kind of tactics they used, and, of course, labor's always in an adversary position . . . we don't control or have any say-so over the media. We're gonna get the black eye, if its possible to get it.[39]

Speaking of a later decade, Darwin Aycock said of Phoenix Newspapers Incorporated, publisher of the *Republic* and *Gazette*, that "it set a tone for the media in this area . . . as a result, it makes it difficult for us to do anything."[40]

The tragic loss of Governor Osborn dealt another blow to organized labor. Throughout a long and painful illness, he had valiantly struggled to defend the rights of workers. His death in 1948, combined with a deteriorating image both locally and nationally, led to a disappointing election day for labor. Remarked the *Arizona Labor Journal*: "Voters, Deceived by Lies of Senate Bill Backers, Toss Workers to Wolves."[41]

One result of this substantial defeat for organized labor was an agonizing reappraisal of its relationship with the Democratic party. Without the liberal leadership of Osborn, or possibly because of a genuine conservative swing on the part of the electorate, the Democratic party found itself more comfortable in the company of the Republicans than the unions. Organized labor made a practice, from this point, to choose its friends by their deeds and not by their labels.

On the city level, organized labor made every attempt to hold its own. Without the legal sanctions for union shops, however, recruiting was difficult, and many of the larger unions had difficulty maintaining their rolls. The Culinary Workers, after the Westward Ho strike, lost appreciable membership. In general, organized labor limped into the fifties. Deprived of its usual organizational tools, the labor movement pondered new methods as it faced a new decade.[42]

## CHAPTER THIRTEEN

# Public Transportation and Streets in Phoenix, 1950–1980

## BY KEVIN R. McCAULEY

ANY analysis of the last thirty years of transportation in Phoenix could begin with this question: What factors contributed to the situation as it existed in 1950? Several points can be made about the attitudes and policies of the city commission before 1950. First, the governing bodies of the city, whether the old common council or the city commission, were very much concerned with the issue of paved streets. To a large degree, this comprised the extent of city transportation planning. Planners exhibited little concern about a transportation system, other than improving the major streets, the streetcars, and later the buses. This is hardly startling, considering that the city of Phoenix encompassed only seventeen square miles and had a population of about one hundred thousand in 1950. Few perceived a need for anything beyond a good system of arterial roads, a small public transportation system, and rudimentary controls to ensure the smooth movement of traffic.

Even given such simple needs, implementation was still a problem. Before 1960 the city used the improvement district method for street paving, whereby property owners formed a paving-improvement district. Once 51 percent of the property owners signed a petition requesting paving, the process could begin. The method proved slow. It featured an inherently complex process that allowed several opportunities for petitioners or nonpetitioners to appear before the city commission to voice complaints. In addition, both the Great Depression and World War II had a retarding effect on the paving process, with the former causing a lack of capital and the latter creating severe manpower and material shortages. Furthermore, because city government mixed politics and patronage, the streets division of the Public Works Department was inefficient, spending most of its time sprinkling water on the streets to keep down the dust as late as 1950.

James Stokely, a former supervisor of the Street Maintenance Division, describes Phoenix's street situation as it appeared around 1950:

Developers were permitted to put down just about any kind of a pavement that they could afford and still sell the homeowners. So, they would put down just a very minimum construction of street surface and it looked good for maybe two or three years, and the homeowner bought the home. . . .

In addition to new development, there were miles and miles of unimproved streets that were being used for traffic. So [C.V.] Cherry [the head of Street Maintenance], pretty much on his own, developed this street oiling policy and with his workforce was able to develop quite an efficient system of grading the dirt roads and applying the road oil. They [Street Maintenance] would bust out like a bunch of bees. . . . Once a year almost every unimproved street in the city was plowed up and re-oiled.[1]

Obviously, the Public Works Department, of which Street Maintenance was a division, had neither the resources nor the workers to keep up with the rapid growth of Phoenix. Formation of improvement districts became the initiative of property owners; the city did very little soliciting of improvement districts. In this respect, the city was at the mercy of the property owners; without the consent of 51 percent of them, the area went unimproved. This situation remained in effect until 1960.

## THE FIRST MASTER STREET PLAN

Recognizing that the street situation was approaching crisis proportions, the city issued its first long-range transportation plan, titled *Master Street Plan* and compiled by the city planning commission, in May 1949. This twelve-year blueprint to promote orderly growth within the city limits featured as its major element a plan for major thoroughfares. In the plan, Twenty-fifth Avenue, Twentieth Street, and Madison and Jefferson streets would be converted into controlled-access roads to facilitate traffic movement. The plan suggested the widening of other major streets, such as Grand, Central and Van Buren avenues and Buckeye Road, and the use of such innovations as synchronized traffic lights, reverse-lane movements, and prohibition of left turns at certain hours. The plan also proposed the separation of Roosevelt Street into a six-lane highway, with a 125-foot right-of-way and interchanges every half-mile—a forerunner of the Papago Freeway. Finally, the plan proposed making both Jefferson and Madison into one-way streets.[2]

For neighborhood and collector streets, the city commission recommended changes in the zoning ordinance to prevent building encroachment onto needed right-of-way and to establish a more vigorous use of the city's power of eminent domain to acquire right-of-way. The new zoning ordinance also favored a more aggressive campaign to solicit right-of-way donations.

Total cost of the package was $33 million, with $16.8 million to be applied within the city limits (roughly from Buckeye Road on the south to Indian School Road on the north to Twenty-eighth Street on the east to Twenty-fifth Avenue on the west). Construction of the major thoroughfare system would cost $9.7 million, of which only $1.4 million was then available. The city commission saw the need to obtain federal aid and a larger share of the state gasoline tax and highway users tax. It noted that although the city accounted for 25 percent of Maricopa County's automobile registration, it received only 7 percent of the state gasoline tax. The thoroughfare program carried a price tag of $7.1 million, which completed the $16.8 million total figure, but since property owners could be assessed for improvements for this class of streets, the planners showed little concern for sufficient revenues. With the master street plan, the city commission suggested that the city's transportation needs would be taken care of for at least the next decade.[3]

The 1949 *Master Street Plan* was the work of the pre–Charter Government city commission, and only parts of it made the transition with the change of government in April 1950. For example, when consultant Wilber Smith presented his "Major Street and Highway Plan" in 1960, he duplicated to a large extent the work of the 1949 study, calling for the Papago Freeway between McDowell and Roosevelt, the Squaw Peak Freeway at approximately Twentieth Street, and the Black Canyon Freeway, already under construction, at Twenty-third Avenue. This compared favorably with the controlled-access roads at Roosevelt, Twentieth Street, and Twenty-fifth Avenue provided for in the 1949 plan. The city, however, took some of Smith's other recommendations to heart. Jefferson and Washington streets were converted into one-way streets on May 14, 1952, and the left-turn program was begun August 1, 1953. The city ignored the reverse-lane recommendation until January 19, 1965, when it finally converted Fifteenth Avenue.[4]

## PLANNING FOR A HIGHWAY

Events moved slowly until the passage of a new federal highway law in 1956. This major piece of legislation proposed forty-one thousand miles of road for national-defense purposes to link a large percentage of cities with populations exceeding fifty thousand. Most important, it increased the federal share of the construction cost of such roads to 90 percent. The Federal Highway Act of 1956 was highly significant for Arizona, whose small population would have difficulty just matching the remaining 10 percent. Under existing law, Arizona could designate 8 percent of its roads eligible for federal highway aid, amounting to about two thousand miles of roadway in the state.[5]

Shortly thereafter, the city issued a document titled *Better Roads for Tomorrow*, a huge origin-destination type of study. The study demonstrated that while car ownership and average daily trips were up 152 percent and 49 percent, respectively, travel into the central business district (CBD) had declined 64 percent in the same period. This decline was considered by some as a harbinger of the CBD's decline and had a substantial effect on policy decisions concerning the fate of the inner city freeway.[6]

On February 28, 1957, the *Arizona Republic* published an article on the state's freeway plan for Phoenix with a map showing the

---

approximate location of projected developments making up the proposed $40 million Phoenix area highway improvement program, subject of a public hearing yesterday, during which it was assailed—principally by motel interests—but supported by other groups and individuals. . . . [The plan] contemplated sixty-five miles of four to six lane super highways, with traffic interchanges every mile, or less in the Phoenix area, most of which would be controlled access routes. [The plan] features development of the Black Canyon Highway from Skunk Creek into Phoenix; building of the Durango Street "through traffic" bypass south of the city . . . building of a Lincoln-Grant truck route to serve a large industrial area; and development of a new route connecting with U.S. 80 near Litchfield Road and leading to a junction with the Durango Street route.[7]

The city purchased the right-of-way for the Grant-Lincoln trafficway and right-of-way for what was then known as the Phoenix Expressway, the section of highway coming south and then east off Black Canyon Highway, which was known by the 1980s as the Maricopa Freeway. The *Republic* reported in October that fifty-nine parcels had been purchased at a cost of $442,323 for the latter road, with the city responsible for $123,983 of the total. The federal government assumed the remainder because the Phoenix Expressway was to be part of the Interstate Highway System. In March 1958 the Maricopa County Superior Court settled the right-of-way for the Grant-Lincoln trafficway, and in August the city awarded the contract for its construction to the Mohamed Earth Moving Company, which entered a low bid of $339,199.[8]

A traffic study titled *Major Street and Highway Plan for the Phoenix Urban Area* appeared in November 1959. Wilber Smith and Associates of San Francisco compiled this ambitious regional proposal, but it was considered somewhat extravagant for the budgets of the cities involved. Sam Mardian, elected mayor in 1960, recalled that Phoenix had problems obtaining a fair share of the state gasoline tax for its street and highway construction and maintenance programs. Frustrated in its attempts to secure more revenue from the state, the city turned its attention to improving the performance of the Street Maintenance Division. James Stokely noted that after 1960 the city "woke up" to the need for setting pavement standards and getting the county to take responsibility for requiring improvement districts.[9]

Another major breakthrough occurred on October 25, 1960, when the council adopted Resolution No. 10592, which changed the policy on improvement districts. According to Mardian, the legislature refused to put up thirty thousand dollars to widen McDowell Street. But since the city had to find the money available, primarily through gasoline taxes, to go ahead with the project, "it accelerated the street improvement program."[10]

The wisdom of the city's transportation policies during this time can be viewed through the perspective of the 1980s. Had Phoenix not hesitated during those ten years and had it begun its program in 1949 as recommended, the later transportation picture might have looked less grim. If work had begun and right-of-way had been purchased, the city would have been in a position to take immediate advantage of the Federal Highway Act of 1956.

## RAISING REVENUES FOR A FREEWAY

More gloomy news came with publication of the 1961 Street Needs Study. It made some salient points about the condition of the streets and the city's financial abilities to deal with the situation:

1. Freeway costs were estimated at $111.9 million, . . . [and it would] require 82 years to correct existing deficiencies in the streets and to construct the Papago, Squaw Peak, and Paradise portions of the freeway system.
2. The projected deficit for 1980 for freeways and all streets in the city was $338.8 million. . . . Based on an annual expenditure of $1.2 million, the city was short $5.6 million a year.

The need for the city to increase its revenues was obvious.[11]

To begin correcting this problem, the Phoenix Growth Committee recommended in May 1961 that the city designate $3 million of the total $103 million to be issued as street bonds. This was all that could be guaranteed by the city's share of existing gasoline tax revenues. But as Ed Hall, the city street improvement administrator at the time, noted, "street funds available would construct less than fifteen miles of major arterial streets and completely eliminate any city freeway right-of-way acquisition and construction during the next five years."[12]

Phoenix then turned to the legislature for an increase in the city's share of the state gasoline tax. At that time, the distribution formula provided for the state to retain 70 percent of the revenues and to give 30 percent to the counties, which then divided 10 percent proportionately among the cities within their jurisdiction. Phoenix tried unsuccessfully during the 1961 and 1962 legislative sessions to secure a three-cent county-option gasoline tax, and it needed an enabling act from the legislature permitting the residents of Maricopa County to vote on an additional countywide tax of three cents per gallon to increase revenues for implementation of the Wilber Smith plan. Legislators failed to pass such legislation during either session.

In April 1962 the city council adopted a resolution calling for state and federal construction of seventeen miles of urban freeways. The resolution also called for the state to designate portions of the Papago and Indian Bend freeways as state highways and to put them in the state's federal aid primary system. In June the Inner Loop portion of the Papago Freeway—the section of road from Black Canyon Highway east—was declared a state highway by the Arizona State Highway Commission. Indian Bend Freeway from Papago Freeway to the Superstition Freeway and the proposed Superstition Freeway were also declared state highways in the same action.

Still desperate for more revenue to improve the city's major streets and purchase advanced rights-of-way for the freeway system, the city council in October 1962 adopted an ordinance imposing a city gasoline tax of two cents per gallon. The state of Arizona, as well as several of the city's large distributors, took immediate exception, filed suit, and on January 24, 1963, the Arizona Supreme Court declared the ordinance illegal.[13]

In November 1962 the United States Bureau of Public Roads agreed to accept the Papago Inner Loop into the federal-aid primary system, making it eligible for 78 percent federal financing. At the same time, the state undertook an aerial study of the proposed freeway route, the first major step in construction of the Papago. It became increasingly obvious that the Papago would be the next freeway constructed, ostensibly to facilitate traffic movement in the CBD and perhaps help revitalize the downtown area.

Not surprisingly then, an April 1963 report titled *A Transportation Plan for Downtown* noted that the average daily traffic movements into downtown had increased 5 percent a year and that the key to revival of the CBD was more accessibility and improved functional design of the downtown area. This required, first and foremost, construction of the Papago Freeway. It also implied the need for additional parking facilities, fewer pedestrian–motor vehicle conflicts, and a residential high-rise development north of the CBD. For those most interested in the urban renewal of the CBD, this study did more than anything else to bind the two together. A rationale for the Papago Freeway, heretofore lacking, was firmly established: it would provide easy access to downtown from both the east and the west, something the Maricopa Freeway, only two and one-half miles to the south in the downtown area, failed to do. Thus the city council pressed ahead to gain approval for construction of the Papago Freeway along the Moreland Corridor route.[14]

A giant step toward eventual construction of the freeway system was taken in April 1963 when the legislature approved a penny-a-gallon increase in the state gasoline tax; 80 percent of the additional revenue was earmarked for Arizona's cities, and 20 percent went to the counties. Some estimated this would give Phoenix an additional $1.7 million for street construction in 1963, allowing construction of an additional three or four miles of arterial streets.[15]

Less than a year later, the Arizona State Highway Commission approved the proposed alignment of Papago Freeway along the Moreland Corridor. Construction cost estimates for the Inner Loop came to seventy million dollars. A month later the city revealed that the cost of Wilber Smith's major street and highway plan had grown at the rate of a million dollars a month. This development showed the lack of coordination among the street administrator's office, the zoning commission, and the Engineering Department, all of whom issued building permits.[16]

On July 10, 1964, the highway commission authorized the purchase of the first right-of-way for Papago Freeway, buying a two-hundred-foot strip of property on the northeast corner of Moreland Street and Central Avenue from developer Leonard Goldman. The commission continued to purchase most of the right-of-way for the freeway system, at least on those routes designated as state highways. Given the meager sums Phoenix had for right-of-way acquisition and the rising costs of such acquisitions, this seemed practical.

In February 1965 the freeway's eventual construction was guaranteed when the U.S. Bureau of Roads approved Papago Freeway as the new Interstate Highway System route through Phoenix (the old alignment provided for Interstate 10, coming east from Los Angeles, to run south of Buckeye Road and join the Maricopa Freeway at the Durango Bend interchange). The Papago would be the recipient of large federal appropriations, relieving some of the financial strain on the city. On the other hand, the new alignment would cost forty million dollars compared to nineteen million dollars for the Durango route, with the differences stemming from right-of-way acquisition costs. This additional difference increased substantially and made the Durango alternative look better at later dates.

More important, the Interstate designation applied only to that portion of the Papago west of Black Canyon Freeway. Accordingly, the *Phoenix Gazette* reported on a "community-wide campaign . . . to secure an interstate route designation for a 4.9 mile, $50 million stretch of the Papago Freeway through the heart of Phoenix." Again the city would gain substantial benefits.[17]

## FREEWAY OPPOSITION

Opposition to the freeway system developed in many sectors; one of the most important opposing forces was the *Arizona Republic*. Editorials portended trouble for the city in its quest for a wide base of support for the freeway system, and some predicted long delays in freeway construction. The influence of the press cannot be underestimated in a one-newspaper-publisher town like Phoenix. Whereas the city council saw an obvious need for freeways, Eugene Pulliam, owner of the *Republic*, found the country's failure to build aesthetically pleasing systems just as obvious. A growing polarization on the issue developed between the local government and the press, with their appointed battleground being the Papago Inner Loop.

For a number of years the city had issued annual studies titled *Six-Year Major Street Program*. A 1966 study typified the diversity of financing for the major street program. It said flooding that year had caused considerable damage that would require $900,000 to repair all river crossings within the city, $465,000 of which would come from federal disaster aid. The six-year program proposed thirty-nine miles of major arterial streets at a cost of $20.6 million: $12.9 million for construction, $6.7 million for right-of-way acquisition, and $896,000 for the drafting of plans. Revenue sources included $5.8 million in federal aid, $11.8 million from the major street fund, $1.13 million from the 1961 bond issue, $941,000 from the five-cent gasoline tax fund, and $640,000 from property owners for sidewalks. Studies like these allowed Phoenix to inventory its progress from year to year and demonstrate the source of funds for street improvements.[18]

The final alignment of Papago Freeway from Black Canyon Highway west to Sixty-seventh Avenue was approved by the U.S. Bureau of Roads in 1967, and right-of-way acquisition had begun. In 1968, Robert Towne, head of the state right-of-way acquisition program, reported that most of the properties awaiting acquisition had been purchased.[19]

In 1968, Arizona made public a document titled *A State-Wide Street and Highway Needs Study*. It included the recommendation that state highway user revenues be placed in one fund and that the distribution formula be changed in such a way as to allow cities to share in all highway funds, not simply gasoline tax revenues. This major policy innovation recognized that the urban areas of Arizona needed more equitable distribution of funds because of the more intensive concentration of people, and need, in the urban areas.[20]

Other recommendations from the 1968 study were more readily implemented. For example, Phoenix's 1968 Six Year Major Street Program noted that the legislature had given the Arizona Highway Department permission to establish a ten-million-dollar fund for advance purchase of right-of-way for major streets and that Phoenix was phasing out funds for this purpose.[21]

With the Papago Inner Loop segment approved for inclusion in the Interstate Highway System, the city had managed for more than eight years to convince state and federal authorities that the Interstate route should run through the heart of Phoenix. Construction costs for running the freeway through town had increased to twice the cost of running it south of the downtown area. Disruption of traffic movements in and out of the CBD for a sustained period of three to five years had not been examined. Furthermore, without a total system of freeways, the benefits of a crosstown freeway would be minimal, since it did little to facilitate north-south traffic movement. Finally, it would bring out-of-town traffic right through the center of the city, adding to the already congested rush-hour traffic peaks. The most direct benefits would seem to be accrued not by the Phoenix motorist, which was the intention from the start, but by the downtown merchant, who exerted increasingly more influence.[22]

Firm commitments for a crosstown freeway allowed the city council to turn its attention to a design. The council hired the consulting firm of Johannessen and Girard, which proposed a one-hundred-foot elevated-freeway design for the Inner Loop at a cost of $79.7 million; this compared favorably with other designs. Although one councilman protested, "Who the hell wants to live under a freeway?" support for the design was widespread. Even the Arizona Republic supported the concept, saying, "It is the sort of dynamic planning that Phoenix needs."[23] The city council approved the design on January 21, 1969, and soon thereafter Mayor Milton Graham announced that construction of the Papago Inner Loop would begin in two and one-half years.

With so much attention focused on freeways, the 1969 Street Needs Study went almost unnoticed, but it provided a yardstick measure to the progress the city had made since the 1961 study. Phoenix had actually witnessed an increase in deficient street mileage. It fell into a constant game of catch-up, a game it was unable to win. The October 1960 change in the financing method, while accelerating the program, merely allowed the city to keep pace with deficiencies. A comparison of the 1961 and 1969 street needs studies shows that in those eight years, with the help of taxpayers and property owners, Phoenix had reduced the number of deficient local and collector streets 160.4 miles, while the number of deficient major streets, financed by the city alone, had increased 1.6 miles.

Such a comparison might have caused the city council to question the wisdom of its standing policy, yet it remained unchanged.[24]

Through an advanced transportation planning team consisting of a city planner, a traffic engineer, and a city engineer, the city issued another report in 1969 titled *Mobility—Phoenix Style: Summary Report on Transportation*. It cited increased population, low density, urban sprawl, and long distances between centers of activity as the sources of transportation problems in the city. It recommended accepting the inevitability of the automobile as the main means of transportation in Phoenix and also recommended building freeways. Ultimately this report created considerable impetus for the freeway system; in effect, it stated that without the freeway system, the city's traffic problems would never be solved.[25]

Such attitudes as this one on the city's part had much to do with the formation of citizens' groups that contended more freeways were only one answer to Phoenix's transportation woes. A group called Citizens for Mass Transit against Freeways, or CMTAF, with J. B. Bowers chair and former Arizona Supreme Court Justice Renz Jennings cochair, sought to propose a mass-transit system for the valley instead of freeways, which it saw as a major contributor to air pollution.[26]

The united front for freeways showed signs of strain from without and from within. In February 1970, several members of the land transportation committee of the Phoenix Forward Task Force issued a minority report claiming their views had not been included in the majority report. The minority report suggested building a valleywide mass-transit system rather than freeways. Rapid transit, they argued, was the only answer to growing urban sprawl, traffic congestion, air pollution, and the growing immobility of the nondriver.[27]

Such opinions, which were undoubtedly in a distinct minority around Phoenix, were quickly countered. Louis C. Lagomarsino, vice-president of Johannessen and Girard, said in March that "mass transit is not a realistic answer for solving growing traffic congestion in Phoenix. . . . Freeways, such as the Papago East Freeway . . . provide a more realistic and economical answer."[28]

Although Lagomarsino had a vested interest in seeing the Papago East Freeway (as the Inner Loop was now called) built as his firm was designing it, he was certainly not alone in his opinion. A 1970 public-opinion survey found that 86 percent of the respondents saw freeways as the solution to Phoenix traffic problems, although it also showed that 53 percent of those surveyed thought a different type of transportation system would be required within the next ten or twenty years.[29]

Other studies appeared, offering mixed reports. In December 1970 the Valley Area Traffic and Transportation Study group (VATTS) issued a report titled *Transit and the Phoenix Metropolitan Area*. Although primarily a transit study, it suggested a "highway compatible system" of rapid transit, looking toward mixed transportation solutions to the valley's problems. The *1970 Six-Year Major Street Program* noted that the city was still unable to sell the remaining 960,000 dollars' worth of 1961 street bonds because of high interest rates. It also noted that in a November 1970 state election, Proposition 104 had passed, abolishing the 1952 gasoline tax distribution formula.[30]

## SUPPORT FOR THE FREEWAY

It had been ten years since the Wilber Smith plan had been adopted, and Phoenix was still without an additional mile of freeway. However, several points should be made about this lapse of time. On January 1, 1970, President Nixon signed the National Environmental Policy Act (NEPA) into law. It required an environmental-impact statement on all federal actions (including the building of freeways) that might have an adverse effect on the environment. Various city councils might have realized (but apparently did not) that the adoption of such a law would give those opposed to the freeway system a legitimate entry into the decision-making process and that the process would become much slower because of it. There also remained the matter of sufficient revenues and rising costs. While certain portions of the freeway system had been approved for federal funds, other portions were completely unfunded. On the surface, the 1960s represented Phoenix's age of consensus. When such a vacuum of interest exists, those who control the decision-making process lean heavily in the direction of their natural constituency; in the case of the Charter Government Committee, the downtown business community was the natural constituency. The decision to pursue a policy of freeway construction eventually showed the mark of Charter's influence. These groups that opposed freeways, such as CMTAF, bereft of a strong political base, were ignored.

Concern about sufficient funds to put both the major street and high-way programs into high gear continued. When asked what caused the transportation problems going into the 1970s, John Driggs, who was the mayor at the time, replied that it was a political attitude. He also cited "the historic rural domination of the Highway Commission."[31]

The *1971 Six-Year Major Street Program* provided for thirty-nine miles of streets at the cost of $32 million—almost a one-to-one ratio—for construction of major streets. Although the 1952 state gasoline tax distribution formula had been voted out, it was up to the legislature to propose a new one. Senate Bill No. 319, introduced in the 1971 session, failed to pass. Without a distribution formula, no funds could be released; therefore, Phoenix received no funds from the five-cent gasoline tax fund, from which it had been averaging a little over $1.5 million a year for the past three years. Not until 1974 did revenue from this particular source again become part of the major street construction budget.

That year the federal government began its Traffic Operations Program to Increase Capacity and Safety (TOPICS). Dan Morgan, traffic engineer, described some of the major innovations that had occurred up to this point, including a "bottleneck removal program." Another major improvement of the traffic system involved computerized signals, which "had tremendous success, probably a ten to fifteen percent increase in capacity or efficiency."[32]

By 1972 a clear line had developed over the Papago Freeway issue. In June, CMTAF released the results of a poll that showed 49 percent of the respondents thought a lawsuit should be filed against the state highway department to halt construction of the Papago and other freeways until the effects of air pollution and the cost of lost taxes could be thoroughly studied. At this time the city council was firmly profreeway and was roundly criticized for such a stance by the *Arizona Republic* in October when it suggested further delays.[33]

Phoenix newspapers seemed to be firmly against the Papago Freeway, a complete switch from their position three years earlier, when they had labeled the elevated Papago East Freeway an innovative design. Even the city planning commission got involved, challenging the council to design the city around a workable transit system rather than the other way around. Said Dwight Bushby, chair of the planning commission: "We need to look at how the city can be structured to make mass transit work and see what the cost would be."[34]

The CMTAF had been busy. Early in 1973 it filed a challenge to the final environmental statement (FES) for Papago Freeway. The Papago, CMTAF claimed, would destroy 12,357 homes and displace 31,758 people, and it further claimed that the state highway department was not offering fair market value for the homes. The CMTAF countered the FES argument that the freeway would have no significant effects on the city by claiming:

1. No data were presented on noise or air pollution to support the FES contention of no significant impact.
2. No alternative studies were done on mass transit.
3. Conflict of interest existed between the Arizona State Highway Department and the real estate interests in the city. CMTAF claimed the real reason for the freeway was pressure from a company called Litchfield Properties, who owned land around the Litchfield area.[35]

The challenge had a significant effect at the federal level. In February the Environmental Protection Agency said that the FES on Papago

Freeway, prepared by the Arizona Highway Department and Federal Highway Administration representatives and already submitted to the Federal Highway Administration in Washington, was "too narrow in scope to evaluate the long range effects of the Phoenix freeway system." This meant more delay for Papago and created a lull in which the city might reexamine its plans. The city council was pressured for a citywide vote on the proposal that Papago be added to the May 8 bond election ballot. Although city council failed to act in time to make the question an advisory vote, it decided to add a straw poll ballot on May 8, setting the stage for the first confrontation over Papago Freeway.[36]

## THE PAPAGO FREEWAY: NO, THEN YES

When the dust had settled on May 8, after almost a month of hard campaigning on both sides, the antifreeway groups had won a major victory. Approximately 58 percent of the electorate had voted against Papago. John Driggs, freeway advocate and mayor at the time, credited the antifreeway victory to the role of the newspaper. With Papago no longer a reality, even though the votes against it had been cast in a straw-poll situation, the city council adopted Resolution No. 14111, which called for abandoning the proposed Inner Loop. In January 1974, Gruen and Associates of California, a consulting firm, received a $490,000 contract to determine the best alternate route for I–10. A Maricopa Association of Government (MAG) committee recommended that the old Papago route be disqualified from further consideration as the Interstate route; it preferred to build the Interstate along the Moreland Corridor alignment as far east as Ninety-first Avenue, where it would turn south to hook up with the Maricopa Freeway.[37]

All this activity left the city of Phoenix in a very difficult position. It had spent a great deal of money on right-of-way acquisition, which now left an empty corridor along Moreland Street. John Driggs recalled that the city council attempted then to salvage the area, at least as a transportation corridor. This idea came to fruition under the succeeding city council. In December 1974, Mayor Timothy Barrow appointed the Moreland Corridor Advisory Committee, headed by architect Joseph Lort, to devise some sort of parkway plan for the corridor. In January 1975, the *Arizona Republic* reported that the parkway as proposed by the committee would cost $53.3 million in addition to the $34 million already spent in right-of-way acquisition costs for the Papago Inner Loop. Despite the cost, the parkway plan was adopted by the advisory committee on March 14, and the city council set itself to the task of finding funds to cover both right-of-way acquisition and construction costs.[38]

In February 1975, Gruen and Associates presented its report to MAG, recommending that I–10 come through Phoenix via the Durango Bend route. This nine-mile route would curve southeast from the original Papago route at Sixty-seventh Avenue and join the Maricopa Freeway at Durango Bend. The plan cost $72.7 million—the smallest estimate of five alternative routes studied by Gruen and Associates—and included $44.3 million for construction of I–10 to the Maricopa Freeway and $28.4 million for widening the Maricopa Freeway from six lanes to eight. This route also had the least adverse effect on the environment because it ran mainly through agricultural lands southwest of Phoenix. MAG formally adopted the recommendation on March 14.[39]

When the issue seemed decided, the Papago Freeway again sparked controversy. On May 8, the second anniversary of the straw-poll vote, a group called UNITE (Use Now I–10 Effectively) took out initiative petitions to put the issue of a crosstown freeway on the November 8 ballot. By July 2, UNITE had gathered 15,205 signatures; only 8,087 were necessary to place the initiative on the ballot.[40]

Meanwhile, the city council continued to support the idea of a tree-lined parkway along the Moreland Corridor. In June, U.S. Sen. Paul Fannin announced that he would seek federal funds for parkways for both Phoenix and Tucson. The newspapers again opposed the idea of a crosstown freeway along the Moreland Corridor. An October 13 editorial

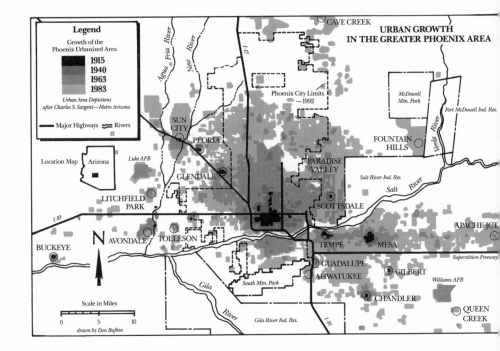

in the Phoenix *Gazette* typified the pressure brought to bear on the profreeway group by asserting that "a 'yes' vote is a vote for nothing," and, conversely, "a 'no' vote on the freeway is all it takes to clear the way for Phoenix to have the best of the situation."[41]

Despite the editorial pressure of the newspapers and continued support for a parkway along the Moreland Corridor by the city council, 54 percent of the voters approved Proposition 201 on November 5. Interestingly enough, the *Gazette* noted, eleven of the fifteen precincts along the Moreland Corridor had voted for the Papago Freeway. City Manager John Wentz believed the "residents in these precincts, more than anyone else, recognized the current traffic congestion along the corridor . . . they wanted something to be done, wanted something to happen right now, and saw the freeway as the quickest way."[42]

Phoenix resurrected the Papago Freeway. The Arizona Senate's transportation committee voted five to four to limit the new Papago Freeway to a depressed design, eliminating the elevated element which most believed was the direct cause of the 1973 defeat. A new environmental-impact statement was prepared, but CMTAF promptly filed a seven-volume challenge to it, claiming in essence that several alternate routes were less costly and had fewer environmental effects. By September the state transportation board had limited consideration of the I–10 route to two options: a $410 million Moreland Corridor route or a $61 million Durango Bend route. After three years of confusion and chaos, the matter, for the moment, had been settled.[43]

More than a year later, City Manager Marvin Andrews recommended that the city council endorse a $1.4 billion freeway system for the Phoenix metropolitan area. Basically, the plan reaffirmed the Wilber Smith plan of 1960, calling for construction of an outer beltway around the city on the north from I–10 on the west to Superstition Freeway on the east, construction of the Squaw Peak Freeway along Twentieth Street, construction of the Paradise Freeway, completion of the Hohokam Freeway into Sky Harbor International Airport, and completion of the Superstition Freeway out to Apache Junction. A $304 million plan had ballooned into a $1.4 billion plan. The city council endorsed and adopted it on December 20, 1977, with Calvin Goode the lone dissident.[44]

In April 1978 the state revealed that some money was available for highway construction and announced an $826 million five-year construction budget. Of this, $457 million was earmarked solely for construction of the Papago Freeway, representing 70 percent of all Interstate Highway System expenditures between 1979 and 1983. Despite the tremendous cost, Phoenix would have its crosstown freeway. Secretary of Transportation Brock Adams approved Papago Freeway as the official I–10 route in October 1978. He granted this designation with certain reservations:

that the freeway be realigned if archaeological sites in its path proved to be significant, that freeways be depressed, that environmental effects upon the city be minimized, that certain soundproof public-use sites be reserved, and that 15 percent of the cost of construction be contracted to minority businesses.[45]

Some believed that city officials had acted in a fiscally irresponsible fashion, proceeding to plan such a freeway in the face of spiraling costs. Out of such an attitude the alternative Phoenix Grid Plan movement was born. Dr. Robert Hurt, Phoenix dentist and one of the original group of six or so who formulated the plan, used a federal law that allowed withdrawal and substitution of already-allocated funds to apply those funds to local roads, bridges, and an outer beltway.[46]

For the first time the question of a specific alternative to the freeway system had been raised, rather than simply the question of whether to build a freeway in a particular spot. Criticism of the Phoenix Grid Plan was heavy. Ed Hall claimed it would cost "Phoenix citizens an extra $9.5 million a year to operate additional buses required by the Grid Plan." He also stated that "there would be no federal dollars to operate the additional fifty-two buses, because the city is already using the maximum available." MAG staffer Dave French claimed that a switch to the plan "would completely bog down the system, because every project would have to go through the standard federal aid process and could get so involved, it would be difficult to have all construction underway by September 1986 as required." Finally, Bill Ross, the state engineer supervising the construction of I–10, estimated that the Grid Plan would involve more than 280 separate construction contracts representing seventy different projects.[47] With such a formidable array of experts opposing the plan, few expressed surprise when the people of Phoenix voted against it by a three-to-one margin. Dr. Hurt suggested that people "were just confused" about the plan.

Although transportation planning had always been the city's strongpoint, the inability to commit plans to action became a debilitating weakness. The early result was an entire decade of inaction after the *1949 Master Street Plan*. Wilber Smith's 1960 "Major Street and Highway Plan" echoed many of the major 1949 recommendations, indicating that little had been accomplished in the period between 1949 and 1960.

Faced with an inadequate transportation system because of the inattentiveness of previous administrations, the policy makers of the 1960s tried to implement Smith's plan. Implementation efforts were hampered, however, by inadequate financing and a bureaucracy incapable of quick decision. As a result, little was accomplished to relieve the growing congestion on the roads of Phoenix. In addition, the policy makers of that time failed to recognize that their planning efforts required adaptation to the ever-changing political situation and the evolving characteristics of physical growth in Phoenix. By the early seventies, it should have occurred to those responsible for transportation planning that the *Major Street and Highway Plan* might never be fully implemented.

The 1970s brought three votes on the Papago Freeway. The inability to move forward on construction of this important segment of interstate highway appears to be caused by a lack of political leadership that was reflected in the indecision among the residents and voters of Phoenix as to the best course of action to pursue.[48]

## CHAPTER FOURTEEN

# *Conclusion*

## BY G. WESLEY JOHNSON, JR.

WE HAVE briefly explored selected themes in the modern history of Phoenix: social groups, minorities, economic development, water resources, and developments in political reform, labor, and transportation. To sum up the Phoenix experience from a different perspective, let us turn to three concepts which cut across these themes: growth (or growing) pains, uniqueness, and personality. Growing pains are typical of all great cities; in this collection we have seen the particular variety which afflicted Phoenix. The communities of the arid American West needed water, and the stories of water thirst (greed) of cities like Los Angeles are well known. Phoenix was no exception, and it was not until the tempestuous Salt River could be tamed, and a reliable source of irrigation water secured, that local farmers could succeed. This created an economic base that allowed Phoenix to become a true state-capital city, its agricultural wealth buttressed by commerce and the state government. This was the foundation for a closed society directed by an aggressive city elite, composed of locals and cosmopolitans. It was the latter, people like W. J. Murphy and his Arizona Canal, B. J. Fowler and Roosevelt Dam, and Dwight Heard and the Chicago mortgage money for valley farms, who made a difference. Their efforts helped lift Phoenix out of the ordinary and capitalize on its location near a major river, its winter climate, and its desert uniqueness—essential for later tourists and retirees.

Looking back from the era of the metropolis, it would be easy to fault these early Phoenicians for lack of vision. The reality of the early-day struggles to build the community—the Arizona Canal was dug with mule teams—and the fact that many successful local businessmen (the Shermans, the Brophys) moved to Southern California when they could suggest the difficulties of pioneering. The acquisition of the state capital for Phoenix was the single most important achievement of this pre–twentieth century period, since it brought a focal point to Phoenix growth that enabled it to surpass older Tucson within several decades. This helped Phoenix gain a spur from the Santa Fe railroad line and laid the foundation for Fowler's effort to gain federal backing for building a permanent water storage solution: Roosevelt Dam. The optimism of frontier boosterism paid off for the early Phoenicians.

Growing pains were less evident between 1910 and 1940, but during that time the foundation was laid for the post–World War II boom period. For example, Phoenix's climate came to be seen as an asset rather than a liability: the first resorts, Ingleside and San Marcos, appeared, and winter visitors now arrived on a regular basis. Many of them eventually became residents and started the pattern of retiree migrants. The 1920s witnessed the building of Phoenix's high structures, the Heard and Luhrs buildings and the Luhrs Tower, whose slender silhouette symbolized the growth from town to city. The city pushed out beyond the boundaries Sherman's electric trolley lines had set before World War I as the automobile came into full use in Phoenix. The suburban subdivisions of the 1920s, designed for a white-collar city, announced the later mass subdivisions of the 1950s, designed for a mass population newly arrived to work in the factories.

The Great Depression created a status-quo period in Phoenix, broken only in 1940 when the federal government built air bases to the east and west of Phoenix. After Pearl Harbor, the location of Phoenix inland from California provided an incentive to locate aircraft factories and support industries away from the Pacific, and Phoenix enjoyed a modest wartime boom. Airmen and war workers alike would prove to be important for Phoenix's future, since at the war's end thousands of them either returned to Phoenix or stayed on, convinced of the desert city's future.

The next decade deserved to be called the Frenzied Fifties, since it was then that the metropolis began to appear and the well-defined small city, with its distinctive downtown, gave way to never-ending rings of concentric circles that grew out from the center as suburbs were added. Eventually Glendale to the west and Scottsdale and Tempe to the east and south had to scurry to preserve their own corporate limits as Phoenix aggressively annexed new subdivisions in all directions. Even the other side of the Salt River to the south, long known as rich agricultural lands, grew as the African-American community was extended and new industrial parks were set in motion; these would transform both sides of the river into Phoenix's major industrial site. As the sixties and seventies approached, growth continued, with the most distinctive landmark in Phoenix now becoming the shopping mall. The first ones, such as Thomas Mall and Chris-Town, were viewed as logical east and west focal points to complement Park Central, the pioneer plaza which had stolen much of the thunder from downtown.

Indeed, these three major shopping malls, plus downtown, did not long remain primary destinations for Phoenix consumers. Rather, following a pattern most popularized in Southern California, minor shopping plazas emerged to service each new subdivision or tract that was added. A proliferation of such facilities forever sealed the fate of downtown, which had lost all of its department and specialty stores by the 1970s and became a center for courts, lawyers, and banks. At one level of analysis, Phoenix had entered a postindustrial phase of growth characterized particularly by a consumer society, and that particular society would be satisfied only with unlimited purchasing arenas. Indeed, a twentieth-century shootout at the O.K. Corral now took place as Texas-based 7–Eleven stores disputed terrain with Phoenix-based Circle K convenience stores.

As we have seen in this volume, these phases of growth were punctuated by important specific developments, such as gaining control of both agricultural and drinking water and developing a new form of city government that would bolster the confidence of investors—all three examples that succeeded. But in transportation, as the final essay shows, Phoenix lost at least three or more decades in developing a transportation system that came to life only in the late 1980s. The economic development of Phoenix is still in motion, reminding us that the struggle to create a foundation for eventual economic takeoff still continues. In the minds of many Phoenicians, economic greatness is still just around the corner.

These growing pains have contributed to the creation of a unique city. But how unique? Phoenix has often been lumped with other Sunbelt cities, yet in its current phase of emphasizing high-tech industries, such as electronics and computers, it is little different from Austin or Tucson. In its thrust into the retirement industry, it resembles San Diego or Tampa. In its earlier emphasis on agriculture, it resembled Los Angeles or Bakersfield. What, then, is unique about Phoenix? Even the dry climate, so touted for winter tourists, is shared by Tucson and Las Vegas. Possibly the most unusual aspects of Phoenix are its desert flora and fauna, which are part of the Sonoran Desert and which (with Tucson) do establish a unique southwestern identity. Phoenix also possesses the unique legacy of its great valleywide system of canals, a priceless asset from the Hohokam peoples and early Anglo pioneers. Therefore, it is the combination of the Sonoran desert and the irrigated green oasis that creates an unusual environment that establishes the uniqueness of Phoenix. Its setting, in a long river valley surrounded by such picturesque mountains as Camelback and Papago Park's hills, creates an unmistakable signature.

Looking beyond the setting, we find Phoenix has been slightly behind Southern California in its move toward more casual outdoor living, with comparable styles to match (the late lamented Goldwater Department Stores' "Desert Fashions"). Hence the promotion of a unique lifestyle, as seen in personal swimming pools, patios for barbecues, lanais, "Arizona rooms," furnishes another clue. Although all of the aforementioned exist in many American cities, it is the concentration and frequency which one notices in Phoenix. The city has during the past two decades also moved toward the exclusive housing development with limited access and guarded gates, a concern for privacy set in motion years earlier in the 1920s with the development of the earliest such property, Country Club Estates. This emphasis on the magnificent home in the exclusive area has meant that Phoenix lagged behind other comparable communities in creating public facilities (Encanto Park and its lagoon are an exception) until quite late when surrounding desert lands were incorporated into a municipal park system. Today a part of the landscape is the ubiquitous Mexican restaurant, but as late as the 1950s, only Jordan's on the North Central and a few others served the entire city. All of these ingredients have contributed to the development of a Phoenix lifestyle which is recognizable by even short-term visitors.

Surprising to most adopted Phoenicians is the notion that Phoenix was not a part of the old Wild West, that compared to Tombstone it was a tame community of farmers rather than a central point for the rough-and-ready Arizona frontier story. This reality gave Phoenix a different personality from Tucson (an old Spanish-Mexican town), or Tombstone and Jerome (mining towns), or Prescott (the outpost of New England). But the agricultural citizenry of Phoenix, mainly locals, was tempered with a continuous but limited number of cosmopolitans, who made the world of commerce go round and furnished a needed dynamic and many connections. The citizens from Illinois, New York, and California, three of the nation's most successful states, were in plentiful supply in settling Phoenix, and their skills provided the leadership know-how that began to separate Phoenix from other Arizona cities. Thus the attraction of well-educated, talented migrants helped create a city with an open, friendly western personality, but a city with a midwestern can-do attitude created in the 1930s during the formative years of the ruling city elite. That group, looking down upon a burgeoning city from its aerie in the Arizona Club, could see a community whose streets hosted the annual Rodeo Parade, symbol of the carefree life of the desert oasis. The isolation of Phoenix ended with World War II, of course, but this sense of separation from the big cities of the Midwest and East—symbols of crime, corruption, and dirt—was a part of the Phoenix prewar psyche. It even lasted into the late 1940s, when Phoenix won awards as the cleanest city in the United States, which, given the lack of industry and a huge population base, was probably true.

When a city metamorphoses into a metropolis, its personality is bound to change. Some observers speak of a loss of innocence for Phoenix, which came with the decline of isolation. More specifically, Phoenix lost its cleanliness with the advent of smog and industry; its universally well-kept homes gave way to square miles of empty, rotting, or ill-cared houses as more citizens sought newer abodes farther out on the desert. Not surprisingly, Phoenix by the 1980s had also lost its unique commercial identity as one business or industry after another sold out to outside firms or investors. Diamond's, Korrick's, Allison Steel, Arizona Bank, Goldwater's, the *Arizona Republic*—all became part of a long list of familiar enterprises no longer owned or headquartered by local people. A bank here, a utility there, a specialty shop elsewhere is all that remained. This created a discontinuity in commercial society and set in place a municipal personality with an instant character. Since people poured into Phoenix by the tens of thousands each year, their expectations were mainly for services to match their newfound southwestern lifestyle. The need to have an identity with the past, to become part of the Phoenix legacy, appealed to only a few newcomers, such as those who might venture to visit the Indian antiquities at the Heard Museum. For others, the attainment of a go-go "Sunbelt modern" lifestyle was reward enough.

In this volume we have explored selected subjects which shed light on the growing pains, uniqueness, and personality of twentieth-century Phoenix. We have looked at elites and minority groups to see how they both have contributed to the city's development. The old families, generation after generation, shored up a city and prepared it to enter the metropolitan era. Phoenix women early on organized into community groups and injected feminine work and energy into the building process. The Indians and Italians, diverse minorities in their own ways, were representative of other ethnics, such as the African Americans, Hispanics, and Asian Americans, who also contributed to the rise of Phoenix. We have also looked at the economic growth of Phoenix, the boosterism that succeeded, the business risks that paid off in such areas as tourism and retiree living. We have also seen the difficulties of establishing a labor movement on the Phoenix frontier.

A special note should be added about Phoenix and good government. As we have seen, the city's municipal organizations literally did not keep up with the pace of economic development and the growing sophistication needed by local government. The response was the mobilization of Phoenix elites for Charter Government, which firmly steered city hall through the decade of perhaps the city's greatest change, the 1950s, and continued to exercise influence down through the 1970s. Elite-based and sanctioned, Charter eventually outlived its early reforming usefulness, and city hall by the 1980s had become more responsive to broader community needs of diverse ethnic, economic, national-origin, and neighborhood communities. But it was precisely at the point when Charter took over at midcentury that Phoenix put behind forever the sheltered climate of localism and entered the national scene as a fast-growing metropolitan area.

Although these essays have focused on Phoenix, one should be mindful of the growth registered by other communities in the Valley of the Sun. Scottsdale in the 1950s emerged as an affluent town that battled Phoenix in the annexation wars for dominion over wealthy northeast suburbs; Tempe grew rapidly as Arizona State College was transformed into a major regional university. Glendale to the west and Chandler to the east abandoned their agricultural past to become major cities, and Mesa, originally a self-contained Mormon settlement of about three thousand during the Depression, mushroomed to more than three hundred thousand souls fifty years later. These surrounding cities played a positive role in stimulating growth of the Phoenix metropolitan region, at times upstaging the old city itself in attracting new industries and new citizens.

Phoenix has benefited from dynamic leadership and entrepreneurs willing to go for the main chance and move the city toward the twenty-first century. In this, Phoenix differs little from Dallas, Houston, or San Diego. But in the process of transformation from desert hamlet to state capital to regional metropolis, Phoenix has acquired a distinctive personality, a clear sense of uniqueness, and a set of growing pains that simply will not stop. Perhaps the next decade will see a loss of momentum, but Phoenix by the early 1990s (despite a few setbacks, such as financial stagnation and growing pollution) was still moving forward: a thrust characterized by a frenzy of commercial building in midtown to give the city a new extended skyline and by construction of the long-awaited freeways. This thrust into the next century suggests how far the village on the Rio Salado has come in the past 120 years. Unlike many other American cities, Phoenix has not yet entered a downturn phase. Reflective citizens and critics alike now ask: How long can growth continue?

## CHAPTER FIFTEEN

# A Hundred Years of Phoenix History

## BY AIMÉE DE POTTER LYKES

THE following chronology is derived from a newspaper chronology and supplementary research for the Phoenix History Project of the Arizona Historical Society.

### The Territorial Years

1865    J. Y. T. Smith sets up camp near the Salt River (about where Sky Harbor Airport would be) to cut wild hay for U.S. Army horses at Fort McDowell. The only white man in the valley, he lays out a wagon road to the fort.

1867    A former Confederate soldier from Georgia, John ("Jack") Swilling, hauls galleta hay for Smith. He sees ancient canal tracings and organizes the Irrigation Canal Company in Wickenburg.

1868    U.S. surveyors Wilfred F. and George P. Ingalls survey the Salt River Valley. Two and three-fourths miles of Swilling's Ditch are completed; ground is broken for cultivation. Yavapai County forms an election precinct of about fifty persons, Phoenix, apparently named by Englishman Brian P. D. ("Darrell") Duppa of Swilling's company. The first Anglo woman, Mary Adeline Gray, arrives with her husband, Columbus.

1870    Darrell Duppa, John Moore, and Martin Griffin are appointed to choose a townsite, later the center of Phoenix. The site is accepted at a meeting on October 20, thereafter the city's birthday.

1871    Part of Yavapai County becomes Maricopa County, with Phoenix the county seat. William Hancock's survey shows a town one by one-half miles; its niney-eight blocks contain about five hundred people, half of whom are Mexican American.

1872    A school district, organized May 21, builds an adobe schoolhouse for about thirty children.

1873  Manano Tisnado is lynched (by hanging) for cow stealing and murder. Helling's Mill, Phoenix's first industry, claims to produce one thousand bags of flour an hour. Phoenix is a distribution point for mining products and for farm products going north.

1878  Phoenix's population is reported to be about fifteen hundred, half Mexican American. There are more than ten stores. The *Salt River Herald* newspaper, to become the *Phoenix Herald*, starts publication.

1879  The Southern Pacific through line arrives in Maricopa. The Bank of Arizona, headquartered in Prescott, opens a Phoenix branch. Murderers Keller and McCloskey are lynched (hanged) August 22.

1880  The Republican and Democratic territorial conventions are held in Phoenix. Farmers form a union to uphold wheat and barley prices, which fall anyway.

1881  Immigrants pour into Phoenix, incorporated by the Territorial Legislature on February 25. John T. Alsap is elected first mayor. The first ordinance specifies the city seal, taxes, and license fees. The Phoenix Rangers are organized against the Apaches in Tonto Basin.

1882  Disincorporation looms as the new city fails to develop adequate revenue. Almost all ordinances are repealed, but new ones show incorporation is needed to centralize canals, move the central cemetery, and provide sanitation and fire and police protection. The *Gazette* now offers a Democratic alternative to the *Herald*.

1883  The Phoenix Mercantile Association is formed to protect the credit system. Cotton has come to the valley, and fruit culture increases.

1884  The fraudulent Peralta-Reavis land-grant claim arouses Phoenicians to unite in a land league against it. Valley Bank organizes with fifty thousand dollars capital. The territorial fairs, held in Phoenix, begin.

1885  The first election is held under a new city charter. The Arizona Canal is completed in June. Livestock raising is becoming important.

1886  Rains continue to swell the Salt River seasonally and impede transportation; roads are poor. The city, now out of debt, starts organizing a fire department. The territorial insane asylum, considered a financial plum for Phoenix, is completed northeast of Phoenix. Governor Zulick, in his annual report, proposes water storage in the mountains.

1887  C. W. Strauss is granted a franchise for a telephone line. The city health department is created. The Maricopa and Phoenix Railroad arrives in Phoenix. M. E. Collins and M. H. Sherman's Arizona Improvement Company puts the first mule-drawn street railway car on line. Phoenix has three banks. The canals north of the Salt River are now all in one system.

1888   City hall is completed. The chamber of commerce is organized.

1889   The territorial capital is moved from Prescott to Phoenix. Phoenix's first sewer franchise is granted; a water system is being built. The U.S. Committee on Irrigation and Reclamation, surveying western states, visits Phoenix. Phoenix merchants organize against railroad freight charges.

1890   Use of electric lights is increasing. Floods cut telegraph wires and close the railroad bridge to Tempe. Walnut Grove Dam, ninety-five miles northwest of Phoenix, bursts, killing more than fifty people. Citrus and cattle production continue to grow. The U.S. census is protested as counting only those within the corporate city: 3,100.

1891   Floods wash out the railroad bridge to Tempe. Bell Telephone puts up a Phoenix system in June. The state constitutional convention meets in Phoenix; its constitution is approved in the territory and by Phoenix but fails in Congress.

1892   Phoenix issues electric, railway, sewer, water, and gas franchises. The Palo Alto and Capitol additions develop the city's outskirts. The statehood movement continues. A mass meeting on the national issue of the silver standard is held in December.

1893   The city contracts for electric lights; the first electric street-railway car appears. The chamber of commerce is emerging as a strong political force. Linville and Montgomery additions are developed.

1894   A city ordinance confines prostitution to Block 41. The vote in the territorial election is a little over 11,000, of which Phoenix registers 4,494. The national railroad strike limits Phoenix buyers to a dollar's worth of groceries per sale. The speed limit in the city is six miles per hour. Paved roads and sidewalks are needed.

1895   Phoenix Union High School District is established. The only meatpacking plant between Denver and Los Angeles opens. Valley agricultural shippers now have the same rates as Los Angeles, opening up eastern markets. The first passenger train from the north reaches Phoenix via Prescott. Sisters of Mercy Hospital (later St. Joseph's Hospital) opens.

1896   Dairy farms form a cooperative creamery. The Salt River Valley gets its first date palms.

1897   The two hundred thousand dollar Adams Hotel, "largest and most magnificent in the southwest," opens. A school census shows 1,452 school-age children in Phoenix.

1898   A Spanish press is started in Phoenix with *El Democratico*. As the Spanish-American War gets under way, Phoenicians rush to enlist in the Phoenix Rough Riders. The red-light district is outlawed. A Phoenix women's club, the Friday Club, organizes a public library.

1899  A bond issue for a municipal waterworks loses. Several additions are annexed.

1900  Iron Springs, a summer retreat near Prescott, coalesces "for the first time, a nucleus of Phoenix society." A bond election for municipal water and sewer systems is voted down in February. Phoenix has twenty-eight saloons, eighteen gaming tables, and the WCTU (Women's Christian Temperance Union). The first automobiles appear. Water storage is becoming the overwhelming issue in the valley; a local water storage committee emerges from meetings. The census of 1900 dismays Phoenix; the count of five thousand five hundred is too small!

1901  Drought wreaks hardship as county-appointed water commissioners begin to study the Tonto Dam site with federal experts. The capitol is dedicated, and the Territorial Legislature moves out of city hall. The public library is turned over to the city; a woman is appointed to the library board. The Phoenix Woman's Club is founded. Both political parties favor municipal ownership of public utilities.

1902  The Newlands reclamation bill passes Congress. The Salt River Valley Water Users Association forms, eventually to include all important valley farmers, and approves the Tonto Basin Water Storage Plan. The building of Tonto Dam, later Roosevelt Dam, will be the valley's dominant economic activity for a decade.

1903  A bond election for a municipal waterworks approves bonds in December.

1904  Telephone companies vie for patronage. Phoenix continues its opposition to joint statehood with New Mexico.

1905  Alfalfa is the biggest valley crop. Floods exacerbate an unsettled canal situation.

1906  The U.S. Reclamation Service is gradually acquiring the valley's canal system. Saloon fees are raised to help city budget problems as the Anti-Saloon League and the WCTU spread their influence. Gambling is voted out in a public opinion poll; an antigambling ordinance follows.

1907  Associated Charities, Phoenix's first attempt at organized charity, faces the problem of indigent, invalid immigrants pouring into the city during the Panic of 1907. The panic otherwise affects Phoenix little. The board of trade starts a new pattern by raising twelve thousand dollars to advertise Phoenix. One hundred thousand dollars is raised in a blazing eleven-day campaign for a YMCA building.

1908  A civic federation of seventy-five members is organized to improve Phoenix.

1909   Pacific Gas and Electric Company, now Phoenix's supplier of those utilities, is attacked all year by citizens' groups wanting alternatives to its rates. Telephone companies form and reorganize. A county election gives the go-ahead for a bridge over the Salt River at Center Street (Central Avenue).

1910   Phoenix is becoming a rail center but also has 329 licensed automobiles. Leading citizens form a committee to secure paved streets. A segregated school system, staunchly opposed by African Americans, is established. The Interstate Commerce Commission takes 30 percent off Phoenix's transcontinental freight rates. The state constitutional convention meets in Phoenix. Even with several additions annexed since 1909, Phoenix has only 11,134 people, still several thousand less than Tucson.

1911   Impending statehood promotes prosperity for Phoenix, the capital, and the city votes 73 percent to 27 percent to ratify the state constitution. Roosevelt Dam is dedicated. The Center Street bridge now unites Phoenix with the south side. The city buys the Phoenix Sewer and Drainage Company to provide a municipal system. Phoenix unions begin organizing for the Arizona Federation of Labor. Phoenix has one-fifth of the new state's banking resources.

## Town Becomes City in the New State

1912   Statehood becomes official as President Taft signs a proclamation on February 14. Phoenix women are leaders in the successful struggle to amend the new state constitution to give women the vote. A New York company buys Pacific Gas and Electric Company. Phoenix leader Dwight Heard organizes the Arizona branch of Teddy Roosevelt's Progressive party, acquiring the twenty-three-year-old Phoenix *Arizona Republican*, the state's largest newspaper.

1913   The Aztec Sun Fete draws thousands in February. Women are about 35 percent of the voters in the city election. A mayor's committee selects one hundred men to choose a charter commission; they decide to include twenty-five women. A new charter with a city-manager plan is adopted in a city election.

1914   W. A. Farish becomes Phoenix's first city manager. Women organize for the national woman-suffrage amendment. The ailing Valley Bank reorganizes as nine thousand depositors remain calm. Arizona votes dry for state prohibition.

1915   At least eight hundred Phoenicians are out of work; the Municipal Free Employment Bureau is set up to help. The charter is amended to give the city commission more supervisory power. Agitation for prohibition and woman suffrage occurs. Movie companies look Phoenix over but choose Hollywood.

1916    The movement for a municipal electric plant continues. Phoenix National Guard companies are sent to the Mexican border to join the U.S. Army in quelling disturbances there. The Home Guard is organized to protect against random violence in the city. A city board of censors, created ad hoc, quarrels with theater managers over Birth of a Nation, a movie resented by African Americans; it is withdrawn after a week's successful run.

1917    The Central School Block is sold for $210,000 for commercial purposes. World War I cuts off Egyptian cotton imports, booming the valley's long-staple cotton as chief supply for Ohio's tire factories. The Goodyear Company buys a huge tract near Tolleson, later named Litchfield after Goodyear's president. Mexican nationals are brought in to pick cotton; the Boys' Food Battalion is organized to pick melons. Liberty Bond drives begin, along with the persecution of bond slackers.

1918    Phoenix oversubscribes in Liberty Bond and Thrift Stamp campaigns. The Spanish flu, eventually affecting three thousand Phoenicians, closes schools, theaters, etc., for two to three months in the fall. Phoenix "boys" are off to the service before armistice is cheered on November 11.

1919    Ten thousand cheer the 158th Regiment's return to Phoenix. The first airline out of Phoenix is planned. The chamber of commerce leads an attack on railroad freight rates. City limits are extended as the 1920 census looms. The Building Trades Council defeats the Contractors' Association to win the closed shop. Dairies vanish as land goes to cotton.

1920    The original Phoenix is now completely paved. The city votes 1.4 million dollars' worth of bonds for water, sewer, and fire systems. County bonds for paving roads help offset postwar depression. Increasing efforts are made to provide for tubercular residents. Women organize for national candidates. Phoenix finally nudges past Tucson as Arizona's largest city, 29,053 to 20,292.

1921    Phoenix's first fifty years are celebrated in its first Pioneer Reunion. A cotton depression affects the whole community. Cooperative marketing is organized, and the Federal Land Bank apportions $400,000 to the valley. The chamber of commerce is reorganized to include almost a thousand members, including women. City charities organize into one welfare league. Runs close Central and Citizens banks temporarily, but Phoenix National and Valley banks survive with California banks' help. Plans to control Cave Creek are expedited when it floods in August. A gigantic paving program and construction of the Verde water system help Phoenix stave off the worst unemployment.

1922   Verde River water starts to supply Phoenix. The struggle for lower railroad freight rates continues before the Interstate Commerce Commission. Colorado River development becomes an issue. Valley Bank gains eight more branches as it merges with Gila Valley Bank. Through Farm Bureau efforts, four agricultural cooperatives are formed: cotton, dairy products, hay, and grain. The Arizona Industrial Congress pushes "Buy Arizona." The Salt River Valley Arizona Club is formed to publicize Phoenix and the valley.

1923   Cave Creek Dam, the Southern Pacific–Santa Fe Union Depot, Deaconess Hospital (later Good Samaritan Hospital), and the county highway system are finished. The city creates the Phoenix Bureau of Charities. Municipal ownership of the street railway is discussed.

1924   Prosperity returns in building, bank deposits, etc. The chamber of commerce, Salt River Valley Arizona Association, and the board of Realtors open an office in Los Angeles.

1925   Phoenix is increasingly a convention center. The street-railway issue peaks and ends as the city takes over. The city also annexes twelve subdivisions, dedicates a municipal airport, and institutes zoning. A high school for African Americans is voted in.

1926   Highway access to Phoenix continues to improve. A mammoth celebration marks achievement of the long-sought mainline joining railroads north and south. Cantaloupe and lettuce are increasingly important. A municipal parks and playgrounds board is created.

1927   The "town ditch," the old Salt River Canal, near the center of the city, finally goes underground for the sake of sanitation. The first regular flight to Los Angeles is instituted. Residential developments, hotels, and real estate are all booming. Verde Water System is failing; investigations begin to uncover the inadequacy of resources used for this.

1928   Phoenix is becoming the financial center of the Southwest. Seventy-four subdivisions have been annexed in the past two years. Neighborhood improvement associations are forming. The city zoning and planning commission is created.

1929   Out-of-town capital continues to pour into Phoenix, now one of the nation's most prosperous cities and an increasingly important airport and convention center. The Frank Lloyd Wright–influenced Biltmore Hotel opens.

1930   A zoning ordinance is passed. Radio is increasing in importance: KTAR joins NBC. Phoenix is still the most prosperous city in the West in a depressed national economy. The movement for a veterans' hospital begins. Progress in parks and playgrounds continues slowly. The census, as usual, counts fewer people than Phoenicians think it should: 49,950.

1931    The Great Depression arrives in Phoenix; by the year's end, unemployment is a major problem. City economies hold down the tax rate, although a parks board is created, a municipal airport is rented, and an annexation program on city-dictated terms proceeds.

1932    The Depression deepens, with pressures for government economy alternating with pressure for relief for the unemployed. With some success, the Create-a-Job Campaign combines private and city aid. The Salt River Valley Water Users Association takes on the administration of the Reconstruction Finance Corporation's loans to farmers. Mayor Paddock reorganizes the city government for thrift as property valuations are reduced to decrease city taxes. Arizona repeals prohibition on November 8.

1933    Phoenix newspapers applaud the national bank holiday. Merchants cooperate with the National Recovery Act on the forty-hour workweek. Phoenix gets a Civilian Conservation Corps camp in South Mountain Park; a transient camp is also set up on the state fairgrounds for crowds of unemployed drifting into the city.

1934    Phoenix strives for and acquires federal funds for municipal projects. Prosperity, as measured by tourists, bank clearings, and retail sales, gradually returns; however, the city still must cope with multitudes of unemployed transients. A riot at the Federal Emergency Relief Administration forces attention on radicals well into 1935. There is antialien agitation against Japanese farmers in the fall.

1935    Federal Public Works Administration (PWA) projects proceed, especially in the parks. The Works Projects Administration (WPA) comes to Phoenix—one project is park development—as Federal Emergency Relief leaves. Of 109 cities nationally, Phoenix leads in FHA loans. The city buys Sky Harbor Airport.

1936    Phoenix becomes the third city in the country in per capita retail sales.

1937    A county scandal focuses on illegal gambling, a hot issue for several years. WPA and PWA projects continue.

1938    The PWA, offering federal aid to local builders, continues its projects. The WPA, emphasizing hiring local labor for federal projects, falls from favor. The city continues to struggle for some years for its share of the state gasoline sales tax. Phoenix continues to grow as an agricultural and wholesale center.

1939    The city continues annexing to be ready for the 1940 census. It secures a metropolitan category, permitting it to claim a larger population. A $1,613,000 slum-clearance project gets under way with federal aid. Construction returns to the 1930 level and city debts are paid on a cash basis for the first time in years. Charter reform continues to be discussed, as it has been throughout the decade. Citrus crops are prime in the valley economy.

1940    Land for a civic center is given to Phoenix by the children of A. C. Bartlett. The census counts 65,434 Phoenicians. The city, now with metropolitan status and new annexations (including the wealthy Country Club district), apparently does not dispute the count. Sky Harbor is developed.

1941    Airport construction and new and major air-training centers reflect the importance of Phoenix defense industries. The USO and Red Cross gear up. Commercial airlines jockey for Phoenix routes. The Phoenix metropolitan area is listed by the census as having 121,828 people. Matthew Henson, the first slum-clearance project, opens in May, Marcos de Niza in August. The Pearl Harbor attack catalyzes defense efforts, such as the Phoenix Civilian Defense Committee, and industries move to Phoenix's inland location, away from the vulnerable West Coast.

1942    Defense and service agencies continue to organize. Labor benefits from the war manpower shortage; women are increasingly on the job scene. Phoenix transportation and housing are very stressed by workers pouring into war industries, such as Goodyear, ALCOA, and AiResearch, and by military personnel from the airfields. Rent control and conversion subsidy are instituted to relieve the housing shortage. Wide-open prostitution brings a ruling from Luke Airfield making Phoenix off-limits to military personnel, but the chamber of commerce and civic organizations combine to demand a reformist city administration and the order is rescinded. Phoenix is deemed secure enough for a prisoner-of-war camp at Papago Park, east of the city. Meat, milk, gasoline, and nylon stockings are scarce.

1943    The Citizens Good Government Council, offshoot of the chamber of commerce, attempts to stiffen the city's antivice stand as its ticket wins a three-way election. By year's end a threatening venereal-disease epidemic is successfully controlled. The city government is making money from both services and taxes in a booming war economy. Scrap-salvage drives, war-bond sales, and labor struggles alternate in the news.

1944    Busy and prosperous, Phoenix tops its war bond quotas, Community Chest, and YMCA drives. Juvenile delinquency, a new phenomenon on Phoenix streets, and recreation are of special concern to the city. A shortage of workers is a chronic concern for farmers and a boost for the unions. Housing is still in very short supply. The city turns to postwar planning and the remediation of wartime blight.

### Peacetime Development as a Sunbelt Metropolis

1945   The city continues to profit from water and transportation charges. War loans and victory-loan drives go over the top. Peace exacerbates housing and employment adjustment. The city hires the Public Administration Service, which proposes reforms. A Securities and Exchange Commission divestiture order results in Phoenix investors' taking control of the Central Arizona Light and Power Company, which, with the Salt River Project (Salt River Valley Water Users Association), is the source of community power. The great war plants—ALCOA, Goodyear, and AiResearch—wind down.

1946   Ariola, Reynolds Aluminum, and the American Institute of Foreign Trade are launched in the Phoenix area. The city continues to be involved in housing for veterans, a major problem. Master zoning plans are worked out in the Public Service Administration. The city becomes aware of the need to cooperate with the county for contiguous county zoning. The chamber of commerce is involved in a statewide plan for roads, freeways, and a $150,000 fund to attract clean, light industry. Unions continue active, but the state right-to-work law passes.

1947   Downtown parking is an increasing problem. The Greater Phoenix Council is created as the city pushes annexation and resists the separation of suburbs. The housing emergency eases as construction booms. Hurting financially with the peacetime economy, the city frantically seeks new sources of revenue. A charter-revision committee is appointed by the mayor to reform city government. Strikes continue as labor tries to minimize the effects of the right-to-work law. Dog racing gets a solid foothold. Phoenix is called a center of illicit drug trade. The professional and permanent Phoenix Symphony Orchestra is organized.

1948   Downtown parking continues to be an issue. The efforts of the Ballot Battalion and the League of Women Voters increase the city vote. The city continues annexing. An election in November brings in the mayor-council-manager form of government, with the mayor and six council members to be elected together. Trolleys have now been completely replaced by buses. Bond issues for airport, water, library, park, and other development pass. Motorola's coming to Phoenix heralds "the wave of Phoenix's future in manufacturing": light, high technology with easily shipped products.

1949   Mayor Nicholas Udall and his council minority continue to feud with City Manager Deppe and the majority. The city wrestles with its budget and levies its first sales tax. At the instigation of community leader Alfred Knight, a new committee is formed and eventually becomes the Charter Government Committee. Udall, as its candidate, wins an election which also brings to the council Barry Goldwater and the first woman to serve at the city's top levels, Margaret Kober, as well as others from Phoenix's "powerful upper middle class asserting itself." Annexations proceed; notable are purchases of outlying private water companies. A professional city manager, Ray Wilson, takes the reins.

1950   Low-cost-housing construction proceeds with disputes. The city tax function is moved to the county. The Phoenix metropolitan area is now coterminous with the county. City finances are back in the black. The misery in farm-labor camps near Phoenix gets national attention. Phoenix African Americans get a state legislative district: Eight. The chamber of commerce program to bring in new industry is succeeding. Air conditioning helps Phoenix become a summer convention city.

1951   Phoenix is the fourth-fastest-growing city in the nation; it is now also an All-American City by award. A new city code is adopted. The civil rights movement arrives in Phoenix.

1952   Barry Goldwater goes from the city council to the U.S. Senate. Central Arizona Light and Power consolidates with Northern Arizona Light and Power to become Arizona Public Service.

1953   Annexation battles continue. Solutions to the problem of downtown parking continue to be debated.

1954   Greyhound Park opens. Phoenix hosts forty-nine conventions. The desegregation of the public schools is, at least legally, complete. An election favors a city sales tax. Phoenix seeks federal aid for streets.

1955   Sale of the city bus system is voted down in June. Annexations in the east bring conflict with Scottsdale. The highest budget in the city's history is adopted without discussion. Segregation is banned in city housing. Phoenix is growing at almost the fastest rate in the United States for cities of one to two hundred thousand.

1956   A Phoenix Growth Committee is again approved to help with bond issues for city services. The Arizona Supreme Court upholds the city sales tax. Strikes shake Mountain States Telephone and Telegraph and Reynolds Aluminum. Freeway plans proceed.

1957   Sperry Rand decides on Deer Valley rather than Sky Harbor. Annexations are carried out, northeast and northwest. The city turns its health functions over to the county; city and county also cooperate on parks and sewers. General Electric builds a major computer production center.

1958   Phoenix doubles its size by annexation. Shopping centers multiply. Pollution becomes an issue.

1959   Phoenix receives its second All-American City award. The municipal bus lines are sold. Annexations continue, involving a race with Glendale for certain areas. Relaxed zoning and industrial codes draw industry. Nationally known Phoenix contractor Del Webb buys land and starts plans for Sun City, a retirement community northwest of Phoenix. Industries continue to arrive.

1960   Maryvale and South Phoenix are annexed. Still a distributing center, Phoenix is now also an electronics center, with Motorola, General Electric, and Sperry Rand. The 1960 federal census shows a 300 percent growth for Phoenix since 1950, from 106,818 to 439,170 residents.

1961   Deer Valley is annexed. Papago Park, now belonging to Phoenix, adds a zoo to its other attractions. An antismog crusade appears in the press. The city housing code is repealed in February, and federal assistance for urban renewal is refused. Local conservatism generates some criticism nationally.

1962   A new housing code is passed. Downtown "looks up" as the city's center with completion of the city-county complex. But crimes and convenience disperse consumers into the multiplying shopping centers. The Volker Report ends a decade-long controversy between Tucson and Phoenix over the establishment of a medical school: Tucson triumphs. Seventy-six new industries come to Phoenix.

1963   The housing code is defeated in a special May election. County hearings are held on pollution. Ways to revive the downtown economy continue to be discussed extensively. The Phoenix Human Relations Commission is appointed as sit-ins gain momentum for the civil rights movement. Sewer and street systems are expanded, high-rises are approved, and retail stores outstrip city growth. The Valley Beautiful Citizens Council organizes to protect the city and suburbs from losing their charm to urbanization.

1964   The Citizens Task Force reports, after an eight-month study, that 60 percent of the area's crime is committed by juveniles, so the city tightens law enforcement for this group. Eight years of annexation feuding with Scottsdale ends with an agreement on boundaries. Civil-rights protests continue, and Phoenix passes Arizona's first ordinance forbidding discrimination in public accommodations. Freeway and street construction costs increase to one million dollars a month as rights-of-way climb. Downtown merchants push for development east of Central and a high-rise zone for downtown.

Lack of a housing code halts federal investment in low-rent public housing. Two hundred–plus inner city leaders are invited to confer on inner city problems; LEAP (Leadership and Education for the Advancement of Phoenix), a private corporation, is created to work with the city on behalf of disadvantaged residents.

1965    Downtown Phoenix continues its efforts to revive, working with city government to devise financing for a downtown auditorium and convention center. The Phoenix Junior Chamber of Commerce secures more than thirty thousand signatures for a housing code; a new code is drawn up. Papago Freeway, designated an Interstate highway, becomes eligible for almost total federal financing. The press fears the freeway will divide and "Los Angelize" Phoenix, but the city administration sees it decreasing traffic congestion and bringing in business. Morrison Warren becomes the first African-American city councilman. Phoenix has about three times the square footage of selling space considered adequate for a city its size—and about 53 percent of the state's business failures. Critics, such as Clare Boothe Luce and the Valley Beautiful Citizens Council, warn of urban blight.

1966    The city-council complex opens. A minimum-standard housing code loses.

1967    The mayor receives emergency powers July 26 to handle a riot at a black housing project; there are no serious injuries. An African-American leader on the Human Relations Commission, Arlena Seneca, is honored as Phoenix Woman of the Year by the Advertising Council. The prosperous "Phoenix area" (a special area including the city and environs designated by the *Republic* and *Gazette* for statistical purposes) hums on, characterized by 23.0 years median age, 31 percent residents of less than five years, $1,615,267,000 retail sales, and 3.4 percent unemployed of a 340,000-member work force.

1968    A study reveals that Phoenix-area heads of households have a median educational level of high school graduates, while the median for inner-city heads of households is grade school or less. Median family income is $7,757 for the Phoenix area, $2,737 for the inner city. Western Electric completes its Phoenix plant, the largest telephone-cable production facility in the world, twenty acres under one roof. Metropolitan Phoenix (Maricopa County) has twenty-six radio stations and five television stations. Phoenix is publicized as a warehouse and distribution center for more than five hundred firms with a thirteen-state and northern Mexico market of 23 million people. The Central Arizona Project to bring the Colorado River closer to the Phoenix area by 1980 is approved.

1969   Segregation is still the Phoenix pattern: of eleven housing projects, three are predominantly white, four completely black. Of the remaining four, two are 90 percent Hispanic, and two are black and Hispanic without whites. The city enacts a luxury tax on cigarettes and liquor to balance its budget. Retail sales pass the two-billion-dollar mark for the first time. In Arizona, metropolitan Phoenix has 80 percent of the manufacturing jobs, 60 percent of all employment, and 48 percent or more of the retail sales in all of nine categories. One hundred twenty thousand people migrate to the Phoenix area during one year.

1970   Phoenix is the twentieth city in the United States in population, with 581,562 residents, a 32 percent growth since 1960. Metropolitan Phoenix has 968,487 people, 46 percent more than in 1960. Most growth is north and east, except Maryvale in the west and Deer and Moon valleys in the northwest. Fifteen companies and the two Air Force bases each employ more than one thousand workers. An intermediate standard of living in Phoenix requires $10,226 for a family of four. Median income is $8,823 in the Phoenix area, with 3.4 the median number of persons in a household. On November 1 the city issues a model commemorating its centennial.

1971   Metropolitan Phoenix, Maricopa County, is now the twenty-fourth most populous county in the United States, with an estimated 1,013,000 people. In 1971 it spends more dollars on construction and builds more housing units than ever before in its history. Since 1960, 60 percent of its households have moved, about a third of them within the county. The county has 54.6 percent of Arizona's population (the city of Phoenix has 60 percent of the county's) and 60 percent of its retail sales. Phoenix has thirteen major shopping centers outside downtown. Greyhound-Armour-Dial Corporation comes to Phoenix. Twenty-five of the thirty-one city-charter amendments proposed by the Charter Review Committee are approved in the city election for the first major overhaul of the charter in more than thirty years.

1972   Phoenix's downtown presents its auditorium and convention center with the opening of Civic Plaza. Housing construction continues at a high level. During the year, the assets of the Phoenix area's ten banks increase 18 percent; of its savings and loan institutions, 36 percent. Sentiment against the midcity Papago Freeway is rising. State Proposition 200 wins; the city's luxury tax, the only one in Arizona, is now preempted by the state. In exchange, Phoenix and other cities will share 15 percent of the state's income-tax collections.

1973  The *Republic* and *Gazette* Consumer Survey shows 12 percent of the Phoenix area's homeowners living in mobile homes, 82 percent in single-family homes, and 6 percent in townhouses. "The trend toward smaller family size has been established"; only 19 percent of households have three or more children. Three-fifths of all households now earn more than $10,000 a year. Citizens Mass Transit against Freeways heads the fight against the Papago Freeway; a public-opinion poll votes down this loop of Interstate 10. Planning for the $2.2 billion Palo Verde Nuclear Generating Station fifty miles west of Phoenix gets under way. The Phoenix Historical Society is founded.

1974  The city's total area is now 248 square miles. More than three times as many conventions come to Phoenix as in 1970. Economic recession, however, brings an unusually high rate of unemployment; housing construction is down more than 31 percent from 1973; tourism is down 1.4 percent. Phoenix's cost of living, now twentieth among twenty-four urban centers, is one of the lowest in the nation. The number of households with full- or part-time working women has zoomed to 26 percent of all households. Women in proprietary or managerial positions have increased 144 percent since 1970.

1975  Margaret Hance becomes Phoenix's first female mayor, making Phoenix the second-largest city in the country to have a female mayor. The most controversial city election issue is the recurring proposal for the Papago Freeway. Opposed by the newspapers, the Phoenix 40 (a group of civic leaders), and all but the American party candidates, the freeway nevertheless wins. Employment is still in the doldrums.

1976  As demand catches up with the overbuilding of 1974 and 1975, housing experiences a rebound, with residential permits gaining 36.2 percent during the year. Tourism moves ahead of livestock and crop marketing as metropolitan Phoenix's number-two income producer; manufacturing continues first. Phoenix proper now has 37 industrial parks and 128 major office buildings. The murder of newspaper reporter Don Bolles brings reporters from all over the nation to investigate Phoenix crime and politics. The city removes the sales tax from food but doubles it on nonfood items, a decision openly fought by the chamber of commerce, which fears Phoenix prices will become less competitive.

1977  Employment begins to recover after the recession years. Residential construction gains 165 percent over 1976. Harsh northern weather conditions bring an unprecedented number of tourists.

1978   Phoenix is now the fifteenth-largest city in the nation, with only four of the larger cities having posted an increase in population since 1970. The University of Arizona reports average farm income in Arizona as highest in the nation and more than 30 percent higher than the second-highest state average, "a pervasive element in the growth of Phoenix." Cotton, alfalfa, durum wheat, vegetables, citrus and other fruits, and beef and dairy cattle are still important to Phoenix, as they have been for most of its history. The first of three annual floods does not prevent more than forty thousand housing starts, making Phoenix the seventh city in the nation for such starts. Almost half of Phoenix area households are now composed of one or two persons; more than half have no children. Private transportation is still overwhelmingly important. Sixty percent of Phoenix-area households report owning more than one vehicle. Mayor Hance initiates a drive for support of the $500 million Papago Freeway in the belief that "a ring of freeways around the Valley will spell doom for central Phoenix." The city's budget for job stimulation programs, home improvements, parks, and elderly housing in low-income areas is $13.4 million. Phoenix's unemployment rate now runs around 5 percent compared to the national 6 percent. The twelve municipal courts have a nightmarish backlog of two hundred thousand cases. Proposition 200, to replace three planned Phoenix area freeways, including Papago, with a ground plan to widen city streets and step up bus service, is opposed by all nineteen valley cities and the county, so it loses in the November election.

1979   Cropland under the Salt River Project, which includes much of Phoenix as well as surrounding land, has shrunk from 152,090 acres in 1971 to 109,278 by the end of 1979, although statewide farmers have converted enough new land to keep pace with urbanization. The Verde and Salt rivers flood again. Retired households now equal one-fourth of Phoenix area families, an increase of 178 percent since 1970, compared to a 90 percent increase for total households. A new $65 million airline terminal is built as three more airlines join the eight serving Phoenix. A prosperous year adds fifty-six thousand jobs in metropolitan Phoenix (now Maricopa County). The tourist season now runs from September 1 to the end of May. Phoenix passes an antipornography ordinance prohibiting sales closer than five hundred feet to churches or schools. An Indian, a Mexican American, and an African American, representing minorities which make up 20 percent of the city, unsuccessfully sue in federal court to enjoin Phoenix from holding its general election, claiming that the at-large election of council members is discriminatory and that the minorities' vote is diluted more than ever by the city's May annexation of 7.9 square miles. With the fading of Charter Government power, the two-term tradition in city government is vanishing. Mayor Hance is opposed only by Dan Fein of the Socialist Workers party in an election, polling 58 percent of those eligible to vote. To increase city revenues, the Urban Infill Committee recommends developing the 30 to 40 percent of Phoenix land that is vacant. The Inner City Planning Committee produces a plan for the city, and it is unanimously adopted by the council.

1980     The city of Phoenix has 764,911 of the 1,509,052 people in metropolitan Phoenix. The metropolitan area has grown 55 percent in the 1970s, making it the fastest growing in the nation, although twenty-sixth in population. The city's housing industry, with buyers pinched by inflation and soaring mortgage rates, touches its lowest mark in five years, although multiple-unit building is at its highest peak ever. Newcomer households drop from 12 percent to only 6 percent of the total; people cannot afford to move to the Sunbelt. Likewise, 1980 is not a good tourist year, although the Phoenix area ranks twenty-second of twenty-four metropolitan areas in cost of living. Metropolitan Phoenix has the second-highest concentration of high technology in the United States. FBI statistics report Phoenix the most crime ridden of the country's ten most populous cities. The city faces a possible water shortage for those parts of it not under the Salt River Project and hopes the post-1985 delivery of Central Arizona Project water will supply what it needs. Arizona's 1980 Groundwater Act creates the Phoenix Active Management Area to bring groundwater into balance. It also provides for an advisory council and a study to be completed by January 1983 to establish per-capita use rates for cities.

1981     Phoenix's first computer-software factory is constructed. The Salt River has its third successive year of flooding, and 27,000 International Lion conventioneers inundate the valley in June! Tourists spend an estimated $1.966 billion in metropolitan Phoenix; 6,641,750 passengers embark and disembark at Sky Harbor. Net migration into the metropolitan area is 20,000 during the year. Mayor Hance wins her fourth term with 70 percent of the vote on one of the most complicated city ballots ever. "Yes" votes are secured for a budget override and civil-service reform, with only 29.8 percent of eligible voters turning out. One hundred thirty-seven scattered housing sites for low-income families, financed by the U.S. Department of Housing and Urban Development, "stir up a hornet's nest," but proceed apace.

Phoenix has been an incorporated city for one hundred years.

# NOTES

## EDITOR'S PREFACE

1. John Alexander Williams, ed., "Public History and Local History," *The Public Historian* 5 (Fall 1983).

## CHAPTER ONE

1. See G. Wesley Johnson, Jr., ed., "Sunbelt Capital: An Introduction," 237–38; Blaine Lamb, "Jews in Early Phoenix," 299–318; and Gary P. Tipton, "Men Out of China," 341–56, all in *Journal of Arizona History* 18 (1977).

2. Charles C. Colley, "Carl T. Hayden, Phoenician," 247–58; and G. Wesley Johnson, Jr., "Dwight Heard in Phoenix," 257–78, both in *Journal of Arizona History* 18 (1977).

## CHAPTER TWO

1. William D. Angel, Jr., "To Make a City: Entrepreneurship on the Sunbelt Frontier," in *The Rise of the Sunbelt Cities*, ed. David C. Perry and Alfred J. Watkins (Beverly Hills, Calif.: Sage Publications, 1977), 125–26.

2. Some materials on Phoenix history had been collected as part of a general collection on Arizona at the Arizona State University Library's Arizona Room, and some materials were on deposit at Phoenix Public Library. Otherwise the first century of history in Phoenix awaited documentation. Newspapers had been preserved at the Arizona State University Library and the State Archives and Library, Phoenix. The situation, however, was not comparable to that in such western cities as Denver or Salt Lake City.

3. Materials and methodology are discussed in a monograph study of Phoenix, "The Modern Phoenicians," by G. Wesley Johnson, Jr. As for a rationale on studying elites in the community, one of the best syntheses is in Robert Presthus, *Men at the Top: A Study in Community Power* (New York: Oxford Press, 1964); see especially chaps. 1, 2, and 12. See also Geraint Parry, *Political Elites* (New York: Praeger, 1969) for a general introduction on elites; Carl V. Harris, *Political Power in Birmingham, 1871–1921* (Knoxville: University of Tennessee Press, 1977), for an informed discussion by a historian using the decisional approach, especially pages 39–95; Jocelyn M. Ghent and Frederic C. Jaher, "The Chicago Business Elite, 1830–1930: A Collective Biography," *Business History* 50, no.3(1976): 288–328; John Walton, "Community Power and the Retreat from Politics: Full Circle after Twenty Years?" *Social Problems* 23 (1976): 292–303; and the imaginative treatment in Edward O. Laumann, Lois M. Verbrugge, and Franz U. Pappi, "A Causal Modelling Approach to the Study of a Community Elite's Influence Structure," *American Sociological Review* 39 (1974): 164–74. Examples of elite analyses in other western cities include Eugene P. Moehring, *Resort City in the Sunbelt: Las Vegas, 1930–1970* (Reno: University of Nevada Press, 1989); Stephen J. Leonard, *Denver: Mining Camp to Metropolis* (Aliwot: University Press of Colorado, 1990); less comprehensive but useful are Anthony M. Orum, *Power, Money, and the People: The Making of Modern Austin* (Austin: Texas Monthly Press, 1987), and E. Kimbark MacColl, *Merchants, Money, and Power: The Portland Establishment* (Portland, Or.: Georgian Press, 1988).

4. Glen Elder, "History and the Life Course," in *Biography and Society: The Life History Approach to the Social Sciences*, ed. Daniel Bertaux (Beverly Hills: Sage Publications, 1981), 88–89.

5. The main approach to urban history of the Phoenix History Project has been to construct an urban biography of the city. This entailed developing a basic chronology, a narrative history, and a number of problems for analysis, such as elite formation, analysis of the census, participation of minorities, economic growth, and public policy.

6. See biographical folders on Smith, Swilling, Hancock, and Alsap in "Biographical Research Files," Phoenix History Project, Phoenix (hereafter cited as Project Biographical Files).

7. Duppa and Hayden, ibid.

8. See U.S. Census for Phoenix and Salt River Valley for 1870 and 1880.

9. For a detailed discussion of some of these early Town Elite members, see Geoffrey Mawn, "Phoenix, Arizona: Central City of the Southwest, 1870–1920" (Ph.D. diss., Arizona State University, 1979).

10. On Christy, see extensive materials furnished by the Christy and Fulwiler families in the Project Biographical Files.

11. Murphy's grandson has published a full portrait of this remarkable entrepreneur: Merwin L. Murphy, *W. J. and the Valley* (Alhambra, Calif.: Merwin L. Murphy, 1975). See also Project Biographical Files and excerpts from National Archives, Washington, D.C., materials on the building of Roosevelt Dam.

12. On Ganz, see Project Biographical Files.

13. Aside from materials at the Phoenix History Project, there are several important bound books of correspondence by Sherman at the Sherman Foundation Library in Corona Del Mar, California.

14. Robert Merton, *Social Theory and Social Structure* (Glencoe, Ill.: The Free Press, 1957); see especially chap. 10, "Patterns of Influence: Local and Cosmopolitan Influentials," 387–420.

15. Recruitment of elites is related to Pareto's concept of the circulation of elites and for this essay is viewed simply as the process by which certain elite cohorts were formed in Phoenix. As Nadel remarked concerning recruitment, it was "the movement of people in and out of positions of pre-eminence." See S. F. Nadel, "The Concept of Social Elites," *International Social Science Bulletin* 8 (1956): 413–24; see also Parry, *Political Elites*, 97–105 for a more specific focus on recruitment and elite background.

16. On Whitelaw Reid, see Bingham Duncan, *Whitelaw Reid: Journalist, Politician, Diplomat* (Athens: University of Georgia Press, 1975), chap. 12; in addition, the letters of Whitelaw Reid in the Library of Congress tell much about his sojourn and impressions of Phoenix life.

17. On the Jewish merchants, see Lamb, "Jews in Early Phoenix, 1870–1920."

18. For a full treatment of Fowler's activities and influence in Phoenix and the best account yet on the winning of the Roosevelt Dam, see Karen L. Smith, *The Magnificent Experiment: Building the Salt River Reclamation Project, 1890–1917* (Tucson: University of Arizona Press, 1986).

19. See discussion of transference of the capital city in Jay J. Wagoner, *Arizona Territory, 1863–1912: A Political History* (Tucson: University of Arizona Press, 1970), 245–47.

20. See materials on boosterism in Arizona Collection, Arizona State University Library, and in the Phoenix History Project file.

21. U.S. Census for 1910.

22. George Mickle, Project Biographical Files.

23. Stauffer left some of his papers to the Arizona Historical Society in Tucson, there are some documents in the Arizona Room and the Arizona Historical Foundation at the Arizona State University Library, and a special collection of materials on Stauffer was given to the Phoenix History Project by his daughter, Sylvia S. Laughlin.

24. See social and civic club files at Phoenix History Project; on the early additions to the townsite, see Karen L. Smith, "From Town to City: A History of Phoenix, 1870-1912" (M.A. thesis, University of California, Santa Barbara, 1978); on the role of Dwight B. Heard in the development of new residential areas mentioned above, see interview with Bartlett Heard, son of Dwight, in tape-recorded interviews by the author at the Phoenix History Project.

25. On the changing role of agriculture, see the series of interviews on agricultural history in Phoenix by Karin Ullmann for the Phoenix History Project.

26. See the excellent article by Sylvia Laughlin, "Iron Springs, Arizona: Timeless Summer Resort," *Journal of Arizona History* 22 (1981): 235-54.

27. See G. Wesley Johnson, Jr., "Dwight B. Heard in Phoenix: The Early Years," *Journal of Arizona History* 18 (1977): 259-78, and the taped interviews with Bartlett Heard at Phoenix History Project.

28. On early charter reform, see Stephen Rockstroh, "An Analysis of Phoenix Municipal Administration, 1881-1952" (M.A. thesis, Arizona State University, 1952), and Joseph C. Smith, "The Phoenix Drive for Municipal Reform and Charter Government, 1911-1915" (MS, Arizona Collection, Arizona State University Library, 1975). On members of the elite mentioned, see Project Biographical Files.

29. On the McArthur brothers, see Project Biographical Files.

30. For information about the building of the Luhrs family properties, see taped interviews with George Luhrs, Phoenix History Project; see also ledgers and other business documents in the Luhrs family manuscript collection, Arizona Room, Arizona State University Library, Tempe.

31. See Michael F. Konig, "Transformation of Postwar Municipal Government in Phoenix," typescript (1982), Phoenix History Project; see also Bradford Luckingham, "Urban Development in Arizona: The Rise of Phoenix," *Journal of Arizona History* 22 (1981): 197-234.

32. On Bimson, see Ernest J. Hopkins, *Financing the Frontier* (Phoenix: Valley National Bank, Arizona Printers, 1950), and files and interviews with Bimson at Phoenix History Project.

33. On the founding of the symphony and art museum in Phoenix and the role of community leaders, see Cultural Files, Phoenix History Project, and interviews with Frank Snell and Walter Bimson; see also interview with Oscar Thoeny, M.D., in Arizona Medical History Collection, Flinn Library, Maricopa County Medical Society, Phoenix.

34. See Snell interviews, Phoenix History Project.

35. See files of the Phoenix Chamber of Commerce at Phoenix History Project; see also "Research Memo Overview on Phoenix Business," a report by Nancy Edwards at Phoenix History Project on interviews with postwar business leaders in Phoenix conducted by Edwards. On Motorola's move to Phoenix, see interview by Richard Lynch with Dr. Dan Noble, vice-president of Motorola, Phoenix History Project.

36. The best overview on postwar politics and charter government is Brent Whiting Brown, "An Analysis of the Phoenix Charter Government Committee as a Political Entity" (M.A. thesis, Arizona State University, 1968); see also Konig, "Transformation," and Konig, "Toward Metropolis Status: Charter Government and the Rise of Phoenix, Arizona, 1945-1960," (Ph.D. diss., Arizona State University, 1983).

37. Brown, "Charter Government Committee," and interview with Dix Price, former Charter Committee chair, Phoenix History Project.

38. See interviews with Williams and Mardian, Phoenix History Project.

39. See interviews with Orme Lewis, Harry Rosenzweig, Newton Rosenzweig, and Frank Snell, Phoenix History Project.

40. See U.S. Census for Phoenix, 1950 and 1960. See also taped interviews with Ralph Burgbacher and Sherman Hazeltine, Phoenix History Project. The two high-rise clusters, distinctly separated by several blocks of much lower buildings, present a dramatic and rather unusual city skyline to those flying into Phoenix for the first time.

41. See demographic and economic figures for changing growth patterns in the Salt River Valley in *Foresight Eighty: Insights and Foresights for the Phoenix Metropolitan Area* (Phoenix: Western Savings, 1980), a compendium issued during Phoenix boom days by the then largest savings and loan in Phoenix.

42. See the interpretation of Charter's demise in G. Wesley Johnson, Jr., *Phoenix: Valley of the Sun* (Tulsa, Okla.: Continental Heritage Publishing, 1982), 159–65. See also interviews with John Driggs, Newton Rosenzweig, Dix Price, and Sam Mardian, Phoenix History Project.

43. No major study has been made of the impact of expatriates, winter visitors, and health seekers on Phoenix. On the activity of a leading community entrepreneur, see interview with Karl Eller, Phoenix History Project.

44. Phylis C. Martinelli, "Beneath the Surface: Ethnic Communities in Phoenix, Arizona," typescript, Phoenix History Project. Martinelli was in charge of carrying out research on ethnic and minority groups at the Phoenix History Project. See also the Martinelli's article in this volume, as well as Trennert's. In addition, on the Phoenix Indian School, see Robert L. Trennert, *The Phoenix Indian School: Forced Assimilation in Arizona, 1891–1935* (Norman: University of Oklahoma Press, 1988).

45. Johnson, *Phoenix: Valley of the Sun*, 144–76.

46. I would like to acknowledge financial support for research on this essay from the National Endowment for the Humanities, Research Division, and the Arizona Humanities Council, and private sponsors of the Phoenix History Project. An earlier version was part of a lecture and occasional-paper series sponsored by the Charles Redd Center at Brigham Young University and is used with permission.

## CHAPTER THREE

1. "Census of Maricopa County 1882" (MS, 1882), Archives of the Secretary of State, Phoenix, passim.

2. *Phoenix Herald, Arizona Republican, Arizona Gazette* to 1912, passim. "Public women" was a euphemism of the day for prostitutes. "Gambling and liquor furnished about the only diversions available to or understood by the pioneer." James H. McClintock, *Arizona, Prehistoric, Aboriginal, Pioneer*, 3 vols. (Chicago: S. J. Clarke, 1916), 2:384; Nancy K. Tisdale, "The Prohibition Crusade in Arizona" (M.A. thesis, University of Arizona, 1965), 5.

3. In 1904, Mrs. W. F. Nichols said in her inaugural address to the Woman's Club: "This club was not instituted as a social organization. It was founded and is maintained not only for study and self-improvement but to be helpful to others . . . to give an uplift to women who by reason of household cares, or other circumstances have little time to spend on study, yet crave and need the mental stimulus . . . of other women who are thoughtful and earnest. . . . I am glad our club bears the name of the Women's [sic] Club. I trust that its platform and policy will be as broad as its name . . . inclusive rather than exclusive." *Arizona Republican*, 12 November 1904.

4. Eleanor Flexner, *Century of Struggle: The Woman's Rights Movement in the United States* (Cambridge, Mass.: Belknap Press, 1975), 185–86, 189.

5. The branch was urged in a letter to Dr. Ingalls from Mrs. Clendenning. *Phoenix Herald*, 11 April 1888, 28 April 1880, 14 December 1881; *Arizona Republican*, 2 May 1909, 31 March 1899; Women's Christian Temperance Union File, Arizona Room, Arizona State University Library; Tisdale, "Prohibition," 12.

6. *Arizona Gazette*, 14 November 1884. The Methodist Church was at Second Avenue. Herb and Dorothy McLaughlin, *Phoenix 1870-1970 in Photographs* (Phoenix: Herb McLaughlin, 1970), 49; *Laws of the Territory of Arizona. Thirteenth Legislative Assembly. Also Memorials and Resolutions* (San Francisco: H. S. Crocker and Co., 1885), 56–57, 82–83, 212–13; *Annual Report of the WCTU, 1884*, WCTU Home, Phoenix, cited in Tisdale, "Prohibition," 19; untitled scrapbook, WCTU Home, Phoenix; Paul Renau Ingles, comp., *Charter and Combined Ordinances and Resolutions of the City of Phoenix* (Phoenix: Phoenix Printing Company, 1910), 78–79; *Annual Report of the WCTU, 1887*, WCTU Home, Phoenix, as cited in Tisdale, "Prohibition," 20–21; McClintock, *Arizona*, 2:384; *Revised Statutes of Arizona* (Prescott, Ariz.: Prescott Courier Print, 1887), 371; *Arizona Daily Star*, 9 March 1889.

7. *Arizona Daily Star*, 9 March 1889, 30 March 1890; *Phoenix Herald*, 27 March 1887, 6 October 1890; *Annual Report of the WCTU, 1887*, as cited in Tisdale, "Prohibition," 20–21, 31; U.S. Bureau of the Census, *Thirteenth Census of the United States Taken in the Year 1910. Population 1910. Reports by States with Statistics for Counties, Cities and Other Civil Divisions. Alabama–Montana* (Washington, D.C.: Department of Commerce, 1911), 2:73.

8. Louise Boehringer, "Josephine Brawley Hughes," *Arizona Historical Review* (January 1930): 102; *Journals of the Seventeenth Legislative Assembly of the Territory of Arizona, 1893* (Phoenix: Herald Book and Job Office, 1893), 27, 30; Louis C. Hughes, *Report of the Governor of the Territory of Arizona to the Secretary of the Interior, 1894*, 55–56.

9. Mrs. A. B. Buckley, *Arizona Republican*, 31 March 1899; *Annual Report of the WCTU, 1887*, as cited in Tisdale, "Prohibition," 20–21, 57, 67; *Minutes of the Thirteenth Annual WCTU Convention, 1901*; *Arizona Gazette*, 9 November 1901. The other locales were in Tucson, Florence, Casa Grande, Flagstaff, Prescott, Mesa, and Tempe.

10. *Arizona Republican*, 14 September, 24 October, 7 November 1900; McClintock, *Arizona*, 2:384–85; *Revised Statutes of Arizona Territory, 1901* (Columbia, Mo.: Press of E. W. Stephens, 1901), 801–6.

11. *Arizona Republican*, 9 July 1902; Tisdale, "Prohibition," 64–66; *Arizona Gazette*, 8 March 1903.

12. *Arizona Republican*, 11, 18 January 1903; *Arizona Gazette*, 17 June 1903; see note 55 for Mrs. McCormick's role in the suffrage movement. *Woman's Club of Phoenix, Arizona* (n.p., n.d., unpaged). Mrs. LaChance, identified with temperance before coming to Arizona in 1895, became president of the territorial WCTU in 1900 and was reelected throughout the decade. Jo Conners, *Who's Who in Arizona*, 2 vols. (Tucson: Daily Star Press, 1913), 1:610. Mrs. LaChance's husband, Leander, was a Methodist, manager of the Wakelin Grocery House. McClintock, *Arizona*, 3:420; Tisdale, "Prohibition," 27; "WCTU Records, Book No. 2" (MS), WCTU Home, 180, 182, 184.

13. *Arizona Republican*, 8, 9, 10 August 1903; *Arizona Gazette*, 30 October 1903, 12 October 1904. In October 1904 a Prohibition party convention met in Good Templars' Hall and nominated a ticket for the fall election.

14. *Arizona Republican*, 14 April, 6 May 1905; Tisdale, "Prohibition," 78–79. One meeting was at the Methodist Church. In August 1904 the city council responded to the WCTU by voting it the cost of a sidewalk—$102. This was through the good offices of "Mr. Clark," probably Vernon Clark. "WCTU Record; Book No. 2" (MS), WCTU Home, 255.

15. Tisdale, "Prohibition," 78–79. The league originated in Oberlin, Ohio, in 1893. John Kobler, *Ardent Spirits: The Rise and Fall of Prohibition* (New York: G. P. Putnam's Sons, 1973), 19; *Arizona Republican*, 28 October 1906. The O'Neills were an instance of Catholic participation in the antigambling and suffrage causes. McClintock, *Arizona*, 3:567.

16. *Arizona Daily Star*, 23 January 1907; Tisdale, "Prohibition," 80–81.

17. An unsuccessful attempt was made to claim before the supervisors that existing prohibition districts could not participate. *Arizona Republican*, 7 April 1908; *Arizona Gazette*, 23 January 1908. The saloon licenses were expiring and Phoenix saloons closed for three days, not wanting to buy licenses they would not need for more than a day if local option prevailed. *Arizona Gazette*, 29, 30 April 1908; Tisdale, "Prohibition," 85–87.

18. *Arizona Gazette*, 28 April, 1 May 1908; *Arizona Republican*, 1, 3 May 1908; *Arizona Democrat*, 2 June 1910; Tisdale, "Prohibition," 85–87; McClintock, *Arizona*, 3:493. Two years later the *Arizona Democrat* accused its rival of taking money to defend a saloon-keeper whereas it (the *Democrat*) opposed prohibition in principle. Coggins, mayor from May 1906 to May 1909, was a Baptist who in 1908 purchased the interest of all other stockholders in the Phoenix Title, Guarantee and Abstract Company. On February 6, 1908, he became adjutant general of Arizona under Governor Kibbey. Mesa's election also had women and children participating. The WCTU, urged on by Dr. Hughes, furnished refreshments and taught the children the songs and yells. Christianna Gilchrist (see note 27) was on the "banner committee" and was vice-chairwoman of the "Ladies' Campaign Committee"; she also invited the colored Sunday school. WCTU minutes headed "April 30, 1908" (MS, unbound), WCTU Home, 3.

19. *Arizona Gazette*, 1, 4 May 1908; Tisdale, "Prohibition," 89.

20. *Arizona Daily Star*, 11, 21 February 1909; *Arizona Republican*, 19 March 1909; Tisdale, "Prohibition," 90–92. Hughes, then over sixty, was superintendent of the Southern Methodist Church Sunday school. "Dr. H. A. Hughes," in McClintock File, Phoenix Public Library.

21. See WCTU minutes, 25 April 1908 (MS, unbound), WCTU Home, unpaged. District Attorney George Bullard announced that thereafter no license would be issued to a saloon within one hundred yards of the old red-light Block 41. Sheriff Carl Hayden (later U.S. senator) pronounced half the crime in the city the result of the association of saloons with the block. *Arizona Gazette*, 23 October 1907; *Arizona Republican*, 24, 26, 27 November 1907. Under the 1909 ordinance, saloons had to be on the ground floor, not less than twelve feet wide, with no bar more than thirty feet long or more than thirty feet from the front. There were to be no doors to other rooms, no liquor served anywhere else, no tables, chairs, or stools. The front of the building had to be entirely of glass, not covered by curtain, paint, or screens, and no more than three feet above the sidewalk. *Arizona Republican*, 7 May 1909; Tisdale, "Prohibition," 80. Judge Ainsworth filed for the Royal Arch and the ordinance was invalidated in November 1909. *Arizona Gazette*, 16 June 1909; *Charter and Compiled Ordinances and Resolutions of the City of Phoenix*, 366–69. Ibid., 283–84. *Arizona Statehood Magazine*, 1, no. 4(December 1910): 12, 14; *Arizona Republican*, 19 September 1910; 1, 2, 9 April 1911; *Session Laws of the 22nd Legislative Assembly of the Territory of Arizona* (Phoenix: N.p., 1903), 132–33; *Arizona Daily Star*, 29 June, 17, 29 December 1910; 30, 31 March 1912; James R. Dunseath, ed., *Reports of Cases Argued and Determined in the Supreme Court of the Territory, January 1910 to May 1911* (San Francisco: Bancroft-Whitney Co., 1911), 13:280–81; Tisdale, "Prohibition," 81, footnote.

22. *Arizona Gazette*, 28 October, 1, 2 November 1910; Tisdale, "Prohibition," 105–12. The league published the *Arizona Issue* in Phoenix from January 1910. Lobbying on the floor of the convention was prohibited.

23. *Arizona Gazette*, 1, 2 April 1911 and until election; Tisdale, "Prohibition," 119–20.

24. *Arizona Republican*, 2, 9, 15 April 1911. Stockholders in the Adams Hotel claimed that construction, stopped for the election, would never resume if prohibition won. *Arizona Democrat*, 15, 30 March, 13, 15 April 1911.

25. *Arizona Republican*, 19, 30 April, 28 May 1911; *Arizona Gazette*, 18, 19 April 1911; *Arizona Democrat*, 19 April 1911; *Minutes of the 1911 WCTU Convention*, cited in Tisdale, "Prohibition," 124–25.

26. Andrew Sinclair, *Prohibition: The Era of Excess* (Boston: Little, Brown and Co., 1962), 107–8; McClintock, *Arizona*, 3:923.

27. *Arizona Republican*, 5 September 1910; 17 April, 12 September, 1, 3 November 1911; *Arizona Democrat*, 12 December 1910. By 1894 the WCTU had forced the closing of the "worst kind of variety theaters" on Washington Street, at various times, by pleas to the city council. *Arizona Republican*, 13 November 1911. The cattle growers' association, the postmasters' convention, the pharmacists' association, and the dental association also had mutual relationships with the fair. Christianna Gilchrist (daughter of Sophia Montfort and Presbyterian minister John Gilchrist) was born January 20, 1862, in Boggstown, Indiana. Her mother was left a widow with five children when Christianna was fifteen months old. A schoolmate of James Whitcomb Riley, Christianna graduated from Hanover College and taught eight years in a Colorado academy before leaving for health reasons. In 1899 she came to Phoenix, drawn by its mild climate, and soon joined the WCTU. Active in the Presbyterian Missionary Society, she had "hosts of friends especially among the younger people whose problems she seemed to understand." She died December 18, 1945. Roberta Clayton, comp. and ed., "Pioneer Women of Arizona" (mimeographed), 165–66; "WCTU Records, Book No. 2" (MS), WCTU Home, 64.

28. *Phoenix Herald*, 27 December 1879, 2 February 1886.

29. Ibid., 24 January 1890; 14, 16, 19 December 1891; *Arizona Gazette*, 10 January, 20 October 1895. The six women signing a letter to the *Herald* on hospital conditions were Mmes Harriet Hine, O. J. Thibodo, E. D. Garlick, Hattie Talbot, J. M. Copes, and M. E. Frakes. Dr. Hughes, later president of the Anti-Saloon League, was county physician in 1891 and carried on something of a feud with the women, sending an ill man to Mrs. Garlick (see note 51 for her work as a temperance and suffrage leader), claiming he had no room for him; she gave the man some of her own money. See note 18 for Hughes's prohibition role. The committee was Mmes Hattie Talbot (Benevolent Society president, whose husband would be mayor and who would be active in the library and suffrage movements [see note 47], regent of the Daughters of the American Revolution, and in 1907 one of the trustees of the Phoenix Woman's Club), E. Ganz, W. C. Budge, L. Chalmers, John Dennis, M. H. Williams, and Leo and Charles Goldman. For Mrs. Talbot, see Margaret Wheeler Ross, *The Tale Is Told: The Arizona Federation of Women's Clubs*, 2 vols. (Phoenix: N.p., 1976?), 1:13; *Arizona Gazette*, 6 March 1907.

30. Dr. Weems was president, Dr. Halsey vice-president, the Reverend Ferguson secretary-treasurer. *Arizona Gazette*, 20 December 1898.

31. The plan was in operation from January 15. The union solicited clothing as well as subscriptions. *Arizona Gazette*, 2 February 1905. For the original plan, see "WCTU Records, Book No. 2" (MS), WCTU Home. The territorial president of WCTU relief had suggested a local relief organization in November 1898, and by February 1902 this was a Phoenix WCTU department under a superintendent, Mrs. M. A. Thomas. Ibid., 39, 153, 268–72; *Arizona Republican*, 13 November 1906.

32. *Arizona Republican*, 7 January 1907. Miss Gilchrist gave Phoenix's population as twelve thousand; one-fourth would have been three thousand. The county had to send the "poor farm" wagon daily to cheap boardinghouses for penniless individuals who were too weak to work. The farm was full to overflowing. John Orme suggested that eastern

philanthropists be contacted to donate a sanitarium. *Arizona Gazette*, 19 October 1907. The sick were often refused lodging. *Arizona Republican*, 17 December 1908. In March 1907, Riis spoke at the Methodist Church under Associated Charities auspices. *Arizona Gazette*, 2 March 1907.

33. *Arizona Republican*, 16 February 1907, 5 November 1908.

34. *Arizona Gazette*, 7, 21 October, 1 November 1907; *Arizona Republican*, 17 January 1907; 17, 18 October 1908.

35. *Arizona Gazette*, 5 May 1908; *Arizona Republican*, 5 November 1908.

36. *Arizona Republican*, 9, 11 March 1909; 15 June, 11 October, 15 December 1911; 14 March, 8 October 1912; Mrs. B. F. Fowler, "Woman's Club Movement in Phoenix and Vicinity," *Call of the Desert*, 1 May 1908, 17. Crittenton Home had received WCTU aid in previous years. *Arizona Republican*, 2 May 1909.

37. *Arizona Republican*, 14 March, 18 November 1912.

38. *Phoenix Herald*, 19 December 1889, 11 April 1888.

39. *Salt River Herald*, 16, 23 November 1878. William NcNulty was librarian. *Phoenix Herald*, 29 November 1879. See Ann Douglas, *The Feminization of American Culture* (New York: Knopf, 1977), passim, for nineteenth-century women's orientation to reading. *Phoenix Herald*, 17 December 1879, 16 October 1880. The association incorporated in 1886, leasing a room behind the post office for twenty dollars a month, including maintenance and librarian. *Phoenix Herald*, 26, 27 April 1888.

40. The first reading room was run by Katie Ingalls, presumably a relative of Dr. Ingalls, for whose prohibition activities see note 5. *Arizona Republican*, 3 May 1894; *Phoenix Herald*, 7 June 1884; 12, 30 March, 6, 12, 16 April 1888; Lillian Crandell, "Crusaders Then and Now," speech given in Glendale at the WCTU state convention, 30 October 1964, WCTU Home, cited by Tisdale, "Prohibition," 16; *Arizona Gazette*, 13 December 1887; 2 January, 25 February, 10 May, 19 December 1889; 6 January 1890; Frank Elwell, "History of Phoenix Churches" (TS), 2. *Phoenix Herald*, 7 December 1888. The WCTU asked the *Herald* to say the opera rooms would be used only until better could be had. *Phoenix Herald*, 8 December 1888.

41. *Arizona Gazette*, 24 November 1892, 19 July 1884, 23 October 1898; *Arizona Republican*, 28 July 1894, 31 March 1899. The Good Templars also maintained a free reading room. Phoenix National Bank, *Phoenix and the Salt River Valley, Arizona* (Phoenix: Phoenix National Bank, 1893–94), 36; "WCTU Records, Book No. 2" (MS), WCTU Home.

42. In 1976 the Friday Club would be, after Prescott's Monday Club, "the oldest continuously operating club" in the state and one of the city's most exclusive, with admission by unanimous vote. Ross, *Tale Is Told*, 16–18; *Arizona Republican*, 24 February 1901; Andrew Downing, *History of the Carnegie Public Library, Phoenix, Arizona* (Phoenix: Carnegie Public Libary, 1914), 10, 11. The library, on the second floor of the Fleming Building—James Fleming donated the rent—was open Tuesdays and Thursdays from nine to four. Miss Catherine Dyer was the first librarian. *Arizona Gazette*, 19 June 1898; James McClintock quoted in the *Gazette*, 30 September 1930. The WCTU's books apparently had not circulated before.

43. Michael F. Konig, "Toward Metropolis Status: Charter Government and the Rise of Phoenix, Arizona, 1945–1960" (Ph.D. diss., Arizona State University, 1983). Konig points out that such cultural attractions as a library, museums, and the arts were to prove necessary in attracting industry to Phoenix in the 1950s. The *Republican* ridiculed the claim that a library would spread disease. *Arizona Republican*, 11 February 1899.

44. No relationship has been found with the old association. See Downing, *Library*, 11. According to a charter member of the Friday Club, the founding meeting was called by the Friday Club. *A Charter Member: The Story of the Friday Club. Being Historical*

*Reminiscences* (Phoenix: The Friday Club, 1936), 7; *Arizona Gazette*, 15 November 1899, 21 March 1900; *Arizona Republican*, 24 August, 21 December 1900. At least at first, Friday Club members took turns as library tenders. "History of the Phoenix Public Library" (mimeographed), unpaged. The Friday Club had contributed 1,200 books to the library, 250 more had been purchased, and 194 others donated. *Arizona Republican*, 9 October 1900.

45. *Arizona Republican*, 28 December 1900; *Arizona Gazette*, 30 March 1901. The librarian and janitor were the only paid personnel; the discrepancy in the published amounts may have resulted because salaries were given in annual amounts and/or small expenses were not listed. The vote for library trustees: W. C. Foster, five; Vernon Clark, five; J. L. B. Alexander, four; T. E. Dalton, three; R. L. Long, three; Mrs. Frazier, two; Mrs. W. K. James, two. *Arizona Gazette*, 2 April 1901.

46. *Arizona Gazette*, 11 March 1900; *Arizona Republican*, 29 August 1930; Ross, *Tale Is Told*; Margaret Wheeler Ross, "Arizona Federation of Women's Clubs," *Arizona* 6 (September 1916): 3. Ross, *Tale Is Told*, passim, and *Woman's Club of Phoenix, Arizona, 1910-1911* (n.p., n.d.), unpaged. Fowler and McClintock, particularly, were Phoenix elites. Under the term of Phoenix Library Association President B. Heyman, Andrew Carnegie had been asked, and refused, to finance a library. B. A. Fowler had also corresponded with Carnegie about the library. Downing, *Library*, 11-12. The *Arizona Gazette*, 17 June 1902, attributed Carnegie's offer to the Friday Club. The Phoenix Woman's Club was simultaneously involved in establishing a free museum. *Arizona Republican*, 31 December 1902; Downing, *Library*, 12-13. For the effect of the 1900 census see B. A. Fowler, *Arizona Republican*, 2 November 1909. Educated at Andover (1862) and Yale (1868), Fowler, outstanding in the valley's reclamation, temperance, and charity movements, was also, with his "ceaseless zeal," important in the library movement's success. *Arizona Gazette*, 5 November 1907. He went to Washington in October 1903 with all kinds of data to support Phoenix's claim to the larger grant. Downing, *Library*, 14-15; Conners, *Who's Who in Arizona*, 2:797; McClintock, *Arizona*, 3:922-23; *Arizona Republican*, 12 January 1904. See also Terry D. Oehler, "B. A. Fowler and the Carnegie Public Library," *Phoenix* (1 July 1980): 65-67.

47. *Arizona Gazette*, 2 February 1904; 7 June, 8 January 1905; 5 November 1907; 13 February 1908; originally (1901) the Woman's Club had resolved to occupy part of the library but withdrew the resolution. Talbot was mayor from May 1901 to May 1903. Downing, *Library*, 12, 13. The Keefer lots were about a block north of the ditch on Center Street (later Central Avenue), the ditch being the Salt River Canal at Center, somewhat north of Van Buren. *Arizona Republican*, 23, 24 November, 6, 9 December 1904. Apparently the city chose the Keefer lots first—December 8, 1904—but when the cash to buy them was not forthcoming within the forty-five days agreed on, the city decided on the park site. Downing, *Library*, 17. Mrs. Morford, a charter Friday Club member, was the wife of the former publisher of the *Herald* (combined with the *Republican* in 1899) who had been director of the original Phoenix Library Association. *Phoenix Herald*, 26 April 1886; Downing, *Library*, 19. On March 3, 1902, the city council had levied an annual five-mill tax for the library. "History of the Phoenix Public Library," unpaged.

48. Boehringer, "Josephine Brawley Hughes," 103; Frances W. Munds to James H. McClintock, 15 April 1915, McClintock Collection, Phoenix Public Library.

49. *Phoenix Herald*, 27 August 1882, 28 June 1886; *Arizona Gazette*, 2 August 1884, 28 September 1886; *Amended School Laws of the Territory of Arizona Enacted by the Twelfth Legislative Assembly, 1883* (Territorial publication, no other data).

50. McClintock, *Arizona*, 2:384; *Phoenix Herald*, 7, 26 February 1889; 15, 18 September 1891. Carrie Chapman Catt and Nettie Roger Shuler, *Woman Suffrage and Politics: The Inner Story of the Suffrage Movement* (New York: Charles Scribner's Sons, 1923), 128;

Mattie L. Williams, "History of Woman Suffrage in Arizona," *Arizona Historical Review* (January 1929): 70, and as quoted in Roscoe Wilson, "Story of Woman's Vote," *Arizona* (11 June 1967): 48. See page 35 for the firming of the prohibition-versus-saloon lines in the 1890s. Legislators, however, responded to the presence of women in the galleries. *Phoenix Herald*, 4 March 1891; Tisdale, "Prohibition," 37.

51. Boehringer, "Josephine Brawley Hughes," 103; *Phoenix Herald*, 23, 24 September 1889; 13, 18, 24, 28 September 1891; *Journal of the Constitutional Convention for the State of Arizona* (Phoenix: Herald Power Print, 1891), 24; *Arizona Republican*, 26 May 1894. Mrs. Garlick was also a leader in the Ladies Benevolent Society (see note 29) and would be president of the territorial WCTU in 1896. Thomas Lauerman, "Desexing the Ballot Box: The History of Woman Suffrage in Arizona, 1883-1912" (Arizona State University, 1973), 28. Mrs. Hughes had asked Mrs. Johns to come to Arizona. McClintock, *Arizona*, 3:11. Apparently there was an NAWSA branch in Phoenix, perhaps mainly for this appearance. Two of the three Maricopa County convention delegates, T. C. Jordan and M. H. Williams, voted against suffrage; Alexander voted for it. *Phoenix Herald*, 24 September 1891; Tisdale, "Prohibition," 42.

52. "The Governor's Message," *Journals of the Seventeenth Assembly*, 30-31, 212-13; *Phoenix Herald*, 29 May 1894; Lauerman, "Desexing the Ballot," 9; Boehringer, "Josephine Brawley Hughes," 103; *Arizona Republican*, 1 May 1894; it also ignored him on the Sunday closing law. *Journals of the Eighteenth Legislative Assembly, 1895* (Phoenix: N.p., 1895), 30-31.

53. *Arizona Daily Star*, 7 December 1895; Catt and Shuler, *Suffrage*, 129-30. Mrs. Hayden, chosen vice-president, was the mother of Carl Hayden, who served as U.S. senator from Arizona for many decades.

54. *Journals of the Legislative Assembly of Arizona, 1897* (Phoenix: N.p., 1897), 112, 115, 119; Tisdale, "Prohibition," 57-60; Susan B. Anthony and Ida H. Harper, eds., *History of Woman Suffrage*, 6 vols. (New York: J. J. Little and Ives Co., 1922), 4:471-74, 6:10; *Journals of the Twentieth Legislative Assembly of the Territory of Arizona* (Phoenix: Arizona Press of J. O. Dunbar, 1899), 449, and see index under House Bill No. 35; Catt and Shuler, *Suffrage*, 128.

55. *Arizona Gazette*, 14 February 1900; 16 July 1902; 5, 6 March 1901; *Arizona Republican*, 11 January 1903, 17 May 1901. Mrs. McCormick's home was at 554 North Fourth Avenue. See page 36 for the WCTU franchise department. Frances Munds, in Anthony and Harper, *Woman Suffrage*, 6:10, says Mrs. Catt and Mrs. Shuler returned in 1900 and organized the first full-fledged suffrage association in the territory. Pauline O'Neill was also president of the Woman's Relief Corps. *Arizona Gazette*, 31 May 1904; McClintock, *Arizona*, 3:7. Munds in Anthony and Harper, *Woman Suffrage*, 6:10, cites Bucky O'Neill as a staunch friend of suffrage. Anna McClatchie, president of the Phoenix Woman's Club, joined the Phoenix WCTU in May 1901. "WCTU Records, Book No. 2" (MS), WCTU Home, 13. Robinson was adjutant general from 1899 to 1901. Jay J. Wagoner, *Arizona Territory, 1863-1912: A Political History* (Tucson: University of Arizona Press, 1970), 501; Munds in Anthony and Harper, *Woman Suffrage*, 6:10-11.

56. Frances W. Munds to James H. McClintock, 4 April 1915, James H. McClintock Collection, Phoenix Public Library. The convention met January 19 through 21 in Padget's Hall. *Arizona Gazette*, 20, 21, 22 January 1903; Tisdale, "Prohibition," 71-75; "First Annual Convention of the Arizona Federation of Women's Clubs," *Arizona Republican*, 1902, James H. McClintock Collection, Phoenix Public Library. Munds to McClintock, 4 April 1915; *Minutes of the 1902 WCTU Convention* (Phoenix: N.p., 1903), cited in Tisdale, "Prohibition," 70.

57. Mrs. Munds called Kibbey an arch foe who gave the governor the Republican vote on another bill in exchange for the veto. Anthony and Harper, *Woman Suffrage*, 6:11.

*Arizona Republican*, 14, 23 February 1903; *Arizona Gazette*, 28 February 1903. Kibbey estimated that with women voting, Arizona would have 36,438 voters to New Mexico's 38,798. Mrs. Kibbey would be president of the Friday Club in 1907 and of the Woman's Club in 1908, when Kibbey would be governor. *Arizona Republican*, 4 March 1908. For the *Republican's* favorable comments, see ibid., 18 March 1903; for the veto, ibid., 20, 21 March 1930. The *New York Times*, 18, 20 March 1903, said the House supposedly passed the bill as a joke. Cited by Wagoner, *Arizona Territory*, 406. McClintock, *Arizona*, 2:386, refers to the *Republican's* turnabout; Tisdale, "Prohibition," 73.

58. *Arizona Republican*, 18 November, 13 December 1903. Maricopa County assembly delegates in 1903 were, besides Kibbey in the council, G. U. Collins, J. D. Marlar, T. Powers (House Speaker) from Phoenix, and J. W. Woolf from Tempe. *Acts, Resolutions and Memorials of the Twenty-Second Legislative Assembly of the Territory of Arizona* (n.p., n.d.), unpaged. Mrs. Munds refers to a "little paper" by Mrs. Robinson. Munds in Anthony and Harper, *Woman Suffrage*, 6:11.

59. Munds in Anthony and Harper, *Woman Suffrage*, 6:11. Kibbey advocated outlawing gambling and female saloon employees and favored Sunday saloon closing in his 1907 address to the legislature, but he did not mention suffrage. *Arizona Daily Star*, 23 January 1907. For the gambling issue, see *Arizona Republican*, 12, 16 May 1905; 21 January, 13 April 1906; and Munds in Anthony and Harper, *Woman Suffrage*, 6:11. It was, according to McClintock, the first referendum in Arizona outside the school districts. McClintock, *Arizona*, 2:385. Phoenix businesses seem generally not to have been unfavorable to liquor, especially after outlying areas went dry. However, they seem to have viewed gambling as competing unfairly for the business dollar. See page 35 for territorial action on gambling and Tisdale, "Prohibition," 83–84.

60. Munds in Anthony and Harper, *Woman Suffrage*, 6:12; Paul Fuller, *Laura Clay and the Woman's Rights Movement* (Lexington: University of Kentucky Press, 1975), 104–5; *Arizona Gazette*, 5 February 1909.

61. Fuller, *Clay*, 106; *Arizona Democrat*, 11 July 1910. The Phoenix unions consisted of the carpenters, barbers, pressmen, electrical workers, plasterers, printers, hod carriers, bricklayers, bookbinders, and three delegates from the Trades Council. Ibid., 12 July 1910. For the convention, see Wagoner, *Arizona Territory*, 412; Conners, *Who's Who in Arizona*, 614. Mrs. Munds, as chairwoman of the Equal Suffrage Campaign Committee (see note 63), received a letter from later Governor Hunt concerning his candidacy for delegate to the convention, of which he would be president, in which he stated that because of Taft's unsympathetic attitude toward equal suffrage, it was better for the convention to press for the initiative, referendum, and recall in the constitution, leaving suffrage until statehood. G. W. Hunt to Frances W. Munds, no date, 1910, G. W. Hunt Collection, Box 1, folders 9, 10, Arizona State University. Mrs. Munds's committee accepted this and asked Hunt as convention president to support the Connolley bill for the referendum. Frances W. Munds to G. W. Hunt, 10 November 1910. "I was not in favor of making the effort to get a suffrage plank in the constitution." Frances W. Munds to James H. McClintock, 4 April 1915, 3.

62. Munds to McClintock, 4 April 1915, 3; *Arizona Daily Star*, 12, 24 April 1912; Mrs. Mattie Williams, "Woman Suffrage in Arizona," *Arizona Historical Review* 1 (January 1929): 70–71; B. E. Marks and L. W. Coggins had charge of petition tables. *Arizona Republican*, 19 April, 16 June, 4, 6 July 1912; *Arizona Democrat*, 14 June 1912; Lauerman, "Desexing the Ballot," 21. Templars and Anti-Saloon League branches may have been the basis for a leaflet distributed October 9 claiming more than eight hundred civic, industrial, labor, religious, fraternal, and political organizations' support. Tisdale, "Prohibition," 133.

63. *Arizona Republican*, 7 December 1895; 1, 8, 15 September, 4, 16 October, 10 November 1912. Mrs. Munds was assisted by a number of prominent women, especially from the WCTU. Williams, "Suffrage," 72. O'Neill and McCormick had been the Phoenix members of the Arizona Equal Suffrage Campaign Committee. G. W. P. Hunt Collection, Box 1, Folder 11, Arizona State University. Mrs. Munds had long affiliation with the WCTU. Cleon Petty, "Mrs. Frances Lillian Willard Munds, Arizona Woman" (mimeographed), unpaged. Debs outpolled Taft in Arizona in 1912, although both ran far behind Wilson and Roosevelt. Lauerman, "Desexing the Ballot," 34. Laura Gregg was sent by NAWSA at a cost of nearly twelve hundred dollars. Press work was in charge of Mrs. Maybelle Craig and Miss Sally Jacobs of Phoenix. For the parties, see Catt and Shuler, *Suffrage*, 177. Among Republican supporters of suffrage was Grace Forbes, who in 1912 became the wife of prominent attorney J. L. B. Alexander. Eleanor Alexander Wiebeck, "My Memories of Grace M. Alexander" (mimeographed), unpaged, in Alexander Collection, Arizona State University. Dr. Shaw had become national superintendent of the WCTU's suffrage work in 1888 and was the first person to secure that group's support for suffrage. Tisdale, "Prohibition," 138-40. *Arizona Daily Star*, 8 October 1912.

64. *Arizona Republican*, 8 November 1912.

65. The Woman's Club had about 125 members in 1908. Mrs. B. A. Fowler, "Woman's Club Movement," 17. Lauerman, "Desexing the Ballot," 29, analyzing support for equal suffrage, notes that active women supporters were of the middle or upper classes.

## CHAPTER FOUR

1. In *1980 Census of Population* (Washington, D.C.: Government Printing Office, 1981), chap. B, vol. I, pt. 1, 209, Phoenix is listed as having an Indian population of 16,781. The entire Phoenix metropolitan area had 22,788 native people. For additional information, see Estelle Fuchs and Robert J. Havinghurst, *To Live on This Earth: American Indian Education*, reprint edition (Albuquerque: University of New Mexico Press, 1983), 273-75; Francis P. Prucha, *The Great Father: The United States Government and the American Indians*, abridged edition (Lincoln: University of Nebraska Press, 1986), 394-95; and Edward B. Liebow, "A Sense of Place: Urban Indians and the History of Pan-Tribal Institutions in Phoenix, Arizona" (Ph.D. diss., Arizona State University, 1986), passim.

2. Bradford Luckingham, *The Urban Southwest: A Profile History of Albuquerque, El Paso, Phoenix and Tucson* (El Paso: Texas Western Press, 1982), 1-16; George Harwood Phillips, "Indians in Los Angeles, 1781-1875: Economic Integration, Social Disintegration," *Pacific Historical Review* (August 1980): 427-51. For general information on urban Indians, see Jack O. Waddell and O. Michael Watson, eds., *The American Indian in Urban Society* (Boston: Little, Brown and Company, 1971).

3. Edward H. Spicer, *Cycles of Conquest: The Impact of Spain, Mexico, and the United States on the Indians of the Southwest, 1533-1960* (Tucson: University of Arizona Press, 1962), 148; Frank Russell, *The Pima Indians*, reprint (Tucson: University of Arizona Press, 1975), 30-34.

4. Gen. A. J. Alexander to Col. J. Sherburne, 2 October 1868 (copy), Arizona Collection, Hayden Library, Arizona State University.

5. Capt. F. E. Grossman to Bvt. Col. George L. Andrews, 19 October 1869, National Archives, Record Group 75, Records of the Bureau of Indian Affairs, Letters Received, Arizona Superintendency (hereafter referred to as BIA and appropriate subdivision); J. H. Stout to H. Bendell, 31 August 1872, in *Annual Report*, Commissioner of Indian

Affairs, 1872 (hereafter referred to as *AR*, CIA, and appropriate year), 317; Stout to J. M. Ferris, 9 May 1872, Stout Letterbook, Special Collections, University of Arizona Library; Stout to Gen. O. O. Howard, 11 May 1872, ibid.

6. *The Pima Indians*, 26th Annual Report, Bureau of American Ethnology, 1904–1905 (Washington, D.C.: Government Printing Office, 1908), 54; Stout to Commissioner, 31 August 1873, in *AR*, CIA, 1873, 281–82; Charles Hudson to Commissioner, 31 August 1875, in *AR*, CIA, 1875, 7; Stout to Commissioner, 31 August 1877, in *AR*, CIA, 1877, 32; Stout to Commissioner, 15 August 1878, in *AR*, CIA, 1878, 3–4; *Arizona Miner* (Prescott), 23 March 1977, 30 January 1879. For a complete history of the circumstances surrounding the creation of the Salt River Reservation, see articles by Earl Zarbin in the *Arizona Republic*, 7–10 January 1979.

7. The report of Clyde M. Johnson of the Pima Agency for 1888, in *AR*, CIA, 1888, 6, lists 3,290 Pimas and 100 Maricopas living on the Gila Reservation, 588 on the Salt River Reserve, and 180 with Mormons in Mesa. Luckingham, *Urban Southwest*, 29, gives the 1880 population of Phoenix as 1,708; Mabel Hancock Latham, Reminiscences of Phoenix, Hancock Family Collection, Box 3, Folder 53, Arizona Historical Foundation; Anna Moore Shaw, *A Pima Past* (Tucson: University of Arizona Press, 1974), 113.

8. Shaw, *A Pima Past*, 113–14; Phoenix City Ordinance, 30 May 1881; James M. Barney, "Famous Indian Ordinance," *Sheriff* (June 1954): 77; *Phoenix Herald*, 25, 29 July 1881. The municipal ordinance was reaffirmed on 22 December 1889 by the city council.

9. *Arizona Gazette*, 22 February 1883; *Phoenix Herald*, 2 March 1883; David F. Myrick, *Railroads of Arizona*, 3 vols. (San Diego: Howell-North Books, 1980), 2:499–500; *Phoenix Daily Herald*, 27 July 1888.

10. *Phoenix Daily Herald*, 20 September 1886; 5 July 1887; 1 September 1888; 12 July, 11 October 1889; *Arizona Gazette*, 8 April, 3 July 1886; 16 December 1887.

11. Robert A. Trennert, "'And the sword will give way to the spelling book': Establishing the Phoenix Indian School," *Journal of Arizona History* 23 (Spring 1982): 42–43; Mawn, "Phoenix," 135–54.

12. *Arizona Republican*, 10, 12, 13, 14 October 1890; *Phoenix Daily Herald*, 13, 14 October, 15 December 1890; T. J. Morgan to R. V. Belt, 12 October 1890, BIA, Letters Received (hereafter LR), 32299–1890; Wellington Rich to Morgan, 18 December 1890, ibid., 39956–1890; John W. Noble to Morgan, 30 December 1890, BIA, Authority, 25378–1890.

13. Rich to Commissioner, 5 August 1891, in *AR*, CIA, 1891, 557–58; Rich to Morgan, 19 March 1891, BIA, LR, 11506–1891; *Phoenix Daily Herald*, 3 April 1891.

14. *Phoenix Daily Herald*, 3, 7 September 1891; 29 April 1892; Rich to Commissioner, 10 September 1892, in *AR*, CIA, 1892, II, 838.

15. Superintendent of Indian Schools to Commissioner, 23 December 1895, BIA, LR, 51510–1895; S. M. McCowan to Commissioner, 31 July 1899, in *AR*, CIA, 1899, 384.

16. Harwood Hall to Commissioner, 10 August 1894, in *AR*, CIA, 1894, 369–71. For a comprehensive review of the Phoenix outing system, see Robert A. Trennert, "From Carlisle to Phoenix: The Rise and Fall of the Indian Outing System, 1878–1930," *Pacific Historical Review* 52 (August 1983): 277–91.

17. *Phoenix Daily Herald*, 1 July 1893; 8 June 1894; 23, 26 December 1895; *Daily Enterprise*, 9, 11 March 1899; S. M. McCowan to Commissioner, 30 July 1898, in *AR*, CIA, 1898, 354. After 1896 the newspapers regularly reported on the progress of Indian athletics, as did *The Native American*, the school magazine established in 1901.

18. Rich to Commissioner, 10 September 1892, in *AR*, CIA, 1892, 656; *Phoenix Daily Herald*, 24 January 1893; McCowan to Commissioner, 4 March 1900, BIA, LR, 13553–1900.

19. Clark M. Carr, "The Salt River Valley, Arizona," *Southwest Illustrated Magazine* (June 1895): 107–11; *Phoenix Daily Herald*, 26 April, 11 July 1890; 5 November 1892; 22 November 1895; 28 November 1898; 23 June 1899; *Phoenix Republican*, 7, 22 March, 19 October 1901; 1 December 1902.

20. *Phoenix Daily Herald*, 25 May 1893.

21. *Arizona Gazette*, 16 November 1890, 12 March 1895; *Phoenix Daily Herald*, 18 February 1896; 15 May, 23 June, 24 November 1897; 28 November 1898.

22. *Phoenix Daily Herald*, 18 February 1896; "Salt River Valley," *Arizona Graphic*, 30 September 1899, 3; Burt Ogburn, "Ancient Stone Relics in the Rio Salado Valley," *Arizona Educator* (September 1897): 11–12.

23. Keith L. Bryant, Jr., *History of the Atchison, Topeka and Santa Fe Railway* (New York: Macmillan, 1974), 118–20.

24. "The Indian and the Kodak," *Arizona Graphic*, 23 September 1899, 3; *Phoenix Daily Herald*, 18, 19, 20 February 1896; 22 February 1898.

25. "The Carnival of Phoenix," *Arizona Graphic*, 2 December 1899, 1–3; "Phoenix Cowboy and Indian Carnival," *Arizona Graphic*, 9 December 1899, 1–3.

26. "The Phoenix Carnival," *Arizona Graphic*, 30 December 1899, 1–2; *Phoenix Daily Herald*, 29 November 1900; *Arizona Republican*, 17 December 1900.

27. *Arizona Republican*, 10, 16, 17 December 1900; 13, 16, 22, 26 November 1902.

28. Ibid., 24, 25, 26, 28 December 1905.

29. Charles W. Goodman to Commissioner, 11 April 1902, BIA, LR, 22877–1902; Mawn, "Phoenix," 412.

30. Goodman to Commissioner, 10 September 1902, BIA, LR, 55054–1902; the Reverend L. McAfee to James B. Alexander, 18 November 1902, ibid., 1360–1903, enclosure #1.

31. Goodman to Commissioner, 10 September, 24 October 1902, 2 January 1903, ibid., 55054–1902, 64577–1902, 1360–1903. *Arizona Republican*, 8 July 1904, reported that prostitution among Indian women in Phoenix was a continuing problem.

32. Goodman to Commissioner, 18 July 1910, BIA, *Annual Narrative and Statistical Reports* (hereafter ANSR), Phoenix, 1910; Outing Matron Report, 7 July 1910, ibid.; Amanda Chingren to J. B. Brown, 2 June 1918, ibid., Phoenix, 1918.

33. Outing Matron Report, 7 July 1910, BIA, ANSR, Phoenix, 1910; Report of E. M. Sweet of the Outing System at Phoenix, 15 July 1916, BIA, Central Files, Phoenix, 76513–1916–806; *Arizona Republican*, 1 May, 13 June, 15 December 1908; 22 January, 27 May 1909; 23 March, 21 May 1910; 17 March 1911. Mawn, "Phoenix," 314–19, provides complete coverage of the bridge construction.

34. A. E. Marden to Goodman, 28 July 1913, BIA, ANSR, Phoenix, 1913; Brown to Cato Sells, 13 August 1915, BIA, Federal Records Center (Laguna Niguel, California), Phoenix Area Office; Annual Reports, Phoenix Indian Sanatorium, 1929, 1931, 1932, BIA, ANSR, Phoenix Sanatorium.

35. *Arizona Republican*, 8 August 1914.

36. Shaw, *A Pima Past*, 142–46; Brown to Commissioner, 2 July 1918, BIA, ANSR, Phoenix, 1918; Phoenix Indian School to Commissioner, 9 May 1918, BIA, Federal Records Center, Phoenix Area Office.

37. *Fourteenth Census of the United States, 1920* (Washington, D.C.: Government Printing Office, 1922), 3:77, 80.

38. Regulations Governing the Conduct and Service of Non-Citizen Indians in Phoenix and Vicinity, 8 June 1922, BIA, Central Files, Phoenix, 87833–1923–824.

39. *Arizona Republican*, 14 February, 26 September 1923; *Annual Report*, Board of Indian Commissioners, 1924, 40–42; Michael John Kotlanger, S.J., "Phoenix, Arizona: 1920–1940" (Ph.D. diss., Arizona State University, 1983), 407–8.

40. *Annual Report*, Board of Indian Commissioners, 1924, 42-43; *Arizona Republican*, 14 December 1924.

41. Adelena O. Warren to C. H. Burke, 8 November 1923, BIA, Central Files, Phoenix, 87833-1923-824; Report on Outing Matron Activities, Phoenix, Arizona (1925), ibid., 40642-1925-824; *Native American*, 10 October 1925.

42. *Native American*, 10 October 1925; Shaw, *A Pima Past*, 151-54.

43. Shaw, *A Pima Past*, 152-54; *Arizona Republican*, 6 April 1927; Kotlanger, "Phoenix," 409.

44. A. F. Duclose to Burke, 29 June 1923, BIA, Central Files, Phoenix, 91218-1917-821; John B. White to Commissioner, 5 September 1923 and Commissioner to White, 22 September 1923, ibid., 71229-1923-821; *Arizona Republican*, 10 July 1923; Kotlanger, "Phoenix," 401.

45. *Annual Report*, Board of Indian Commissioners, 1927, 29-30; Amanda M. Chingren to J. B. Brown, 2 November 1927, BIA, Federal Records Center, Phoenix Area Office; *Arizona Republican*, 6 April 1927.

46. *Fifteenth Census of the United States, 1930* (Washington, D.C.: Government Printing Office, 1932), 3:157; Brown to School Superintendents, 31 July 1929, Brown to Arthur C. Plake, 25 July 1929, Brown to Commissioner, 8 January and 12 February 1930, BIA, Federal Records Center, Phoenix Area Office; Goldie Weisberg, "Panorama: Phoenix, Arizona," *American Mercury* 17 (May 1929): 97-98.

47. Liebow, "A Sense of Place," 122-24, 140-42.

## CHAPTER FIVE

1. Donald Tricarico, *The Italians of Greenwich Village* (New York: Center for Migration Studies, 1984); William De Marco, *Ethnics and Enclaves: Boston's Italian North End* (Boston: UMI Research, 1981); Humbert Nelli, *The Italians in Chicago: 1880-1930* (New York: Oxford University Press, 1970); Leonard Moss, "Voluntary Association in South Italy and Detroit," in *The Family and Community Life of Italian Americans*, ed. Richard Juliani (New York: American Italian Historical Association, 1983), 11-22; Robert Park and Ernest Burgess, *The City* (Chicago: University of Chicago Press, 1925); Anthony Pizzo, "The Italian Heritage in Tampa," in *Little Italies in North America*, ed. Robert Harney and J. Vincenza Scarpaci (Toronto: Multicultural History Society of Ontario, 1981), 123- 40; *United States Census Reports*, vol. 1, Twelfth Census (Washington, D.C.: Government Printing Office, 1901); Lawrence Larsen, *The Urban West at the End of the Frontier* (Lawrence: Regents Press of Kansas, 1978), 21-27.

2. Ralph Mahoney, "Our Italian-American Heritage," *Arizona Days and Ways Magazine*, 11, 18, 25 August 1957; Phylis Cancilla Martinelli, "Beneath the Surface: Ethnic Communities in Phoenix, Arizona," in *Culture, Ethnicity, and Identity*, ed. William McCready (New York: Academic Press, 1983), 181-93; Amitai Etzioni, "The Ghetto: A Reevaluation," *Social Forces* (March 1959): 255-62; Phylis Cancilla Martinelli, "Pioneer paesani in Globe, Arizona," in *Italian Immigrants in Rural and Small Town America*, ed. Rudolph J. Vecoli (New York: Italian American Historical Association, 1987).

3. *Great Registers of Voters*, Maricopa County 1882-1910 (microfilm, Arizona State Department of Library and Archives, Archive Division); *Phoenix City Directories*, 1882, 1892, 1895, 1897, 1898, 1899, 1905, 1913, 1914.

4. Sacks Collection, Arizona Historical Foundation, Hayden Library, Arizona State University; *Great Registers of Voters*, Maricopa County 1882.

5. Felix Bertino, interview with author, Phoenix, July 1976.

6. *United States Census Reports*, Special Reports, 313, Occupations, Twelfth Census (Washington, D.C.: Government Printing Office, 1904), 225–27.

7. Edna Bonacich, "A Theory of Middleman Minorities," *American Sociological Review* 38 (October 1973): 583–94; *Phoenix City Directory* (Phoenix: Phoenix Directory Company, 1892–98).

8. "The Magnani Gambling Case," *Arizona Republican*, 18 February 1908; Geoffrey P. Mawn, "Phoenix, Arizona: Central City of the Southwest, 1870–1920" (Ph.D. diss., Arizona State University, 1979), 413–17.

9. Mawn, "Phoenix, Arizona," 413–17.

10. *Phoenix City Directory*.

11. *Annual Report of the Commissioner-General of Immigration* (Washington, D.C.: Government Printing Office, 1904).

12. David Nicandri, *Italians in Washington State* (Tacoma: Washington State Bicentennial Commission, 1978), 26; Andrew Rolle, *The Immigrant Upraised* (Norman: University of Oklahoma Press, 1968), 96.

13. Phylis Cancilla Martinelli, "Italy in Phoenix," *Journal of Arizona History* 18 (Autumn 1977): 321.

14. Frederick G. Bohme, "A History of the Italians in New Mexico" (Ph.D. diss., University of New Mexico, 1958), 196. The towns would include Morenci, Globe, Miami, and Jerome.

15. Phylis Cancilla Martinelli, "Italian Immigrant Women in the Southwest," in *Italian Immigrant Women in North America*, ed. Betty Boyd Caroli, Robert Harney, and Lydio Tomasi (Toronto: Multicultural History Society of Ontario, 1978), 324–40.

16. Mary E. Gill and John S. Goff, "Joseph H. Kibbey and School Segregation in Arizona," *Journal of Arizona History* 21 (Winter 1980): 418; *Arizona Gazette*, 3 July 1901; Rolle, *Immigrant Upraised*, 101–2; Jean Ann Scarpaci, *Italian Immigrants in Louisiana's Sugar Parishes* (New York: Arno Press, 1980), 278.

17. "A Gathering of Italian Boys," *Arizona Republic*, 21 June 1912; *Arizona Gazette*, 29 September 1897, 6 November 1915.

18. Judge Francis Donofrio, interview with author, Phoenix, July 1976; George Grosso, interview with Jim Stokely, Phoenix, February 1976.

19. Robert Barrett, "The Man Who Made It a Rodeo," *Arizona*, 9 March 1980, 8–11.

20. Al Ruland, "A Fantasy in Rocks," *Arizona Days and Ways Magazine*, 15 June 1958, 13; Rolle, *Immigrant Upraised*, 284–87.

21. *Arizona Republic*, 4 March 1982.

22. Ruby Cudia, interview with K. Trimble, Phoenix, January 1977.

23. "POWs Were in Guarded Condition," *Arizona*, 3 December 1978, 54–59.

24. *United States Census Reports*, Summary Tape File 3A (Arizona), Census of 1980 Population and Housing, Phoenix, Arizona, SMSA (Washington, D.C.: Government Printing Office); *United States Census Reports*, PUMSP Tape File Data Dictionary Record P (Arizona), 1984.

25. Helen Gagliardo, telephone interview with author, Phoenix, 13 November 1981.

26. *Arizona Republic*, 28 February 1981.

27. Doris Pane, "Cook's Tour of the Valley's Ethnic Markets," *Phoenix* (May 1978), 49.

28. *United States Census Reports*, Occupations, 225–27.

29. *Arizona Republic*, 16 April 1982.

30. "Phoenix—Where Worlds Meet" (Phoenix: PACT, 1982).

31. Joseph Ryan, ed., *White Ethnics: Life in Working Class America* (Englewood Cliffs, N.J.: Prentice-Hall, 1973). For the assimilation point of view, see, for example, Orlando Patterson, *Ethnic Chauvinism* (New York: Stein and Day, 1977), Stephen Steinberg, *The Ethnic Myth* (New York: Atheneum Press, 1981), or Pierre Van den Berghe,

*The Ethnic Phenomenon* (New York: Elsevier, 1981). For the views of those seeing continued ethnic identity, see Andrew Greeley, *Ethnicity in the United States* (New York: John Wiley, 1974); Jack Kinton, ed., *American Ethnic Revival* (Aurora, Ill.: Social Science and Sociological Resources, 1977); or Michael Novak, *The Rise of the Unmeltable Ethnics* (New York: Macmillan, 1973).

32. Leonard Gordon, "Social Issues in Post Cybernetic Age Arid Area Cities," in *Urban Life and the Struggle to Be Human*, ed. Albert J. Mayer and Leonard Gordon (Dubuque: Kendall/Hunt Publishing Co., 1979), 24–45; Amitai Etzioni, "The Ghetto— A Reevaluation," *Social Forces* (1959): 255–62; William Yancey, Eugene Ericksen, and Richard Juliani, "Emergent Ethnicity: A Review and Reformulation," *American Sociological Review* (1976): 391–94; *Columbus Day Magazine* (Phoenix: Arizona Columbus Day Committee, 1986).

33. Phylis Cancilla Martinelli, *Ethnicity in the Sunbelt: Italian American Migrants to Scottsdale, Arizona* (New York: AMS Press, 1989); idem, "Testing McKay and Lewin's Ethnic Typology: Italian Americans Defend Columbus Day in Arizona" (paper presented at the 1992 Pacific Sociological Association Conference, Oakland, Calif.); idem, "Traditional Values in Italian American Families," *Family Perspectives* (August 1987); idem, "A Test of the McKay and Lewin's Typology," *Ethnic and Racial Studies* (April 1986); idem, "Exploring Ethnicity in the Sunbelt: Italian Americans in Scottsdale, Arizona," *Humbolt Journal of Social Relations* (Spring/Summer 1985).

## CHAPTER SIX

1. Geoffrey P. Mawn, "Promoters, Speculators, and the Selection of the Phoenix Townsite," *Arizona and the West* 19 (Fall 1977): 207–24; Charles S. Sargent, "Towns of the Salt River Valley, 1870–1930," *Historical Geography* 5 (Fall 1975): 1–3; San Diego *Union*, 5 March 1872.

2. Geoffrey P. Mawn, "Phoenix, Arizona: Central City of the Southwest, 1870–1920" (Ph.D. diss., Arizona State University, 1979), 38–68; George H. Kelly, comp., *Legislative History: Arizona, 1864–1912* (Phoenix: Manufacturing Stationers, 1926), 132–35.

3. Sargent, "Towns of the Salt River Valley," 1–2; Mawn, "Phoenix, Arizona," 162–64.

4. Mawn, "Phoenix, Arizona," 172–74; Sargent, "Towns of the Salt River Valley," 3–4; John A. Black, *Arizona: The Land of Sunshine and Silver, Health and Prosperity; The Place of Ideal Homes* (Phoenix: Republican Book and Job Print, 1890), 64–66.

5. Mawn, "Phoenix, Arizona," 219–62; H. L. Meredith, "Reclamation in the Salt River Valley, 1902–1917," *Journal of the West* 7 (January 1968): 76–83.

6. Joseph C. McGowan, *History of Extra-Long Staple Cottons* (El Paso: Texas Western Press), 79–92; Bradford Luckingham, "The Southwestern Urban Frontier, 1880–1930," *Journal of the West* 18 (July 1979): 40–50.

7. *Arizona Republican*, 28 January 1920; 8 May 1921; 28 December 1924; 27 December 1925; 26 November, 26, 30 December 1926; 17, 23 November, 12, 25 December 1927; 15, 30 December 1928; 23 February, 9 June, 29 December 1929; 24 February 1930; *Arizona Republic*, 25 February 1931 (the *Arizona Republican* became the *Arizona Republic* in November of 1930).

8. *Arizona Republic*, 8 November 1934; 24 July 1935; 12 April, 20 May 1936; 17 November 1940; 16 November 1934; Arthur G. Horton, *An Economic, Political and Social Survey of Phoenix and the Valley of the Sun* (Tempe: Southside Progress, 1941), 105.

9. Horton, *Survey of Phoenix*, 145; *Arizona Republic*, 30 August 1933, 3 November 1934, 24 February 1936, 24 November 1940.

10. *Arizona Republic*, 3 May, 16, 28 November 1940; 5 June, 20 November 1941; 17, 24 November 1954; Horton, *Survey of Phoenix*, 43, 134–36. A movement to change the name from Salt River Valley to Roosevelt Valley received considerable support in the 1920s, but it failed to gain acceptance. In 1960 Barry Goldwater staged a successful campaign to change the name of Roosevelt Dam to Theodore Roosevelt Dam to lessen the danger that the "wrong Roosevelt" might get the credit. *Arizona Republican*, 24, 25, 28, 30 April 1925; "Water for Phoenix: Building the Roosevelt Dam," *Journal of Arizona History* 18 (Autumn 1977): 293–94.

11. *Arizona Republic*, 24 November 1940; 29 June, 17 July, 29 September, 20 November 1941; 22 November 1942; 5, 10 January 1945; 11 March 1956; 12 February 1961; Charles S. Sargent, "Arizona's Urban Frontier: Myths and Realities," in *The Conflict between Frontier Values and Land Use Control in Greater Phoenix*, ed. Charles S. Sargent (Tempe: Arizona State University Center for Public Affairs, 1976), 19–23; Charles C. Colley, "Carl T. Hayden—Phoenician," *Journal of Arizona History* 18 (Autumn 1977): 247–57.

12. *Arizona Republic*, 6 February 1946; 3, 16 November 1948; 2 January 1949; 22 May, 14 December 1954; 15 May 1955; 11 March 1956; 9 May, 21 June 1957; 4 January 1958; 1 January, 12 February 1961; "Disinterested Outsiders Say Phoenix Best Publicized City in the U.S.," *Phoenix Action* (February 1950): 4; Thomas Lee McKnight, *Manufacturing in Arizona* (Berkeley: University of California Press, 1962), 325–30, passim. Phoenix organizations invested more time and money attracting people and business than the other cities of the Southwest. During the 1950s the annual budget of the Phoenix Chamber of Commerce, for example, contained more funds for national advertising than any similar organization in the other cities. Some leaders in the other cities noticed this disadvantage and told their own booster organizations, calling for larger advertising budgets for their own chambers of commerce. See, for example, *Albuquerque Journal*, 22 November 1959.

13. Daniel E. Noble, "Motorola Expands in Phoenix," *Arizona Business and Economic Review* (June 1959); 1–2.

14. *Arizona Republic*, 16 August, 10, 22 December 1955; 1 January, 24 December 1961; 11 February 1962; McKnight, *Manufacturing in Arizona*, 312–40; Mark and Gertrude Adams, *A Report on Politics in El Paso* (Cambridge: Joint Center for Urban Studies of the Massachusetts Institute of Technology and Harvard University, 1963), 26–27.

15. Bradford Luckingham, "Urban Development in Arizona: The Rise of Phoenix," *Journal of Arizona History* 22 (Summer 1981): 224–28; *U.S. Census of Population*, various years.

16. Neil Morgan, *Westward Tilt: The American West Today* (New York: Random House, 1961), 344. See also Bradford Luckingham, "Phoenix, Arizona: The Desert Metropolis," in *Sunbelt Cities: Politics and Growth since World War II* (Austin: University of Texas Press, 1983); and Bradford Luckingham, *Phoenix: The History of a Southwestern Metropolis* (Tucson: University of Arizona Press, 1989).

## CHAPTER SEVEN

1. Bradford Luckingham, "The Southwestern Urban Frontier, 1880–1930," *Journal of the West* 18 (July 1979): 47; Geoffrey P. Mawn, "Phoenix, Arizona: Central City of the Southwest, 1870–1920" (Ph.D. diss., Arizona State University, 1979), 556–59; Charles S. Sargent, "Towns of the Salt River Valley, 1870–1930," *Historical Geography Newsletter* 5 (1975): 1–5; Jeffrey Cook, "Patterns of Desert Urbanization: The Evolution of Metropolitan Phoenix," in *Urban Planning for Arid Zones: American Experiences and Directions*, ed. Gideon Golany (New York: John Wiley and Sons, 1978), 212–14.

2. Joseph C. McGowan, "History of Extra-Long Staple Cottons" (M.A. thesis, University of Arizona, 1960), 143, 163–65; Walter Woehlke, "What Cotton Did to Arizona," *Sunset Magazine* (July 1927): 21–23, 62–64.

3. U.S. Works Progress Administration, Writers Project, *Arizona: A State Guide* (New York: Hastings House, 1941), 75–86; Arthur G. Horton, *An Economic, Political, and Social Survey of Phoenix and the Valley of the Sun* (Tempe: Southside Progress, 1941), 79–90.

4. Salt River Valley Water Users Association, *Salt River Project, Arizona* (Phoenix: Salt River Valley Water Users Association, 1940), 1–4; Carol Osman Brown, "A Happy Birthday SRP," *Phoenix Magazine* 13 (February 1978): 53–54; Salt River Project pamphlet, *A Valley Reborn: The Story of the Salt River Project* (Phoenix: Salt River Project, 1978), 1–8.

5. James Vance, Jr., "Focus on Downtown," *Community Planning Review* 16 (Summer 1966): 11–23; Kevin Lynch, *The Image of the City* (Cambridge, Mass.: M.I.T. Press, 1960), 2; Truman Hartshorn, *Interpreting the City: An Urban Geography* (New York: John Wiley and Sons, 1980), 362.

6. Horton, *An Economic, Political, and Social Survey*, 176–88; Janus Associates, *Historical and Architectural Resources along the Inner Loop Corridor, Phoenix, Arizona* (Tempe: Janus Associates, 1981), 7–65; Leland Roth, *A Concise History of American Architecture* (New York: Harper and Row, 1979), 360–62; *Arizona: A State Guide*, 144–45.

7. David F. Myrick, *Railroads of Arizona*, 3 vols. (Berkeley, Calif.: Howell-North Books, 1980), 781–84; Bradford Luckingham, *The Urban Southwest: A Profile History of Albuquerque, El Paso, Phoenix and Tucson* (El Paso: Texas Western Press, 1982), 30–31; D. W. Meinig, *Southwest: Three Peoples in Geographical Change, 1600–1970* (New York: Oxford University Press, 1971), 38–52, 77–81; Arizona Directory Company, *Phoenix City and Salt River Valley Directory, 1931* (Phoenix: Arizona Directory Company, 1931), 8. A fine collection of photographs of the various topics discussed in this paper can be found in Herb and Dorothy McLaughlin, *Phoenix 1870–1970 Photographs* (Phoenix: Herb McLaughlin, 1970).

8. For more information on this period, see Michael John Kotlanger, S.J., "Phoenix, Arizona: 1920–1940" (Ph.D. diss., Arizona State University, 1983).

## CHAPTER EIGHT

1. For background on this period see Larry Schweikart, *A History of Banking in Arizona* (Tucson: University of Arizona Press, 1982). General works on the period include Ernest J. Hopkins, *Financing the Frontier* (Phoenix: Arizona Printers, 1949); Paul Hughes, *Bank Notes* (Phoenix: Phoenician Books, 1971); and G. Clarke Bean, *The Spirit of the Arizona Bank* (Princeton, N.J.: Newcomen Society, 1972). As shown in the Schweikart's bibliographical essay, each has distinct and serious weaknesses, particularly regarding the period in question.

2. Other banks are discussed in James Simmons, *Banking on Arizona's Future* (Princeton, N.J.: Newcomen Society, 1980), and A. R. Gutowsky, *Arizona Banking* (Tempe: Arizona State University, College of Business, 1967). See also Don C. Bridenstine, "Commercial Banking in Arizona, Past and Present" (Ph.D. diss., University of Southern California, 1958), and a booklet published by Southern Arizona Bank and Trust in 1953 titled *Fifty Years of Growth in Tucson* (no author).

3. Articles on Walter Reed Bimson are numerous. In addition to Hopkins's descriptions (*Financing*, 206–71), see Don Dedera, "Walter Reed Bimson: Arizona's Indispensable Man, Complete Banker," *Arizona Highways* (April 1973): 1, 21–29; "The Brash Banker of Arizona," *Saturday Evening Post* (10 April 1954): 23; Keith Monroe, "Bank Knight in Arizona," *American Magazine* (November 1945): 24–25, 116–22. See also a reprint of

a speech by Carl A. Bimson, Walter's brother, before the Newcomen Society in North America titled "Transformation in the Desert—The Story of Arizona's Valley Bank," 20 March 1962 (Arizona State University Library [cited hereafter as ASUL]); "The Eagle," May 1980; and the *Arizona Republic*, 25 October 1961. Several other less useful articles have been produced from these sources. Additional material was provided through interviews with Carl Bimson in March and April of 1980. Different dates will be cited as they apply. One tape of an interview is on file at ASUL, and Mr. Bimson generously typed his observations on some of the other conversations (copies on file at ASUL). For the figures quoted, see *Speeches of Carl Bimson* (Phoenix: Valley National Bank, 1956), 232–37, and Joseph Stocker, "Financing America's Most Flourishing Frontier," *Arizona Highways* (November 1956): 2–7, 35–38.

4. Hopkins, *Financing*, 252–53; *Speeches of Carl Bimson*, 232–37.

5. See Schweikart, *History*, chaps. 5 and 6, for a more thorough discussion of Carl Bimson's role.

6. Raymond Kent, *Money and Banking*, 3rd ed. (New York: Rinehart and Company, 1956), 794; "Brash Banker," 23; Bridenstine, "Commercial Banking," 229; Carl Bimson, interview with author, 7 April 1980 (tape on file at ASUL); Hopkins, *Financing*, 247, 249; Monroe, "Bank Knight," 117. As he left the federal buildings in Washington, he caught a glimpse of the committee's "secret" report in a closet and picked up a copy. The statistics it contained were virtually unavailable elsewhere, and Valley Bank made good use of the figures to forecast loans and buying trends. Some have implied that Valley Bank had sufficient cash to lend through Bimson's relationship with Harris Trust Company in Chicago. This available source of money allowed Valley to make loans in the face of the Great Depression. While this hypothesis is logical, little evidence has been produced to support it.

7. Bridenstine, "Commercial Banking," 267–68; Condensed Statements of the Arizona State Superintendent of Banks, 1939–49 (hereafter Condensed Statements, with year designated); Board of Governors of the Federal Reserve System, *Federal Reserve Bulletin* (January 1957): 45; Hopkins, *Financing*, 259.

8. Frank C. Brophy to Lewis Douglas, January 6, 1934, Box 77, File 6, Douglas Collection (hereafter DC), University of Arizona Library (hereafter UAL); "Arizona's New Bank Tax Law," *Banking* 38 (April 1946): 127; Bridenstine, "Commercial Banking," 281–82. According to Bridenstine, some of the banks' real-estate holdings were the result of defaults. This property "would have surely been a source of consternation to the state because of the resulting high rate of tax delinquency." The Eighth Legislature decreed that banks must report real estate taken in payment of due debts. These holdings had to be disposed of within five years unless granted extensions by the superintendent of banks. See Regular Session of the State Legislature, 1927, chap. 92, secs. 9–10, 285. See also Frank C. Brophy to Lewis Chalmers, 10 December 1930, Box 34, File 1097, Brophy Collection (hereafter BC), Arizona Historical Society (hereafter AHS); Frank C. Brophy to W. L. Honnold, 5 September 1931, Box 34, File 1097, BC, AHS; Frank C. Brophy to Sam Applewhite, 4 December 1933, Box 36, File 1164, BC, AHS.

9. *Coast Banker* 62 (February 1939): 91; *Coast Banker* 66 (February 1941): 104; *Coast Banker* 52 (February 1934): 118. See also John B. Crowell to J. S. Douglas, 10 June 1933, Box 36, File 1164, BC, AHS.

10. "Know Your Bank Taxes," *Banking* 33 (March 1941): 97.

11. *Banking* 38 (April 1946): 127; Regular Session of the Sixteenth Legislature of the State of Arizona, 1943, chap. 11, sec. 1, 16; ibid., sec. 3, 16. It was also stipulated that bank-held real estate "shall be assessed and taxed as other real estate in this state and in the political subdivisions thereof in which the real estate is situated," ibid. See also *Arizona Taxpayers Magazine* 32 (July–August 1945).

12. Gerald Nash, *The American West in the Twentieth Century* (Englewood Cliffs, N.J.: Prentice-Hall, 1973), 219. See also Howard Lamar, "The Persistent Frontier: The West in the Twentieth Century," *Western Historical Quarterly* 4 (January 1973): 5-22. Michael F. Konig, "Phoenix during the 1950s: Narrative of Growth," *Student History Forum* (Tempe: Arizona State University, Phi Alpha Theta, 1980), 50-77, and "Phoenix during the 1950s: An Example of Urban Growth in the Sunbelt," *Arizona and the West* (Spring 1982).

13. Carol Osman Brown, "Phoenix, 1870-1970," *Arizona Highways* (April 1970): 15, and "Happenings along the Way," *Phoenix Magazine* (October 1970): 46; Bradford Luckingham, "People, Water, Cars, and Air Conditioning Add Up to Growth," *Arizona Republic* 19 (June 1973): 3. Reynolds Aluminum took over the ALCOA plant, and the AiResearch plant, closed in 1946, reopened in 1951. L. V. Smith to Frank C. Brophy, 19 September 1951, Box 1, File M-34, BC, AHS; Carl Bimson, October 1952 speech, "Evolution of the Arizona Economy," Valley National Bank (hereafter VNB), 135; Konig, "Phoenix during the 1950s," 52. See also James E. Buchanan, ed., *Phoenix: A Chronological and Documentary History* (Dobbs Ferry, N.Y.: Oceana Publications, 1976), 39, and *The Phoenix Story* (Phoenix: Phoenix Chamber of Commerce, 1960), 8. Carl Bimson noted almost all of these factors in his discussion with the author on 25 March 1980 (notes on file at ASUL).

14. The struggle for control of the Bank of Douglas represents one of the fascinating stories in Arizona economic development. See Schweikart, *History*, chap. 5.

15. Bimson, conversation with the author, 14 August 1980; Bean, *Spirit of the Arizona Bank*, 11-13.

16. Frank C. Brophy to Henry Brume, Empire Trust Company of New York, 23 December 1948, Box 1, File E-23, BC, AHS; Frank C. Brophy to Lewis Douglas, 19 February 1946, Box 77, DC, UAL; Frank C. Brophy to Walter Rounsevel, 25 November 1949, Box 1, File C-13, BC, AHS; Frank C. Brophy to Roy Drachman, 13 January 1950, Box 1, File D-20, BC, AHS; Frank C. Brophy to Victor H. Rossetti, 28 September 1950, Box 1, File F-24, BC, AHS. See also Bean, *Spirit of the Arizona Bank*, 11-13. *Bank of Douglas*, passim.

17. Gene McLain, "Bank of Douglas's Robbery: Arizona's Biggest Crime Unsolved after 4½ Years," *Arizona Days and Ways*, 25 July 1954, 15.

18. Frank C. Brophy to Warren Tremaine, Metalcraft Manufacturing, 3 December 1951, Box 1, File M-34, BC, AHS; Bean, *Spirit of the Arizona Bank*, 13; memo to W. R. Montgomery, 13 April 1953, Box 1, File G-28, BC, AHS. See also Brophy's request for a new safe because the old one "looks rather ragged" (Frank C. Brophy to H. Albert DeWit, Mosler Safe Company, 30 November 1949, Box 1, File M-34, BC, AHS).

19. "100 Years of Banking," First Interstate Bank, 5; *Coast Banker* 83 (September 1949): 122; ibid., 96 (March 1956): 178; ibid., 83 (October 1949): 272; ibid., 86 (June 1953): 353; ibid., 94 (October 1955): 257; ibid., 94 (March 1955): 182; *Arizona Republic*, 27 September 1949, 14 January 1953, 19 November 1955; *Bisbee Daily Review*, 4 February 1956; *Arizona Daily Star*, 19 November 1955; *Wall Street Journal*, 19 March 1957. First National also purchased the White Mountain Bank in McNary in 1955.

20. *Coast Banker* 75 (September 1945): 118, 77; ibid., 76 (July 1946): 64, 93; ibid., 92 (October 1954): 228; Condensed Statements, 1945, 1946, 1954. Interview with H. L. ("Doc") Dunham, VNB, 1959, 8. The First National Bank of Nogales was established in 1903, and by June 1945 it had assets of $7,104,190.63. R. C. Kaufman had founded First National Bank of Winslow in 1921 under the name Union Bank and Trust Company. By 1946 its resources were $3,871,812.94. Buckeye Valley Bank, founded in 1911 by Hugh M. Watson, reported assets of $2,497,131.11 in 1954.

21. *Coast Banker* 90 (March 1953): 162; Bean, *Spirit of the Arizona Bank*, 13–14. According to Brophy, "the bank has grown so fast and so big that I . . . have to neglect other interests which are actually more important, in a financial way." Frank C. Brophy to Lewis Douglas, 29 December 1951, Box 77, DC, UAL.

22. Carl Bimson, interview with author, 15 August 1980; *Coast Banker* 90 (January 1953): 60. See also Bridenstine, "Commercial Banking," 296. Typescript copy of Bimson's comments in author's files, courtesy of Carl Bimson.

23. *Coast Banker* 90 (January 1953): 60; *Arizona Republic*, 4 July 1955. Arizona Bancorporation issued two hundred thousand shares of initial stock to Valley Bank stockholders to act as payment of transfer of the Professional Building to the holding company. The Bank Holding Company Act, passed on May 9, 1956, also defined a bank holding company as one which "controls in any manner the election of a majority of the directors of each of two or more banks, or . . . for the benefit of whose shareholders or members 25 per centum or more of the voting shares of each of two or more banks or a bank holding company is held by trustees; and for the purpose of this Act, any successor to any such company shall be deemed to be a bank holding company from the date as of which such predecessor company becomes a bank holding company." *Federal Reserve Bulletin* (May 1956): 444. The purpose of this law was to limit banks' control of nonbank institutions (see Sec. 4, ibid., 446).

24. Walter Bimson, Letter to Stockholders, 31 July 1956, 7. Because the First State Bank of Arizona had already been merged, Bimson did not list its ownership. See also Condensed Statements, 14 March 1957.

25. Condensed Statements, 1939, 1956; Bridenstine, "Commercial Banking," 300; Gutowsky, *Arizona Banking*, 25, and Condensed Statements, 1959; interview with H. L. ("Doc") Dunham, VNB, 1959, 1–140, passim.

26. Condensed Statements and State Banking Department Records. See Gutowsky's chart, *Arizona Banking*, 24.

27. Minton Moore, interview with author, 20 August 1980.

28. Ibid.

29. Federal Reserve Bank of San Francisco, *Investigation of Banking in Arizona*, 2 vols. (1956), 2:119–20, 276–78, 283–86, 293–300. This was only a part of a larger investigation of Transamerica's holdings in the western United States. See Edward S. Hermann, "Board of Governors v. Transamerica: Victory out of Defeat," *Antitrust Bulletin* 4 (March 1964): 521–39, and Edward S. Hermann, "The Transamerica Case: A Study of the Federal Reserve Board Antitrust Proceedings" (Ph.D. diss., University of California, Berkeley, 1953). See also the Bank Holding Company Act of 1956. For a recent analysis of this period, see Larry Schweikart, "Collusion or Competition? Another look at Banking during Arizona's Boom Years, 1950–1965," *Journal of Arizona History* 28 (Summer 1987): 189–200.

30. *Investigation*, 101–2.

31. Ibid., 352, 366–69; Gutowsky, *Arizona Banking*, 29. See also *Phoenix Gazette*, 28 December 1962, and *United States of America v. the Valley Bank of Arizona, the Arizona Bank, and Arizona Bancorporation*, Civil No. 4550 (Phoenix, 28 December 1962), 10; Walter Bimson, Letter to Stockholders, 2 January 1963, VNB; Subpoena, 7 March 1963, VNB; *Arizona Republic* 14 October 1966; Consent Decree 4550-Phoenix, *United States of America v. Valley National Bank*, 23 November 1966. The Arizona Bank was prohibited from acquiring other banks for five years, Valley National for fifteen; *The President's 66th Annual Report of the Valley National Bank* (Phoenix: Valley National Bank, 1967), 10.

32. For the growth of other banks during this time, see Simmons, *Banking*, passim, and Schweikart, *History*, chaps. 7 and 8.

33. A. B. Robbs Trust Company "Dispatch," June 1959, p. 1, Box 1, Folder 4, Continental Bank (now Chase Bank) Archives (hereafter CB), Financial Center, Scottsdale, Ariz.; interview with A. B. Robbs, Jr., 27 June 1985, Tape #3; A. B. Robbs Trust Company Minutes, 26 July 1950, Box 6, CB.

34. Interview with A. B. Robbs, Jr., 27 June 1985, Tape #3; Larry Schweikart, *That Quality Image: The History of Continental Bank* (Tappan, N.Y.: Custombook, 1985).

35. See Larry Schweikart, "A Dynamic Legacy: Thunderbird Bank, 1964–1985," privately published, 1985; Schweikart, *That Quality Image*, 80–89; "Arizona Banking Changed Forever in '85 as Major Firms Were Bought," *Arizona Republic*, 2 January 1986; interview with A. B. Robbs, Jr., 29 November 1985, Tape #12, CB.

36. Edwin H. Jelliff, interview with author, 28 August 1980.

37. Except for Continental Bank's administrative headquarters in Scottsdale, a Phoenix suburb, all of the major banks now have headquarters in central Phoenix. Each even has a new headquarters building constructed in the last decade. See Schweikart, *History*, chap. 8.

38. For mergers and absorpsions under interstate banking in the 1980s, see Lynne Pierson Doti and Larry Schweikart, *Banking in the American West from the Gold Rush to Deregulation* (Norman: University of Oklahoma Press, 1991), 199–240.

39. Recent developments involving Valley National Bank are covered in Doti and Schweikart, *Banking in the American West*, chaps. 6–7, passim, as well as "Arizona's Deepening Real-Estate Slump Is Hammering Hard at Banking Firms," *Wall Street Journal*, 23 October 1989; "Commercial Real-Estate Bog Muddying Valley Banks [sic] Boots," *Arizona Republic*, 26 June 1989; "Big Banks Form 'Bad Banks' to Discard Problem Loans," ibid., 20 November 1988; "Arizona Bank Performance 48th in Nation," ibid., 25 July 1989; and Terry Greene, "And the Money Kept Flowing," *New Times*, 21–27 June 1989.

## CHAPTER NINE

1. *Arizona Gazette* (Phoenix), 27 October 1884.

2. Ibid.

3. *Phoenix Herald*, 30 October 1884; *Arizona Republican* (Phoenix), 19 March 1911; *Arizona*, American Guide Series (New York: Hastings House, 1940), 454; *Phoenix Herald*, 15 June 1888.

4. *Phoenix Herald*, 30 June 1884; *Arizona Citizen* (Tucson), 12 July, 15 November 1873.

5. *Salt River Herald* (Phoenix), 4 May 1878; interview with Howard Alexander, Salt River Project, 21 August 1981; Joseph H. Kibbey, *M. Wormser v. The Salt River Valley Canal Company, et al.*, Decision, 31 March 1892, 5, as reprinted by the Salt River Project Archives; Alfred J. McClatchie, *Utilizing Our Water Supply*, University of Arizona Agricultural Experiment Station, Bulletin 43 (Tucson, 28 July 1902), 63.

6. *Salt River Herald*, 6 July, 17 August 1878; *Phoenix Herald*, 11 April 1888, 15 January 1892.

7. *Territorial Expositor* (Phoenix), 9 May 1879; *Phoenix Herald*, 12 July, 20 August 1879.

8. *Territorial Expositor*, 12 September, 31 October, 7 November 1879; 20 August 1880; *Phoenix Herald*, 10 September, 15 December 1879.

9. *Territorial Expositor*, 25 February, 4, 11 March 1881; *Arizona Gazette*, 7 March 1881.

10. *Arizona Gazette*, 19 May, 20 December 1882; 8 May 1883; 24 May 1887; 3 April 1892; *Phoenix Herald*, 7 May, 11 July, 19 September, 24, 29 December 1883; 19 September 1884; 4 February 1887; Kibbey, *Wormser v. Canal Company*, 5; McClatchie, *Water Supply*, 88; Argument of Clark Churchill, *Wormser v. Canal Company*, 211, Phoenix Public Library.

11. *Phoenix Herald*, 9 July 1887, 8 September 1888.

12. F. H. Newell, *The History of the Irrigation Movement*, First Annual Report of the U.S. Reclamation Service (Washington, D.C.: Government Printing Office, 1903), 20–21, as reprinted by Salt River Project Archives.

13. Ibid., 4–5; *Phoenix Herald*, 9, 16 April 1889.

14. *Phoenix Herald*, 2, 6, 13, 19 July, 14, 15, 20 August 1889; Minutes of the Maricopa County Board of Supervisors, Book No. 3 (1884–1889), 564.

15. Ibid., 18 July 1890, 12 January 1891; *Arizona Gazette*, reprinted in *Tempe Daily News*, 30 July 1892.

16. Newell, *Irrigation Movement*, 6.

17. *Phoenix Herald*, 18, 21 December 1891; *Arizona Gazette*, 28 April 1893; 5 March, 16 April 1896.

18. *Phoenix Herald*, 16 May 1892.

19. *Arizona Gazette*, 19 February, 4, 16 June 1893; *Arizona Republican*, 20, 16 April, 10, 16, 21 June, 16 July 1893; *Arizona Weekly Gazette* (Phoenix), 20 July 1893; *Phoenix Herald*, 23 February 1895.

20. Arthur Davis, *Report of the Irrigation Investigation of the Pima and Other Indians on the Gila River Reservation, Arizona* (Washington, D.C.: Government Printing Office, 1897), reprinted by Salt River Project Archives; F. H. Newell to C. D. Walcott, 11 November 1896, quoted in Davis, *Irrigation Investigation*.

21. Samuel Hays, *Conservation and the Gospel of Efficiency: The Progressive Conservation Movement, 1890–1920* (Cambridge, Mass.: Harvard University Press: 1959), 39–50, as cited by Karen L. Smith in "The Campaign for Water in Central Arizona, 1890–1903," *Arizona and the West* 23 (Summer 1981): 137; *Phoenix Herald*, 16, 18 December 1896.

22. Arthur Davis, "Irrigation near Phoenix, Arizona," U.S. Geological Survey, Water Supply and Irrigation Paper No. 2 (Washington, D.C.: Government Printing Office, 1897), as reprinted by Salt River Project Archives.

23. *Arizona Gazette*, 16 April 1898.

24. *Daily Enterprise*, 30 November 1898; *Arizona Gazette*, 1 December 1898; 28 February, 4 March, 5 April 1899; Dwight B. Heard to Aaron Goldberg, 30 December 1898, reprinted in *Arizona Weekly Gazette*, 14 January 1899; F. H. Newell to Thomas Boyle, 28 March 1899, reprinted in *Arizona Gazette*, 5 April 1899.

25. *Arizona Gazette*, 27 September 1899; *Daily Enterprise*, 28 September 1899.

26. *Daily Enterprise*, 27 December 1899; *Arizona Gazette*, 4 June, 31 December 1899; Newell, *Irrigation Movement*, 8.

27. *Arizona Republican*, 20 April, 2 May 1900; *Arizona Gazette*, 18 April, 2 May 1900; Committee on Water Storage, "A Report to the Phoenix and Maricopa Board of Trade," April 1900, as printed by Salt River Project Archives.

28. *Arizona Republican*, 19 July, 3 August 1900.

29. *Arizona Gazette*, 1, 15 August 1900; *Arizona Republican*, 23 August 1900.

30. *Arizona Gazette*, 31 August 1900; *Daily Enterprise*, 1 September 1900.

31. *Arizona Republican*, 4 November 1901; *Daily Enterprise*, 15 November 1900; B. A. Fowler to E. A. Hitchcock, 20 November 1900, Salt River Project Archives.

32. *Arizona Gazette*, 11 December 1900; *Arizona Republican*, 1 January 1901.

33. Charles D. Walcott to E. A. Hitchcock, 14 January 1901, Salt River Project Archives; *Arizona Republican*, 1 January 1901.

34. *Arizona Republican*, 4, 15, 18 January 1901.

35. Ibid., 6, 13 February 1901.

36. Ibid., 24 February, 10, 12 March 1901; *Daily Enterprise*, 15 March 1901.

37. *Arizona Republican*, 12, 19, 28 March 1901; *Daily Enterprise*, 27 March 1901.

38. *Arizona Republican*, 21 March, 16, 17, 22, 29 April, 1 May 1901; *Daily Enterprise*, 18, 20 March, 27 April 1901.

39. *Arizona Republican*, 6 July, 20 December 1901; 4 February 1902.

40. Ibid., 7, 14 September, 4 December 1901.

41. Ibid., 20 March 1901; *Arizona Gazette*, 7 December 1901; *Daily Enterprise*, 19 December 1901.

42. *Arizona Republican*, 16 January 1902; *Arizona Gazette*, 16 January 1902.

43. *Arizona Republican*, 4 February 1902.

44. Ibid., 6, 8 March 1902; *Arizona Gazette*, 5 February, 8 March 1902.

45. *Arizona Republican*, 2 March 1902; *Arizona Gazette*, 9 February 1902.

46. *Arizona Republican*, 13 March, 4, 5, 8, 9 April 1902; *Arizona Gazette*, 13 March 1902; *Daily Enterprise*, 31 March, 7 April 1902.

47. *Arizona Republican*, 8, 20, 27 April, 18, 20 May 1902.

48. Ibid., 28, 29 May 1902; *Arizona Gazette*, 29 May 1902.

49. *Arizona Republican*, 5, 9, 10, 11 June 1902.

50. Ibid., 13 June 1902.

51. Ibid., 14 June 1902.

52. Ibid., 28 June 1902.

## CHAPTER TEN

1. Glen Wells, City of Phoenix Water Department, telephone interview with author, 5 January 1982. As of 1977, the American Water Works Association estimated the national average rate per capita at 150 gallons. See *The Story of Water Supply*, a pamphlet published by the American Water Works Association, Denver, Colorado.

2. *Arizona Republic* (Phoenix), 4 July 1951.

3. "Phoenix Artesian Water," *Arizona: The New State Magazine* (December 1918): 7; *Arizona Republican*, 4 April, 15 May 1900.

4. Act of 16 April 1906, 34 Stat. 116; General Reclamation Circular, 1913, 39 L. D., 501; H. J. Roth to Dario Travaini, 25 April 1952, Salt River Project (hereafter SRP) Secretary's Office; Jim Brassfield, SRP Water Resources and Services, telephone interview with author, 8 January 1982.

5. Rober Wiebe, *The Search for Order, 1877–1920* (New York: Hill and Wang), 1967; Karen L. Smith, "From Town to City: A History of Phoenix, 1870–1912" (M.A. thesis, University of Califonia, Santa Barbara, 1978), 168–69.

6. *Arizona Republican*, 11 January 1903; Kenneth MacNichol, "Phoenix—The Growing City," *Arizona: The New State Magazine* (September 1912): 8; "Water System in Brief," City of Phoenix Department of Water and Sewers. Verde Park is at Ninth Street and Polk.

7. MacNichol, "Phoenix," 8; *Verde River Project of the City of Phoenix* (no author, no date [c. May 1923]), City of Phoenix Department of Water and Sewers, 7.

8. *Verde River Project*, 8.

9. Ibid., 8, 9, 11–12, 32; "Data in Chronological Order Relative to Verde District," SRP Archives.

10. *Verde River Project*, 13, 16–17, 19–20, 24–25, 33, 41.

11. Ibid., 35; *Phoenix Gazette*, 28 May 1946; *Arizona Republic*, 31 May 1946.

12. *Arizona Republic*, 29 May, 21 June 1946.

13. *Phoenix Gazette*, 27 May 1946.

14. *Arizona Republic*, 12 July, 1946.

15. *Phoenix Gazette*, 28 May 1946.

16. *Arizona Republic*, 17 August, 17 November 1946; Agreement with Roosevelt Irrigation District, 30 June 1946, Microfiche C1534, City Clerk's Office, Phoenix; Certificate of Water Right, 3 December 1954, Microfiche 1604, City Clerk's Office, Phoenix.

17. *Arizona Republic*, 4 July 1951, 1:7.

18. Ibid., 5, 15 July 1951.

19. Agreement between the Salt River Valley Water Users Association and the City of Phoenix, a Municipal Corporation, 1 January 1952, SRP Secretary's Office.


CHAPTER ELEVEN

1. Brent Brown, "An Analysis of Phoenix Charter Government as a Political Entity" (M.A. thesis, Arizona State University, 1968), 86; Stephen Rockstroh, "An Analysis of Phoenix Municipal Administration, 1881–1952" (M.A. thesis, Arizona State University, 1952), 89.

2. Rockstroh, "Phoenix Municipal Administration," 90, 91; *Record of the Commission and Council, City of Phoenix* (hereafter referred to as *Commission and Council*), 24:217. See also Charles A. Esser, "Busey Foes Fire Bill Richards," *Arizona Republic*, 22 October 1947, 1, 2. According to Esser, Mayor Ray Busey and Commissioner Walter Maxwell composed the minority bloc of the city commission and opposed the firing of Richards and the appointment of Deppe. Commissioners Gordon Smith, Roy D. Stone, and Nicholas Udall, who together made up the majority bloc, favored the replacement of Richards, claiming that he had become subservient to the mayor.

3. Charles A. Esser, "Deppe Lays City Hall Confession to Busey," *Arizona Republic*, 9 December 1947, 2; Charles A. Esser, "Deppe–Busey Feud Flares at Hearing," *Arizona Republic*, 11 December 1947, 1, 3. See also editorial, "Cooling Things Off," *Arizona Times*, 4 December 1947, 6.

4. "City Manager Ruling Upset," *Arizona Republic*, 27 February 1948, 10.

5. Henry Fuller, "Udall Takes Mayor Post Amid Peace," *Arizona Republic*, 2 May 1948, 1, 5; "Group Gets Assurance from Udall," *Arizona Republic*, 30 March 1948, 1, 7; "Revised City Charter Draft Is Authorized," *Arizona Republic*, 8 April 1948, 12. The strong manager form of government proposed by the Charter Revision Committee was designed along the lines suggested by a model charter recommended by the Public Administration Service. Some citizens and municipal employees feared the new amendments provided tempting opportunities for graft by the city manager, and they also complained that the amended charter would fail to protect civil service within the municipal government. See "Strong Manager Plan Hits Snag," *Arizona Republic*, 4 June 1948, 19.

6. Phoenix Title and Trust Company, *City Directory: Phoenix, 1947–1948* (Phoenix: Arizona Directory Company, 1948), 114, 435, 475; Charles A. Esser, "Deppe Ouster Attempt Fails," *Arizona Republic*, 3 August 1948, 1, 2. According to Esser, strife occurred during the campaign preceding the May 1948 election of Mayor Udall and Commissioners William Tate and Jack Blaine. The Scheumack forces, then represented by Udall and Tate, were opposed by the politically ambitious organization of city business leaders and World War II veterans called the Biz-Vets. The Biz-Vets, led by Duke Burks, owner of the Town House Hotel, and Paul Primock, an employee of the state tax commission, supported Blaine for a city commission seat. After the election, conflict over the seating of a new commissioner continued between the Scheumack forces and the Burks–Primock faction. Udall refused to select a commissioner favorable to either side. Finally Walters was chosen, and he subsequently sided with Udall in opposing attempts by the Scheumack forces and the Burks–Primock group to control city hall. Blaine's failure to vote to remove Deppe must be interpreted as an attempt to secure a concession from

Udall with regard to the city-clerk position only. The Burks–Primock forces could not profit by combining with the Scheumack forces.

7. Charles A. Esser, "Udall Urges Election on Mayoralty Set Up," *Arizona Republic*, 10 August 1948, 1, 8.

8. Charles A. Esser, "City Charter Revision Vote Called Likely," *Arizona Republic*, 5 August 1948, 2; *Commission and Council*, 28:101-2.

9. Orren Beaty, "City Clerk Is Fired; Boyer Named to Post," *Arizona Republic*, 15 September 1949, 1, 2.

10. "Referendum Vote Sighted," *Arizona Republic*, 13 August 1948, 1; Orren Beaty, "Charter Revision Vote Set," *Arizona Republic*, 25 August 1948, 1; *Commission and Council*, 26:153. See also "Charter Vote Call Delayed," *Arizona Republic*, 1 September 1948, 1; Orren Beaty, "Commission Again Pledges Intention to Call Charter Vote Set November 16," *Arizona Republic*, 29 September 1948, 1. The more liberal newspaper circulating in Phoenix at this time also supported the proposed charter amendments. See Ernest Mancinelli, "Here's Summary of Charter Revision Plan," *Arizona Times*, 15 November 1948, 1.

11. "Deppe, Union Deal Charged," *Arizona Republic*, 11 November 1948, 1, 2. Conflicting opinions regarding support for the charter amendments came from the city-employee labor unions. While the Central Labor Council staunchly opposed the strong-manager proposals, William J. Eden, business representative of the Arizona Council of Federal, State, County, and Municipal Employees, endorsed the proposals, declaring he felt that city employees would benefit under a strong manager with full administrative responsibility.

12. Editorial, "The *Republic*'s Stand," *Arizona Republic*, 15 August 1948, 6; Brown, "Analysis of Phoenix Charter Government," 29; Charles A. Esser, "Strong Manager, Bonds Pass," *Arizona Republic*, 17 November 1948, 1, 4.

13. Rockstroh, "Phoenix Municipal Administration," 94; Mancinelli, "Charter Revision Plan," 9.

14. Charles A. Esser, "Critics Claim Deppe Padded City Budget by More Than $800,000," *Arizona Republic*, 20 November 1948, 1, 3; Charles A. Esser, "Deppe's Job Is Revealed Precarious," *Arizona Republic*, 18 November 1949, 1, 2; "City Charter Vote Canvass Is Completed," *Arizona Republic*, 24 November 1948, 1, 2; Charles A. Esser, "City Council Appoints Deppe," *Arizona Republic*, 30 November 1948, 1, 4; Pete Bluemle, "City Gets New Councilmen; Deppe Retained as Manager," *Arizona Times*, 30 November 1949, 1, 2; Brown, "Analysis of Phoenix Charter Government," 29, 30.

15. "Udall Refuses to Make Radio Speech," *Arizona Republic*, 12 December 1948, 1; Al Leach, "Deppe Fires Boyer as Showdown Vote on Council Looms," *Arizona Republic*, 10 January 1949, 1, 3; Pete Bluemle, "Deppe Fires Boyer; Stone Quits Post," *Arizona Times*, 10 January 1949, 1, 2; "Deppe Fires Auditor, Puts Alice Mosien, Aide in Former Job," *Arizona Republic*, 30 January 1949, 1, 5. According to the *Arizona Republic*, information regarding the city manager's motivation in firing Williams was supplied by a city employee who remained anonymous in fear of reprisals by Deppe. It must also be noted that Williams, according to the same *Arizona Republic* article, had been ticketed ninety times for parking violations by the traffic division. These violations, Deppe claimed, were the reason for his removal of the auditor. See also "Deppe Backs Ouster Move," *Arizona Times*, 31 January 1949, 1.

16. "Council Manager Exchange Verbal Blows, Shift Blame for City Financial Plight," *Arizona Republic*, 2 March 1949, 10; "Money Lack Still Plagues City Council," *Arizona Republic*, 7 March 1949, 1, 2; Lou Witzeman, "City Faces Money Troubles," *Arizona Times*, 19 February 1949, 1, 2; Al Leach, "City Tax Protest Is Mapped," *Arizona Republic*, 22 March 1949, 1, 13, 24 March 1949, 1. See also City of Phoenix, *Annual Budget*,

1948–1949 (Phoenix: City of Phoenix, 1948), 1, 2. Also consult Al Leach, "City to Delay Tax Decision," *Arizona Republic*, 29 March 1949, 1, 4; "Battle to Kill City Sales Tax Is Begun," *Arizona Times*, 21 March 1949, 1, 2.

17. "Deppe Fires Five in City Job Shuffle," *Arizona Republic*, 6 April 1949, 1, 10; Orren Beaty, "Attorney Aide Bucks Ouster," *Arizona Republic*, 7 April 1949, 1, 3; "Kinney Fired Twice in City Hall Reshuffle," *Arizona Republic*, 9 April 1949, 4.

18. Bob Sherill, "Deppe Answers Charges of Buying without Regard to Purchase Laws," *Arizona Times*, 3 March 1949, 1.

19. Orren Beaty, "Blaine Fails in Effort to Oust Deppe," *Arizona Republic*, 15 June 1949, 1, 2; "Councilman Charges Vice Rampant," *Arizona Times*, 14 June 1949, 1, 2; Orren Beaty, "New Attack on Manager Is Defeated," *Arizona Republic*, 22 June 1949, 1, 8. Regarding Blaine's accusations against Deppe, Udall said, "It sounds as though he [Blaine] had just delivered his opening speech in the campaign for mayor in November." See "Probe Vice Squad Head Gifts," *Arizona Times*, 22 June 1949, 1.

20. "Mayor Demands Report on Phoenix Vice: Vote on Motion Lost in Shuffle," *Arizona Republic*, 28 September 1949, 1, 2; *Commission and Council*, 28:44, 45, 61.

21. "Phoenix Free of Organized Vice, Deppe Report Declares to Council," *Arizona Republic*, 12 October 1949, 1; *Commission and Council*, 28:102.

22. Claiborne Nuckolls, "Acting Governor Bolin Orders Phoenix Vice Probe," *Arizona Republic*, 23 June 1949, 1; "County, State Probing Death in City's Jail," *Arizona Times*, 23 June 1949, 1, 2; Claiborne Nuckolls, "State Vice Probe of Phoenix Vice Folds," *Arizona Republic*, 25 June 1949, 1; "Governor Says State Dropping Probe of City," *Arizona Times*, 24 June 1949, 1, 3.

23. Gene McLain, "O'Clair Backs Antivice Men, Denies Graft," *Arizona Republic*, 25 June 1949, 1, 7; Al Pierce, "O'Clair, Cop Shop Win National Pat," *Arizona Times*, 19 August 1949, 1; "Deppe Brands Blaine a Contemptible Liar," *Arizona Republic*, 14 July 1949, 1; Pete Bluemle, "City Manager Brands Blaine 'Malicious Liar,'" *Arizona Times*, 13 July 1949, 1, 2; Orren Beaty, "Deppe Pay Increased by Council," *Arizona Republic*, 20 July 1949, 1, 2.

24. The Charter Government Committee represented the combined efforts of Dix Price, president of the Arizona Young Democrats; Ronald Webster, president of the Arizona Young Republicans; and Alfred Knight, Phoenix philanthropist and patron of the arts, to ensure the execution of the reforms of the charter amendments. "The Time to Start a Campaign Is Now," *Phoenix Gazette*, 15 April 1949, 6; "Charter Group's Bid Launched," *Phoenix Gazette*, 6 July 1949, 1; Brown, "Analysis of Phoenix Charter Government," 31–33; Paul Kelso, "Phoenix Charter Rises Anew," *National Municipal Review* (April 1949), 177.

25. Henry Fuller, "Charter Group Hit by Smear," *Arizona Republic*, 10 July 1949, 1.

26. "Udall Says Deppe Grabs Free Radio for Politics," *Arizona Republic*, 27 August 1949, 1, 9; "Deppe Brands Udall Blast as 'Innuendo,'" *Arizona Times*, 27 August 1949, 1, 2.

27. Orren Beaty, "Phoenix Political Uproar May Boil into Open Soon," *Arizona Republic*, 2 September 1949, 9; Pete Bluemle, "Bitter Battle Looms for November 8 Election," *Arizona Times*, 20 August 1949, 1, 2; Orren Beaty, "Udall Heads First Full City State," *Arizona Republic*, 9 September 1949, 1, 7; *Commission and Council*, 28:135.

28. Beaty, "Phoenix Political Uproar," 9; "Blaine Puts in Bid for Mayoralty," *Arizona Times*, 3 October 1949, 1.

29. "Busey Enters Mayor's Race," *Arizona Republic*, 12 October 1949; "All Mayor, Most Council Candidates Are Active," *Arizona Republic*, 5 November 1949, 12; *Commission and Council*, 28:135.

30. "Four Amendments to City Charter on Ballot for November 8 Election," *Arizona Republic*, 16 October 1949, 1. The proposed charter amendment would eliminate

the inventory tax and limit the city tax on equipment and machinery to 30 percent of its value. Supporters claimed this would encourage the development of manufacturing in the city. See also "City Council Candidate Hits Repeal of Tax," *Arizona Republic*, 25 October 1949, and *Commission and Council*, 28:15, 19.

31. "Mayor Udall Takes Off Gloves, Flays Busey for Turmoil in Own Regime," *Arizona Republic*, 3 November 1949, 10; "Mayor Aspirants Back More Jobs, Amendments," *Arizona Republic*, 4 November 1949, Sec. 2, 9.

32. "Goldwater Brands Imler Ticket's Claims of City Achievements False," *Arizona Republic*, 26 October 1949, 13.

33. "Udall Unlimbers Big Guns, Blasts Opponent in Mayor's Race by Name," *Arizona Republic*, 27 October 1949, 10.

34. Ibid.; "Deppe Through as Manager Whoever Wins City Election, Busey Claims," *Arizona Republic*, 2 November 1949, 11; "Udall Takes Off Gloves," 10.

35. "Ministerial Association Approves Charter Ticket, Busey Raps Mayor," *Arizona Republic*, 27 October 1949, 10.

36. Ibid.; "Boss Control of City Hall Raised as Major Issue at Campaign Rally," *Arizona Republic*, 28 October 1949; "Every Citizen's Duty," *Arizona Republic*, 7 November 1949, 1. See also cartoon on editorial page of *Arizona Republic*, 30 October 1949, depicting the newspaper's support for the Charter Government Committee ticket and its opposition to the Imler slate, Deppe, and "Boss" Scheumack. See also "Record City Vote Turnout Is Expected," *Arizona Republic*, 7 November 1949, 1, 2.

37. "All Mayor, Most Council Candidates Are Active," 12. Caywood and Scheumack obviously referred to Phoenix Newspapers Incorporated owner Eugene G. Pulliam. During the 1949 municipal elections, Pulliam was living in Indianapolis, Indiana, where he merged the *Indianapolis News* with his *Indianapolis Star*. See Fenwick Anderson, "Bricks without Straw: The Mirage of Competition in the Desert of Phoenix Daily Journalism since 1947" (Ph.D. diss., University of Illinois at Urbana-Champaign, 1980), 79.

38. "All Mayor, Most Council Candidates Are Active," 12; "Deppe Says Papers Ask Privileges," *Arizona Times*, 12 March 1949, 1, 2.

39. Orren Beaty, "Live Issues Keynote City Political Campaign," *Arizona Republic*, 6 November 1949, 1, 2.

40. "Boss Control of City Hall Raised as Major Issue at Campaign Rally," 9; "Deppe Through as Manager Whoever Wins City Election, Busey Claims," 11.

41. Beaty, "Live Issues Keynote City Political Campaign," 2.

42. "Udall Is Reelected Mayor," *Arizona Republic*, 9 November 1949, 1; Orren Beaty, "Election Victors Plan Study of City Problems," *Arizona Republic*, 10 November 1949, 1; *Commission and Council*, 28:169-A. Support for the Charter Government Committee was overwhelming, not only in the northern voting precincts of the city but also in the less-affluent southern and western voting precincts. See "Record of Voting Tallies by Precinct: Phoenix, 1949," on file at Office of the City Clerk, Phoenix.

43. "Action Taken to Get Trained City Manager," *Arizona Republic*, 19 November 1949, 10; "New Regime Takes City Reins Today," *Arizona Republic*, 3 January 1950, 1; *Commission and Council*, 28:301.

44. "New Council Suspends Deppe as City Manager," *Arizona Republic*, 4 January 1950, 1, 8; *Commission and Council*, 28:301, 302.

45. "James Deppe, Former City Manager, Takes Life," *Arizona Republic*, 15 June 1950, 1.

46. During the 1950s the population of Phoenix quadrupled to more than 439,000, while the value of manufactured products increased by nearly 1,500 percent. See U.S. Bureau of the Census, *U.S. Census of Population: 1960, Characteristics of the Population* (Washington, D.C.: Government Printing Office, 1963), 51; U.S. Bureau of the Census,

*U.S. Census of Manufacturers: 1954, Area Statistics* (Washington, D.C.: Government Printing Office, 1963), 102; and U.S. Bureau of the Census, *U.S. Census of Manufacturers: 1958, Area Statistics* (Washington, D.C.: Government Printing Office, 1963), 3, 4.

## CHAPTER TWELVE

1. *Arizona Daily Star*, 8 July 1910.
2. Charles Buxton Harrison, "The Development of the Arizona Labor Movement" (M.A. thesis, Arizona State College, Tempe, 1954), 14.
3. Alfred H. Kelly and Winifred A. Harbinson, *The American Constitution: Its Origins and Development* (New York: W. W. Norton, 1948), 701.
4. John Mills, interview by Phoenix History Project, 26 April 1978.
5. Angela Hammer, unpublished autobiographical fragment, Phoenix History Project; M. A. DeFrance, interview by Phoenix History Project, 15 August 1978.
6. *Arizona Producer*, 15 March 1938.
7. Michael S. Wade, *The Bitter Issue* (Tucson: Arizona Historical Society, 1976), 2.
8. *Arizona Labor Journal*, 1 February 1940.
9. Ibid.
10. *National Labor Relations Act* (Wagner Act), 19 Statute 449–50 (1935). "An act to diminish the causes of labor disputes burdening or obstructing interstate and foreign commerce, to create a National Labor Relations Board, and for other purposes," as quoted in Leon Litwack, *The American Labor Movement* (Englewood Cliffs, N.J.: Prentice-Hall, 1962), 117.
11. Kelly and Harbinson, *American Constitution*, 701.
12. *Arizona Labor Journal*, quoted in Wade, *The Bitter Issue*, 39.
13. M. A. DeFrance, interview by Phoenix History Project, 15 August 1978.
14. Max Faulkner, interview by Phoenix History Project, 13 October 1978.
15. Archie Campbell, interview by Phoenix History Project, 30 January 1976.
16. *Arizona Labor Journal*, 1 August, 26 December, 20 June, 27 June 1940; 30 January 1941.
17. Ibid., 14 January 1943.
18. Wade Church, interview by Phoenix History Project, 28 September 1978; Darwin Aycock, interview by Phoenix History Project, 5 September 1978.
19. Wade Church, interview by Phoenix History Project, 28 September 1978.
20. Ibid.
21. *Arizona Labor Journal*, February 28, 1946.
22. The Reverend Bernard Black, interview by Phoenix History Project, 28 October 1978.
23. M. A. DeFrance, interview by Phoenix History Project, 15 August 1978.
24. *Arizona Labor Journal*, 22 July 1943; M. A. DeFrance, interview by Phoenix History Project, 15 August 1978; the Reverend Bernard Black, interview by Phoenix History Project, 28 October 1978.
25. *Arizona Labor Journal*, 13 May 1943; 17, 31 January 1946.
26. U.S. Bureau of the Census, *United States Census of Population: 1950* (Washington, D.C.: Government Printing Office), vol. 2, *Characteristics of the Population*, pt. 3, Arizona.
27. John Mills, interview by Phoenix History Project, 26 April 1978.
28. Wade, *The Bitter Issue*, 5.
29. Ibid., 27; Wade Church, interview by Phoenix History Project, 28 September 1978.
30. Wade, *The Bitter Issue*, 28.
31. Ibid., 36

32. Ibid., 39.
33. Wade Church, interview by Phoenix History Project, 28 September 1978.
34. M. A. DeFrance, interview by Phoenix History Project, 15 August 1978.
35. *Arizona Labor Journal*, 11 April 1946.
36. Ibid., 14 March, 23 May 1946.
37. Ibid., 7 November 1946.
38. Wade, *The Bitter Issue*, 91.
39. M. A. DeFrance, interview by Phoenix History Project, 15 August 1978.
40. Darwin Aycock, interview by Phoenix History Project, 5 September 1978.
41. *Arizona Labor Journal*, 4 November 1948.
42. M. A. DeFrance, interview by Phoenix History Project, 15 August 1978.

## CHAPTER THIRTEEN

1. James Stokely, interview with author, 15 January 1980.
2. *Master Street Plan* (Phoenix: City of Phoenix, 1949), 7–12.
3. Ibid., 9–17.
4. Don Morgan, traffic engineer, interview with author, 4 March 1980.
5. *Historical Notes: Existing Road System and Current Regulations of Highway Transportation in Arizona* (Phoenix: Arizona Department of Transportation, 1977), 25.
6. *Better Roads for Tomorrow* (Phoenix: City of Phoenix, 1957), 31.
7. *Arizona Republic*, 28 February 1957.
8. *Arizona Republic*, 18 October 1957, 12 August 1958. *Phoenix Gazette*, 21 March 1958.
9. *Arizona Republic*, 21 November 1959; *A Major Street and Highway Plan for the Phoenix Urban Area* (San Francisco: Wilber Smith and Associates, 1960), 6–7; Sam Mardian, interview with author, 23 January 1980; James Stokely, interview with author, 15 January 1980.
10. Sam Mardian, interview with author, 15 January 1980.
11. *1961 Street Needs Study* (Phoenix: City of Phoenix, 1961), 4–10, 39.
12. *Phoenix Gazette*, 15 May 1961.
13. Ed Hall, street development administrator, interview with author, 4 March 1980; and *Street Improvement Needs Study* (Phoenix: City of Phoenix, 1979), 8; *City of Phoenix, et al. v. Sidney Popkin, et al.*, in *Report of Cases Argued and Determined in the Supreme Court of Arizona* (St. Paul, Minn.: West Publishing Co., 1963), 93:14–16.
14. *Arizona Republic*, 6 November 1962; *A Transportation Plan for Downtown* (Phoenix: City of Phoenix, 1963), 2–4, 16, 24.
15. *Six-Year Street Needs Study* (Phoenix: City of Phoenix, 1963), 1, 21.
16. *Phoenix Gazette*, 8 January 1964; *Arizona Republic*, 17 February 1964.
17. *Phoenix Gazette*, 31 March 1965.
18. *Six-Year Major Street Program* (Phoenix: City of Phoenix, 1966), ii, 3.
19. *Arizona Republic*, 4 January 1967; "Freeway Clearance Under Way," *Phoenix Gazette*, 12 January 1968.
20. *Capital Improvement Needs Study* (Phoenix: City of Phoenix, 1979), 8.
21. *Six-Year Major Street Program* (Phoenix: City of Phoenix, 1969), 12.
22. *Phoenix Gazette*, 14 December 1968, 10 January 1969.
23. *Phoenix Gazette*, 10 January 1964; *Arizona Republic*, 10 January 1969.
24. *Street Needs Study* (Phoenix: City of Phoenix, 1969), 16. The 1961 study showed 124.7 deficient miles of collector streets and 472.5 deficient miles of local streets for a total of 597.2 miles. The 1969 study showed 56.3 deficient miles of collector streets and 380.5 miles of local streets for a total of 436.8 miles. Subtracting the latter total from

the former total gives us a sum of 160.4 miles, which is the reduction from 1961 to 1969 in total miles of deficient collector and local streets.

25. *Mobility—Phoenix Style: A Summary Report on Transportation* (Phoenix: City of Phoenix, 1969), 1, 8.

26. "Anti-Freeway Group Names Head," *Phoenix Gazette*, 5 December 1969.

27. *Minority Report—Land Transportation Committee—Phoenix Forward Task Force* (Phoenix: City of Phoenix, 1970), 5–10.

28. *Arizona Republic*, 15 March 1970.

29. *Arizona Republic*, 17 November, 27 December 1970.

30. *Transit and the Phoenix Metropolitan Area* (Phoenix: City of Phoenix, 1970), 56; *Six-Year Major Street Program* (Phoenix: City of Phoenix, 1970), 2–3.

31. John Driggs, interview with author, 23 January 1980.

32. Don Morgan, interview with author, 24 January 1980.

33. *Phoenix Gazette*, 7 June 1972; "Stubborn Council Hangs On," *Arizona Republic*, 5 October 1972.

34. *Arizona Republic*, 15 October 1972.

35. *Second Citizen Challenge to the Final Environmental Impact Statement* (Phoenix: Citizens for Mass Transit against Freeways, 1973), 4–5.

36. *Arizona Republic*, 16 February 1973. See also *Arizona Republic*, 18 April 1973. The decision to add such a question to the ballot needed to be decided on by April 17; the council failed to act by that date, but added a straw poll ballot later in the week.

37. Resolution No. 14111, "A Resolution officially requesting the Arizona Highway Commission to abandon present plans for the construction of the Inner Loop portion of the Papago Freeway," Resolutions of the Phoenix City Council; *Phoenix Gazette*, 14 June 1973; *Arizona Republic*, 23 January, 4 March 1974.

38. *Arizona Republic*, 18 December 1974, 24 January 1975.

39. *Interstate 10 Transportation Corridor Alternatives Study* (Phoenix: Gruen and Associates, 1975), table F; *Arizona Republic*, 14 March 1975.

40. *Arizona Republic*, 25 May 1975; *Phoenix Gazette*, 2 July 1975.

41. *Phoenix Gazette*, 21 June 1975; "Yes Means Nothing," *Phoenix Gazette*, 13 October 1975. It is generally admitted by even the most casual observer that the newspapers lost all pretense of journalistic objectivity during this campaign, up to the point that "hard news" stories concerning the issue began to reflect the editorial bias of the papers. Rarely were UNITE's viewpoints presented, except to be ridiculed. The October 23 and 24 issues of the *Phoenix Gazette* and the October 29 and 31 issues of the *Arizona Republic* are good illustrations of this.

42. *Arizona Republic*, 5 November 1975; *Phoenix Gazette*, 6 November 1975.

43. *Phoenix Gazette*, 19 May, 24 September 1976; *Arizona Republic*, 3 September, 22 October 1976.

44. "Freeways Win Backing," *Phoenix Gazette*, 15, 20 December 1977.

45. *Phoenix Gazette*, 10 April, 20 October, 27 December 1978.

46. Dr. Robert Hurt, interview with author, 31 January 1980.

47. *Phoenix Gazette*, 21 September 1979.

48. For those readers interested in recent developments regarding transportation in Phoenix, the author recommends the following texts: "I-17/I-10 Corridor Study: Executive Summary," Arizona Department of Transportation, 1986; G. L. Flanagan, "Threading the Needle in Phoenix: Location and Preliminary Design of a New Urban Freeway," in *Proceedings, Institute of Transportation Engineers, District 6 Meeting, Reno, Nev., 1987*; T. R. Warne, "Papago, the End in Sight," in *Proceedings, Arizona Conference on Roads and Streets, 1988*.

# BIBLIOGRAPHY

Abbitt, Jerry W. "A History of Public Transportation in Phoenix, Arizona, 1887–1989." M.A. thesis, Arizona State University, 1989.

Alltop, David. "The Valley Bank of Phoenix, 1883–1914." Manuscript, Arizona Collection, Arizona State University Library, 1976.

Alsap, John Taber. "Resources of the Salt River Valley, 1872." *Arizona Historical Review* 3 (1936): 50–54.

Arizona Days and Ways. Sunday supplement to the *Arizona Republic*. Phoenix, 11 February 1962.

Arizona Republican. *Phoenix and Arizona Guide Book*. Phoenix: Arizona Republican, 1926.

Babbitt, George. *Arizona Mosaic*. Scottsdale: B. and H. Publishing Company, 1977.

Barney, James M. "Phoenix: A History of Its Pioneer Days and People." *Arizona Historical Review* 5 (1933): 264–85.

Bates, Walter G. "Water Storage in the West." *Scribner's Magazine* 7 (1890): 3–17.

Beasley, Al D., ed. *Twentieth Century Phoenix, Illustrated*. Phoenix: N.p., 1910.

Black, John A. *Arizona, the Land of Sunshine and Silver, Health and Prosperity, the Place for Ideal Homes*. Tucson: N.p., 1890.

Blanchard, C. J. "The Call of the West: Homes Are Being Made for Millions of People in the Arid West." *National Geographic* 20 (1909): 403–37.

Brown, Brent Whiting. "An Analysis of the Phoenix Charter Government Committee as a Political Entity." M.A. thesis, Arizona State University, 1968.

Buchanan, James E., ed. *Phoenix: A Chronological and Documentary History*. Dobbs Ferry, N.Y.: Oceana Publications, 1978.

Cable, John, Susan L. Henry, and David E. Doyel. *City of Phoenix, Archaeology of the Original Townsite, Block 28 North*. Phoenix: Professional Service Industries, 1983.

Carter, Oscar. "The Government Irrigation Project at Roosevelt Dam, Salt River, Arizona." *Journal of the Franklin Institute* 163 (1907): 277–301.

Chaudhuri, Joyotpaul. *Urban Indians of Arizona: Phoenix, Tucson, and Flagstaff*. Tucson: University of Arizona Press, 1974.

Christy, Lloyd B. *Life of Col. William Christy*. Phoenix: Lloyd B. Christy, 1930.

Cook, Jeffrey. "Patterns of Desert Urbanization: The Evolution of Metropolitan Phoenix." In Gideon S. Golany, ed., *Urban Planning for Arid Zones: American Experiences and Directions*. New York: John Wiley and Sons, 1978.

Cookridge, E. H. *The Baron of Arizona*. New York: John Day, 1967.

Cross, Jack et al. *Arizona: Its Peoples and Resources*. Tucson: University of Arizona Press, 1960.

Davis, Daniel C. "Phoenix, Arizona, 1907–1913." Manuscript, Arizona Collection, Arizona State University Library, 1988.

Daws, A. George, comp. *The Commercial History of Maricopa County*. Phoenix: Daws Publishing Company, 1919.

_____. *What Made Arizona Men*. Phoenix: Daws Publishing Company, 192?.

Delong, Sidney R. *The History of Arizona to 1903*. San Francisco: Whitaker and Ray Company, 1905.

Dick, George. *One of a Kind: An Informal History of Phoenix Zoo, 1961–1982*. Phoenix: Arizona Zoological Society, 1982.

*Directory of the Performing Arts in Metropolitan Phoenix*. Phoenix: J. A. Hard Associates, 1974.

Driggs, Junius E. *Junius E. Driggs: Looking Over My Life*. Phoenix: J. E. Driggs, 1988.

Dukes, Homer D. *Washington and Central, 1922–1979*. Phoenix: H. D. Dukes, 1979.

Dunbar, John O. *Irrigation, the Great Water System of the Salt River Valley*. Phoenix: Maricopa County Supervisors, 1904.

——. *The Peerless Valley of the Salt River: Phoenix, Its Capital City*. Phoenix: Maricopa County Supervisors, 1903.

Duncan, Bingham. *Whitelaw Reid: Journalist, Politician, Diplomat*. Athens: University of Georgia Press, 1975.

Dutton, Allen A. *Phoenix Then and Now*. Phoenix: Allen A. Dutton, 1984.

Farish, Thomas E. *History of Arizona*. 8 vols. Phoenix: Office of the State Historian, 1915–18.

First Institutional Baptist Church, Phoenix. *Eighty Years of Serving, Seeking, Saving and Sending*. Phoenix: First Institutional Baptist Church, 1987.

Fleming, Lawrence J. *Ride a Mile and Smile the While: A History of the Phoenix Street Railway, 1887–1948*. Phoenix: Swaine Publications, 1977.

Foreman, Richard Lane. "A Brief History of Phoenix, 1890–1899." Honors thesis, Arizona State University, 1976.

——. "The Rise of Council-Manager Government in Phoenix. How Responsive Is It?" Manuscript, Arizona Historical Foundation, Arizona State University Library, 1976.

Fortier, L. E. "Early Irrigation Systems in the Salt River Valley." Manuscript, Arizona Historical Foundation, Arizona State University Library, 1971.

Gladwin, Harold, Emil Haury et al. *Excavations at Snaketown: Material Culture*. Reprint. Tucson: University of Arizona Press, 1965.

Goldsmith, Maxine. *The Place of Yiddish in a Changing Jewish Ethnicity*. M.A. thesis, Arizona State University, 1988.

Goodall, Leonard E. "Phoenix Reformers at Work." In Leonard E. Goodall, ed., *Urban Politics in the Southwest*. Tempe: Arizona State University Institute of Public Administration, 1967.

Greenwald, David H., and Richard Ciolek-Torrello, eds. *Archaeological Investigations at the Dutch Canal Ruin, Phoenix, Arizona: Archaeology and History along the Papago Freeway Corridor*. Flagstaff: Museum of Northern Arizona, 1988.

Halseth, Odd S. "Arizona's 1500 Years of Irrigation History." *Reclamation Era* 33 (1947): 251–54.

Hamilton, Patrick. *The Resources of Arizona*. Prescott: Arizona Territorial Legislative Assembly, 1881.

Hardt, Athia L. *Phoenix, America's Shining Star: A Celebration of Phoenix Enterprise*. Northridge, Calif.: Windsor Publications, 1989.

Hawkins, Helen B. "A History of Wickenburg to 1975." M.A. thesis, Arizona State University, 1950.

Heard, Dwight B. "The Roosevelt Dam." *World To-Day* 11 (1906): 1103–1105.

Hendricks, William O. M. H. *Sherman: A Pioneer Developer of the Pacific Southwest*. Corona del Mar, Calif.: Sherman Foundation, 1973.

Hermonson, G. M. "Urbanization of Agricultural Lands in Maricopa County, Arizona." M.A. thesis, Arizona State University, 1968.

Hildebrand, Robert William. "Metropolitan Area Government: Miami, Nashville, Phoenix in Perspective." M.A. thesis, Arizona State University, 1974.

Hinton, Richard J. *The Hand-Book to Arizona*. San Francisco: Payot, Upham and Company, 1878.

Hodge, F. W. "Prehistoric Irrigation in Arizona." *American Anthropologist* 6 (1893): 323–30.

Hodge, Hiram C. *Arizona as It Is, or, the Coming Country*. New York: Hurd and Houghton, 1877.

Hopkins, Ernest J. *Financing the Frontier*. Phoenix: Valley National Bank, 1950.

Horton, Arthur G. *An Economic, Political, and Social Survey of Phoenix and the Valley of the Sun*. Tempe, Ariz.: Southside Progress, 1941.

James, George W. *Arizona the Wonderland*. Boston: Page Company, 1917.

————. "In the Egypt of America: The Salt River Project." *Twentieth Century Magazine* 3 (1911): 483–91 (pt.1), 4 (1911): 3–11 (pt. 2).

James Associates for the Arizona Department of Transportation. *An Overview of Subdivision Development along the Inner Loop Corridor, Phoenix, Arizona*. Tempe, Ariz.: James Associates, 1981.

John C. Lincoln Hospital. *From Desert to Distinction: A History of John C. Lincoln Hospital*. Phoenix: John C. Lincoln Hospital, 1981.

Johnson, G. Wesley, Jr. "Dwight Heard in Phoenix: The Early Years." *Journal of Arizona History* 18 (1977): 259–78.

————. "Men of Vision: Phoenix." In Karen Dahood, ed., *The Golden West: The Literature of Comprehension*, 17–25. Tucson: Tucson Public Library, 1981,

————. *Phoenix: Valley of the Sun*. Tulsa, Okla.: Continental Heritage Publishing, 1982.

Kaney, Eunice E. "Original Phoenix Townsite." Manuscript based on James Barney's writings, *The Phoenix City Directory*, editions of 1895 and 1908. Arizona Historical Foundation, Arizona State University Library, 198?.

Kelly, George H., comp. *Legislative History: Arizona, 1864–1912*. Phoenix: Manufacturing Stationers, 1926.

Kelso, Paul. *A Decade of Council-Manager Government in Phoenix*. Phoenix: N.p., 1960.

King, Cameron H. *The Citrus and Fruit Belt of Southern Arizona*. Phoenix: Commissioner of Immigration, 1887.

Konig, Michael F. "Toward Metropolis Status: Charter Government and the Rise of Phoenix, Arizona, 1945–1960." Ph.D. diss., Arizona State University, 1983.

Kotlanger, Michael John, S.J. "Phoenix, Arizona: 1920–1940." Ph.D. diss., Arizona State University, 1983.

Lamb, Blaine. "Jews in Early Phoenix, 1870–1920." *Journal of Arizona History* 18 (1977): 299–318.

Laughlin, Sylvia. "Iron Springs, Arizona: Timeless Summer Resort." *Journal of Arizona History* 22 (1981): 235–54.

Lewis, Christine. "The Early History of the Tempe Canal Company." *Arizona and the West* 7 (1965): 227–38.

Liebow, Edward B. "A Sense of Place: Urban Indians and the History of Pan-Tribal Institutions in Phoenix, Arizona." Ph.D. diss., Arizona State University, 1986.

Lockwood, Frank C. *Pioneer Days in Arizona from the Spanish Occupation to Statehood*. New York: Macmillan Company, 1932.

Luckingham, Bradford. *Phoenix: The History of a Southwestern Metropolis*. Tucson: University of Arizona Press, 1989.

———. "Urban Development in Arizona: The Rise of Phoenix." *Journal of Arizona History* 22 (Summer 1981): 197–234.

———. *The Urban Southwest: A Profile History of Albuquerque, El Paso, Phoenix and Tucson*. El Paso: Texas Western Press, 1982.

Lykes, Aimée de Potter. "Phoenix Women in the Development of Public Policy: Territorial Beginnings." Manuscript, Arizona Historical Foundation, Arizona State University Library.

Lynch, Richard E. *Winfield Scott*. Scottsdale, Ariz.: City of Scottsdale, 1978.

McCauley, Kevin. "Twentieth Century Phoenix." M.A. thesis, University of California, Santa Barbara, 1982.

McClintock, James H. "An American Community in the Making." *Arizona, the New State Magazine* 1 (1911): 14–17.

———. *Arizona: Prehistoric, Aboriginal, Pioneer, Modern*. 3 vols. Chicago: S. J. Clarke, 1916.

McCroskey, Mona L. "The Luhrs Tower: Art Deco Comes to Phoenix." Manuscript, Arizona Collection, Arizona State University Library.

McFarland and Poole, comps. *A Historical and Biographical Record of the Territory of Arizona*. Chicago: McFarland and Poole, 1896.

McGrath, Gaylord M. "The Evolution of Resorts and Guest Ranches in Greater Phoenix, Arizona." Typescript, Arizona Collection, Arizona State University, 1973.

McKnight, Thomas Lee. *Manufacturing in Arizona*. Berkeley: University of California Press, 1962.

McLaughlin, Herb and Dorothy. *Phoenix 1870–1970 in Photographs*. Phoenix: Herb McLaughlin, 1970.

McLoughlin, Emmett. *People's Padre: An Autobiography*. Boston: Beacon Press, 1954.

Madden, Huan. *The Codac Story: The History of the Community Organization for Drug Abuse Control*. Phoenix: Office of Information Coordinator, 1975.

Mann, Dean E. *The Politics of Water in Arizona*. Tucson: University of Arizona Press, 1963.

Mawn, Geoffrey P. "Blacks in Phoenix, 1890–1930." Manuscript, Arizona Historical Foundation, Arizona State University Library.

———. "Phoenix, Arizona: Central City of the Southwest, 1870–1920." Ph.D. diss., Arizona State University, 1979.

———. "Phoenix, 1870–1912." Manuscript, Arizona Collection, Arizona State University Library.

———. "Promoters, Speculators, and the Selection of the Phoenix Townsite." *Arizona and the West* 19 (1977): 207–24.

Mead, Elwood, W. L. Marshall, and I. D. O'Donnell. "Report of the Central Board of Review on the Salt River Project, Arizona." *Reclamation Record* 8 (1917): 14–21.

Meyer, A. Leonard. *Meyer's Business Directory of the City of Phoenix, Arizona.* Phoenix: A. L. Meyer, 1888.

Meyer, Louis S. "Federal Aid and Its Impact on the State of Arizona." M.A. thesis, Arizona State University, 1962.

Monk, Janice, and Alice Schlegel, eds. *Women and the Arizona Economy.* Tucson: Southwest Institute for Research on Women/Women's Studies, University of Arizona, 1986.

Murphy, Merwin. *W. J. and the Valley.* Alhambra, Calif.: Merwin Murphy, 1975.

Myrick, David F. *Railroads of Arizona.* 3 vols. Berkeley, Calif.: Howell-North Books, 1980.

Niebur, Jay Edward. "The Social and Economic Effects of the Great Depression on Phoenix, Arizona, 1929–1934." M.A. thesis, Arizona State University, 1967.

Oxford, Elizabeth S. "Phoenix: American Oasis in the Great American Desert." M.A. thesis, University of Washington, 1951.

Patrick, Herbert R. *The Ancient Canal Systems and Pueblos of the Salt River Valley, Arizona.* Phoenix: Phoenix Free Museum, 1903.

Peplow, Edward H., Jr. *History of Arizona,* 3 vols. New York: Lewis Historical Publishing Company, 1958.

"Phoenix: One Hundred Years Young, 1870–1970." *Arizona Highways* (April 1970).

"Phoenix—The Blemishes in Boomtown." *Business Week,* November 15, 1969, 144–46.

Phoenix Aviation Department. *Phoenix Sky Harbor International Airport: History and Development.* Phoenix: Phoenix Aviation Department, 1983.

Phoenix Fine Arts Association. *Festival of Arts.* Phoenix: Arizona Arts Publications, 1958.

Phoenix Historic Preservation Commission (prepared by Don M. Ryden). *The Union Station: Phoenix Portal to the Nation.* Phoenix: Phoenix Historic Preservation Commission, 1990.

*Phoenix Magazine.* "The People, Places and Events: 20 years of Valley History and a Vision of the Future: Scottsdale, Mesa, Tempe, Chandler, Glendale, and West Valley." Phoenix: Phoenix Publishing Company, 1986.

———. "Phoenix: The First Century: Special 100th Anniversary Issue." October 1970.

Phoenix Planning Department. "Central Phoenix Plan." Phoenix: Phoenix Planning Commission, 1969.

_____. *History of the City of Phoenix, Arizona*. Phoenix: City of Phoenix Planning Department, 1975.

_____. *Phoenix Historic Building Survey* (prepared by Charles Hall Page and Associates, San Francisco). Phoenix: City of Phoenix Planning Department, 1979.

Phoenix Police Department. *A History of the Phoenix Police Department*. Phoenix: Phoenix Police Department, 1978.

Phoenix Union High School. *A Bicentennial Commemorative History of the Phoenix Union High School System, 1895–1976*. Phoenix: Phoenix Union High School, 1976.

Pierson, Katie. "History of the Phoenix Indian School." Typescript, Phoenix, 1963, in Arizona Collection, Hayden Library, Arizona State University.

Plancor, Inc., Research Division. *Economic Impact of the Proposed Interstate Program on the Phoenix, Arizona, Area*. Phoenix: Plancor, 1957.

Pollack, Paul W. *Arizona's Men of Achievement*, vol. 1. Phoenix: Paul W. Pollack, 1958.

Prince, John Frederick. "A Biography of E. W. Montgomery, 1925–1953." M.A. thesis, University of Arizona, 1960.

Pry, Mark E. "The Growth of an Early Sunbelt City: Urban Structure in Phoenix, Arizona, 1880–1910." M.A. thesis, Arizona State University, 1988.

Reynolds, Jerry. *The Golden Days of Theaters in Phoenix: A Dramatic Tableau of the Theaters and Amusements in Greater Phoenix from 1877 to 1982*. Glendale, Calif.: Associated Media Services, 1982.

Richards, J. Morris. *Western Savings and Loan: A History*. Phoenix: Western Savings and Loan, 1979.

Roberts, Shirley J. "Minority Group Poverty in Phoenix." *Journal of Arizona History* 14 (1973): 348–54.

Rockstroh, Stephen S. "An Analysis of Phoenix Municipal Administration, 1881–1952." M.A. thesis, Arizona State University, 1952.

Roosevelt Action Association, Inc. (prepared by Gerald A. Doyle and Associates). *The Roosevelt Neighborhood Historic Buildings Survey*. Phoenix: Roosevelt Action Association, 1983.

Rotary Club of Phoenix. *A History of the Rotary Club, 1914–1955*. Phoenix: Rotary Club of Phoenix, 1955.

Russell, Peter Lee. "Downtown's Downturn: A Historical Geography of the Phoenix, Arizona, Central Business District, 1890–1986." M.A. thesis, Arizona State University, 1986.

Ryerson, Jennie S. "An Early History of Phoenix and the Salt River Valley from the Hohokam to 1891." M.A. thesis, Arizona State University, 1948.

Salt River Project. *The Taming of the Salt*. Phoenix: Salt River Project, 1979.

Sargent, Charles S. "Towns of the Salt River Valley, 1870–1970." *Historical Geography Newsletter* 5 (1975): 1–9.

_____, ed. *The Conflict between Frontier Values and Land-Use Control in Greater Phoenix*. Phoenix: Arizona Council on the Humanities and Public Policy, 1976.

Schmieder, Ruby Harkey. *Sulphur Smoke: Stories of a Pioneer Family in Arizona*. Phoenix: Ruby H. Schmieder, 1983.

Shaddegg, Stephen C. *Century One: One Hundred Years of Water Development in the Salt River Valley*. Phoenix: Stephen C. Shaddegg, 1969.

———. *Miss Lulu's Legacy*. Tempe: Arizona State University, 1984.

Shell, Harrold, and Tim Simmons. *Up from the Ashes: The Real Story about the Phoenix Fire Department*. Phoenix: International Print Company, 1986.

Sheridan, Jan Booth. "Public Sculpture in Phoenix." M.A. thesis, Arizona State University, 1985.

Sloan, Richard E., and Ward R. Adams. *History of Arizona*. 4 vols. Phoenix: Record Publishing Company, 1930.

Smith, Albert W. *What Happened to Vacant Lots?* Phoenix: Trails West Publishing Company, 1973.

Smith, Courtland L. *The Salt River Project: A Case Study in Cultural Adaptation to an Urbanizing Community*. Tucson: University of Arizona Press, 1972.

Smith, Joseph C. "The Phoenix Drive for Municipal Reform and Charter Government, 1911–1915." Manuscript, Arizona Collection, Arizona State University Library, 1975.

Smith, Karen L. "From Town to City: A History of Phoenix, 1870–1912." M.A. thesis, University of California, Santa Barbara, 1978.

———. *The Magnificent Experiment: Building the Salt River Reclamation Project, 1890–1917*. Tucson: University of Arizona Press, 1986.

Stewart, Warren H., Sr. *Seventy-five Years of Mission-minded Ministry: First Institutional Baptist Church, Phoenix, Arizona, 1905–1980*. Phoenix: First Institutional Baptist Church, 1980.

Tipton, Gary P. "Men Out of China." *Journal of Arizona History* 18 (1977): 341–56.

Tisdale, Nancy K. "The Prohibition Crusade in Arizona." M.A. thesis, University of Arizona, Tucson, 1965.

Titcomb, Mary Ruth. "Americanization and Mexicans in the Southwest: A History of Phoenix's Friendly House, 1920–1983." M.A. thesis, University of California, Santa Barbara, 1984.

Trennert, Robert A. *The Phoenix Indian School: Forced Assimilation in Arizona, 1891–1935*. Norman: University of Oklahoma Press, 1988.

Trimble, Marshall. *Arizona*. New York: Doubleday, 1977.

Turney, Omar. *Prehistoric Irrigation*. Phoenix: Arizona State Historian, 1929.

Wagoner, Jay J. *Arizona Territory, 1863–1912: A Political History*. Tucson: University of Arizona Press, 1970.

Wallingford, V. C. "Social Conditions in Phoenix." *Earth* 13 (1916): 12–13.

Weisiger, Marsha. *Boosters, Streetcars, and Bungalows*. Phoenix: Roosevelt Action Association, 1984.

Wenum, John D. "Annexation as a Technique for Metropolitan Growth: The Case of Phoenix." M.A. thesis, Arizona State University, 1970.

———. "Spatial Growth and the Central City—(Case of Phoenix)." Ph.D. diss., Northwestern University, 1968.

Williams, Jack. Introduction to *City of Phoenix 75th Anniversary, 1881–1956*. Phoenix: Phoenix City Council, 1956.

Yancey, Farrell E. "Judge Wells and the Phoenix Post Office." Manuscript, Arizona Historical Foundation, Arizona State University Library.

Young, Herbert V. *Water by the Inch: Adventures of a Pioneer Family on an Arizona Desert Homestead*. Flagstaff: Northland Press, 1983.

Zarbin, Earl. *Salt River Project: Four Steps Forward, 1902–1910*. Phoenix: Salt River Project, 1986.

Zeimann, Jay C. "The Modernization of the Salt River Project: The Impact of the Rehabitation and Betterment Program." M.A. thesis, Arizona State University, 1988.

# CONTRIBUTORS

MARGARET FINNERTY, after serving on the staff of Sen. Robert F. Kennedy in Washington, D.C., took her B.A. and M.A. degrees in history at Arizona State University. She won the Johnson Prize for local history at ASU, served as archivist of the Phoenix History Project, and became curator of education for the Arizona Historical Society. She is currently a historical consultant for the Heard Museum, Capitol Museum, and Salt River Project, and a faculty member of Ottawa University in Phoenix. She has written *Del Webb, A Man, A Company*.

G. WESLEY JOHNSON, JR., a native of Phoenix, studied history for his A.B. degree (honors) at Harvard and Ph.D. at Columbia. He lived in California for twenty-one years, serving as Research Associate at Hoover Institution and a member of the history faculty of Stanford; he later taught at the University of California, Santa Barbara, where he directed the Graduate Program in Public Historical Studies and was editor in chief of *The Public Historian* quarterly published by the University of California Press. He is author of several books on community history including *Phoenix, Valley of the Sun* and *Naissance du Sénégal Contemporain*, published in Paris. He has received major fellowships from the Ford and Rockefeller foundations and the Social Science Research Council. He is currently professor of history, Brigham Young University.

MICHAEL F. KONIG is associate professor of history at Westfield State College in Massachusetts, where he specialized in urban history. He took his B.A. degree at United States International University, M.A. at San Diego State, and Ph.D. at Arizona State University. He has served as an urban planner and is particularly interested in the Sunbelt/ Frostbelt historical dichotomy. He has written *A Case Study of Leadership: Springfield, Massachusetts, and Its Mayors, 1945 to the Present* and *Creating an Image: A History of Downtown Development in Springfield, Massachusetts*.

MICHAEL KOTLANGER, S.J., is currently a lecturer in history and archivist of the University of San Francisco. He is a member of the Society of Jesus and took his B.A. at the University of San Francisco, M.A. at Loyola University of Los Angeles, M.Div. at the Jesuit School of Theology at Berkeley, and Ph.D. in history at Arizona State University. He has also worked as a historical consultant and academic counselor at his present university.

BRADFORD LUCKINGHAM is a well-known urban historian of the American West who has taught for many years at Arizona State University. He studied for his B.S. at Northern Arizona University, M.A. at University of Missouri, Columbia, and Ph.D. in history at University of California, Davis. He has published *The Urban Southwest: A Profile History of Albuquerque, El Paso, Phoenix, and Tucson* and, more recently, *Phoenix: The History of a Southwestern Metropolis*.

AIMÉE DE POTTER LYKES of Branford, Connecticut, formerly taught at Phoenix College and served as a Research Associate on the Phoenix History Project. She took her B.A. at Wellesley College and M.A. in history at Yale. She also did graduate work at Columbia University, the University of Chicago, and Arizona State University. She has most recently become interested in doing advanced study and research in Chinese, has traveled to China several times, and has published "A Dream on the Strings," a translation in Y. H. Wang, ed., *Perspectives in Contemporary Chinese Literature*.

PHYLIS CANCILLA MARTINELLI, originally from San Francisco, earned her doctorate in sociology from Arizona State University. She was a Research Associate of the Phoenix History Project in charge of ethnic studies, worked on the history of the Roosevelt Dam labor camp, and has won several awards for historic photo displays of ethnic communities. She has specialized in the study of interaction between ethnic groups in the West—in particular, the Hispanics and Italians. She is currently associate professor of sociology at St. Mary's College in Moraga, California.

KEVIN R. McCAULEY is currently Principal Analyst, Office of the President, University of California, and administers the Academic Geriatric Resource Program. He makes his home in San Francisco. He took his B.A. and M.A. in history at University of California, Santa Barbara, where he held a Rockefeller Foundation fellowship. He continued his education at Carnegie-Mellon University, where he was awarded the M.S. in Applied History and was a Mellon Fellow. He also served as a Public Information Office Intern in the Mayor's Office of Phoenix for one year and was associated with the Phoenix History Project. He has published "The Federal Role in Transit Investment Decisions: The Case of Baltimore, Maryland" in Joel Tarr, ed., *Duke/Rand Collegiate Case Studies Series*.

LARRY SCHWEIKART studied for his M.A. in history at Arizona State University and his Ph.D. at University of California, Santa Barbara. He has taught in the University of Wisconsin system and is at present associate professor of history at University of Dayton in Ohio. He is also a professional consultant and serves as chairman of Discover the Past, Inc. He has published *A History of Banking in Arizona* and numerous articles on the history of American banking. He is currently completing a history of banking in California for the California Bankers Association with co-author Lynne Pierson Doti of Chapman College. He also maintains a lively interest in sports and has completed a history of the Phoenix Suns basketball team.

KAREN L. SMITH took her B.A., M.A. and Ph.D. degrees in history at University of California, Santa Barbara, where she was a Rockefeller Fellow in the Graduate Program in Public Historical Studies. She was a Research Associate on the Phoenix History Project, where she investigated the history of Phoenix neighborhoods and problems of water. She did an internship at Salt River Project, which she later joined in a professional capacity. She is currently Manager, Information Systems. She has published *The Magnificent Experiment:*

*Building the Salt River Reclamation Project, 1890–1917*. Her contribution to this volume was originally given as part of a research panel for the Arizona Humanities Council conference, "Phoenix: Emergence of a Sunbelt Metropolis."

ROBERT A. TRENNERT has just completed several terms as chair of the history department of Arizona State University. He took his B.A. at Occidental College and his Ph.D. in history at University of California, Santa Barbara, served as associate director of the Phoenix History Project, and has specialized in the history of images of the American Indian, federal Indian policy, and the history of Arizona. He has published numerous articles and books on American Indian history, including *The Phoenix Indian School*. He has served on the board of the Arizona Humanities Council, was a founding member of the Western History Association, and is widely known as a discriminating amateur of model railroads.

EARL ZARBIN was a newspaperman until his retirement several years ago. He worked for the *Kansas City Star*, the *Arizona Daily Star* in Tucson, and the *Arizona Republic* in Phoenix. He also was a correspondent for *Life* magazine and Fairchild publications. He took his B.A. degree at the University of Arizona. He is the author of *Roosevelt Dam: A History to 1911*, *The Swilling Legacy*, and *All the Time a Newspaper*. He makes his home in Phoenix and is at present a free-lance writer and editor.

# INDEX